Reparative Citizenship for Sephardi Descendants

Remapping Cultural History
General Editor: Jo Labanyi, New York University

This series challenges theoretical paradigms by exploring areas of culture that have previously received little attention. Its volumes discuss parts of the world that do not easily fit within dominant northern European or North American theoretical models, or that make a significant contribution to rethinking the ways in which cultural history is theorized and narrated.

Volume 2
Images of Power: Iconography, Culture and the State in Latin America
Edited by Jens Andermann and William Rowe

Volume 3
The Art of the Project: Projects and Experiments in Modern French Culture
Edited by Johnnie Gratton and Michael Sheringham

Volume 4
Locating Memory: Photographic Acts
Edited by Annette Kuhn and Kirsten Emiko McAllister

Volume 5
Intersected Identities: Strategies of Visualization in 19th and 20th Century Mexican Culture
Erica Segre

Volume 6
Fetishes and Monuments: Afro-Brazilian Art and Culture in the 20th Century
Roger Sansi

Volume 7
Journeys Through Fascism: Italian Travel-Writing between the Wars
Charles Burdett

Volume 8
Border Interrogations: Questioning Spanish Frontiers
Edited by Benita Sampedro Vizcaya and Simon Doubleday

Volume 9
Love and the Idea of Europe
Luisa Passerina

Volume 10
Indispensable Eyesores: An Anthropology of Undesired Buildings
Mélanie van der Hoorn

Volume 11
Rethinking the Informal City: Critical Perspectives from Latin America
Edited by Felipe Hernández, Peter Kellett and Lea K. Allen

Volume 12
Grassroots Memorials: The Politics of Memorializing Traumatic Death
Edited by Peter Jan Margry and Cristina Sánchez-Carretero

Volume 13
Tuff City: Urban Change and Contested Space in Central Naples
Nick Dines

Volume 14
Silence, Screen, and Spectacle: Rethinking Social Memory in the Age of Information and New Media
Edited by Lindsey A. Freeman, Benjamin Nienass, and Rachel Daniell

Volume 15
Narratives in Motion: Journalism and Modernist Events in 1920s Portugal
Luís Trindade

Volume 16
Reparative Citizenship for Sephardi Descendants: Returning to the Jewish Past in Spain and Portugal
Edited by Dalia Kandiyoti and Rina Benmayor

Reparative Citizenship for Sephardi Descendants

*Returning to the Jewish Past
in Spain and Portugal*

Edited by
Dalia Kandiyoti and Rina Benmayor

berghahn
NEW YORK · OXFORD
www.berghahnbooks.com

First published in 2023 by
Berghahn Books
www.berghahnbooks.com

© 2023, 2026 Dalia Kandiyoti and Rina Benmayor
First paperback edition published in 2026

All rights reserved. Except for the quotation of short passages
for the purposes of criticism and review, no part of this book
may be reproduced in any form or by any means, electronic
or mechanical, including photocopying, recording, or any information
storage and retrieval system now known or to be invented,
without written permission of Berghahn Books.

Library of Congress Cataloging-in-Publication Data

Names: Kandiyoti, Dalia, editor. | Benmayor, Rina, editor.
Title: Reparative citizenship for Sephardi descendants : returning to the Jewish past in Spain and Portugal / edited by Dalia Kandiyoti, Rina Benmayor.
Description: 1st. | New York : Berghahn Books, 2023. | Series: Remapping cultural history; 16 | Includes bibliographical references and index.
Identifiers: LCCN 2022036437 (print) | LCCN 2022036438 (ebook) | ISBN 9781800738249 (hardback) | ISBN 9781800738256 (ebook)
Subjects: LCSH: Sephardim—Spain—Reparations. | Sephardim—Portugal—Reparations. | Reparation (Criminal justice)—Spain. | Reparation (Criminal justice)—Portugal. | Restorative justice—Spain. | Restorative justice—Portugal. | Citizenship—Spain. | Citizenship—Portugal. | Jews—Iberian Peninsula—History.
Classification: LCC DS135.S7 R47 2023 (print) | LCC DS135.S7 (ebook) | DDC 305.6/96046—dc23/eng/20220815
LC record available at https://lccn.loc.gov/2022036437
LC ebook record available at https://lccn.loc.gov/2022036438

British Library Cataloguing in Publication Data
A catalogue record for this book is available from the British Library.

EU GPSR Authorized Representative
LOGOS EUROPE, 9 rue Nicolas Poussin, 17000, LA ROCHELLE, France
Email: Contact@logoseurope.eu

ISBN 978-1-80073-824-9 hardback
ISBN 978-1-83695-361-6 paperback
ISBN 978-1-83695-362-3 epub
ISBN 978-1-80073-825-6 web pdf

https://doi.org/10.3167/9781800738249

Contents

List of Illustrations   viii

Acknowledgments   x

Introduction
   Sephardi Jews, Citizenship, and Reparation in
   Historical Context   1
   Dalia Kandiyoti and Rina Benmayor

I. Reparation and Reconciliation?
Legal and Political Perspectives on the 2015 Laws

1. "Reparative Citizenship": Confronting Injustices of the Past or Building Modern Nationalisms?   37
Alfons Aragoneses

2. Beyond Reparatory Justice: The Portuguese "Law of Return" as Nation Branding   53
Isabel David and Gabriela Anouck Côrte-Real Pinto

3. Reparations in Spanish Parliamentary Debates about the 2015 Nationality Law for Descendants of Sephardi Jews   73
Davide Aliberti

4. Personal Essay: Passport to the Past, Passport to the Future   94
Colette Capriles

II. Roots of "Returns":
Early Uses of Jewish and Muslim History

5. "Spaniards We Were, Spaniards We Are, and Spaniards We Will Be": Salonica's Sephardic Jews and the Instrumentalization of the Spanish Past, 1898–1944   107
Devin E. Naar

6. "Spanish Jews" and "Friendly Muslims": The Historical Absence of a Citizenship Campaign for Muslims of Iberian Descent 137
Elisabeth Bolorinos Allard

7. Personal Essay: The Story of a Spanish Dönme 153
Uluç Özüyener

III. Negotiating the Present: Between States and Official Communities

8. *Moriscos Andalusíes*: Historical Reparation, Reconciliation, and the Duty of Memory 166
Elena Arigita and Laura Galián

9. Negotiating Historical Redress: The Spanish Law of Nationality for Sephardi Descendants and Spain's Jewish Communities 183
Daniela Flesler and Michal Rose Friedman

10. Personal Essay: "Congratulations, You Are Portuguese!" Reflections on Identity and Nationality 202
Rita Ender

11. Personal Essay: Sefarad Postponed 213
Ruth Behar

IV. Sephardi Descendants: Emotions, Identities, and Bureaucracies

12. "*La Nostalgia de Sefarad Tira Mucho, Pero No Tanto*": Attachment, Sentiment, and the Ethics of Refusal 223
Charles A. McDonald

13. Affective Citizenship and Iberian Sephardi Descendants 238
Rina Benmayor

14. Descendants of Conversos in the Americas: The Ancestral Past, Sephardi Identity, and Citizenship in Spain and Portugal 257
Dalia Kandiyoti

15. Portuguese Citizenship for Brazilian Descendants of Sephardic Jews: A Netnography 277
Marina Pignatelli

Appendix. Certifying Origins for Sephardic Descendants in Portugal: A Snapshot of the Evaluation Process 295
Teresa Santos and Heraldo Bento

16. Personal Essay: The Fez in the Water—Exile and Return 304
Victor Silverman

Coda. Directions in Citizenship and Historical Repair 315
Dalia Kandiyoti and Rina Benmayor

Index 319

Illustrations

Figures

Front cover image: Santa María la Blanca (Toledo, Spain) was a synagogue built in the second half of the thirteenth century and converted into a place of Catholic worship two centuries later. Currently, it belongs to the Catholic Church. Contemporary efforts to restore it to the Jewish community and the state have been unsuccessful, and its iconic *mudéjar* arches remain a symbol of the ongoing quest for historical reparations.

3.1. Timeline. Created by Davide Aliberti. 80

3.2. Summary of Legislative Activity. Created by Davide Aliberti. 86

5.1. Photograph of Isaac Alcheh y Saporta published in his pamphlet, *Los españoles sin patria de Salónica* (1917), accompanied by a poem in honor of his mother in which he explains that he added her surname to that of his father's in line with Spanish custom. He also alludes to Spain as *nuestro Sión* (our Zion), or, in other words, as the Sephardic homeland. Public domain. 108

5.2. Cadastral document for the Katalan Hadash (New Catalan) synagogue issued to the Jewish Community of Salonica in 1922, after the synagogue, along with thirty-one others, had been destroyed by the fire of 1917. Source: The Jewish Museum of Thessaloniki, used with permission. 123

5.3. Title page of the *Mahzor Katalan*, a high holiday prayer book published by the Katalan Hadash congregation in Salonica in 1927 in honor of the four-hundredth anniversary of its first printing in 1527 and with the hope that the new prayer book would inspire the congregation's members to rebuild their synagogue. Source: New York Public Library, used with permission. 124

5.4. Birth registration issued by the Spanish consul of Salonica for Jacques, son of Isidor Abravanel and Dora née Aruch, 1932. Jacques's grandfather Yakov (d. 1939), after whom he was named, was a prominent merchant and a notable in the Jewish community of Salonica. Jacques, his parents, and his brother numbered among the 511 Salonican Jews recognized as Spanish nationals at the onset of the Nazi occupation in 1943. Source: Abravanel's granddaughter, Makena Mezistrano, used with permission. 127

5.5. Spanish passport for Salonican Bergen Belson survivor Jacques Abravanel (1932–2012). After the war, Abravanel returned to Salonica where he became a star soccer player for Iraklis (Hercules) before eventually settling in Seattle, Washington. Source: Abravanel's granddaughter, Makena Mezistrano, used with permission. 128

15.1. Number of Sephardic applications for Portuguese citizenship by year. Graph produced by Santos and Bento, based on raw data provided to the authors by the Instituto de Registos Centrais e do Notariado. 298

15.2. Countries with largest number of applications, by year. Graph produced by Santos and Bento, using raw data provided by the Comunidade Israelita de Lisboa, November 2020. 299

Acknowledgments

The seeds of this book were planted with our personal responses to the Spanish and Portuguese Nationality Laws for Sephardi Descendants, just after they went into effect in 2015. In early 2016 Rina Benmayor initiated her two-year application process to Spain. Although not a pursuant, Dalia Kandiyoti was intrigued by the possible impact of the laws on the applicants and on changing discourses about Sephardism, diasporas, and nationalism. As we shared ideas and experiences of the application process, heard from friends and relatives who were interested in trying their luck, and read reports in the Jewish, Spanish, and Portuguese press, we decided to explore how other Sephardi Jews might be reacting to this unusual invitation. In early in 2017, we designed and launched the Spanish and Portuguese Citizenship for Sephardi Jewish Descendants: An Oral History Collection (2017–22), which now comprises some seventy in-depth interviews. Long before the Covid-19 pandemic, we were using the Zoom platform to interview applicants from all over the world—Europe, the Americas, the Middle East, and Africa —about their family histories, Sephardi identities, and reasons for seeking Spanish or Portuguese nationality. We presented our first joint papers on this research in Madrid (2018), and Salamanca and Lisbon (2019), and, together, with small group of scholars studying Jews in Spain and Portugal, formed the ongoing Genealogies of Sepharad/Genealogías de Sefarad research group.

Through this collaboration and further research, we became convinced that our work on the citizenship laws was not only timely but that it also warranted a book. Collecting various disciplinary and personal perspectives was best suited, we decided, to the layered, multidimensional set of issues the nationality provisions have presented. The concept and contours of the volume took shape in the Fall of 2019; despite the significant physical and emotional Covid-19 fog that engulfed the world in 2020, our contributors and the press moved forward with this project, to our great encouragement. Receiving National Endowment for the Humanities (NEH) faculty awards to develop our respective chapters, which also advanced our work for this volume, was icing on the cake. We are very grateful to the NEH for its support.

We also acknowledge with much appreciation the editorial board and staff of Berghahn Books—Series Editor Jo Labanyi, Editorial Board member Kostis Kornetis, and Associate Editor Amanda Horn for their heartening green light and guidance during the worst of the Covid-19 period and for the inclusion of this project in the series "Remapping Cultural History." Sulaiman Ahmad and Keara Hagerty's skillful direction of production was very helpful at various stages. We also thank Alison Hope for her detailed and careful copy editing. To the authors included in this volume go our profound thanks for their original contributions and perseverance through the rigorous revision processes at a time when coping with health and safety was the overwhelming priority. Michal Friedman shared her wealth of historical knowledge and gave us support and constructive comments on our drafts in her unfailingly generous way. Our thanks to Mary Louise Pratt for her enthusiastic support of our project, and to Linda Shopes for her smart editorial feedback and suggestions in the proposal stage of this book. As always, Robert Latham offered his experience and support whenever asked. The Genealogies of Sepharad research group, some of whose members' articles are included in the volume, has encouraged and inspired us to continue this work.

Introduction

Sephardi Jews, Citizenship, and Reparation in Historical Context

Dalia Kandiyoti and Rina Benmayor

"¡Cuánto os hemos echado de menos!" (How we have missed you!) declared Spain's King Felipe VI at the ceremony in June 2015 celebrating the passage of the new Spanish nationality for descendants of Sephardi Jews (Alberola 2015).[1] Just months earlier, during a press conference heralding Portugal's amendment to its nationality law (Decreto-Lei no. 30-A/2015) to incorporate Sephardi descendants, Minister of Justice Paula Teixeira da Cruz emphasized, "I would not say that this is a case of historical reparation, because I understand that what was done is impossible to repair. I would say that this [amendment] is about the attribution of a right. . . . We took a long time to deal with this matter. Therefore, I think today is a noteworthy day" (*Lusa e Público* 2015). Between February and June 2015, the two countries that comprise the Iberian Peninsula passed historic nationality laws allowing dual nonresidential citizenship to those whose Jewish ancestors had been victims of expulsion and forced conversion.[2] The Spanish law is described as a reencounter and reconciliation with the global Sephardi community after more than half a millennium; the Portuguese amendment is called a law of return to the homeland. Without having to renounce their current citizenships or establish residency, the descendants of those Jews who were expelled or forcibly converted to Catholicism during the fifteenth and sixteenth centuries could now reclaim a right to nationality through ancestry, based on genealogical proof of lineage, even if they do not identify as Jewish.

Recognition of genocides, ethnic cleansings, expulsions, and land appropriations can have powerful reparative effects. Yet few countries in the world have held themselves accountable for past injustices perpetrated against their populations or have offered citizenship as a form of apology, atonement, or repair. Nationality restitution in Europe has applied to twentieth-century citizenship deprivations during World War II. Germany, Austria, and Greece reformed their laws to restore citizenship rights and reparations to Holocaust survivors and descendants of the Nazi genocide. Ghana's right of abode program, positioned as a homecoming for Africans in the diaspora, speaks to a history that stretches back three centuries. Though all three laws in Spain, Portugal, and Ghana concern the recovery of national belonging predating the formation of contemporary nation-states, only Spain and Portugal offer nonresidential dual citizenship with the goal of reconnecting to its roots a people wronged long ago.

The news of these laws, which had been under development for several years, reverberated in Sephardi communities throughout the Jewish world. The *Times of Israel* proclaimed, "Citizenship for Sephardic Jews 'Corrects Historical Wrong'" (Lipschitz 2015), and the *LA Times* declared, "Welcome Home, 500 Years Later: Spain Offers Citizenship to Sephardic Jews" (Chu 2015). Similarly, *The Forward* ran the headline: "Portugal Issues First Passport Under Sephardic 'Law of Return'" (JTA 2015). Despite various historical and political precedents of citizenship dispensations for Sephardi Jews, as we explain below in this introduction, the press and government officials hailed these laws as unique and historic in offering citizenship to set right the wrongs committed more than five centuries ago.

Since the passage of the laws, the positive response from Sephardi communities became evident in the combined number of applicants, at slightly over 300,000, to both Spain and Portugal, based on governmental data.[3] The global nature of this response is in part a consequence of the widespread dispersal and movement of Sephardi Jews and the descendants of New Christians over many continents and centuries, resulting from expulsions and Inquisitions. It is difficult to encapsulate the complexity of these migratory movements in a short space, as they formed a dense web of back-and-forth routes, often via Italy, to the Ottoman Empire (Turkey, Greece, and the Balkans) (Benbassa and Rodrigue 2000; Ben-Ur 2009, 1–22; Díaz-Mas 1986, 53–94). The Ottoman Empire received the largest concentration of Sephardi exiles, referred to as Eastern Sephardis, the speakers of Ladino. Others fled Spain to closer regions, resettling primarily in Morocco, where Spanish influence was already established, and where Haketia became a Sephardi vernacular. A great number of Spanish Jews also sought refuge in Portugal, only to face a forced conversion decree in Portugal four years later (1496), triggering more border-crossings to evade Inquisitorial forces. By the eighteenth century many Portuguese converts had migrated to urban centers in Northern Europe, predominantly in Amsterdam, Hamburg, and London, where reconversions to Judaism took place freely. These European cities also became the springboards to the Americas, first to Brazil and later to the Caribbean and elsewhere on the continent, including the East Coast of the United States, forming the Western Sephardi branch of the diaspora. Those who retained their Portuguese roots are referred to in the 2015 law with the historical term *Judeus da nação* (Jews of the nation). Nineteenth- and twentieth-century migrations, driven in large part by the Balkan Wars of 1912 and World Wars I and II, would extend the diaspora farther across the north of Africa, and throughout the United States, the Southern Cone countries of South America, and southern Africa. At different times over these centuries India, China, and Japan would become home to Jews of Spanish and Portuguese origin. The vastness and complexity of dispersal and resettlements set the stage for the tens of thousands of citizenship applications received from every continent.

Given the passage of centuries since the original expulsions, persecutions, and forced conversions, what motivated Spain and Portugal to take such actions at this moment? What does it mean, legally, historically, and rhetorically, that Spain seeks to reconnect and reconcile with the Sephardi world, and Portugal offers a right of return? Why were the descendants of Moriscos—Spanish Muslims forcibly converted to Christianity in the sixteenth century and expelled in the seventeenth—not included in the law? In what ways did the Spanish and Portuguese Jewish communities push for these laws? What has motivated descendants to seek these new nationalities, and how have they negotiated the process institutionally, legally, and personally? Why have some eligible individuals chosen not to apply? And what is the meaning of these laws to the Sephardi descendants themselves in terms of identity, belonging, and collective memory? These are the questions that motivated this book.

A key aspect that inspired this undertaking is the novelty of the laws and the unprecedented response to them, which piqued the interest of both the general public and scholars. Our own curiosity led to an extensive oral history project, interviewing some sixty descendants from four continents who applied to one or, in a handful of instances, to both countries (Benmayor and Kandiyoti 2017–22).[4] As this book was being finalized in early 2022, a number of academic journal articles and book chapters about these provisions appeared (e.g., Aliberti 2018; Benmayor and Kandiyoti 2020; Goldschläger and Orjuela 2021; Kerem 2021; Ojeda-Mata 2018; Schammah Gesser and Pinheiro 2019). *Reparative Citizenship* is, however, the first academic book of articles and essays on the topic, bringing together a geographical and disciplinary diversity of perspectives—legal, historical, institutional, cultural, and testimonial—to analyze the significance and impact of the laws.

The sixteen original chapters written for this volume are by an international and multidisciplinary group of twenty-one scholars and writers from Italy, Portugal, Spain, Turkey, the United Kingdom, the United States, and Venezuela. The authors are legal scholars, political scientists, historians, oral historians, anthropologists, ethnographers, philosophers, literary and cultural studies scholars, filmmakers, and creative writers. One of the volume's unique features is its combination of academic and personal writing, a practice uncommon in scholarly literature. Interspersed among eleven analytical chapters are five testimonial essays; these are reflections penned by Sephardi descendants who applied for or received citizenship and represent the diasporic and ethnic complexities of Sephardi identity. This stylistic mixture affords readers a rigorous and intimate look into the contemporary meanings of these two ancestry-based citizenships. Both the scholarly discussions and the personal narratives shed light on Sephardi identities, the import of ancestral pasts, and ideas and feelings about becoming Spanish or Portuguese nationals. Together, they provide a grounded understanding of the role that remote histories and collective memory play for nations, communities, and individuals in the present. Also notable is the fact that four of the critical chapters are jointly researched and authored, breaking with individualistic modes of scholarship. As coauthors of papers on the citizenship laws and now as coeditors of this volume, we appreciate the added value and pleasure of joint thinking, research, and writing.

Why "Reparative" Citizenship?

Despite the Spanish king's impassioned words of welcome, Spain, unlike Portugal, has never rescinded the Edict of Expulsion, nor has it issued a formal apology for the sufferings of the expulsion and Inquisition. And while the Portuguese minister used the word "reparative," she was quick to explain that the law does not constitute a reparation, but rather the restoration of a right. In fact, both laws carefully avoid using any form of the term "reparation" (as various chapters in this volume explain). Why then, are we calling these citizenships "reparative"?

Both terms, "reparative" and "citizenship," have complex multiple meanings and interpretive uses. From a strictly legal standpoint and in accordance with internationally accepted definitions of "reparations" (see Aliberti chap. 3 in this volume), the Spanish and Portuguese nationality laws cannot be called reparative, since material compensation is not the goal, and it is impossible to calculate damages from a distance of five centuries. In addition, holding modern states responsible for historical acts is problematic, since at a time of the expulsions and Inquisitions neither Portugal nor Spain existed as nation-states. Extending reparations for something that happened so long ago would have implications in the present, in particular as regards Spain's Law of Historical Memory and compensations claims for victims of the Spanish Civil War and the Franco dictatorship. At the same time, as Alfons Aragoneses and Davide Aliberti point out in chapters 1 and 3, respectively, in recent decades the concept of reparations has broadened from its compensatory postwar origins, and has acquired new meanings when connected to human rights and social justice movements, such as reparative justice and transitional justice (Carranza 2009; Torpey 2006). As the International Center for Transitional Justice (ICTJ) explains, "Reparations initiatives seek to recognize and address the harms suffered by victims of human rights violations. They can be designed in many ways and may include symbolic as well as financial or practical measures" (ICTJ n.d.). In recent years, reparations and reconciliation have become more closely aligned with their underlying symbolic, moral, and ethical dimensions, as evidenced in international laws, declarations of human rights, and post-conflict peace and rights efforts to come to terms with national pasts. The Truth and Reconciliation commissions in Latin America and South Africa (Avruch and Vejarano 2002; Mamdani 2002), and Spain's Law of Historical Memory, as well as reparations movements for Atlantic slavery (Araujo 2017) and colonial land grabs (Lenzerini 2017) are a few salient examples. However, rarely has citizenship been offered as a form of symbolic reparation or reconciliation, and, as we noted earlier, never at such a historical distance. Whether the laws actually achieve repair is a question that hangs in the balance. Many of our contributors, in fact, are unconvinced that they do. The laws, however, constitute, in Aragoneses's words, "a strong gesture that has a rights and legal dimension and shows a commitment to the values of democracy and human rights" (chap. 1 in this volume).

In proposing citizenship and these laws as forms of reparation, we are also influenced by the metaphorical value of colloquial speech. "Reparative," "repair," and "reparation" are all terms that have been widely used in vernacular reference to the laws—by the governmental architects, by parliamentarians throughout their debates, by the press in all languages, and by the applicants themselves. Vernacular usage is less constrained in recognizing the laws' underlying impulses, be they restorative (Benmayor and Kandiyoti 2020) or symbolic. Along with the Portuguese minister of justice cited above, the former Spanish minister of justice, Alberto Ruiz-Gallardón, the main governmental force behind the Spanish law, has publicly referred to the law as a symbolic reparation (see Flesler and Friedman, chap. 9; and McDonald, chap.12 in this volume).

If the laws trigger an expansion of our understanding of reparation, they also contain within them the potential to destabilize traditional constructs of citizenship. Although they are based on a condition of genealogical, cultural, and territorial origin, the citizenships are not automatically granted but rather are attained through a multistage naturalization process based on rigorous genealogical proof, especially for non-Jewish descendants. Such requirements raise questions as to whether these laws can be considered truly reparative, since multiple conditions are placed on the attainment of citizenship. At the same time, their uniqueness, particularly as regards the lifting of residency and single-state loyalty, suggests a more malleable concept of membership and belonging. Globalization and trans-nationalization processes have led a growing number of countries to recognize the existence of simultaneous allegiances and acknowledge dual and multiple citizenships to be held by its peoples. For instance, states may offer dual citizenship for strategic reasons (Harpaz and Mateos 2019) or in exchange for substantial investments (Joppke 2019). Moreover, scholars now pose citizenship as "an 'institution' mediating rights between the subjects of politics and the polity to which these subjects belong" (Isin and Nyers 2014, 1). The European Union as a polity, to cite the most relevant example, challenges traditional nationalist legal frameworks of belonging and their cultural moorings, as the reactions of movements and parties on the political Right decry. At the same time, the blurring of pre-Schengen borders is accompanied by the strengthening of North-South apartheid logics (Cabot 2019) and by expanded policies of immigrant detention (e.g., Klaus 2017).

Despite the growth of detentionary regimes and the hardening of immigration and refugee policies in Europe and the United States, when seen from the perspectives of the diverse peoples who now comprise multicultural nation-states, citizenship is no longer the sole purview of the state to define. Demands for rights by social actors and communities produce new meanings of national belonging that go beyond legal frameworks (Flores and Benmayor 1997; Kabir 2005; Maestri and Hughes 2017). Struggles for educational and citizenship rights by undocumented immigrant minors in the United States, known as Dreamers, who are beneficiaries of the Development, Relief, and Education for Alien Minors Act (DREAM Act), for instance, rely on and at the same time destabilize normative citizenship frames (Patler 2018). Citizenship, in this sense, can be understood as more than just national membership status; it acquires new meanings through the expression of social and cultural practices. Spanish and Portuguese citizenship may represent reconciliatory efforts by the state to reembrace its Sephardi descendants, but the applicants themselves can also expand the meaning of reparative citizenship, as does Colette Capriles, a Venezuelan of Sephardi ancestry born into a Catholic family, by proudly declaring herself the holder of a "Sephardi passport" (chap. 4 in this volume). Interestingly, given the extraterritorial location of most applicants and citizenship recipients, the passport, rather than the national identity card, becomes the documentary representation of their membership in the nation-state.

The negotiation between subjects and states also has a historical dimension, one that is unique in the case of the 2015 Spanish and Portuguese laws. Bearing novel features, these laws also are tied to the ways in which the two states have related to Sephardi Jewry since the nineteenth century, when they abolished their Inquisitions, and the absolute authority of the Catholic Church was challenged. The relationship has been variable and not necessarily consistent, yet the sense of a continuum is expressed in the present by politicians and other state representatives. However, the complications of the reconnection following the extreme ruptures of expulsion, conversion, and the Inquisition are revealed by many of our contributors. Next, we trace this connection between the Iberian Peninsula and the descendants of exiled and converted Sephardi Jews, with a focus on the tangled story of their reintegration through special nationality dispensations.

Routes of Spanish Nationality and the Sephardi Jewish Past

Spain's 2015 citizenship law draws on a very long and nonlinear history of the reincorporation of Sephardi Jews into the national body and the national imaginary. Scholars have written extensively on the reappearance of Sephardi Jews in liberal political and cultural discourses of the nineteenth century, when Jewish and Muslim cultures were presented as key to Spain's own culture and their absence a keen loss, though such discourses did not lack ambivalence or self-serving formulations (Friedman 2011; Menny 2010; Rohr 2005, 2011). Colonial conquests and ambitions led to the concretization of some of these ideas: the "discovery of" and "reconnection with" Moroccan Sephardi Jews in the context of Spain's early twentieth-century colonization of part of the North African country played a particularly important role, though Sephardi Jews elsewhere, especially in the Ottoman Empire, too were of interest (Bolorinos

Allard 2021; Calderwood 2018; Ojeda-Mata 2018; Rohr 2011). The descendants of the expelled Jews, who retained forms of Spanish such as Ladino and Haketia, and customs that evolved in the centuries after exile, were recruited to serve as so-called middlemen and agents of Spain from the Balkans to North Africa. This effort, undergirded by intellectuals and diplomats, most notably by Senator Ángel Pulido, was in some ways remarkable (see, e.g., Bolorinos Allard, chap. 6 and Naar, chap. 5 in this volume; Rohr 2007). It stood in contrast to the conservative antisemitic political forces in Spain and the centuries-long ban on Jews and Judaism, along with the ban on Muslims and Islam. Cultural and ethnoracial discourses sought to undo the legacy of the Inquisition, which was originally established to root out "judaizers" and, later, other "heretics." The newer views were undergirded by the political and economic motivations for the cultivating of Moroccan and Ottoman Jews. In what scholars now refer to as philosephardic discourse, the cultural continuity with Iberia that Sephardi Jews bore in their pastoral and toponymic Peninsular surnames, medieval Spanish tongue, culinary traditions, and religious rituals were lauded and positioned as markers of a timeless love and nostalgia for their Iberian homelands, just as they would be later in the preambles of both of the 2015 laws. Culturally hybridized groups of Ladino-speaking North African and Balkan Jews who had absorbed many aspects of their local cultures were reconstructed as "Spaniards without a homeland," in an often-cited term coined by Pulido. This projection of affect and above all loyalty onto the inheritors of historical Sepharad (the Hebrew word for Spain) lent them a different image than the virulently antisemitic one (Álvarez Chillida 2002) that had characterized Spanish history and the attitudes of those opposing liberalization. But, for the more liberal thinkers and actors, reimagined Sephardi Jews were key to the historical foundations of a multicultural, tolerant, tricultural Spain characterized by *convivencia* (peaceful coexistence), the term made influential by mid-twentieth-century scholar Américo Castro, and not by the "mistakes" of expulsions and persecutions.[5]

It was not only their perceived loyalty and longing that led to the conditional, partial, and periodic legal reincorporation of Sephardi Jews into the national body. This reintegration had begun in the nineteenth century despite the staunchness of national Catholicism that began waning only with the death of Francisco Franco in 1975. Other notions also paved the way to citizenship initiatives, most relevantly, the conception of a shared identity posited as a historical mixture between Jews and Spaniards (Ojeda-Mata 2016), with a racializing bent (Goode 2009). These discourses of Sephardi Jews as belonging to the Spanish *raza* (race) constituted a way of folding them into the Hispanism of the early twentieth century and of the Franco period, when prominent Spaniard intellectuals claimed *hispanidad* (being Hispanic) as a force that united Spain with its lost possessions in Spanish-speaking Latin America. Language was primary to an *hispanidad* branded as spiritual. This made it possible for the Spanish-speaking, but not Spanish-identifying, Ottoman and Moroccan Jews to be incorporated into this neocolonial and postimperial vision, advocated variously by liberal, nationalist, right-wing, conservative, proto-fascist, and fascist ideologues in different periods (Friedman 2011; Ginio 2007; Rohr 2007). Scholars have pointed out that the idea of a spiritual kind of race of Spanish-speaking peoples, seemingly going beyond racial ideas, did not in fact displace biological race or blood logics (Goode 2009; Martín-Márquez 2008, 50; Ojeda-Mata 2016). The perception of Jewish economic power, an antisemitic trope, in areas of interest to Spain played an important role in the rapprochement, signalling the overlap between antisemitism and philosephardism.

What did all this mean for the restitution of Sephardi legal status in Spain? Degrees of integration into the Spanish nation were practiced already in the nineteenth century for a small number of Sephardi Jews belonging to the elites. As early as the 1840s, these included consular protections and later what Ojeda-Mata (2018, 45) described as "fourth-class Spanish citizenship by naturalization" in Morocco.[6] Remarkably, in the second decade of the twentieth century, the Spanish consul in Salonica, who was influenced by Pulido's vision of Spanish national restoration through the Sephardi Jews, made "an ambitious outreach" and sought to extend Spanish nationality to the Ottoman Sephardi Jews in insecure status due to the Balkan wars and Greek nationalism (Stein 2016, 29). In 1924 a Royal Decree of the dictatorial regime of Primo de Rivera offered naturalization to Sephardi Jews who were consular protégés of Spain, or were descended from them. The motive was to make Spanish nationals out of those who had been displaced and/or found themselves without nationality following the breakup of the Balkans and Ottoman Empires. Similar to the 2015 Spanish law, the dispensation came with an expiration date: 1930. By then, several thousand had received nationality though, as Isabelle Rohr explains it, many "missed the opportunity" and became stateless because of the nonrecognition of protégés locally and by Spain. Moreover, as minorities, some feared consequences in the nationalist environments of Turkey or Greece, where ideologies of ethnic and religious homogeneity became dominant. Others found the requirements "quite arduous" or impossible to fulfill (Rohr 2007, 27). Notably, the decree included a warning that "the petitioner should assert that he will not settle in Spain" (quoted on 27). The special nationality allowances to Jews also took place during the brief period of the Spanish Republic and even under Franco's dictatorship, which incessantly decried a fabricated Judeo-Masonic conspiracy, both during its pro-Nazi war years and afterward (Avni 1982; Baer 2011; Rohr 2007). The regime also denationalized thousands of Jews during World War II (Ojeda-Mata 2018; see also Naar, chap. 5 in this volume).

World War II, when many Sephardi Jews were in desperate need of protection, presented a tragic litmus test of philosephardism. Individual consuls, acting on their own and not under state directives, helped save Jews from the Holocaust by providing Spanish documentation, which protected them in their countries or helped them leave. These papers constituted a déclassé form of nationality, which did not allow them refuge or permanent residence in Spain (Rother 2005). Because of the non-settlement stipulation, Spain refused permanent repatriation, including to those who had been naturalized under the 1924 decree and were at great risk. Protection was not automatic even for those held in concentration camps while holding Spanish citizenship (Avni 1982). For example, the hundreds of Salonican Jews who had Spanish papers and were deported from Greece to Bergen-Belsen were at the camp for months while Spain equivocated about claiming their Jewish nationals. Eventually, the Salonicans were sent to Morocco or Palestine with no stay in Spain (Avni 1982). The Spanish government intervened, and these lives were saved, but the Jewish nationals of Spain were not treated like citizens with the right of abode in their own country. Most of those who *were* repatriated were treated as stateless in Spain and sent to third countries as quickly as possible. Nevertheless, in the postwar period and under the new world order, Spain successfully built a narrative about having been a savior of Jews, appropriating the individual work and sacrifices of some consuls as decisions of the state, obfuscating the experiences of the refugees and other facts that scholars, beginning with Haim Avni, later unearthed in detail. In 1948 another Royal Decree offered national-abroad status to Sephardi Jews in Greece and Egypt who were about to lose their position as protégés at the termination of the Ottoman era Capitulations, agreed on in the Montreux Treaty of 1937. By then, the philosephardism of the liberals and Republicans had long given way to the fascist, nationalist antisemitism of Francoism, though it still became an instrument at certain junctures after the dictator's allies lost the war and his regime tried to construct a different image of Spain. Flowery language about a shared past and the 1948 dispensation disguised the partial and conditional nature of the legal and cultural reincorporation of Sephardi Jews and the virulent Judeophobia of the regime.

The period that shaped the 2015 law began after Franco's death in 1975, during the early 1980s transition to democracy, when significant legal developments allowed the freedom of practice and organization to religions other than Catholicism. Also, during this time, the Civil Code was revised to add Sephardi Jews to the list of those with reduced requirements of residency (from ten to two years) in Spain for acquiring citizenship, along with citizens of Latin American countries, Andorra, Equatorial Guinea, and the Philippines. The special treatment of these groups was due to the way "Spain has traditionally considered nationals of some countries as forming part of a joint cultural community and acknowledges a certain historical debt towards other communities" (quoted in Howard 2009, 108). Citizenship scholar Christian Joppke has observed that Spain and Portugal have a special place among individual European states that have preferential provisions of nationality to those with pre-existing ethnic ties or, in the case of former empires with overseas conquests, to citizens of former territories viewed as a part of their "postcolonial constellations" (2005, 112-13). The "historical and cultural links" with the regions and peoples that their former empires ruled "have taken on cultural and panethnic contours, pointing to a . . . state-transcending community that calls for privileged treatment" in matters of immigration and citizenship (112). However, as always there are limitations. Despite the wide-ranging idea of a historical and cultural community, the expelled Morisco descendants were not acknowledged, and Sephardi Jews were the only group for whom dual citizenship was *not* admissible. This 1982 modification, leading to the special law of 2015, was made during a period in which we still find ourselves: what we might call a neo-philosephardism, or as Aragoneses put it, *"filosefardismo* 2.0" (2016, 30). Couched in both longstanding national discourses and contemporary references to collective memory, rights, and genocide, the 2015 dispensation was positioned as the culmination of Spain's striving to reconcile with Sephardi Jews. Alberto Ruiz-Gallardón, the minister of justice who proposed the bill, explained that Spain, which had a "historical debt" to Sephardi Jews who had "always wanted to be Spaniards," needed to correct a "historical mistake." This law, he declared, is the culmination of the reencounter with the Sephardi Jews (Aliberti 2018, 195; *La Vanguardia* 2014; also see Flesler and Friedman, chap. 9 in this volume).

The post-Franco era, anchored in discourses of *convivencia*, promoted Jewish Spain as integral to the national culture through diplomatic and institutional relations with the Jewish world, the creation of a large network of medieval Jewish neighborhoods and museums, and the encouragement of Jewish tourism (Flesler and Pérez Melgosa 2020; Linhard 2016). These developments had their parallels in Portugal as we will see in this introduction, including in terms of creating new nation-branding (see David and Côrte-Real Pinto, chap. 2 in this volume). Key related events in Spain have included the granting of the Prince of Asturias Concord Award to Sephardi communities in 1990, King Juan Carlos I's historic 1992 speech in a Madrid synagogue welcoming home the Sephardi Jews (paving the way to 2015), the cultural efforts of the Instituto Cervantes to incorporate Ladino/Judeo-Spanish into its programs, the change of name of a town that had been called Castrillo Matajudios (Fort Kill The Jews) to Castrillo Mota de Judios (Fort Hill of Jews), the 2018 announcement by the Real Academia Española of the creation of a Ladino academy, and much more.[7] The pre-expulsion Jewish past has had a substantial role to play in Spain's long transition to democracy and its efforts to reverse or overcome the intertwined legacies of empire, the Inquisition, and dictatorship. The 2007 Law of Historical Memory, whose provisions include right of return and citizenship for Spanish Civil War political exiles and their descendants, is connected to the inclusion of Sephardi Jews in the newer practices and discourses of recovery, restitution, and rights in Spain. As numerous scholars have shown, the transnational rise of collective memory discourses characterizing the late twentieth century have had multiple dimensions in Spain, where civil war memory practices and narratives (Labanyi 2008) have been imbricated with Holocaust memory *and* the Spanish Jewish past (Baer 2011; Flesler and Pérez Melgosa 2020, 12–16; Linhard 2014). The inclusion of citizenship restoration within a landscape of historical memory, for both the descendants of the civil war exiles and of Sephardi Jews, taking place within less than a decade of one another, is viewed as part and parcel of an ethical relationship to the past and the postdictatorial reconstruction of national image. Spotlighting and augmenting the few Jewish material traces that have survived bans and persecutions and the invitations to Sephardi Jews to return through the offer of nationality have helped shape Spain as a worthy European partner bearing a vision of democracy, rights, and tolerance.

The preamble of the law is a testament to the ways in which this neo-philosephardism combines antediluvian and current discourses. Although there is little evidence for the claim, it asserts that "the children of Sepharad maintained an abundance of nostalgia immune to the transformation of languages and generations" (Law 12/2015). Citing Sephardi Jews' maintenance of language and custom, it adds, "Pulsating through time is a love for a Spain that is at last aware of the historical and emotional load the Sephardim have carried 12/2015" (Law 12/2015).[8] Coupled with these well-worn projections of nostalgia and loyalty, true only of a few Sephardi elites but key to Spain's rapprochement with Sephardi Jews for more than a century, are references in the preamble to the Holocaust and its place in Spanish memory.⁹ The text also speaks to the global identity of Sephardi Jews. Such characterizations, along with contemporary notions about collective memory and reconciliation, update philosephardism.

The Reception of the Spanish Law

From the start, the Spanish law was both praised and criticized for its discursive pitch as well as its dispensations. As Flesler and Friedman show in chapter 9 of this volume, the Federation of Jewish Communities of Spain, also established in the early 1980s, initiated this law, whose major improvements over earlier dispensations were eliminating any residency requirement and allowing dual citizenship. Well received by the state, the proposition was debated and eventually implemented through the time-honored claims about Sephardi Jews. The evocative words of the new king, Felipe VI, addressed to Sephardi Jews in 2015 "How we have missed you," which we quoted at the outset, also had a positive and even inspiring effect on many potential applicants (e.g., Assouline 2019). Benmayor and Kandiyoti's extensive oral history project (2017–22), and Benmayor's chapter 13 on affective citizenship in this volume indicate that many Sephardi Jews were moved by such discourses, both the Spanish and the Portuguese, of home, invitation, and restitution, whether or not they had any prior place for Spain or Portugal in their identities or family narratives. More often than not, the Peninsula itself, though not its diasporic culture, was a remote place of origin of little relevance. However, other Sephardi Jews had more practical motives that made little space for an emotional attachment to the past (Benmayor and Kandiyoti 2020; Kerem 2021) or held rather critical perspectives, like those of some scholars and authors, in which they questioned the countries' motives (see McDonald, chap. 12 in this volume). For Maite Ojeda-Mata, this law has few advantages over the old and is part of a "long Spanish tradition, one of recognition of Sephardi Jews' rights in small doses and never in an absolute or universal way" (Ojeda-Mata 2015, 49). The unexplained three-year expiration date (2018, later changed to 2019) and the demanding and costly requirements of eligibility and travel for in-person signings, all of which could add up to thousands of dollars if also handled by lawyers, were roundly critiqued. Perhaps symbolically the least digestible condition was to pass an intermediate-level Spanish language test (in addition to a Spanish culture and history exam). That most Jews of Spanish origin outside of Iberia and Latin America no longer speak Spanish or Judeo-Spanish precisely because of the extremely long gap between the loss of rights and their restitution, constituted a bitter irony for some, as Rita Ender expresses in chapter 10.

The rigors of the evidence and documentation process in both Spain and Portugal (see Bento and Santos's appendix to chap. 15 in this volume) have been controversial and detailed in much media coverage and some scholarly articles (e.g., Aragoneses 2016; Goldschläger and Orjuela 2021; Kerem 2021; McDonald 2021; Schammah Gesser 2019). The requirements to provide extensive genealogical evidence have been challenging for everyone, but particularly for those who have no present connection to historical Sephardi communities and congregations, especially the non-Jewish applicants of Sephardi descent from Christian, Muslim, Dönme, or other backgrounds. Finally, the 2,519 denials of citizenship by the Spanish Ministry of Justice as of 30 June 2022 (out of 45,186 cases reviewed to that date), have been controversial, generating an appellate process that some applicants are pursuing. These and any future rejections will merit investigative attention, as the review process is completed and more information becomes available. Also hanging in the balance is the impact of the Covid-19 pandemic on the application process, preventing or making it exceedingly risky for aspirants to travel to Spain and sign their applications before the notarial deadline, as Ruth Behar's essay, chapter 11 in this volume, attests.

Neo-philosephardism as a discourse deployed in the 2015 citizenship process seems to have a larger, more-global and rights-based vision than in the past, but its reliance on old tropes symbolically excludes many applicants who are eligible, including the non-Jewish descendants. For example, as Kandiyoti points out in chapter 14, the loyalty discourse cannot be applied to most of the converso descendants of the Americas whose families have been Christian without normative Jewish knowledge or practice since the medieval or early Modern era. Yet they, too, can be and have been beneficiaries of the law, since discrimination based on current religion is not allowed, and descent is the sine qua non of eligibility.

The linear narrative of cultural continuity bolsters Spain's (and Portugal's, as we will explain shortly) image as having an enduring cultural and identitarian impact on its historical victims. It also legitimizes the laws on these terms without acknowledging the nonconformity of converso, Dönme/Sabbatean, and other such pasts to this neat story. Furthermore, the emphasis on loyalty and cultural preservation reinforces the exclusion of the Morisco descendants expelled en masse at the beginning of the seventeenth century. Dispersed thereafter, mostly to North Africa and elsewhere in the Muslim world, Spanish Muslim descendants are sidelined for having assimilated to their places of exile and lost their Spanishness, as Arigita and Galián explain in chapter 8. As is well known, the primary reason for the Sephardi retention in diaspora of culture and language from the Peninsula was not a unilateral resistance to assimilation or loyalty, but rather the particular conditions of the Ottoman *millet* system that allowed religious communities' autonomy. But this is overlooked and set off against the Morisco exiles' adaptation to the local languages, religions, and cultures. Within the context of these contradictory discourses and practices, the reception of the laws, then, have been strikingly mixed within the Jewish, Muslim, Spanish, Latin American, and other contexts: on the one side, the law's exclusions (of Morisco descendants as well as Western Saharans/Sahrawis), rhetorical framing, and stringent demands have been subject to critique. On the other, there has been positive response and enthusiasm among the diverse actors and observers.

Portugal's Path

As other observers have remarked (e.g., Schammah Gesser 2019), Portugal's relationship with its Jewish past and its road to citizenship for Sephardi Jews is nowhere near as extensive as Spain's. A reencounter with its Jewish history became significant only in the aftermath of António de Oliveira Salazar's dictatorial rule in 1974 and in the process of democratization that followed. A massive de-Judaizing process had taken place with the 1496 forced conversion of the entire Portuguese Jewish community, estimated at a remarkable 20 percent of the population, and heavily consisting of the Spanish exiles of 1492. The effort to rid Portugal of its Jews was almost entirely successful because of Christianization; the flight of persecuted conversos, accused of judaizing, to safer European locations or the Ottoman Empire; and the victimization and murders carried out by the Inquisition and pogroms. However, Portuguese Jewish and converso identity persisted in diaspora as *nação* (the nation). So widespread was the *nação* that in the Americas and Europe of the early modern era, the label "Portuguese" often indicated "Jewish." But in Portugal itself, it would take a long time before there was a positive recognition to replace hateful banishment. The reforms of the Marquis de Pombal, the abolishment of the Inquisition, and the creation of a new constitution in the 1820s were critical to the gradual and very modest repopulation of Jews, mostly Moroccans and some non-Sephardi Eastern Europeans, during the nineteenth century. While Portugal also experienced liberalization, a turn away from the Church, and denunciations of

Judeophobia in that century, there was comparatively less philosephardic pulsion than in Spain (Martins 2006, v.1, v.2).

In the first decades of the twentieth century, the "discovery" of the "*judeus*" of northern Portugal by Samuel Schwarz, a Polish Jew, drew some attention to the Jewish past. Largely endogamous groups practicing secretly a transformed Judaism amalgamated with Catholicism fascinated the Jewish world. Although during the more tolerant years of the Portuguese Republic (1911–26), these crypto-Jews, or *marranos* as they are known in Portugal, garnered sympathy, they had relatively little impact on Portugal's policies or outlook. Early in the Salazar dictatorship, the persecution of an army officer claiming converso descent, Artur Barros Basto, "the apostle of the Marranos" who founded the Porto community and its still-active synagogue, played a role in the emergence of this history.

Sephardi Jews elsewhere played a role in Portugal's empire and its desire to carry influence in the Balkans and in Africa. In 1893 Livornese Jews of Portuguese origin in Tunis received from Portugal protégé status, which had been denied to them by the French and the British (Stein 2016, 28). For Portugal, this meant "embracing as protégés a wealthy mercantile population while vying with other European powers to deepen its commercial and cultural toehold in the Mediterranean" (28). In 1913 Portugal took advantage of the Balkan wars and the uncertain future faced by Ottoman Jews, some of whom sought protective naturalization by other empires. Wishing to extend its influence from Europe to Africa, and prompted by the requests of some Sephardi Jews in Salonica, where the Lisbon, Évora, and other synagogues of exiled Portuguese Jews still stood, Portugal recruited a select number of Jews as protégés. One senator combined the state's colonial future and responsibilities toward the past in a revealing 1913 speech in which he suggested that the proposed law would enable naturalized Jews to be settled in Angola (Franco 2004; Martins 2010; Stein 2016), which Portugal had begun occupying in the sixteenth century and settling in the nineteenth. The Sephardi Jews would be of much use there, owing to their "dotes de energia no trabalho e espírito de economia" (talent for energetic work and economical spirit). Furthermore, he asserted, "In addition to the advantage that should result for the province of Angola, the proposed law represents an act of *justice and reparation* for a race that has been so persecuted at all times and whose mass expulsion in December 1496 from the territory of Portugal by Manuel I and after 1532 by D. João III, by the evil action of the Inquisition, the tragic slaughter in the streets and squares of Lisbon in April 1506 . . . constitute the darkest stains in the entire history of the country." (Quoted in Franco 2004, 137; emphasis added). As with the Spanish case, this recognition and reparation through nationality went hand in hand with political projects in ways that sought to instrumentalize the Sephardi past in the service of Portugal's settler colonialism.

In the end, however, the Portuguese approach to the reincorporation of Sephardi Jews was as ambivalent and partial as the Spanish and even more so during World War II, despite Portugal's reputation as a haven. As a result of Salazar's compulsion to overturn the Republicans' limited 1913 provisions, Greek Sephardi Jews were not able to get protection during the war. "Salazar exhibited greater tolerance toward Jews who had no historical relationship to Portugal then [*sic*] he showed those who held 'provisional [Portuguese] registration' and, indeed, had once been embraced by Portugal" (Stein 2016, 121). Staying out of the war, Salazar maintained "neutrality," which meant sympathy for and business with the German regime, albeit without antisemitism serving as a motor of policy. Yet, because of the regime's claims that the consuls had produced false documents, Greek Jews with Portuguese papers and other Jews of Portuguese background in Holland and elsewhere met their fate at the hands of the Nazis (Milgram 2011). Brave consuls such as Aristides de Sousa Mendes in Bordeaux saved thousands *contra* Salazar, only to be both exploited and punished for it: "While sanctioning him professionally, Salazar ultimately profited from his actions in the postwar period by presenting Portugal as a rescuer of Jewish refugees" (Pimentel and Ninhos 2015, 113). Avraham Milgram has argued that it was not antisemitism but xenophobia and the right-wing fear of liberals and communists that motivated the dictator (Milgram 2011). The extent of Portugal's helping hand was significant because it affected tens of thousands. At the same time, it was basically limited to the offer of temporary passage to those not of Portuguese background on the way to real refuge in other ports. This changed in 1944, thanks to pressure from the United States and efforts of consuls, this time one in Budapest, who issued papers to about 1,000 Jews, with the proviso, again, of denial of refuge in Portugal. Much more than Spain, then, Portugal vacillated in its reincorporation of Sephardi Jews for the better part of the twentieth century.

But in 2013 the proposal to extend a citizenship possibility to descendants of Sephardi Jews was met with little controversy in the Portuguese Parliament or the society at large. Instead of developing a special law like Spain, the existing naturalization law was amended to include Sephardi Jews. This effort was part and parcel of the post-1974 period, characterized by the efforts to modernize, Europeanize, and democratize Portugal. The mobilization of the Portuguese Jewish past through the nationality dispensation was connected to efforts to project a tolerant and mixed Portuguese society. An official discourse of a multiracial and tolerant Portuguese Empire that downplayed slavery and racial hierarchy also characterized the Salazar period, even while protracted colonial wars in Africa were taking place. The post-dictatorship models of coexistence differed but also extended from such earlier ideas about the racially hybrid legacy of the Portuguese Empire, as David and Côrte-Real Pinto explain in chapter 2. Along these lines and connecting also to the memory, reconciliation, and reparation discourses of the moment, Portugal extensively recalled the Jewish past. Unlike in Spain, a head of state, President Mário Soares of the Socialist Party, gave an official apology for the Inquisition's persecution of Portuguese Jews in 1988. As in Spain, a Rede de Judiarias, network of Jewish neighborhoods, was established (in 2001) to promote the Jewish past and tourism, as were new museums, monuments, and festivals, along with the resignifications of the few Jewish remnants.

What distinguishes the Portuguese projects from all other such large-scale Jewish heritage efforts in Spain or elsewhere is the prominence of the converso past and crypto-Jewish groups, and their inclusion in Jewish heritage projects, especially in the north of the country. The awareness of this history of forced mass conversions and crypto-Jewish practice experienced a resurgence in the 1920s and 1930s, as we have seen, but especially in the 1970s and 1980s (Leite 2017; Pignatelli 2019). As a result, the notion that most Portuguese must have Jewish ancestry is popular in Portugal today (Leite 2017). Yet, despite this consciousness and the legal eligibility of converso or other non-Jewish descendants of Sephardi Jews for the citizenship opportunity, the Portuguese preamble, too, focuses by and large on unconverted Jews and New Christians who returned to Judaism outside of Portugal, as this passage indicates: "Despite the persecutions and the separation from their ancestral territory, many Sephardic Jews of Portuguese origin and their descendants kept not only the Portuguese language but also the traditional rites of the ancient Jewish religion in Portugal, preserving their family surnames, objects and documents proving their Portuguese origin, together with a strong memorial relationship that leads them to call themselves 'Portuguese Jews' or 'Jews of the Portuguese Nation [*nação*]'" (Decreto-Lei no. 30-A/2015 2015). Unlike in the Spanish preamble, the forced conversions and the de-Judaification of Portugal after 1496 is mentioned. However, it is the fidelity to the Portuguese language and customs on various continents, following the Jews' exile, that is described, as is the presence of some Jews in Portugal as of the nineteenth century. The fate of the converted non-Jewish descendants is not invoked in the historical overview.

Many Sephardi Jewish descendants have chosen to seek Portuguese rather than Spanish nationality, because Portugal does not demand knowledge of language or civics tests; nor does it require signing with a notary in the country, which also reduces costs, especially compared to Spanish applications, though costs are still substantial for many who hire lawyers and genealogists.[10] As a result, Portugal had been the target of less overt criticism than Spain. While the Portuguese requirements for eligibility had been much less stringent, some applicants have expressed disappointment in the inconsistencies with regard to the process. For example, the Jewish community organizations have played a decisive role in verifying eligibility, but each of them—the Lisbon (Comunidade Israelita de Lisboa) and the Porto (Comunidade Israelita de Porto)—has had different profiles. On social media and in interviews conducted for the Benmayor and Kandiyoti oral history project (2017–22), applicants voiced their concerns about these communities' differential treatment. The Porto community was known to entertain only those with normative Jewish identity or with generationally close Jewish family members, although both Jewish and non-Jewish seekers are eligible under the law as descendants (Kerem 2021). Non-normative Jewish descendants, like Dönmes or Sabbateans, have also remarked on the general lack of historical knowledge about their unique history, at least at the outset (Benmayor and Kandiyoti 2017–22). Despite the obstacles, so many applications had been filed (137,087 as of February 2022 [*Diario de Noticias* 2022]), that in 2021 a member of parliament tried unsuccessfully to amend the 2015 law by imposing a prior residency requirement and other restrictions, claiming that the commercialization of Portuguese citizenship was cheapening the national brand and sovereignty (Almeida 2020). The developments in early 2022, regarding Porto's granting of certifications of Sephardi origin to oligarchs, further complicated the Portuguese picture, leading to the termination of the Porto community as a certification site altogether. In September 2022, the parliament tightened evidentiary requirements, restricting the pool of potential claimants to those who can prove material connections to Portugal (Decreto-Lei 26/2022).

Mobilizing the Past and the Future

This overview of the development of the laws in Spain and Portugal helps us understand something about the special ways in which the past gets mobilized in citizenship regimes. As we have observed in this introduction and elsewhere (e.g., Benmayor and Kandiyoti 2020), Spain and

Portugal's special recognition of Sephardi Jewish descendants as potential nationals has taken place in a period of democratization and Europeanization in the Peninsula (although now these ideals have been put to the test with the upsurge of a far-right wing in Spain). The laws are also related to the contemporary rise in potential new citizens, whom other European states are also "selecting by origin" (Joppke 2005; 2019). According to the state-transcending conception of belonging (25), those considered fellow ethnics are eligible for returning to the nationality of their ancestors. For example, ethnic Hungarians in Serbia, Luso-Hispanics from Latin America, or Bulgarians in Macedonia are subject to preferential treatment in Hungary, Spain, Portugal, and Bulgaria, respectively (e.g., Joppke 2005; Pogonyi 2019). However, unlike in those cases, the selection of Sephardi Jewish descendants is presented as an act of repair and reconciliation on the basis of historical victimization. Also distinctive are the descendants' dispersals from origins that are uncommonly distant in time. Nevertheless, as we have shown above, the laws are predicated on loyalty to roots, demonstrated through linguistic and cultural transmission and/or affiliations with Spain and Portugal. And, as Charles McDonald (2021) has underlined about Spain, a lack of rancor for the victimization is presumed. Such approaches to the past and the present are telling about the conditionality of the intent to repair, which conforms to longstanding ideas about the nation without acknowledging ruptures to belonging. And, they symbolically exclude many potential beneficiaries whose Sephardi roots may be less perceptible.

Yet, never before have the concessions of belonging, whether as protégés or second-class or full citizens, included many non-Jews who are descendants of converts to Christianity and Islam or Sabbateanism. Long inside the Christian Luso-Hispanic or Muslim Turkish worlds, these descendants return to the current Sephardi moment (Kandiyoti 2020), though they were not necessarily the laws' primary targeted individuals. The converso, Dönme, and other non-normative Sephardi descendants exemplify the forked roads, twists, and turns in the path of Iberian-Sephardi "reconciliation" (as Spain refers to it), which are unacknowledged or under-recognized in official discourses. The chapters in this volume by Capriles (chap. 4), Kandiyoti (chap. 14), Özüyener (chap. 7), Flesler and Friedman (chap. 9), and Pignatelli (chap. 15) highlighting the variances and ruptures resulting from centuries long processes of conversions and exiles teach us about the gaps of the historical record and the violence behind them. Reconciliatory and reparative acts, then, may find unexpected historical actors on the stage of citizenship and inconvenient reminders of omissions in collective memories.

The Chapters

The chapters that comprise the four parts of this book divide along two main lines. The first establishes the legal, political, and historical frameworks that shape the development of the laws, including the role of institutions and key players in the current moment as well as in the past, such as during Spain's imperial period, World War II, and the 1992 quincentennial commemorations. The authors offering historical perspectives variously analyze the Ottoman, Moroccan, and Greek contexts as well as the Spanish and the Portuguese, given the import of diasporas to the trajectory of legal dispensations for Sephardi Jews and their differentiation from Muslim Spanish descendants.

A second set of analytical chapters brings the contemporary descendants, the beneficiaries of the laws, into view. Original ethnographic, oral history, media, and cultural research shed light on our understanding of the potential beneficiaries' and applicants' motivations, feelings, and experiences with the process as well the implications of the laws for individual and collective identity, belonging, and memory. Five intercalated personal essays both complement and provide alternative perspectives to the research articles, with their reflective narratives about diasporas and identities in the countries of Curaçao, Venezuela, Turkey, and Cuba, and in the cities of Salonica (Greece) and New York (United States), and their experiential insights into the meanings and processes of acquiring citizenship today.

Alfons Aragoneses's chapter 1, "'Reparative Citizenship:' Confronting Injustices of the Past or Building Modern Nationalisms?" examines the concept of historical injustice from a legal perspective that is integrated with historical and cultural dimensions. Shedding historical light on our understanding of citizenship, Aragoneses first traces the evolving legal and symbolic meanings of reparations and the link between citizenship, the nation, and loyalty, the latter a key concept in this book. After bringing us to the current "conception of citizenship and the loss of part of its nationalistic content," Aragoneses asks whether the new flexibility of citizenship can also serve to repair injustices, particularly of those committed in the distant past. Examining the Spanish and Portuguese reparations legislations comparatively with those of Germany, Austria, and Ghana, he distinguishes between reparations and other measures of citizenship restitution (following denationalization). His conclusions about the significance of the laws concern not their reparative quality but rather the symbolism in establishing a link between identity and justice and between nation and rights.

A specific answer to the often-asked question, "Why did Spain and Portugal offer this citizenship now?" is found in Isabel David and Anouck Côrte-Real Pinto's "Beyond Reparatory Justice: The Portuguese 'Law of Return' as Nation Branding" (chap. 2). Centering on the motivators for Portugal, the authors investigate the link between national identity and nation branding, and the role that reparative citizenship plays within this connection. The aim of branding is embedded in Portugal's contemporary identity as exceptionally tolerant and racially mixed. The authors trace these two intertwined central elements to longstanding ideas, such as Gilberto Freyre's "Lusotropicalism," which rebranded the Portuguese past, transforming conquest and slavery into a narrative of encounters and racial mixing. Through interviews with decision-making and community elites, participant observation at cultural events, and documentary research, David and Côrte-Real Pinto detail the participation of political and community actors, including the designation of Portuguese Jews as brand ambassadors, in recasting and covering over undesirable aspects of the past. The law for Sephardi descendants is part and parcel of Portugal's contemporary branding as tolerant, whose success the authors also evaluate.

In "Reparations in Spanish Parliamentary Debates: About the 2015 Nationality Law for Descendants of Sephardi Jews" (chap. 3) Davide Aliberti furthers our understanding of the valences of reparations. He helpfully parses concepts such as reparations, reconciliation, and transitional justice in order to evaluate whether Spain's is a reparations politics as defined by international rights regimes. In exploring this concept, his essay answers another frequently asked question: What were the political processes that shaped this particular law? Aliberti provides an illuminating response in his detailed analyses of the parliamentary discussions, debates, and detours that paved the legislative path. The research he shares of dramatic and revealing statements by politicians discloses not only the primarily rhetorical use of the reparations concept but also the differences and overlaps among political parties and factions regarding Spain's relationship to its Jewish past and its restoration.

"Passports are used to move through space, but for me they serve to move through time," writes Venezuelan academic and author Colette Capriles, apropos of her new Spanish nationality (chap. 4). In her reflective and lyrical personal essay, she traverses both time and space, tracing the paths and detours of her Sephardi ancestors and her mixed Jewish, Christian, German, Venezuelan family. Her narrative is a portal to the world of Spanish and Portuguese Jews in the Americas, whose fortunes and misfortunes propelled them from Iberia to elsewhere in Europe, to the Caribbean, to the island of Curaçao, and finally to the Venezuelan cities of Coro and Caracas. Capriles shares the paradigmatic history of her Sephardi ancestors, who included a friend of Simon Bolívar's and one Joseph Capriles Teixeira who was born in the Veneto in 1723, educated in Padova, practiced medicine in Tunisia, and ended in Curaçao, but not before first converting to Catholicism, then to Islam, and finally returning to Judaism in the Dutch Caribbean. The past two centuries have been no less circuitous and eventful than in such early modern Sephardi stories of displacement and adaptation. But Curaçaoan rootedness and Venezuelan cosmopolitanism prevailed for Capriles and her family and now will incorporate Spanish nationality, which Capriles sees as an instrument of a possible shared future for her country.

"'Spaniards We Were, Spaniards We Are, and Spaniards We Will Be': Salonica's Sephardic Jews and the Instrumentalization of the Spanish Past, 1898–1944" (chap. 5) by Devin Naar, centers on philosephardism, one of the key terms of this volume, and demonstrates its impact on the vital Sephardi community of Salonica. The instrumentalization of the Jewish past, Naar shows, works both ways. If Spain sought to further imperial and diplomatic ambitions through representations of Sephardi Jews as "Spaniards without a homeland," as we have explained above, Sephardi leaders in the key city of Salonica could attempt to manipulate philosephardism to serve the needs of Sephardi Jews at a critical time of wars in Europe. Fascinatingly, when it seemed necessary, they even drew on the experience of Spanish Jewish exile in order to fold Sephardi history into a Greek nationalist one. Yet the unequal nature of the vaunted Spanish-Sephardi relationship, underscored by feverish rhetoric about shared blood and kinship ties, reveals itself particularly during moments of crisis. As Naar makes clear in his exposition of insufficiently known movements of Salonican refugees between their native city and Spain during World War I and the tragic abandonments of World War II, philosephardism proved to be an unreliable narrative, whose costs and disappointments accrued only to Sephardi Jews and never to Spain.

In "'Spanish Jews' and 'Friendly Muslims': The Historical Absence of a Citizenship Campaign for Muslims of Iberian Descent," Elisabeth Bolorinos Allard (chap. 6) asks, "If Spain desired to remedy the past and recover the ideal of *convivencia* associated with medieval al-Andalus, why hasn't the offer of citizenship been extended to the descendants of the Moriscos?" The answer lies in the historical distinctions made between Spanish Jews, *hispanidad*, and philosephardism on the one side and Muslims, Moriscos, and Africanism (emphasizing a Spain-Islam-North Africa connection) on the other. The nineteenth-century conjuncture of liberalism, nationalism, and Orientalism reinscribed the "Jews of Spain" and "Spanish Islam" in the national imaginary, as essential elements of a usable past in which *convivencia*, rather than the Inquisition, was positioned as a Spanish characteristic. The colonization of northern Morocco led to the divergent treatment. Although both Sephardis and "the Moors" were situated as "brothers," Africanism and philosephardism served distinct purposes that largely excluded the Moriscos, who were subjected to civilizational discourses of primitivism and uplift. Bolorinos Allard concludes that the partial and ambivalent incorporation of Sephardi Jews through citizenship did not displace antisemitism, and the exclusion of Morisco descendants from a "return" to Spain did not prevent them from being interpellated as colonized kin.

Uluç Özüyener's personal essay, "The Story of a Spanish Dönme" (chap. 7) is a rare narrative: it is the first testimony by the first Dönme, or Sabbatean, to receive Spanish citizenship. The author is also one of the very few Sabbateans willing to be open about his identity and share his story. Born in Turkey to a secular Muslim family that hid its Sabbatean roots from his generation, Özüyener discovered the secret Jewish origins and Sabbatean history and practices only gradually. Mindful of the discretion that has been necessary for centuries for safety and integration in Turkey, he tells about Sephardi identity, language, and customs and their transformations within Sabbatean communities. At the center is Salonica, or Selanik as Özüyener refers to it, marking through Turkish orthography its special character and meaning for Dönmes. It is in this storied city that a majority of Sabbateans flourished, and it is the same city that became a lost home due to the 1923 Greek-Turkish population exchange. Özüyener's prismatic narrative reveals his path toward greater knowledge of and strong identification with respect to his Dönme roots and draws on both his own and the wider Dönme past in Zaragoza, Spain, Portugal, Livorno, Selanik, and Istanbul. As he tells it, embracing Spanish citizenship was a consequence of his self-discovery as a Dönme.

Elena Arigita and Laura Galián provide the tools to understand the roots of the differentiation between Sephardi Jewish and Morisco descendants in the eyes of the Spanish state in the contemporary moment (chap. 8). They analyze the ongoing and changing attitudes and practices toward the Morisco past and present in light of reparations and reconciliation discourses. They show that, just as reparations are incomplete for Sephardi Jewish descendants (argued also by Aliberti and Aragoneses), Spain's post-dictatorship attempts to reconcile with its own past are also partial because of the lack of a similar acknowledgment of the expulsion and persecution of Moriscos. Through the analysis of official discourses produced in the key moment of the 1992 commemorations and reinvented currently, Arigita and Galián explain how conquest and conflict were resignified in ways that have resulted in the rejection of reparations for Morisco descendants. The authors reveal the complex ways in which the duty of memory is mobilized and immobilized in the efforts to achieve symbolic repair of Morisco history, and also demonstrate the ways in which Sephardi and Morisco pasts converge and diverge in Spain's present-day memory practices.

Through a set of timely interviews conducted with key governmental and Jewish community architects of the 2015 Spanish law, Daniela Flesler and Michal Friedman present in "Negotiating Historical Redress: The Spanish Law of Nationality for Sephardi Descendants and Spain's Jewish Communities" (chap. 9) a behind-the-scenes account of the law's genesis and development. Based on twelve in-depth investigative conversations and contextual analysis, the authors reveal an inside story that addresses questions such as, why this law and why now? Who were the main negotiators and how did this matter? How and why did it evolve into its final form? The story begins with the Federation of Jewish Communities of Spain and unfolds through a complex web of governmental relationships, connections, and negotiations. Flesler and Friedman's conclusions about the role of the official Jewish community in the creation and implementation of the law draws on some strikingly frank interviews as well as analysis of Spain's vision of Sephardi identity and belonging. The authors lay bare the motivations and limits of negotiating with the state and adapting to its double-edged discourses of rescue, gratitude, indebtedness, and loyalty.

With the stroke of an email, Rita Ender (chap. 10) became Portuguese. A Turkish lawyer who assists clients with their citizenship applications, she and her family were among the first to apply for citizenship, for practical but also existential reasons, given the political regime in Turkey and the difficulties of being a Jewish woman whose name, appearance, and professional profile identify her as non-Turkish. Ender reflects on the challenges of amassing documentary proof of heritage, noting that, in her own case, her ancestral family name of Alburquerque, extant vital records, and the presence of Ladino in her family were sufficient, though in each instance of proof lies a gap of knowledge lost to exile and diasporization. Her documentary film, *Las Ultimas Palavras* (The final words), about the loss of Ladino within her own and younger generations, takes her on her first trip to Portugal at the invitation of the Porto Jewish community. Examining her relationship to this country, not known to her but one that offers her a return, Ender reflects on the meanings of her own belongings, new and old, as she also considers the challenges faced by some of her clients in proving their ancestry: "There is Sephardiness in the story of the people who lack Judaism," she asserts and wonders whether it is "appropriate to make decisions about belonging on someone else's behalf." Rephrasing José Saramago, she concludes that becoming Portuguese may be "a chance to step outside of ourselves and discover a new part of who we are."

Ruth Behar, Cuban American writer and anthropologist, closes Part 3 with "Sefarad Postponed" (chap. 11), a reflection on her decision to apply for Spanish citizenship and on its ultimate impossibility. Caught between her love for Spain, where she became an anthropologist, her passion for her native Spanish language, pride in her Sephardic heritage, and fear of bureaucracies and state controls, Behar leads us through her feelings of ambivalence about applying and her ultimate decision to proceed, encouraged by her encounter with a Spanish lawyer. Written at the beginning of the global pandemic, Behar is left, and leaves us, with a litany of "maybes," given the difficulty of completing the application process and planning for the future. Citizenship and Sefarad, she says, are indefinitely postponed. In an epilogue, penned a year later, postponement became impossibility. With only two steps left in the application process, Behar's dream about becoming a citizen in a Spain in which she would no longer feel the need to hide her Jewish identity was thwarted by the official intransigence to adjust the procedures and deadlines to the realities of the pandemic. Given this turn of events, Behar questions the ultimate sincerity of Spain's offer of citizenship.

Beginning with chapter 12, the articles and essays shift from legal and historical concerns to considerations of the beneficiaries of the laws. In "'*La Nostalgia de Sefarad Tira Mucho, Pero No Tanto*:' Attachment, Sentiment, and the Ethics of Refusal," Charles McDonald (chap. 12) offers a counternarrative to the Spanish law as reparation. Derived from ethnographic interviews with Sephardi descendants, McDonald's focus is on those who have chosen not to seek citizenship and who critique the gesture on ethical and practical grounds. Through three in-depth conversations with normative Sephardi Jews, he highlights some of the salient perspectives on refusal: the ethical concern of "confer[ring] unwarranted legitimacy" on the law; the superficiality of the law and the lack of supportive educational resources to combat antisemitism; indifference and lack of practical need; at best a lack of affective attachment to Spain and preference among Jews for US or Israeli citizenship; and discomfort with a law that casts Sephardis as essentially Spanish. McDonald proposes that, in rejecting the law's philosephardic premise of Sephardi nostalgia and attachment to Spain, refusals are expressions of sentiment that warrant consideration alongside state rhetorics of attachment. From the perspective of refusal, the law is better understood as a gift bestowed rather than as a true act of reparation and mutual reconciliation.

In "Affective Citizenship and Iberian Sephardi Descendants," Rina Benmayor (chap. 13) proposes an alternative understanding of citizenship through the lens of emotion and affective meaning. Affective citizenship, she submits, encompasses the emotions, feelings, and sentiments that come into play in the process of affirming heritage involved in acquiring citizenship. She posits that the invitation to citizenship triggers affective responses, which in turn reshape the intended consequences of the laws. Based on some fourteen original videotaped oral histories with applicants, including her own, she examines how the pursuit of new citizenship kindles feelings about the historical and familial past and unexpected framings of identity and belonging. Close affective readings of the narratives and their verbal and somatic performances reveal a reinforced attachment to heritage and the imagined past, the power of discovering new roots, and the force of historical longing, allowing us to understand how applicants rewrite these invitations to rejoin the nation-state. Close textual readings reveal that more than becoming new Spaniards or Portuguese, acquiring reparative citizenship comes to signify an affective re/turn to and reinforcement of Sephardi belonging.

Dalia Kandiyoti's "Descendants of Conversos in the Americas: The Ancestral Past, Sephardi Identity, and Citizenship in Spain and Portugal" (chap. 14) is the first study of converso descendants in the Americas who have pursued Spanish or Portuguese nationality. Focusing on the key role of genealogy, she draws on eighteen oral histories with individuals who have identified ancestors who converted to Christianity in Inquisitionary times and settled in the Americas. The extensive ancestral information required for eligibility by both laws and the uncovering of hidden and repressed crypto-Jewish ancestors cause narrators to recalibrate their connection not only to Spain or Portugal, but also to the collective settlement stories in their own regions and nations on the continent. Moreover, for many narrators a Sephardi historical consciousness emerges through genealogy, which is discovered or reinforced in the application process. Kandiyoti also traces the implications of the ways some applicants reconfigure Sephardi identity as being based on descent. She shows that descendants of conversos, a set of applicants who figure little in the discursive construction of the laws, narrate ruptures and loss, and sometimes a recent reattachment, rather than a presumed loyalty to and continuity of Iberia and its Jewish afterlives. Ancestral citizenship for those more recently uncovering or rediscovering an ancient belonging has surprising permutations, unanticipated by prevailing conceptions of ethnicity, religion, or nation.

In "Portuguese Citizenship for Brazilian Descendants of Sephardic Jews," Marina Pignatelli (chap. 15) introduces a netnographic approach to analyze "how Brazilian applicants engage with virtual groups in online spaces to reconstruct the narrative and symbolic meanings of 'Sephardiness' in support of their [citizenship] applications." Scrutinizing social network services, such as topically dedicated public and private Facebook groups and public and private YouTube channels, Pignatelli examines the narrative identities of the applicants, as shared in these online spaces, and the ways in which descendants of New Christians construct and use these virtual communities. Sephardiness, she argues, should be understood as a broad spectrum of genealogical, cultural, and historical affinities in which individuals may self-identify simultaneously as Iberian Sephardi, Brazilian, Christian, or Bnei Anusim (descendants of converts). Through information gleaned from popular online groups, this chapter details the information, concerns, and support that applicants seek and share, as well as their expectations and reactions upon receiving citizenship. Pignatelli concludes that, by reconnecting to Portugal, the Brazilians in her study, who are diverse in age, gender, occupation, and location "are in a process of creating their Sephardiness as a chosen, voluntary identity, planted in symbolic, cultural, historical, and religious grounds" and should be considered "active co-players" in the reimagination and regeneration of Sephardism today.

Appended to Pignatelli's chapter is a snapshot of the procedures and challenges of certifying Sephardi origins experienced by the Jewish Community of Lisbon (CIL). In this appendix, "Certifying Origins for Sephardic Descendants in Portugal: A Snapshot of the Evaluation Process," Teresa Santos and Heraldo Bento draw from 2020 government documents and Santos's first-hand experience as an assistant in the CIL's evaluation team. Their synopsis describes the diversity of historical, cultural, and testimonial evidence presented by applicants from throughout the Sephardi diaspora, a complexity that required special preparation by evaluators. Including 2020 aggregated data from the Portuguese government, the appendix offers details on applications from Israelis, Brazilians (both Jews and descendants of converts), and Turkish Dönme (converts to Islam).

Closing the volume, historian and filmmaker Victor Silverman writes, "Migration, exile, and diaspora and their complicated relationships with identity and place, with memory and present experience, run through my family's history." His essay "The Fez in the Water: Exile and Return" (chap. 16) alternates between family tableaus and personal and political reflections, beginning with Silverman's grandfather tossing his Turkish fez into the waters of Izmir, and symbolically letting go of his Ottomanness as he embarked on his adventure to embrace the American Dream. Later, we see his mother and aunts, dubbed the "Boreka

Babies," shelling beans on their stoop in Brighton Beach and making comments in Ladino about the passers-by, an antidote to their own sense of immigrant insecurity. Entwined with such snapshots are Silverman's considerations of the post-memory of exile, nostalgia, the brutality of state nationalisms, and his political and intellectual beliefs. He is fully aware that, with the citizenship amendment, Portugal is rewriting its history and his familial identity. Acknowledging the emotional power of identity transformations he writes, "My hope for humanity and my distrust of nationalisms don't blind me to the emotional significance of national citizenship." The law "promises my family and me that we can be part of something that we (both the Portuguese and the Sephardim) have told ourselves we lost."

Through interdisciplinary and multifaceted optics, *Reparative Citizenship* makes apparent the expansive conceptual import of the unusual reconciliatory gestures of the Spanish and Portuguese laws. The volume as a whole asks us to view the subject of nationality for Sephardi descendants prismatically, in regard to questions of citizenship, belonging, and the repair of historical injustices in a contemporary world.

Dalia Kandiyoti is professor of English at the City University of New York, College of Staten Island, and the author of *The Converso's Return: Conversion and Sephardi History in Contemporary Literature and Culture* (Stanford University Press 2020), *Migrant Sites: America, Place, and Diaspora Literatures* (Dartmouth College/University Press of New England 2009), and numerous articles on contemporary Sephardi, Latinx, and migration/diaspora literatures. With Rina Benmayor, she has developed an oral history project of Sephardi descendants applying for Spanish or Portuguese citizenship. The interviews are archived in the University of Washington Sephardic Studies Digital Collection.

Rina Benmayor is Professor Emerita in the School of Humanities and Communication, California State University Monterey Bay, where she taught oral history, literature, and digital storytelling. She is the author of *Romances judeo-españoles de Oriente* (Gredos 1979); and coauthor and coeditor of *Latino Cultural Citizenship* (Beacon Press 1997); *Telling to Live: Latina Feminist Testimonios* (Duke University Press 2001); and *Memory, Subjectivities, and Representation: Approaches to Oral History in Latin America, Portugal, and Spain* (Palgrave 2016; Oral History Association Book Award 2016). With Dalia Kandiyoti, she has conducted extensive oral histories with Sephardi citizenship applicants. These interviews are archived in the University of Washington Sephardic Studies Digital Collection.

Notes

1. In this volume we favor the designation of "Sephardi" to name and describe Jews originating in the Iberian Peninsula, the biblical Sepharad. However, we recognize that "Sephardic" is more commonly used. We have left the choice of descriptor to the individual authors; consequently, readers will find both forms used.
2. The Spanish and Portuguese laws are legally titled laws of nationality. Whereas the Spanish and Portuguese draw a distinction between nationality (legal status) and citizenship (civic practices), English commonly uses the word "citizenship" as an umbrella term to designate all aspects of national membership. In this book we prefer the term "citizenship," although readers will find both terms used, sometimes interchangeably and other times adhering to a more strictly to legal vocabulary.
3. As of 30 June 2022, the official Spanish government Bulletin (*Boletín Oficial del Estado*) reported that 153,774 applications had been received on the electronic platform of the General Council of Spanish Notaries (CGNE) ("Datos estadísticos básicos de nacionalidad a 30/06/2022"). Of these, 83,484 applications, fewer than half, were formally signed in the presence of a *notario* (special lawyer assigned to this process) in Spain, and subsequently forwarded to the Dirección General de Seguridad Jurídica y Fe Pública (DGSJFP), of the Ministry of Justice, the entity that is charged with making the final decision. Of the 83,484 forwarded applications, 45,186 were reviewed and adjudicated: 42,636 citizenships were granted and 2,519 were denied. 37,710 applications were yet to be reviewed and resolved. Applications from Mexico, Colombia, and Venezuela number in the seven digits each, and alone represent some three-quarters of the applications from seventy-six countries that were forwarded to the ministry of justice. As of February 2022, the Portuguese Instituto de Registos Centrais e do Notariado (Institute of Registries and Notary) reported receipt of 137,087 applicants for Sephardi naturalization. It had approved 56,685 citizenships and denied 300, leaving 80,102 to be reviewed and resolved (*Diario de Noticias* 2022). Together with the Spanish data, these numbers indicate a high level of positive response among descendants, numbering close to 300,000 electronically submitted applications, although not all of these would end up being forwarded to the respective ministry of justice.
4. Benmayor and Kandiyoti's "Spanish and Portuguese Citizenship for Sephardi Jewish Descendants: An Oral History Collection (2017-2022)" is the first and to date the most extensive collection of in-depth interviews with Sephardi descendants on the 2015 citizenship laws. The University of Washington Sephardic Studies Digital Collection is the online repository of the corpus.
5. On philosephardism and Pulido, see Aliberti (2018); Bolorinos Allard (2020, and chap. 6 in this volume), Flesler and Pérez Melgosa (2020); Friedman (2011); Ginio (2007); Goode (2009); Linhard (2014); and Ojeda-Mata (2018). For a critical perspective on Castro, see, e.g., Menny (2010).
6. See Stein (2016, 12) who suggests that the experience of those in the protégé regime exercised by European powers in the Ottoman Empire was in many ways a precursor to the current ones. See also Escudero (2016).
7. For details and analysis of these events, see, e.g., Aliberti (2018); Flesler and Pérez Melgosa (2020); Lisbona (1993); Rozenberg (2006).
8. The translations are ours. For reasons of space, throughout this volume we provide the quotes only in English translation and not in their original languages.

9. According to some scholars, this link often whitewashes Spanish history, including the alliance with Nazism. See Aragoneses (2016, 3); and Baer (2011).
10. See Schammah Gesser (2019, 199–201) for a further comparison between the Spanish and Portuguese laws.

References

Alberola, Miquel. 2015. "El Rey, a los sefardíes: "¡Cuánto os hemos echado de menos!" *El País*, 30 November 2015.
Aliberti, Davide. 2018. *Sefarad: Una comunidad imaginada (1924-2015)*. Madrid: Marcial Pons Historia.
Almeida, Sao José. 2020. "PS abandona exigencia de dois anos de residencia a sefarditas." *Público*, 19 May 2020. https://www.publico.pt/2020/05/19/politica/noticia/ps-deixa-cair-exigencia-dois-anos-residencia-sefarditas-1917154.
Álvarez Chillida, Gonzalo. 2002. *El antisemitismo en España: La imagen del judío, 1812–2002*. Madrid: Marcial Pons.
Aragoneses, Alfons. 2016. "Convivencia and Filosefardismo in Spanish Nation-Building." *Max Planck Institute for European Legal History Research Paper Series* 5, 1–34.
Araujo, Ana Lucia. 2017. *Reparations for Slavery and the Slave Trade: A Transnational and Comparative History*. London: Bloomsbury.
Assouline, Pierre. 2019. *Retour à Sefarad*. Paris: Gallimard.
Avni, Haim. 1982. *Spain, the Jews, and Franco*. Philadelphia: Jewish Publication Society of America.
Avruch, Kevin, and Beatriz Vejarano. 2002. "Truth and Reconciliation Commissions: A Review Essay and Annotated Bibliography." *OJPCR: The Online Journal of Peace and Conflict Resolution* 4, no. 2.
Baer, Alejandro. 2011. "The Voids of Sepharad: The Memory of the Holocaust in Spain." In *Revisiting Jewish Spain in the Modern Era*, edited by Daniela Flesler, Tabea Linhard, Adrián Pérez Melgosa, special issue of *Journal of Spanish Cultural Studies* 12, no. 1: 95–120.
Benbassa, Esther, and Aron Rodrigue. 2000. *History of Sephardic Jewry, XIVth–XXth Centuries*. Berkeley: University of California Press.
Benmayor, Rina, and Dalia Kandiyoti. 2017–22. "Spanish and Portuguese Citizenship for Sephardi Jewish Descendants: An Oral History Collection (2017–2022)." University of Washington Sephardic Studies Digital Collection.
———. 2020. "Ancestry, Genealogy, and Restorative Citizenship: Oral Histories of Sephardi.Descendants Reclaiming Spanish and Portuguese Nationality." *Quest. Issues in Contemporary Jewish History* 18 (December). https://www.quest-cdecjournal.it/wp-content/uploads/2021/01/9-Q18_03_Benmayor-Kandiyoti.pdf.
Ben-Ur, Aviva. 2009. *Sephardic Jews in America: A Diasporic History*. New York: New York University Press.
Bolorinos Allard, Elisabeth. 2021. *Spanish National Identity, Colonial Power, and the Portrayal of Muslims and Jews during the Rif War*. Woodbridge: Tamesis.
Cabot, Heath. 2019. "The European Refugee Crisis and Humanitarian Citizenship in Greece." *Ethnos*, 84, no. 5: 747–71.
Calderwood, Eric. 2018. *Colonial al-Andalus: Spain and the Making of Modern Moroccan Culture*. Cambridge: Harvard University Press.

Carranza, Ruben. 2009. "ICTJ Briefing." International Center for Transitional Justice. https://www.ictj.org/sites/default/files/ICTJ-Global-Right-Reparation-2009-English.pdf.

Chu, Henry. 2015. "Welcome Home, 500 Years Later: Spain Offers Citizenship to Sephardic Jews." *LA Times*, 1 October 2015. https://www.latimes.com/world/europe/la-fg-spain-sephardic-jews-20151001-story.html.

"Datos estadísticos básicos de nacionalidad a 30/06/2022." 2022. Ministerio de Justicia de España. https://www.mjusticia.gob.es/es/ciudadania/nacionalidad/estadisticas-datos-basicos.

Decreto-Lei no. 30-A/2015. 27 February 2015. *Diário da República Eletrónico* 41: 92–93.

Decreto-Lei no. 26/2022. 18 March 2022. *Diário da República Eletrónico* 55: 2–59.

Diario de Noticias. 2022. "Portugal rejeitou 300 em quase 57 mil processos de naturalizaçao de judeus sefarditas." 6 February 2022. https://www.dn.pt/sociedade/portugal-rejeitou-300-em-quase-57-mil-processos-de-naturalizacao-de-judeus-sefarditas-14564419.html.

Díaz-Mas, Paloma. 1986. *Los sefardíes: historia, lengua, y cultura*. Barcelona: Riopiedras.

Escudero, Mónica Manrique. 2016. "¿1868? Retorno a Sefarad." *Liburna* 1: 109–21. https://dialnet.unirioja.es/descarga/articulo/3643191.pdf.

Flesler, Daniela, and Adrián Pérez Melgosa. 2020. *The Memory Work of Jewish Spain*. Bloomington: University of Indiana Press.

Flores, William V., and Rina Benmayor. 1997. *Latino Cultural Citizenship: Claiming Identity, Space, and Rights*. Boston: Beacon Press.

Franco, Manuela. 2004. "Diversão balcânica: os israelitas portugueses de Salónica." *Análise Social* XXXIX, no. 170: 119–47. http://analisesocial.ics.ul.pt/documentos/1218704861X4bGT3ny7Zm31GA0.pdf.

Friedman, Michal Rose. 2011. "Reconquering 'Sepharad': Hispanism and Proto-Fascism in Giménez Caballero's Sephardist Crusade." In *Revisiting Jewish Spain in the Modern Era*, edited by Daniela Flesler, Tabea Linhard, and Adrián Pérez Melgosa. *Journal of Spanish Cultural Studies* 12, no. 1: 35–60.

Ginio, Alisa Meyuhas. 2007. "Reencuentro y despedida: Dr. Ángel Pulido Fernández y la diáspora sefardí." In *España e Israel. Veinte años después*, edited by Raanan Rein, 57–66. Sevilla: Fundación Tres Culturas del Mediterráneo.

Goldschläger, Arielle and Camilla Orjuela. 2021. "Return After 500 Years?: Spanish and Portuguese Repatriation Laws and the Reconstruction of Sephardic Identity." *Diaspora Studies* 14, no. 1: 97–115.

Goode, Joshua. 2009. *Impurity of Blood: Defining Race in Spain, 1870–1930*. Baton Rouge: Louisiana State University Press.

Harpaz, Yossi, and Pablo Mateos. 2019. "Introduction. Strategic Citizenship: Negotiating Membership in the Age of Dual Nationality." *Journal of Ethnic and Migration Studies* 45, no. 6: 843–57. https://www.tandfonline.com/doi/full/10.1080/1369183X.2018.1440482.

Howard, Marc Morjé. 2009. *The Politics of Citizenship in Europe*. Cambridge: Cambridge University Press.

International Center for Transitional Justice (ICTJ). n.d. "What is Transitional Justice?" https://www.ictj.org/what-transitional-justice.

Isin, Engin F., and Peter Nyers. 2014. "Introduction: Globalizing Citizenship Studies." In *Routledge Handbook of Global Citizenship Studies*, edited by Egin F. Isin and Peter Nyers, 1–11. New York: Routledge.

Joppke, Christian. 2005. *Selecting by Origin: Ethnic Migration in the Liberal State*. Cambridge: Harvard University Press.

———. 2019. "The Instrumental Turn of Citizenship." *Journal of Ethnic and Migration Studies* 45, no. 6: 858–78. doi:10.1080/1369183X.2018.1440484.
JTA. 2015. "Portugal Issues First Passport Under Sephardic 'Law of Return.'" *The Forward*, 14 October 2015. https://forward.com/news/breaking-news/322572/portugal-issues-first-passport-under-sephardic-law-of-return.
Kabir, Naila, ed. 2005. *Inclusive Citizenship: Meanings and Expressions*. London: Zed Books.
Kandiyoti, Dalia. 2020. *The Converso's Return: Conversion and Sephardi History in Contemporary Literature and Culture*. Stanford, CA: Stanford University Press.
Kerem, Yitzhak. 2021. "Portugal's Citizenship for Sephardic Jewry: A Golden Fountainhead." *Contemporary Jewry* 26: 1–24.
La Vanguardía. 2014. "Los judíos sefardíes tendrán la nacionalidad española con sólo acreditar su condición." 2 July 2014. https://www.lavanguardia.com/politica/20140207/54400938718/judios-sefardies-nacionalidad-espanola-acreditar-condicion.html.
Labanyi, Jo. 2008. "The Politics of Memory in Contemporary Spain." *Journal of Spanish Cultural Studies* 9, no. 2: 119–25. https://www.tandfonline.com/doi/full/10.1080/1463620080228362.
Leite, Naomi. 2017. *Unorthodox Kin: Portuguese Marranos and the Global Search for Belonging*. Berkeley and Los Angeles: University of California Press.
Lenzerini, Federico. 2017. "The Land Rights of Indigenous Peoples Under International Law." In *Comparative Property Law: Global Perspectives*, edited by Michelle Graziadei and Lionel Smith. Research Handbooks in International Law Series, 393–411. Elgaronline https://doi.org/10.4337/9781785369162.
Law 12/2015. 2015. "Ley 12/2015 de 24 de junio, en materia de concesión de la nacionalidad española a los sefardíes originarios de España" [Law 12/2015 of 24 June, granting Spanish nationality to Sephardi Jews originating from Spain]. *Boletín Oficial del Estado*, 25 June 2015, no. 151.
Linhard, Tabea. 2014. *Jewish Spain: A Mediterranean Memory*. Stanford, Calif.: Stanford University Press.
———. 2016. *Jewish Spain: A Mediterranean Memory*. Stanford, CA: Stanford University Press.
Lipschitz, Cnaan. 2015. "Citizenship for Sephardic Jews 'Corrects Historical Wrong.'" *Times of Israel*, 12 April 2015. https://www.timesofisrael.com/citizenship-for-sephardic-jews-corrects-historical-wrong/.
Lisbona, José Antonio. 1993. *Retorno a Sefarad: la política de España hacia sus judíos en el siglo XX*. Barcelona: Riopiedras.
Lusa e Público. 2015. "Descendentes de judeus sefarditas já vão poder pedir a nacionalidade." *Lusa e Público*, 29 January 2015. https://www.publico.pt/2015/01/29/politica/noticia/descendentes-de-judeus-sefarditas-ja-vao-poder-pedir-a-nacionalidade-1684394.
Maestri, Gaja and Sarah M. Hughes. 2017. "Contested Spaces of Citizenship: Camps, Borders, and Urban Encounters." *Citizenship Studies* 21, no. 6: 625–39.
Mamdani, Mahmood. 2002. "Amnesty or Impunity?: A Preliminary Critique of the Report of the Truth and Reconciliation Commission of South Africa (TRC)." *Diacritics* 32, nos. 3–4 (Autumn, Winter): 32–59.
Martín-Márquez, Susan. 2008. *Disorientations: Spanish Colonialism in Africa and the Performance of Identity*. New Haven, CT: Yale University Press.
Martins, Jorge. 2006. *Portugal e os Judeus*, vol. 1, *Dos primórdios da nacionalidade à legislação pombalina*. Lisbon: Vega.

———. 2010. *A República e os judeus*. Lisbon: Vega.
Martins, Jorge. 2012. *Portugal e os Judeus*, vol. 2, *Do ressurgimento das comunidades judaicas à Primeira República*. Lisbon: Vega.
McDonald, Charles. 2021. "Rancor: Sephardi Jews, Spanish Citizenship, and the Politics of Sentiment." *Comparative Studies in Society and History* 63, no. 3: 722–51.
Menny, Ana. 2010. "Entre reconocimiento y rechazo: los judíos en la obra de Américo Castro." *Iberoamericana. América Latina—España—Portugal* 10, no. 38: 143–50.
Milgram, Avraham. 2011. *Portugal, Salazar, and the Jews*. Translated by Naftali Greenwood. Jerusalem: Yad Vashem.
Ojeda-Mata, Maite. 2015. "La ciudadanía española y los sefardíes: identidades legitimadoras, ideologías étnicas y derechos políticos." *Quaderns-e de l'Institut Català d'Antropologia* 20, no. 2: 36–52. https://raco.cat/index.php/QuadernseICA/article/view/302784.
———. 2016. "'Spanish' but 'Jewish:' Race and National Identity in Nineteenth- and Twentieth-Century Spain." *Jewish Culture and History* 16, no. 1: 64–81. https://doi.org/10.1080/1462169X.2015.1032013.
———. 2018. *Modern Spain and the Sephardim: Legitimizing Identities*. Lanham, MD: Lexington.
Patler, Caitlin. 2018. "'Citizens but for Papers': Undocumented Youth Organizations, Anti-Deportation Campaigns, and the Reframing of Citizenship." *Social Problems* 65, no. 1 (February): 96–115. https://doi.org/10.1093/socpro/spw045.
Pignatelli, Marina. 2019. *Cadernos de oraçoes cripto-judaicas e notas etnográficas dos judeus e cristãos-novos de Bragança*. Lisbon: Etnográfica Press.
Pimentel, Flunser Irene, and Cláudia Ninhos. 2015. "Portugal, Jewish Refugees, and the Holocaust." *Dapim: Studies on the Holocaust* 29, no. 2: 101–13.
Pogonyi, Szabolcs. 2019. "The Passport as Means of Identity Management: Making and Unmaking Ethnic Boundaries through Citizenship." *Journal of Ethnic and Migration Studies* 46, no. 6: 975–93.
Rohr, Isabelle. 2005. "Philosephardism and Antisemitism in Turn-of-the-Century Spain." *Historical Reflections* 31, no. 3: 373–92.
———. 2007. *The Spanish Right and the Jews (1898–1945): Antisemitism and Opportunism*. Eastbourne: Sussex Academic Press.
———. 2011. "'Spaniards of the Jewish Type': Philosephardism in the Service of Imperialism in Early Twentieth-Century Spanish Morocco." *Journal of Spanish Cultural Studies* 12, no. 1: 61–75.
Rother, Bernd. 2005. *Franco y el Holocausto*. Madrid: Marcial Pons.
Rozenberg, Danielle. 2006. *L'espagne contemporaine et la question juive: Les fils renoués de la mémoire*. Toulouse: Presses Universitaires du Mirail.
Schammah Gesser, Silvina. 2019. "Virtually Sephardic? The Marketing and Exception of the New Iberian Laws of Nationality in Israel." *Lusotopie* 18: 192–217.
Schammah Gesser and Teresa Pinheiro. 2019. "Revisiting Isomorphism: The Routes of Sefarad in Spain and Portugal." In *Iberian Studies: Reflections Across Borders and Disciplines*, edited by Nuria Codina Sola and Teresa Pinheiro, 295–320. Berlin: Peter Lang.
Stein, Sarah. 2016. *Extraterritorial Dreams: European Citizenship, Sephardi Jews, and the Ottoman Twentieth Century*. Chicago: University of Chicago Press.
Torpey, John. 2006. *Making Whole What Has Been Smashed: On Reparations Politics*. Cambridge: Harvard University Press.

Part I.

Reparation and Reconciliation?

Legal and Political Perspectives on the 2015 Laws

Chapter 1

"Reparative Citizenship"
Confronting Injustices of the Past
or Building Modern Nationalisms?

Alfons Aragoneses

Introduction:
On the Difficulties of Combining Reparation and Citizenship

In 2015 both Spain and Portugal passed laws facilitating the acquisition of Spanish and Portuguese citizenship by Sephardi Jews. Neither Spanish Law 12/2015 nor Portuguese Decree-Law 30-1/2015 mentions reparation for the unjust expulsion of Jews from the Iberian kingdoms. However, political and mass media discourses frequently refer to the reparative dimension of these laws. It is easy to find press articles or political statements that mention terms such as "reparation," "reconciliation," or "law of return."[1] Moreover, the enactment of the Spanish law generated debate about recognizing Spanish citizenship for Western Saharans, in reparation for their abandonment by Spain in 1975 (Arregui 2015). In the minds of many, and as the title of this volume illustrates, these actually are laws of reparation. A similar situation occurred with other recent reforms of citizenship or right of abode laws in Germany and Ghana. Although these measures did not expressly refer to injustices of the past or reparation for them, media and political discourses associated the German legislation with the expulsion of Jews under the Nazi regime (*Deutsche Welle* 2020) and the Ghanaian reform with the slave trade (Dovi 2015). Citizenship, justice, reparation, and reconciliation are today difficult to separate in political discourses on the topic of historical injustices.

It is therefore clear that the idea of reparative citizenship is present in politics and society. However, from a formalist legal perspective, it is difficult to combine the concepts of "citizenship," "reparation," and "reparative." On the one hand, citizenship today is a link between a state and an individual that generates rights and obligations for both parties. It is a link of a political nature and cannot easily be conceived as a prize or reparation. On the other hand, also from a formalist legal perspective, reparation must refer to a harm suffered by an individual or group of individuals, with an identifiable cause and an identifiable liable subject. In the case of the expulsion of Jews from the Iberian Peninsula, neither the liable subject nor the harm is easily identifiable.

Thus, it is difficult to maintain that citizenship laws such as those analyzed here can repair a historical injustice. It is worthwhile, nonetheless, to conduct a legal or legal-historical analysis of reparative citizenship because, beyond their formal and normative content, laws (and citizenship laws are no exception) have a political, cultural, and symbolic dimension that can be analyzed. In the case not only of the Spanish and Portuguese laws, but also of German and Ghanaian legislation, it is very easy to observe how reparative citizenship is a field in which law, history, politics, and culture are deeply entangled.

In the following pages I attempt to explain, from a legal-historical perspective, the uses of reparative citizenship in various contexts in order to determine the possible intentions of lawmakers in drafting citizenship laws that are interpreted as reparative. I first analyze the historical evolution of the legal concept of citizenship in the past centuries and then address the legal concept of reparation in cases of historical injustices. I conclude by presenting the potential of citizenship regulations as a tool of memory politics and diplomacy.

I use the tools of legal science, while also considering the legal, political, and cultural dimensions of legal discourses and the fact that laws are always produced in a specific historical moment. Citizenship laws are no exception. Therefore, after analyzing the historical evolution of the concept of citizenship, I examine the possibility of repairing historical injustices. I explore whether there have been other cases of reparative citizenship and present my interpretation of the binomial of citizenship and reparation in the case of the Spanish and Portuguese laws.

The Transformations of Citizenship in the Twentieth Century

From a legal perspective, citizenship is the political and legal link between an individual and a state. In a modern democratic state, this link is ideologically, religiously, and ethnically neutral and presupposes no special identity or condition other than that of belonging to a political community. This link results from birth, long-term residence, or naturalization, and it creates rights and obligations. It cannot be understood as a prize, reparation, or compensation, because it has no economic or symbolic content. Citizenship laws govern the requirements, conditions, and procedures for acquiring citizenship from a technical, nonpolitical point of view.

However, if we go beyond the formalist legal-positivist approach, it is clear that citizenship has a political and symbolic dimension linked to the historical regime in which it originated. In the past, citizenship has been linked to nationality, nation-building processes, and conflicts among national groups. These conflicts and processes have political connotations. Analysis of citizenship laws should therefore take a political and historical perspective into account.

We find the word "citizenship" not only today, but also in ancient Roman legal texts, in the Middle Ages, and in nineteenth-century documents on rights and liberalism. There is certainly a terminological continuity of this word from ancient times to today. However, there is no semantic continuity: ancient Roman citizenship is not the citizenship of the nineteenth century. As with all legal terms, there is a "gap existing between the apparent permanence of words and their changing, deeper meaning" (Hespanha 2004, 43). Our modern concept of citizenship appears alongside the modern concepts of nation and state in the late eighteenth century. However, as José María Espinar Vicente explained, the citizenship of the first liberal codes and constitutions of the nineteenth and twentieth centuries has experienced dramatic shifts in meaning in the past fifty years (Espinar Vicente 2012, 50). Globalization has undoubtedly influenced this change and allowed a more flexible and less traditional approach to citizenship in countries all around the world. But from a historical point of view, this is a very recent development.

The first modern regulations of citizenship date from the late eighteenth and early nineteenth centuries. The modern concept of citizenship was a by-product of the invention of nations and states in legal and political texts in Europe and the Americas. During and after the liberal revolutions that created the concept of nation and national sovereignty, it became necessary to identify the citizens forming the nation and, therefore, exercising the power that was previously in the hands of monarchs. This explains the political dimension of citizenship: in theory it was designed as a neutral link between the individual and the nation-state, even though the nation-state was anything but neutral.

However, as Giorgio Agamben has indicated, citizenship had a bio-political content. In the newly created liberal regimes, an individual was integrated into the political nation as a subject of sovereignty simply by being born (Agamben 2006, 163). And yet the concepts of nation and state were political inventions of the national elites imagining national communities, in the sense used by Benedict Anderson (1983). Therefore, citizenship had—and still has—a nationalistic dimension, although it was much stronger and more exclusive two hundred years ago. In the nineteenth and twentieth centuries, citizenship was conceived as "the title by which each national group certified the belonging of a specific subject to the social community exercising sovereignty" (Espinar Vicente 2012, 45). This link with the national group seems neutral today, but in the nineteenth and twentieth centuries it was not: citizenship was directly designed and projected by the majority ethnoracial group of a nation-state and usually excluded servants, women, and members of other groups.

To determine the citizens of a state, it was necessary to imagine the nation. This task corresponded to the—usually white—elites. Consequently, those elites established the requirements for being a citizen: they imagined the national community and the cultural or ethnic features of its members. Nationals, and therefore citizens, had to behave as such and be loyal to the national community as projected by the elites. This happened in the United States, where native peoples and blacks were not considered citizens, and in Europe, where citizenship was exclusive to white Christians during the nineteenth and part of the twentieth centuries. As a result, Jews were accepted as citizens in several European countries (Germany, France, and Italy) in what is considered an example of emancipation. This process took place after assimilation. First, Jews had to assimilate; after that they would be recognized as citizens, as happened in France in 1789 (Sznaider 2019, 456). This is the actual meaning of the famous speech by Clermont-Tonnerre before the Assemblée Nationale in 1789: "We must refuse everything to the Jews as a nation and accord everything to Jews as individuals. We must withdraw recognition from their judges; they should only have our judges. We must refuse legal protection to the maintenance of the so-called laws of their Judaic organization; they should not be allowed to form in the state either a political body or an order. They must be citizens individually" (Clermont Tonnerre, 1789, quoted in Hunt 1996, 86–88).

The link to an ethnic or national community was one pillar of citizenship. The other was the opposite notion of nonnational or foreigner. The concept of citizen was construed in opposition to the concept of foreigner. Nonnationals (noncitizens) were strangers, foreigners (*extranjeros, étrangers, Ausländer*). The essence of this dichotomy between citizen and noncitizen (foreigner) can be found in the origins of constitutionalism. As Giorgio Agamben explains, "In the phrase *déclara-*

tion des droits de l'homme et du citoyen, it is not clear whether the two terms *homme* and *citoyen* name two autonomous beings or instead form a unitary system in which the first is always already included in the second. And if the latter is the case, the kind of relation that exists between *homme* and *citoyen* still remains unclear" (Agamben 2006, 161).

The implications of this concept of citizenship were various and significant. As a member of a national group, a citizen was endowed with political rights and, more importantly, was presumed to be loyal to the state and to the national community. This nationalistic idea of loyalty was directly incorporated into legal texts. Most legal systems considered citizenship to be an exclusive link between subject and state: individuals were not allowed to hold more than one citizenship, because their loyalty could not be divided or shared. In practice, a male citizen could serve only one country in a war or for military service. This explains the suspicion toward European Jews as lacking loyalty to their country, or for having different loyalties, as was dramatically exemplified in the Dreyfus affair.

This was also reflected by international law. In the important The Hague Convention of 1930 on conflict of laws we read "that it [was] in the general interest of the international community to secure that all its members should recognize that every person should have a nationality and should have one nationality only" and, "accordingly that the ideal towards which the efforts of humanity should be directed in this domain is the abolition of all cases both of statelessness and of double nationality" ("The Hague Convention" 1930, 192). All member states had to achieve the ideal of one single citizenship for every human being.

One could argue that processes of naturalization of foreigners occurred in the first half of the twentieth century. An example of this is the naturalization of Sephardi Jews in Spain in the 1910s, 1920s, and 1930s. But these Sephardi Jews, and foreigners in general, had to renounce—or at least not exercise—their former citizenship. Spain's naturalization of Sephardi Jews, mostly in Morocco and the Balkans, is a good illustration of how citizenship (theoretically a neutral legal condition) was used as a tool of colonial politics: in the old antisemitic/philosemitic argument, Jews were seen as wealthy, but the Sephardi in particular, the *españoles sin patria*, stateless Spaniards, according to the expression of Angel Pulido (1905), were seen as potential national agents abroad (Aragoneses 2018, 208–9). Citizenship was granted for political reasons and in exchange for a future benefit to the nation. No reparative intention was behind these processes.

The conception of citizenship as linked to an ethnic or national community and in opposition to the notion of foreigner remained intact until the second half of the twentieth century. But, as Espinar Vicente (2012) explains, this nationalistic conception has been superseded. In most democracies, citizenship today is a "stable political link and a guarantor of rights" (41) and not a link of an ethnic or cultural nature (50). It has no ethnic connotation and is not in direct opposition to the concept of foreigner. He adds, "Not all nationals have the same standing in the legal system, and the same applies to foreigners: they are not all in the same legal position" (41). Being a resident national or a nonresident national is not the same. Likewise, a foreign "European citizen" is not the same as an individual from a country in our "historical community of nations," or a citizen of Australia. According to this author, these three foreigners have different rights in Spain. But, more importantly, in many countries citizenship is no longer "the expression of current and effective social ties" (41).

This shift in the conception of citizenship and the loss of part of its nationalistic content opens the door to changes in the regulation and political function of citizenship. The old idea of exclusive loyalty has given way to the possibility of multiple loyalties. The old idea of an exclusive and homogeneous nation has faded, to be replaced by the possibility of different ethnic, religious, or linguistic communities sharing the bond of citizenship. As a consequence, many states perceive dual nationals outside their territory as an opportunity rather than a threat.

Dual citizenship has a direct link with what Benedict Anderson called "long-distance nationalism" (2002, 73). For Anderson, this concept refers to the nationalism practiced by nationals living as migrants in other countries and enjoying, in some cases, dual citizenship, in a direct consequence of the revolution in communications and transportation. Nina Glick Schiller defined it as "a set of identity claims and practices that connect people living in various geographical locations to a specific territory that they see as their ancestral home" (2002, 570). Long-distance nationalism makes the old nationalistic idea of national loyalty unsustainable: citizens can have more than one cultural or national identity and more than one loyalty. Shabrina Amelia Ronny et al. explain that "while previously both citizenship and political loyalty towards a specific national community was determined as one package, today the rise of multiple citizenships in the world has made countries to [sic] acknowledge dual or multiple citizenships" (2020, 480). This situation is viewed as "disrupting the idealized definition of what it means to be a member of a country and a nation, as a result of the large volume and increase of movement across states that stretches out wide the national community" (480).

In their analysis of the Indian and Indonesian cases, these authors note that the reform of citizenship laws is now an instrument to redefine the national community: "In contrast to the [*sic*] nationalism, which has been interpreted conventionally, the concept of long-distance nationalism can be a justification for the Government to recognize the presence of a transnational community" (Ronny et al. 2020, 482). This new approach to nation and nationalism paves the way for law reform to recognize the citizenship of national communities in the diaspora.

India recently adopted this approach. Because the Indian Constitution forbids dual citizenship, descendants of Indian migrants are not recognized as Indian citizens, depriving the Indian state of the economic and political networks of Indians in the diaspora. To remedy this, the Citizenship Act of 2005 introduced Overseas Citizenship of India, which grants an indefinite right of abode for Indians of the diaspora. The aim of this reform was to attract the sympathies of more than 30 million Indians abroad and to use their potential as economic and diplomatic agents to defend India (Ministry of External Affairs 2018).

The Indian case is an example of long-distance nationalism and how citizenship laws can be used in a totally different manner from the time when citizenship was dominated by the old nationalist idea. Following this reasoning, citizenship could also be used as an instrument of nation branding—that is, as an instrument for enhancing the reputation of a country in international relations (Kerr 2013, 354). Nation branding has been theorized and used in several cases to improve a country's image, especially during crises (see David and Côrte-Real Pinto in this volume).[2] If citizenship laws can be an instrument to promote long-distance nationalism, they can also be used as an instrument to improve the image of a country abroad, either among its citizens in the diaspora or among other national communities.

Now that the old nationalistic idea of citizenship and exclusive loyalty has been superseded, citizenship has become a flexible condition used to build ties with nationals in the diaspora or for economic and political diplomacy. The question now is whether citizenship laws can be instruments of reparation for historical injustice.

The Difficulties of Repairing Historical Injustices of the Distant Past

Returning to the title of this paper, I will now ask whether citizenship and the granting of citizenship can be used to repair a harm caused by historical injustice. According to international law, the expulsion of a community is a crime, and the responsible state is under an obligation to make full reparation for the harm caused by the wrongful act. This is clear in theory but, also according to international law, the state is responsible only if it is bound by the obligation in question at the time the act occurred. These same international laws state that the wrongs of a particular moment must be tried according to the laws of that time. While this is not problematic when trying the crimes of the Nazi regime or other twentieth-century crimes, it poses problems when trying historical injustices from the distant past.

Andrea Caligiuri has studied the application of the rules of international law to the slave trade and slavery. Today slavery is a crime under domestic and international law. Caligiuri notes that, according to the doctrine of international law, no liability can be considered for slavery in the nineteenth century because at that time slavery was not held to be a crime against humanity (Caligiuri 2005, 469–70). However, states are still reluctant to apologize for any possible liability that could be inferred from slavery (479).

When discussing the Spanish and Portuguese laws and possible reparation for the expulsion of the Jews, the problem is different, because it is not a matter of a crime or of a historical injustice committed by specific states 150 years ago. Instead, it is a historical episode, certainly an unjust one, that occurred more than five hundred years ago, when the concepts of citizenship, nation, and state as we understand them today did not exist. This raises a preliminary question: Is it possible to provide justice for the victims of a historical injustice of the distant past?

As Berber Bevernage points out, "The relationship between history and justice has been dominated by the idea of the past as distant or absent" (2008, 149). What happened in the past is absent in the present time. This is not the main problem from a legal perspective, because the time of history and the time of law do not always coincide. A historical episode of the past can still produce legal effects in the present. This is the case with the serious crimes committed in the twentieth century, especially the Holocaust, because they still generate rights for the victims and their relatives and obligations for states. The legal time of the rights and the historical time of the episode coincide. There is not, in this case, a "conceptual contrast" between "the time of jurisdiction and the time of history" (150). In this instance, the time of injustice and the time of rights and justice coincide or, in the words of Michael Ignatieff, "The past continues to torment because it is not past" (1996, 119). Thus, there are still victims of the Holocaust who receive compensation from the German state and executioners who are brought to trial. This is why claims for damages by Spanish Jews who were de facto denationalized by the Spanish authorities in 1943 and ended up being deported to Nazi concentration camps (Aragoneses 2019, 130–31), or claims by their immediate descendants, could succeed. In this particular case, the rights and obligations deriving from the historic episode remain in force today.

But the case we are studying here, the expulsion of Jews from the Iberian kingdoms in the fifteenth and sixteenth centuries, is more difficult to assess. From a legal perspective, reparation or reversal of the harm is almost impossible, given that no living persons were directly affected by the political decisions. The time of the expulsion and the time of the rights do not coincide. A further difficulty is that, in 1492, Spain did not exist as a state, and the modern concepts of nation, state, and citizenship were not created until centuries later. Considering fifteenth-century Spain a country, and its inhabitants citizens, would be an anachronism: as already mentioned, terminological continuity does not entail semantic continuity (Hespanha 2004, 43).

Moreover, Sephardi Jews living around the world do not form a homogeneous community. This makes it difficult to identify the consequences of the harm for the identity of Sephardi Jews today. It is therefore very difficult, if not impossible, to determine what form any reparation for the expulsion of their ancestors could take, symbolic or otherwise. To seek reparation for harm, it is first necessary to identify the victim of the harm who will receive the reparation and, of course, the liable subject. It is difficult to think of the Sephardi Jews now living in Israel, France, or the United States as victims, even if what happened to their ancestors was unjust and barbaric.

But let us assume for a moment that the Jews who lived in the Iberian Peninsula had a right, in the modern sense of the term, to live there. We are then confronted with the question of the victims' rights to reparation. Does it still exist today, or has it been superseded? Jeremy Waldron addressed this issue for the case of land expropriation from indigenous communities in the nineteenth and twentieth centuries. According to him, "Some rights are capable of 'fading' in their moral importance by virtue of the passage of time and by the sheer persistence of what was originally a wrongful infringement" (Waldron 1992, 15). Legally, we recognize the importance of prescription and deadlines in both criminal and civil law. Actions are not eternal, except for the case of crimes against humanity. Waldron writes, "Claims about justice and injustice must be responsive to changes in circumstances" (28). The circumstances of Sephardi Jews in the fifteenth and sixteenth centuries, immediately after they were expelled from the Iberian Peninsula, are radically different from the circumstances of Sephardi Jews today. Therefore, it is a complex matter to claim reparation or justice for an episode that took place under circumstances radically different from those of today (28). This does not mean that the historical injustice of the Expulsion should not be acknowledged or politically repaired. As Aleida Assmann (2009, 62) asserts, "We define ourselves through what we remember and forget." Remembrance has to do with justice and also with identity. Therefore, "our comprehension of the past should be the reflection of our moral and political values" (Waldron 1992, 24). Moreover, because "identity is bound up with symbolism, a symbolic gesture may be as important to people as any material compensation" (7). Granting Spanish or Portuguese citizenship to Sephardi Jews is "only" that: a symbolic but nonetheless very strong gesture, expressing a moral and political position in very solemn terms.

In his contribution to this book, Davide Aliberti (chap. 3) has delved more deeply into the concept of political reparation present during the discussion of the Spanish law of 2015. Political reparation is not only a political gesture: it can have an actual effect on victims' perceptions of justice and relief. In 2014 Farida Shaheed, the United Nations special rapporteur in the field of cultural rights, stated, "Collective reparations for mass or grave violations of human rights can take the form of legal but also non-legal measures, the latter entering the field of symbolism and memory, which is too often overlooked (Shaheed 2014, 24). Public apologies are considered in this document to be a memorial expression. Political reparation, also in the form of citizenship laws, therefore, would be a reparative measure of legal and human rights dimensions.

From Germany to Ghana and the Iberian Peninsula: Reparative Citizenship Laws?

After introducing the possibility of granting citizenship as a means of reparation and analyzing the difficulties of legally repairing a historical injustice of the distant past, I will now analyze some cases of citizenship laws presented as reparative. These are the German laws facilitating the acquisition of German citizenship for Jews of German descent, Ghana's right of abode for Africans in the Diaspora, and the Spanish and Portuguese laws granting citizenship to Sephardi Jews.

As we are well aware, Nazi Germany denaturalized its Jewish citizens. The process started in 1933 and culminated with the Reich Citizenship Law of 1935 that denationalized German Jews and members of other groups. That is, any German who could not prove he was "of German or related blood" or who could not show "by his conduct that he [was] willing and fit to faithfully serve the German People and Reich" (*Reichsgesetzblatt*, I, 1935, 1333). This law was necessary in order to strip the rights of Jews and members of other groups with an appearance of legality. It was an important stage in initiating the deportation and murder of Jews because, as Agamben wrote, "Jews could only be sent to the concentration camps once they had been completely deprived of their citizenship" (Agamben 2006, 168). Evidence of this is that in 1940, when the final instructions were approved for mass denaturalization of German Jews (Dean 2002, 227).

After the defeat of National Socialism, these rules were repealed by an Allied Council in 1945. The German Basic Law established, in Article 116.2, "Former German citizens who between 30 January 1933 and 8 May 1945 were deprived of their citizenship on political, racial, or religious grounds and their descendants shall, on application, have their citizenship restored. They shall be deemed never to have been deprived of their citizenship if they have established their domicile in Germany after 1945 and have not expressed a contrary intention." This article and the legislation that developed it cannot be presented as reparatory. It is an instruction aimed at the formal restitution of German citizenship that had been illegally and illegitimately stripped from German citizens.

What is interesting here is that the recovery of citizenship or renationalization of German Jews was hindered by pre-Nazi German legislation that did not allow dual citizenship or recognize the children of a German mother and a foreign father as citizens. As explained above, this ban on dual citizenship was the norm in the citizenship law before the most recent reforms in this matter. German Jews denaturalized and expelled from Germany were formally stateless, and many had obtained citizenship from other countries by 1945. In some cases, Jewish women married foreign men and had children with them. These obstacles remained in place until 2000, although, until 2019, legislative shortcomings prevented nationalization of the children of German women married to foreigners (*Deutsche Welle* 2019; *Jüdische Allgemeine* 2019). These obstacles disappeared in 2019 with the promulgation of two decrees, and in 2021 with legislation reforming the German citizenship law that facilitated the nationalization of descendants of former German citizens (Viertes Gesetz 2021). In the bill, presented by the German government in April 2021, the word "staatsangehörigkeitsrechtliche Wiedergutmachung" (reparation by law of citizenship) appeared (Entwurf eines Vierten Gesetzes 2021).

The situation was similar in Austria. Two laws of 1945 restored the legal status of Austrian Jews to their situation before 13 March 1938. However, a problem arose for the one-third of Austrian Jewish emigrants who, to avoid statelessness, had acquired the citizenship of the countries that accepted them after fleeing the Reich. Dual citizenship was not permitted under Austrian legislation. This, of course, was an obstacle not only for the exercise of political rights, but also for their reception and economic reparation as victims of National Socialism. This explains why, by 1947, only 5,000 of the 110,000 Austrian Jews living in Austria before 1938 had returned (Burger 2014, 167).

Amendments were introduced to Austrian citizenship laws in 1949, 1966, and 1973 to prevent Jewish Austrian emigrants from losing their Austrian citizenship for a second time (Burger 2014, 166). In 1993, amid the process of a revision of Austria's past and its responsibility in the Third Reich, the procedures for recovering Austrian citizenship were simplified for Austrian Jews expelled under National Socialism (171). As in the German case, reparation took other forms rather than reparative citizenship.

The case of Ghana is different. In the 1960s Ghanaian and Pan-Africanist leader Kwame Nkrumah invited African Americans, as descendants of enslaved Africans, to settle in Ghana. The invitation was accepted by a number of African Americans. In 2000 a new immigration act entered into force, granting the right of abode to persons "of African descent in the Diaspora" who met certain criteria, such as having attained the age of eighteen years, having no convictions for criminal offenses, and being financially independent (Ghana Immigration Act 2000, Art. 17). This law grants a right of abode rather than citizenship. With this law, Ghana is indirectly acknowledging a harm perpetrated by the ancestors of American, British, Ghanaian, and other slave traders or slave exploiters. But, from a formal legal point of view, it is not a case of reparative citizenship (or reparative right of abode) since neither the harm nor the liable institutions are clear. It is an example of the previously explained long-distance nationalism, or Pan-Africanism in this case. The act was intended to attract new residents and investors from countries in Europe and North America. The language used in the press and political discourses was associated more with Pan-Africanism and long-distance nationalism than with reparation.

The Spanish and Portuguese citizenship laws of 2015 do not mention reparation, neither in their preambles nor in the articles. They have been described as reparative laws in media and political discourses, as explained by Davide Aliberti in his chapter (chap. 3). This is not due to the regulation of the naturalization procedures, but rather is due to the indirect references to historical injustice in the preambles of the two laws, especially the Spanish one. In both cases, the "song of the law," as Marie Theres Fögen calls preambles (2007), rewrite history by mentioning the injustice of the Expulsion, although the reference is more indirect in the Spanish law. "The Portuguese decree law mentions the right of return, while the Spanish law only refers to reconciliation and reencounter with Sephardic Jews" (Aliberti 2020, 258). However, no direct apology or intention of reparation are to be read in either law. Moreover, the Spanish law does not repeal or make critical reference to the Catholic monarchs' *Edicto* forcing the Jews to abandon their kingdoms, and does not mention the Spanish Jews who were not protected by Spain during the Holocaust. Other references to history and some historical silences are problematic in the Spanish preamble, as I have explained in a recent paper (Aragoneses 2018).

Conclusion: Citizenship Laws Between Reparation and Long-distance Nationalism

From a formal legal perspective, citizenship cannot be considered a measure of reparation for a crime or historical injustice committed by a country in the past. Neither can historical injustice in the distant past be repaired from a legal perspective. However, citizenship law has evolved significantly, making citizenship a potential instrument of diplomacy, country branding or long-distance nationalism. Therefore, granting citizenship to descendants of victims of a historical injustice can also be used as a symbolic mechanism of reparation. Use of this instrument is compatible with diplomatic efforts to improve the perception of a country in the international community or to build ties with one or several countries. Granting citizenship can also help to reshape the image and reputation of a country, especially in times of crisis.

If the aim of these laws is one or several of those mentioned above, the absence of an apology or references to reparation is difficult to understand. Admitting guilt would not mean admitting liability: the more than five hundred years since 1492 make it almost impossible, from a legal perspective, to claim damages against Spain and Portugal. In the Spanish case, the absence of any intention to symbolically repeal the *Edicto* of the Catholic monarchs is even more surprising.

Despite the lack of apology in the two laws, and the overly formal language of the preamble to the Spanish law, along with the difficult and expensive procedures it establishes for acquiring Spanish citizenship, these laws mark a difference in the Spanish and Portuguese approach to the Expulsion episode and to the Jewish world in general. Both countries have demonstrated that they have superseded old nineteenth-century nationalism with regard to citizenship and that they have adopted a more modern approach to this concept.

The symbolism of these operations must not be underestimated. As Aleida Assmann notes, "We define ourselves through what we remember and forget" (2009, 62). Therefore, recognition of a historical injustice and symbolic reparation can be very important tools to create or reinforce consensus in institutions and to foster tolerance and diversity. At a time when homogeneous visions of national communities are no longer sustainable, recognizing a harm done to a group of individuals ten, fifty, or five hundred years ago, and including their descendants in it, is a strong gesture that has a rights and legal dimension and that shows a commitment to the values of democracy and human rights.

Alfons Aragoneses lectures in legal history at Pompeu Fabra University, Barcelona, and is associate researcher at the Max Planck Institute for Legal History, Frankfurt/Main. His doctoral thesis is on the history of comparative law in France (2004). He has written on French and Spanish private law, Francoist law, and memory laws. His recent research is on the links between memory, law, and collective identity in Spain. He coordinated the Database of Spanish Deportees to Nazi Concentration Camps and has assisted the Catalan government on legislative and public policies regarding remembrance projects.

Notes

1. "Sephardi Jews give lukewarm reception to their law. Only 3,843 Jews have obtained Spanish nationality under the regulation intended to make reparation for their expulsion." *El País*, 18 November 2018; "A Questão sefardita: reunir Portugal" [The Sephardi question: reuniting Portugal] *Público* 27 May 2020.
2. A recent and well-known example is the Spanish one. In 2012 the Spanish government created the position of high commissioner for the brand Marca España, with the aim of "improving the image of Spain abroad" (Real Decreto 998/2012 2012).

References

Agamben, Giorgio. 2006. *Homo sacer. El poder soberano y la nuda vida*. Valencia: Pre-Textos.
Aliberti, Davide. 2020. "Back to Sefarad? Comparative Analysis of the 2015 Iberian Citizenship Laws for Sephardic Jews." In *Transcultural Spaces and Identities in Iberian Studies*, edited by Mark Gant, Susana Rocha Relvas, 236–58. Cambridge: Cambridge Scholars Publishing.
Anderson, Benedict. 1983. *Imagined Communities: Reflections on the Origin and Spread of Nationalism*. London: Verso.
———. 2002. *The Spectre of Comparisons. Nationalism, Southeast Asia and the World*. London: Verso.
Aragoneses, Alfons. 2018. "Uses of Convivencia and Filosefardismo in Spanish Legal Discourses." *Rechtsgeschichte—Legal History Rg* 26: 200–19.

———. 2019. "Judaism and Spanish Identities. Between Filosefardismo and Antisemitism." In *Modern Antisemitisms in the Peripheries. Europe and its Colonies 1880–1945*, edited by Raul Castorcea and Eva Kovács, 111–32. Vienna: Wiener Wiesenthal Institute.

Arregui Tena, Rodrigo. 2015. "La concesión de la nacionalidad española a los saharahuis (o habitants de la provincial 53)." *Hay Derecho*, 13 April 2015. https://www.hayderecho.com/2015/04/13/la-concesion-de-la-nacionalidad-espanola-a-los-saharauis-o-habitantes-de-la-provincia-53/.

Assmann, Aleida. 2009. *Erinnerungsräume. Formen und Wandlungen des kulturellen Gedächtnisses*. München: C. H. Beck.

Bevernage, Berber. 2008. "Time, Presence, and Historical Injustice." *History and Theory* 47: 149–67.

Burger, Hannelore. 2014. *Heimatrecht und Staatsbürgerschaft österreichischer Juden Vom Ende des 18. Jahrhunderts bis in die Gegenwart*. Wien: Böhlau.

Caligiuri, Andrea. 2005. *Reparation for Past Slavery. A Critical Approach*. Siena: Università degli Studi di Siena.

Dean, Martin. 2002. "The Development and Implementation of Nazi Denaturalization and Confiscation Policy up to the Eleventh Decree to the Reich Citizenship Law." *Holocaust and Genocide Studies* 16: 217–42.

Deutsche Welle. 2019. "Deutsche Pässe für die Nachfahren verfolgter Juden." 30 August 2019. https://www.dw.com/de/deutsche-pässe-für-die-nachfahren-verfolgter-juden/a-50226772.

———. 2020. "Descendants of Nazi Victims Continue Fight for German Citizenship." 12 February 2020. https://www.dw.com/en/descendants-of-nazi-victims-continue-fight-for-german-citizenship/a-52295031.

Dovi, Efam. 2015. "African-American Resettle in Africa." *Africa Renewal*. April 2015. un.org/africarenewal/magazine/Afric-2015/African-americans-resettle-africa.

Entwurf eines Vierten Gesetzes zur Änderung des Staatsangehörigkeitsgesetzes. Drucksache 19/28674. 19.04.2021. 1–32. https://dserver.bundestag.de/btd/19/286/1928674.pdf.

Espinar Vicente, José María. 2012. "La función de la nacionalidad y la extranjería en el derecho internacional privado contemporáneo." *Anuario Español de Derecho Internacional Privado* 12: 39–64.

Fögen, Marie Theres. 2007. *Das Lied vom Gesetz*. München: Carl Friedrich von Siemens Stiftung.

German Basic Law Article 116.2. https://www.gesetze-im-internet.de/englisch_gg/englisch_gg.pdf.

Ghana Immigration Act. 2000 (Act 573). https://www.gis.gov.gh/ACTS%20AND%20REGULATIONS/ACT%20573.pdf.

Glick Schiller, Nina. 2002. "Long-Distance Nationalism." In *Encyclopedia of Diasporas: Immigrant and Refugee Cultures around the World*, edited by M. Ember, 570–80. New York: Springer.

Hespanha, António Manuel. 2004. "Legal History and Legal Education." *Rechtsgeschichte—Legal History Rg* 4: 41–56.

Hunt, Lynn. 1996. *The French Revolution and Human Rights: A Brief Documentary History*, translated, edited and with an introduction. Boston: St. Martin's.

Ignatieff, Michael. 1996. "Articles of Faith." *Index on Censorship* 5: 110–22.

Jüdische Allgemeine. 2019. "Die deutsche Rechtspraxis ist ein Skandal." *Jüdische Allgemeine*, 13 January 2019. https://www.juedische-allgemeine.de/politik/die-deutsche-rechtspraxis-ist-ein-skandal/.

Kerr, Pauline. 2013. *Diplomacy in a Globalizing World: Theories and Practices*. New York: Oxford University Press.
Ministry of External Affairs. 2018. "Question 2885: Population of Overseas Indians. To be answered on 18.07.2019 at Rajya Sabha." https://www.mea.gov.in/rajya-sabha.htm?dtl/31625/question+no2885+number+of+overseas+indians+abroad.
The Hague Convention on Certain Questions Relating to the Conflict of Nationality Laws, 12 April. (1930). *American Journal of International Law, 24* (S3), 192–200.
Pulido, Ángel. 1905. *Españoles sin patria y la raza sefardí*. Madrid, Establecimiento tipográfico de E. Teodoro Palau.
Real Decreto 998/2012. 2012. "Real Decreto, por el que se crea el Alto Comisionado del Gobierno para la Marca España." *Boletín Oficial del Estado* 155, 29 June 2012: 46129–32. https://www.boe.es/eli/es/rd/2012/06/28/998.
Ronny, Shabrina Amelia, Helda Risman, and Surryanto Djoko Waluyo. 2020. "Diaspora Causatum: Enhancing Defense Diplomacy through Alterations in Citizenship Laws." *Technium Social Sciences Journal* 9: 479–94.
Shaheed, Farida. 2014. United Nations. "Report of the Special Rapporteur in the Field of Cultural Rights." https://digitallibrary.un.org/record/766862?ln=en.
Sznaider, Natan. 2019. "The Burden and Dignity of Jewish Difference." In *Modern Antisemitisms in the Peripheries. Europe and its Colonies 1880–1945*, edited by Raul Castorcea and Eva Kovács, 449–58. Vienna: Wiener Wiesenthal Institute.
Viertes Gesetz zur Änderung des Staatsangehörigkeitsgesetzes vom 12. 2021. *Bundesgesetzblatt* 54 (2021): 3538–41.
Waldron, Jeremy. 1992. "Superseding Historic Injustice." *Ethics* 103: 4–28.

Chapter 2

Beyond Reparatory Justice
The Portuguese "Law of Return" as Nation Branding

Isabel David and Gabriela Anouck Côrte-Real Pinto

The 2015 Portuguese law of return, as it is commonly referred to, illuminates the centrality of contemporary nation branding to citizenship policies that concern the national past. Portugal's amendment to its citizenship law, passed unanimously in 2013 by parties from across the political spectrum,[1] granted descendants of Sephardi Jews, who fled expulsion, forced conversion to Catholicism (1496), and the Inquisition (1536–1821), the right to apply for Portuguese citizenship (Law 43/2013). The law came into effect two years later, in 2015, and can be situated among similar laws seeking to repair past injustices (see "Introduction" and Aragoneses chap. 1, both in this volume). These multiplying reparations laws have drawn scholarly attention with regard to their motivations (e.g., Côrte-Real Pinto and David 2019; Goldschläger and Orjuela 2020; Stein 2016; and this volume). Our chapter extends this work, exploring the link between citizenship laws and policies and nation branding. Since nation branding is anchored in national identity, the literature needs to address citizenship laws, as these define the constituent elements of that national identity. This is particularly important in the case of reparation laws because of the reputation that they project of a country, and reputation is at the heart of nation branding.

The Portuguese case is relevant for scholarship because, unlike the other reparation laws, it portrays an understanding of identity based on a concept of racial exceptionalism grounded in miscegenation. In this chapter, we advance two arguments: (1) The law of return articulates a post–World War II shared belief and hegemonic discourse among the Portuguese that Portugal is a tolerant country; and (2) The law can be interpreted as nation branding. The reclaiming of its Sephardi cultural heritage in the international sphere and the combination of this hegemonic discourse and nation branding fortifies Portugal's image and international standing in a context of global capitalism and competition among states. This reinforced image helps attract human, social, and economic capital and addresses demographic issues. Our chapter's novel contribution is its articulation of citizenship laws with nation branding through the Portuguese case study.

Branding the Nation

The concept of nation branding was created by brand consultant Simon Anholt (1998 2005, 2007, 2010) as a strategy suitable for both developed and developing countries in a context of global capitalism, where states increasingly compete for investment, trade, skills, immigrants, technology, and funds. Nation branding consists in wielding power by "making people want to pay attention to a country's achievements and believe in its qualities" (Anholt 2005, 13).

Nation branding combines brand management, public diplomacy and trade, investment, tourism, and export promotion (Anholt 2007, 3), as states need to build competitive advantages. As Kaneva (2016, 188) aptly argues, "Nation brands are symbolic commodities, produced for the purpose of generating different forms of capital," meaning intellectual, symbolic, social, economic, and financial capital. In our usage, the term "state branding" refers to the nation as the *entrepreneurial state* and nation branding as a form of *state entrepreneurship* that aims at the marketization of the nation to create consumers (e.g., investors, tourists, and immigrants) in other countries. As van Ham (2001) emphasizes, politicians need to find a brand niche, produce competitive marketing strategies, ensure customer satisfaction, and create brand loyalty. This loyalty is ensured by the country's reputation—in other words, the brand.

Brand reputation is based on brand values (main qualities and characteristics), that are built through actions and behaviors on the one hand, and by how people are personally affected by a place on the other (Anholt 2007, 48). The novelty of nation branding is that "national cultural specificity" becomes the "competitive edge" over other countries (Aronczyk 2008, 44). In other words, for Anholt, image is anchored in national identity. As he explains, "The process of arriving at the . . . [branding] strategy . . . needs to be dug out of the history, the culture, the geography, the society of the place. . . . Unless the overall strategy chimes with something fundamentally true about the place and its people, there is little chance that it will be believed or endorsed by the population, let alone the rest of the world" (Anholt 2007, 75). Indeed, branding needs both a nationwide public-private partnership (local and national government, tourist boards, corporations, brands, airlines) and the involvement of the population of the country, supporting the strategy and living the brand by reproducing the country's values and characteristics in their dealings as brand ambassadors with the outside public (Anholt 2005, 119, 130; Anholt 2007, 14, 74). As Aronczyk (2008, 42) notes, drawing from Herbert Simon, under increasing competition for scarce resources, nation branding reaps the benefits of the "attention economy" by attracting positive recognition through a distinctive image. Volcic and Andrejevic (2011, 598) note that, by branding the nation, states promote national interest and a neoliberal nationalism that "combines the obligations of citizenship with the responsibilities and risks of the entrepreneur" (601).

The Changing Face of Portuguese Collective Memory

The nation branding offered by the Portuguese reparation law promotes the image of a tolerant country seeking to correct past injustices. We contend that this image draws from a fundamental trait of Portuguese collective memory: a shared belief and hegemonic discourse portraying Portugal as tolerant. This discourse originated with Brazilian anthropologist Gilberto Freyre (1940, 2003), who coined the term "*lusotropicalismo*" to depict the interactions of the Portuguese with other peoples and cultures. The theory presents the Portuguese as a mixture of different physical types (from northern Europe to Africa), religions (Catholicism and Islam), and customs. For Freyre (2003, 67, 69, 70, 84, 274), this ethnic and cultural indecisiveness favored the erasure of race and class issues while promoting the social and physical adaptability of the Portuguese, leading to miscegenation and cosmopolitanism as a natural outcome at home and in the colonial spaces. While acknowledging mistreatment of slaves, the Portuguese were, in his view, the European colonizers that best coexisted with what he considered "inferior races" and the least cruel in relations with their slaves (265). Freyre (79) contrasts this approach with the extermination policy conducted by Spain and England. As Anderson, Roque, and Ventura Santos (2019) assert, the Portuguese racial regime, presented as benign and unique because of "race mixing," has been the cornerstone in the narrative of a "Latin and particularly a Lusophone racial exceptionalism, in contrast to Northern Hemisphere racial formations" (4).

While initially rejecting Freyre's ideas, after World War II the dictatorship (1926–74) welcomed Lusotropicalism, which became instrumental in defending the legitimacy of the colonial regime in the face of emerging liberation movements and growing international pressure to decolonize (Almeida and Corkill 2015; Marques 2008). Indeed, Freyre's romanticization of slavery and colonialism erased "the racialized, gendered and classed relations within the coloniality of power," based on the cultural, economic, and political hegemony of the whites (Almeida and Corkill 2015, 158).

The overthrow of the dictatorship in 1974 and subsequent transition to democracy and decolonization transformed the political, economic, cultural, and social narratives and practices. Portugal applied for European Economic Community membership, gaining access in 1986. It was then that the country reconstructed its collective memory, seeking to harmonize the experiences of the past with a modern, democratic, postcolonial present. In order to shed the negative connotations of imperialism and to rebuild relations with the Lusophone world, the past was redefined as a "meeting of cultures" (*encontro de culturas*), and the Portuguese language was promoted as the symbol of union (Almeida and Corkill 2015, 164; Hespanha 1999, 18–19). Thus, this redefinition, conducted by the left and the right of the political spectrum, rebranded the Lusotropicalist narrative, adapting it to the democratic context, portraying the country as humanist, tolerant, and nonracist. The new narrative materialized in the creation of the Community of Portuguese Speaking Countries (CPLP) and Lusophony (the community of states that share Portuguese language and culture). As Almeida and Corkill (2015, 164) contend, this reconceptualization was particularly useful for the redefinition of Portugal's semi-peripheric role in the world. The multicultural ethos of the Lusotropicalist narrative has continued to shape the self-perceptions of the Portuguese, their ways of interpreting the world, and the politics of nationhood and citizenship (158). With regime transition, elite change, and decolonization in 1974, the new political leadership successfully rebranded the previous five hundred years in a way that was compatible with the values of the liberal international order, changing the image of the country from a poor, colonialist, retrograde country into a modern, progressive nation. Under this narrative, outbursts of racism are discarded as peripheral to the essentially humanistic core values of the Portuguese, precluding further debate on the issue.

Methodology

The findings of this chapter stem from a qualitative process tracing method in Political Science. Process tracing consists of examining "histories, archival documents, interview transcripts, and other sources to see whether the causal process a theory hypothesizes or implies in a case is in fact evident in the sequence and values of the intervening variables in that case" (George and Bennett 2005, 6). The aim is to "obtain information about well-defined and specific events and processes, and the most appropriate sampling procedures are thus those that identify the key political actors that have had most involvement with the processes of interest" (Tansey 2007, 2). Like Tansey, we considered elite interviews as the most effective means of collecting data in process-tracing studies (see also Richards 1996). To this end, we used a nonprobability, purposive sampling that used positional criteria to identify key elites. This approach implies that the researcher has sufficient knowledge of political structures to identify the most relevant actors (Tansey 2007, 19), according to their knowledge and experience. For the purposes of this chapter, we define elites as the members of parliament involved in the amendment to the law granting citizenship to descendants of Sephardi Jews, the members of government who promote nation branding, and the officials of the Portuguese Jewish Communities of Oporto and Lisbon, whose consultative role was fundamental to the enactment of the amendment to the law.

We conducted nine semistructured interviews in person, via Zoom, Skype, Microsoft Teams, and by telephone between October 2017 and October 2020. Interviewees included Michael Rothwell, board member of the Jewish Community of Oporto; Esther Mucznik, board member of the Jewish Community of Lisbon; Teresa Santos, staff member of the Jewish Community of Lisbon; the members of parliament who authored the amendment—Maria de Belém Roseira (Socialist Party) and José Ribeiro e Castro (Democratic Social Center-People's Party);[2] Adolfo Mesquita Nunes, secretary of state of tourism between 2011 and 2015; Celeste Varum, advisor to the secretary of state of tourism between 2019 and 2022; Constança Urbano de Sousa (Socialist Party), a member of parliament between 2019 and 2022; and Carlos Zorrinho, leader of the parliamentary group of the Socialist Party in 2013. We tried to interview representatives from the other political parties represented in parliament in 2013 (Social Democratic Party, Portuguese Communist Party, Left Bloc, Greens), but they did not reply to our requests.

We were also participant observers at a Shabbaton of the Jewish Community of Oporto,[3] on the weekend of 9–10 March 2018. We attended religious services, lectures, and meals at the synagogue, and spoke to several participants and attendees. Additionally, we consulted parliamentary archives, parliamentary speeches, statistics on bilateral trade, statistics on citizenship requests, documents from the official websites of Portuguese tourism, and Jewish news outlets (newspapers and Jewish association websites).

Living the Brand

According to Anholt (2007, 2008), nation branding must reflect national identity. Our contention is that the concession of Portuguese citizenship to descendants of Sephardi Jews results from the country's self-image as tolerant and, to some extent, solves the flagrant incompatibility between the Inquisition and Expulsion of Jews with this essentialized image of Portugal promoted after World War II. This idea was present in all our interviews. As former Secretary of State of Tourism Adolfo Mesquita Nunes explained, "There is a link between the brand and the identity of Portugal. We cannot promote what is not true at a time of so much information and viralization of content. . . . The amendment to the law on citizenship is coherent with the message that Portugal is an open and tolerant country" (Mesquita Nunes 2020).[4] Maria de Belém Roseira, the author of the amendment, also neatly articulated the shared belief:

> . . . The Inquisition . . . did not originate from the population. It was imposed on king Manuel to allow him to marry the Spanish princess. The Inquisition served petty spirits as a way to annul the debts of royalty to Jews. . . . The persecution of Jews has nothing to do with our essential identitarian traits. . . . The fact that [the amendment] passed unanimously is significant, meaning that the Portuguese people did not want the Inquisition and it was a matter of reparatory justice (*justiça reparativa*). The Portuguese are not persecutors. We are accustomed to living with difference. We mixed with other peoples and we can incorporate a practice [into law] that reflects that way of being. . . . Other peoples invaded lands but they did not mix because they thought they were superior to the colonized. . . . In Portugal, there is a peaceful and natural integration of other forms of being. (De Belém Roseira 2017)

Interviewees from the Portuguese Jewish communities of Lisbon and Oporto concur with this shared belief, living the brand and participating as cocreators. Michael Rothwell from Oporto told us, "Portugal is the safest country for Jews in Europe. . . . The Portuguese are curious about Judaism and they know that they have Jewish ancestry . . . the inhabitants of Oporto frequently tell us that they are happy to see us back and that Portugal should never have expelled the Jews" (Rothwell 2017). Esther Mucznik explained how the founders of the Jewish Community of Lisbon, who arrived in the late eighteenth and early nineteenth centuries, were "welcomed in Portugal and immediately integrated, unlike what was happening in Europe then. In the second half of the 19th century and the beginning of the 20th century there was antisemitism, as exemplified by the Dreyfus case. Antisemitism in Poland and Russia sparked the arrival of the first Ashkenazim in Portugal. In the 1930s, the first refugees from Nazism arrived" (Mucznik 2017). This historical account is tainted, however, by several cases. First, in the so-called Portuguese Dreyfus case, Army captain Barros Basto, founder of the Jewish Community of

Oporto in 1923, sought to bring Marranos back to official Judaism and was expelled from the military in 1937 for behavior considered inappropriate for the office he held.[5] Second, the refusal of the dictatorship to grant citizenship or residency to the circa 250,000 Jews who passed through Portugal fleeing Nazism caused tension with the Jewish community. Only a few remained, as Portugal became a country of transit, not of exile, mostly to North and South America (see also the Introduction to this volume). Third, Aristides de Sousa Mendes, the Portuguese consul in Bordeaux during World War II and who is now designated Righteous Among the Nations, was disowned by the dictatorship for the thousands of visas he issued to Jews (Pimentel 2008).

Mucznik (2017) also stressed the "absence of organized antisemitism" in Portugal today. According to a Eurobarometer on perceptions of antisemitism, only 10 percent of respondents believe antisemitism is a problem in Portugal (European Commission 2019). This image contrasts with the most recent survey on discrimination and hate crimes against Jews in the European Union (European Union Agency for Fundamental Rights 2018), in which 85 percent of respondents considered antisemitism to be the most pressing problem in their country of origin.

José Ribeiro e Castro, former member of parliament and author of another proposal to grant Portuguese citizenship to descendants of Sephardim, presented Jews as a historically integral part of the Portuguese nation: "Jews . . . emigrated to Portugal from the 2nd and 3rd centuries. . . . When Portugal became independent, Jews participated in the formation of the kingdom. After their expulsion . . . they kept their identity traits and rites. In 1821, when the parliament revoked king Manuel's expulsion edict, they . . . returned. . . . There is a cultural and social identification of the Sephardim with the Portuguese nation. . . . The law is . . . how we repair the mistake and recover the Portuguese community that was amputated at the end of the 15th century" (Ribeiro e Castro 2020).

In line with brand values of tolerance, the law was presented by several interviewees (Roseira and Rothwell) as the culmination of a path initiated in 1989, when president of the republic Mário Soares apologized for the persecution of Jews. This was followed in 1996 by a solemn session of parliament, on the fifth centenary of the Expulsion edict, in the presence of president of the republic Jorge Sampaio, who has maternal Jewish roots (see Assembleia da República 1996). According to Carlos Zorrinho (2020), former parliamentary leader of the Socialist Party, "The possibility of reparation is part of a process that a people that is one thousand years old must complete—[to] heal the wounds . . . that makes us a better people."[6] As explained, this path partakes in the rewriting of collective memory initiated in the 1980s. A recent example is the unanimous rehabilitation of Barros Basto by the Portuguese Parliament in 2012. Another is the symbolic burial of Aristides de Sousa Mendes at the national Pantheon in 2020, also approved unanimously by parliament (Lusa 2020a).

As Anholt (2005, 2007) suggests, a successful strategy should avoid negative nation branding. In April 2020, Socialist member of parliament Constança Urbano de Sousa, a former minister of internal affairs, introduced a bill to amend the article on the concession of citizenship to descendants of Sephardi Jews, calling for a minimum of two years of residency in Portugal (Partido Socialista 2020).[7] The proposal was supported by the Social Democratic Party and part of the left. Urbano de Sousa (2020), an academic expert on citizenship, told us that her motivation was to limit the commodification of Portuguese citizenship and "allow for an increase of the Portuguese Jewish community." Even though the law reflects a "noble cause" and "Portugal's tradition of humanism," Urbano de Sousa told us that "the title of the law is 'return' but most of them [descendants of Sephardi Jews who benefited from the law] do not come to Portugal. They have a pragmatic approach. A passport is not a citizenship. Portuguese citizenship is being commercialized by specialized companies that advertise it solely as an EU passport. . . . There is a serious risk of this having negative consequences for the image of Portugal and its relations with the EU partners. . . . Other than a historical link, there needs to be an actual link with today's Portuguese community. The genuine link should be reinforced".

Her proposal was heavily criticized by fellow Socialist Party members, including Roseira (Alegre et al. 2020), the Portuguese Jewish communities (Mucznik 2020; Rothwell 2020), and Jewish communities abroad (Kaufman 2020). Ribeiro e Castro articulated the negative branding associated with it, arguing, "This [proposal] raised antisemitism, even if unintentionally. It implies that [applicants] are criminals . . . this adheres to the stereotype associated with the Jews: "cosmopolitans without roots." . . . We would have gained the label of antisemitic (Ribeiro e Castro 2020). Shortly after the backlash, Urbano de Sousa withdrew the proposal. The international image of Portugal as a tolerant country, however, was partly damaged among Jewish communities (see Liphshiz 2020; Sharon 2020a, 2020b).

Promoting the Brand

Promoting the brand is a continuous effort to develop innovative products, services, policies, and initiatives in order to attract attention, demonstrate the truth of the narrative, and prove the country's reputation

(Anholt 2010, 7). Involvement of the political leadership is fundamental. Since 2013 the Portuguese governments have conducted initiatives via a nationwide public-private partnership with local governments, tourist boards, corporations, brands, and airlines. Mesquita Nunes explained the first initiatives conducted by the center-right government of the Social Democratic Party and Democratic Social Center-People's Party: "The change to the law on citizenship is a conversation starter with niche markets. We prepared a strategy for the Jewish target . . . and organized a mission to Israel, in partnership with companies, tourism operators and the Portuguese Jewish communities" (Mesquita Nunes 2020).

This state entrepreneurship has been followed and enhanced by the subsequent governments of the Socialist Party. Prime Minister António Costa, former Secretary of State of Tourism Ana Mendes Godinho, Secretary of State of Industry Ana Lehmann, and Portuguese diplomats have visited Sephardi communities in the United States, together with the president of the republic, Marcelo Rebelo de Sousa, and the leaders of the Portuguese Jewish communities, to promote the law and tourism, and to advocate for a greater Jewish presence in Portugal. They have stressed the presence of multiple Jewish heritage sites, the role of Portuguese Sephardi Jews in science and culture, and the Jewish ancestry of about 20 percent of the Portuguese population. In particular, they have promoted the brand values of tolerance that portray Portugal as a safe haven for Jews, stressing the country's peaceful nature (the third-most-peaceful country in the world), the absence of visible antisemitism, and the role of Portugal as a transit country during World War II (European Jewish Congress 2018; Glickman 2018; *Times of Israel* 2018).

The Portuguese government has also promoted the brand in Israel. Godinho (2018) published an article in the *Jerusalem Post* promoting tourism and investment, and inviting Jews to live in Portugal. Together with representatives of various companies, Secretary of State of Industry Ana Lehmann visited Israel in 2018 to attract investment in the technological sector (Hinchliffe 2018). The president of the republic, Rebelo de Sousa, visited Israel in January 2020 to attend the World Holocaust Forum and meet the Israeli president (Lusa 2020b). Portugal established relations with the World Sephardi Federation, culminating in 2019 with a visit to Portugal by leaders of Sephardi communities from around the world.

The promotion of Jewish tourism in Portugal is one of the main arenas of nation branding. It involves several stakeholders, among which are national and regional entities and municipalities. Public investment contributed to increasing the number of tourist locations around the country. These are publicized through dedicated websites on religious tourism

("Jewish Heritage;" Rede). These locations include, in Oporto, a Jewish museum and the recently opened Holocaust Museum (branded as the first in the Iberian Peninsula), run by the local Jewish community. In 2019 the largest Chabad center opened in Cascais, in a location donated by the municipality. Celeste Varum (2020), adviser to the secretary of state of tourism between 2019 and 2022, described several initiatives, articulating the public and private sector: exhibitions, events and workshops, economic diplomacy missions, training, and visits (targeting, for example, tour operators, journalists, opinion leaders, and leaders of Jewish communities around the world). Highly relevant markets for this tourism are Israel, Argentina, Brazil, Canada, and the United States. The private sector has also invested in complementary activities, hotels and restaurants serving kosher food and drinks in Jewish heritage locations. Significantly, from November 2017, Portugal and Israel became connected through direct flights (Marketeer 2017).

Another branding strategy is the enhanced visibility of Judaism in Portugal. Members of the Portuguese Jewish communities are regularly interviewed in the Portuguese media, together with articles on Jewish heritage and life in Portugal (Alves 2020; Lusa 2019a). In the cultural sphere, one example is the book *4 Gerações em Lisboa* (*Four generations in Lisbon*), edited by the Lisbon Municipality and the former leader of the Jewish Community of Lisbon, Joshua Benoliel Ruah (Ferreira 2018). Another is the 2019 drama film *Sefarad*, sponsored by the Jewish Community of Oporto, telling the story of Barros Basto. The film premiered on Amazon Prime and was exhibited at international Jewish film festivals in Miami and Moscow (Lusa 2019b).[8] And, in 2018, the Portuguese Parliament passed a resolution launching the Day of Memory of the Victims of the Inquisition, observed annually on 31 March (Lusa 2019c).

Portugal has also been reclaiming and promoting its Jewish heritage in academia, until recently largely dominated by Spanish scholarship. We participated in an international conference titled "Jews of Portugal and the Spanish-Portuguese Jewish Diaspora," held in Portugal in 2018. The conference reception at the Lisbon synagogue was attended by Secretary of State of Tourism Godinho, who addressed the audience to reinforce Portugal's openness to Jews. In December 2020 the Portuguese Foundation for Science and Technology authorized financial support for research and development projects within the framework of the National Program for Holocaust Remembrance (FCT 2021).

This branding strategy has met with little resistance. One example is the local opposition to the construction of a Jewish Museum in Alfama, in Lisbon, because it "breaks with neighborhood traditions" (JTA 2017).

This led to the museum location being transferred to the Belém area. The sheikh of Al Azhar University in Cairo criticized the double standards of the Portuguese law, asking for its extension to the descendants of the Muslims who were also persecuted and expelled from the Iberian Peninsula (Agência Lusa 2018).[9] The greater visibility of the Jewish community has also prompted antisemitism, linked to conspiracy theories, worsened by the Covid-19 pandemic (Rudee 2021). So, to what extent has the branding strategy been effective?

Consuming the Brand

Media attention is a key criterion for measuring consumption. As Mesquita Nunes (2020) told us, "One of the main elements to promote the country is to make others talk about us. . . . If there is news [in the media], this helps project the image of the country. There is a permanent need to invent, in order to foster interest." Indeed, the brand promotion initiatives mentioned in the previous section have been featured regularly in the international media, especially the media linked to Jewish communities (e.g., *Haaretz* 2015). This helps replicate the brand promotion strategy by building on the aforementioned concept of attention economy.

Another parameter to assess the effectiveness of the strategy is the number of applicants for Portuguese citizenship. Between 2015 and December 2021, 137,087 people applied for citizenship: 466 in 2015, 5,100 in 2016, 7,044 in 2017, 13,995 in 2018, 25,199 in 2019, 34,876 in 2020, and 50,407 in 2021. Of these, 56,685 have already received their citizenship.[10] There are multiple motivations for applying, such as sentimental reasons, safety reasons in the country of origin, to obtain a European passport, or to improve business, travel, and education opportunities (Benmayor and Kandiyoti 2020; Côrte-Real Pinto and David 2019; Goldschläger and Orjuela 2020). But the growing numbers can be interpreted as a result of the constructed reputation of Portugal as a welcoming, tolerant country and a safe haven for Jews in a context of global recrudescence of antisemitism. This was confirmed to us by multiple attendees of the Shabatton at the Oporto synagogue in 2018 and by the officials of the Jewish communities of Lisbon and Oporto. The absence of language requirements or of a deadline for applying for Portuguese citizenship reinforces the reputation of Portugal, especially compared to the Spanish, Greek, German, or Austrian laws. In fact, the absence of these requirements can be seen as proof of genuine reparation. As the author of the amendment, Belém Roseira told us, "Reparatory justice cannot be dated."

The brand reputation of tolerance can be assessed by the growing number of Jews living in Portugal, from around seven hundred prior to the law to between five thousand and six thousand in 2021.[11] This growth is mainly fed by new recipients of citizenship. We interviewed several new residents at the 2018 Oporto Shabbaton. One of them was a twenty-five-year-old French man who moved to Portugal because, as he put it, "I feel safe here. The level of acceptance of Jews reflects the social evolution of a country." Catering to a growing community, several newcomers launched small businesses like restaurants or grocery stores, selling kosher goods. Several Israeli families told us that they moved to Portugal because of the high cost of living in Israel.

Similarly, Jewish Israelis with alternative lifestyles who want to create rural communities are moving to the interior of Portugal, which is increasingly depopulated and aging due to younger Portuguese generations relocating to the coasts. Feeling welcomed by the local populations, the new settlers are reviving these regions, moved by visions of a dream life made possible by the low price of land and the slower pace of life in contrast with Israel (Arad 2019; Lidman 2019). As Anholt (2007, 112) argues, successful nation branding should not only be efficient and effective: it "needs to persuade, to inspire and to motivate."

Another measure to assess brand consumption is the economy. Portuguese exports to Israel have grown steadily since 2015, as seen in Table 2.1, and the balance of trade became positive for the first time since 2016.

Israeli investment in Portugal has grown considerably, ranging from information technology, start-ups, medicine, and telecommunications, to real estate (Freire 2019; Idealista 2020; Justo n.d.; Link to Leaders 2020; Steemit n.d.). Portugal and Israel have recently increased military cooperation, as is illustrated by the purchase of Israeli electronic technology by the Portuguese Ministry of Defense, and have engaged in bilateral governmental talks on cooperation in security, science, and technology (Azulai 2019; Dias and Marques 2019; FCT 2019).

Particularly important is Jewish tourism in Portugal. We were unable to obtain official numbers, since Jewish tourists have multiple nationalities. Only scattered data can be found in several newspaper articles, showing a strong increase: from circa 5,000 in the early 2010s to 105,000 in 2017 (Rodrigues 2018). The numbers are particularly significant in the small towns of the interior, where Jewish life was abundant before the Expulsion in 1496. Mayors mention that Jewish tourism, along with Israeli immigrants, are reviving the regions through increased jobs in tourism, the production of kosher food, the opening of new hotels and restaurants, the establishment of companies (namely agricultural) that

Table 2.1. Exports of Portuguese Goods to Israel 2015-2019.

	2015	2016	2017	2018	2019
Exports	112,429,000€	151,298,000€	191,114,000€	217,775,000€	228,821,000€

Source: Adapted from Gabinete de Estratégia e Estudos 2020, 3.

supply the tourist sector, and the demand for historians hired by applicants searching for proof of their Portuguese ancestry (Rodrigues 2018).

Sephardi Jews (both foreign and new recipients of Portuguese citizenship) have engaged in philanthropic donations in Portugal. For example, the grandson of the founder of the Danone yogurt conglomerate contributed 50 million euros to the Champalimaud Foundation for oncological research. Another Sephardi Jew donated to Torre do Tombo, which hosts the national archives, to recover and digitize the files of the Inquisition. Patrick Drahi, a French-Israeli recipient of Portuguese citizenship, donated 1 million euros to the future Jewish Museum of Lisbon. In 2015 he acquired PT, the Portuguese national telecommunications company (*Correio da Manhã* 2018; Rothwell 2020).

As we have seen, the types of capital attracted by the branding efforts of the entrepreneurial state are multiple—social, human, financial, economic—, fulfilling the goal of nation branding.

Conclusion

In this chapter we have argued that the law of return can be portrayed as nation branding. Branding involves constructing a reputation that is anchored in the core values of national identity. We contend that these values stem from a shared belief and hegemonic discourse among the Portuguese that Portugal is a tolerant country. Our interviews confirmed this narrative. The Portuguese state has engaged in continuous entrepreneurship, mobilizing public and private institutions and the Portuguese people as cocreators of the brand, with an important role being played by the Portuguese Jewish communities as brand ambassadors.

The commitment to creating continuous activities, policies, and products has generated varied types of capital, with the increase of Jewish consumers in several segments such as investment, trade, skills, immigrants, technology, and tourism. In this sense, the strategy of nation branding has ensured brand loyalty. From a nation branding viewpoint, Portugal is thus advantageous for Jewish consumers, particularly at a time of heightened antisemitism around the world.

An interesting conclusion that has arisen from our research is that the Portuguese branding involves an implicit yet omnipresent comparison with Spain. In fact, Spain—not Portugal—is painted as the original persecutor of the Jews, while the absence of requirements (other than proof of Sephardi ancestry) and of a deadline for applying is flaunted abundantly by the Portuguese officials and Jewish communities, in contrast with the Spanish law.

There are, however, limits to the positive outcomes of Portugal's nation branding strategy. The attempt to amend the law in 2020, supported by an important number of parties in parliament, partly damaged the image of the country. The negative consequences remain to be seen. So far, there has been no impact on the number of applications for citizenship, which have increased, despite the Covid-19 pandemic. In addition, the selectivity of the law, exclusively benefitting Sephardi descendants, excludes the descendants of Muslims, who were also expelled. Together with this, Portugal's greater proximity to Israel risks harming Portugal's image in some Muslim countries.

By analyzing the Portuguese regime of citizenship pertaining to descendants of Sephardim, we hope that this chapter initiates a dialogue between two strands of scholarship until now unrelated: citizenship studies and nation branding. We have suggested that citizenship regimes create entrepreneurial states seeking to attract social, human, economic, and financial capital. This is done through a brand reputation generated by changes in understandings of citizenship. We therefore suggest that future research linking these two strands has great potential, due to the multiplication of regimes of citizenship in the European Union and beyond.

Isabel David is a political scientist and assistant professor at the Institute of Social and Political Sciences, University of Lisbon (Universidade de Lisboa). She has published in journals such as *Turkish Studies, Journal of Civil Society, Journal of Contemporary European Studies, Mediterranean Quarterly*, and in edited volumes by Rowman & Littlefield, Palgrave Macmillan, Bloomsbury, Routledge, Lexington, Amsterdam University Press, and ABC-CLIO. She is coeditor (with Kumru F. Toktamis) of the recently launched "Culture, Society and Political Economy in Turkey" book series published by Peter Lang.

Gabriela Anouck Côrte-Real Pinto is a political scientist and member of the French think-tank Noria Research. She received her PhD from the Paris Institute of Political Studies (Sciences Po Paris). She held a postdoctorate at EHESS (École des Hautes Études en Sciences Sociales) and taught at Galatasaray University. She has published in journals such as *Journal of Civil Society, International Development Policy, British Journal of Middle Eastern Studies*, and in edited volumes. Her areas of research include Turkey, the European Union, privatization, civilian-military relations, citizenship, and social movements.

Notes

1. The parties are the Socialist Party (PS), center-right Social Democratic Party (PSD), center-right Democratic Social Center-People's Party (CDS-PP), Portuguese Communist Party (PCP), Left Bloc (BE), and The Greens (PEV).
2. Ribeiro e Castro's project merged with that of Roseira. Ribeiro e Castro had been asking governments about granting Portuguese citizenship to descendants of Sephardim since 2010.
3. Shabbaton is a cultural and educational multigenerational event held during the Sabbath.
4. All translations from the Portuguese are by the authors of the chapter.
5. In Portugal, the term "*Marranos*" is synonymous with crypto-Jews—in other words, baptized Jews forced to convert to Catholicism and their descendants who secretly practiced Judaism. The term lost its pejorative connotation in the twentieth century, emphasizing the resistance of Judaism against the Inquisition. Its etymology remains unclear (see Mea and Steinhardt 1997).
6. Referring to the foundation of Portugal as an independent country in 1143.
7. Minister of Justice Francisca van Dunen suggested a ten-year time limit for applications (Silva 2020).
8. The community has produced four films in total.
9. In fact, any individual is eligible to obtain Portuguese citizenship through Article 6, No. 6, of the law, provided they descend from Portuguese citizens or if they are members of communities of Portuguese ancestry. The 2015 amendment, however, created a specific provision for the Sephardim, facilitating their naturalization.
10. These data are from the Institute of Registries and Notary.
11. These figures were provided by our interviewee Michael Rothwell. In the 2011 census, however, 3,061 people identified as Jewish.

References

Agência Lusa. 2018. "Líder islâmico pede que lei para judeus sefarditas seja alargada aos muçulmanos." *Observador*, 16 March 2018. https://observador.pt/2018/03/16/li der-islamico-pede-que-lei-para-judeus-sefarditas-seja-alargada-aos-muculmanos.

Alegre, Manuel, Alberto Martins, Maria de Belém Roseira, and José Vera Jardim. 2020. "Não aceitamos." *Público*, 23 May 2020. https://www.publico.pt/2020/05/23/politica/noticia/nao-aceitamos-1917821.

Almeida, José Carlos Pina, and David Corkill. 2015. "On Being Portuguese: *Luso-tropicalism*, Migrations and the Politics of Citizenship." In *Creolizing Europe: Legacies and Transformations*, edited by Encarnación Gutiérrez Rodríguez and Shirley Anne Tate, 157–74. Liverpool: Liverpool University Press.

Alves, Marco. 2020. "Como 63 grandes famílias judaicas revolucionaram Portugal." *Sábado*, 19 August 2020. https://www.sabado.pt/vida/detalhe/como-63-grandes-familias-judaicas-revolucionaram-portugal.

Anderson, Warwick, Ricardo Roque, and Ricardo Ventura Santos. 2019. "Introduction." In *Luso-tropicalism and its Discontents: The Making and Unmaking of Racial Exceptionalism*, edited by Warwick Anderson, Ricardo Roque, and Ricardo Ventura Santos, 1–20. New York: Berghahn.

Anholt, Simon. 1998. "Nation Brands of the Twenty-first Century." *Journal of Brand Management* 5, no. 6: 395–406.

———. 2005. *Brand New Justice. How Branding Places and Products can Help the Developing World*. Oxford: Elsevier Butterworth-Heinemann.

———. 2007. *Competitive Identity. The New Brand Management for Nations, Cities and Regions*. New York: Palgrave Macmillan.

———. 2010. *Places. Identity, Image and Reputation*. New York: Palgrave Macmillan.

Arad, Roy. 2019. "In Israel, They Felt Unwanted. They Found Paradise in Portugal." *Haaretz*, 16 May 2019. https://www.haaretz.com/israel-news/.premium.MAGAZINE-in-israel-they-felt-unwanted-they-found-paradise-in-portugal-1.7248624.

Aronczyk, Melissa. 2008. "Living the Brand: Nationality, Globality and the Identity Strategies of Nation Branding Consultants." *International Journal of Communication* 2: 41–65.

Assembleia da República. 1996. "Sessão evocativa dos 500 anos do decreto de expulsão dos judeus em Portugal." VII Legislatura, 2ª Sessão Legislativa (1996–1997). https://debates.parlamento.pt/catalogo/r3/dar/01/07/02/015/1996-12-06?sft=true&org=PLC&plcdf=true#p529.

Azulai, Yuval. 2019. "Elbit Systems Wins $50m Contract with Portuguese Air Force." *Globes*, 31 October 2019. https://en.globes.co.il/en/article-elbit-systems-wins-50m-contract-with-portugese-air-force-1001305483.

Benmayor, Rina, and Dalia Kandiyoti. 2020. "Ancestry, Genealogy, and Restorative Citizenship. Oral Histories of Sephardi Descendants Reclaiming Spanish and Portuguese Nationality." *Quest. Issues in Contemporary Jewish History* 18. https://www.quest-cdecjournal.it/ancestry-genealogy-and-restorative-citizenship.

Correio da Manhã. 2018. "Neto do fundador da Danone dá 50 milhões à Champalimaud para estudar cancro." 4 September 2018. https://www.cmjornal.pt/sociedade/detalhe/20180904_1905_fundacao-champalimaud-recebe-50-milhoes-de-euros-para-novo-centro-dedicado-ao-cancro-do-pancreas.

Côrte-Real Pinto, Gabriela Anouck, and Isabel David. 2019. "Choosing Second Citizenship in Troubled Times: The Jewish Minority in Turkey." *British Journal of Middle East Studies* 46, no. 5: 781–96.

De Belém Roseira, Maria. 2017. Interview by Gabriela Anouck Côrte-Real Pinto and Isabel David. 7 October. Audio, 1:07:56.

Dias, João de Almeida, and Ana Cristina Marques. 2019. "Netanyahu reúne-se com Pompeo em Lisboa para lançar campanha—e atira Costa para segundo plano." *Observador*, 4 December 2019. https://observador.pt/2019/12/04/netanyahu-reune-se-com-pompeo-em-lisboa-para-lancar-campanha-e-atira-costa-para-segundo-plano.

European Commission. 2019. "Special Eurobarometer 484. Perceptions of Antisemitism." Kantar Public Brussels. https://europa.eu/eurobarometer/surveys/detail/2220.

European Jewish Congress. 2018. "Portugal Actively Seeks a Greater Jewish Presence." 15 February. https://eurojewcong.org/news/communities-news/portugal/portugal-actively-seeks-greater-jewish-presence.

European Union Agency for Fundamental Rights. 2018. "Experiences and Perceptions of Antisemitism. Second Survey on Discrimination and Hate Crime against Jews in the EU." https://fra.europa.eu/en/publication/2018/experiences-and-perceptions-antisemitism-second-survey-discrimination-and-hate.

Ferreira, Leonídio Paulo. 2018. "Portugal, ao expulsar os judeus, deu mundos ao mundo. E ficou a perder." *Diário de Notícias*, 21 November 2018. https://www.dn.pt/mundo/portugal-ao-expulsar-os-judeus-deu-mundos-ao-mundo-e-ficou-a-perder-10211135.html.

Freire, Mafalda. 2019. "Empresa israelita Checkmarx investe em Portugal." *Business. IT*, 29 July 2019. https://business-it.pt/2019/07/29/empresa-israelita-checkmarx-investe-em-portugal.

Freyre, Gilberto. 1940. *O mundo que o português criou. Aspectos das relações sociais e de cultura do Brasil com Portugal e as colônias portuguesas*. Rio de Janeiro: José Olympio.

———. 2003. *Casa-grande & senzala. Formação da família brasileira sob o regime da economia patriarcal*. Recife: Fundação Gilberto Freyre.

Gabinete de Estratégia e Estudos. 2020. "Comércio Internacional Portugal-Israel." https://www.gee.gov.pt/pt/documentos/publicacoes/estatisticas-de-comercio-bilateral/israel/1599-comercio-internacional-de-portugal-com-israel/file.

George, Alexander L. and Andrew Bennett. 2005. "Case Studies and Theory Development." In *Case Studies and Theory Development in the Social Sciences*, edited by Alexander L. George and Andrew Bennett, 3–36. Cambridge: MIT Press.

Glickman, Elyse. 2018. "Portugal Touts its Jewish 'Law of Return.'" *Jewish Journal*, 14 February 2018. https://jewishjournal.com/culture/travel/230826/portugal-touts-jewish-law-return.

Godinho, Ana Mendes. 2018. "Portugal Is Becoming a 'Must Visit,' Particularly for Jews." *Jerusalem Post*, 27 February 2018. https://www.jpost.com/opinion/portugal-is-becoming-a-must-visit-particularly-for-jews-543798.

Goldschläger, Arielle, and Camilla Orjuela. 2020. "Return After 500 Years? Spanish and Portuguese Repatriation Laws and the Reconstruction of Sephardi Identity." *Diaspora Studies* 14, no. 1: 97–115.

Haaretz. 2015. "Watch: Portugal Rediscovers Its Jewish Heritage." *Haaretz*, 13 August 2015. https://www.haaretz.com/israel-news/watch-portugal-rediscovers-its-jewish-heritage-1.5386531.

Hespanha, António Manuel. 1999. *Há 500 anos. Balanço de três anos de comemorações dos descobrimentos portugueses 1996–1998*. Comissão Nacional para as Comemorações dos Descobrimentos Portugueses.

Hinchliffe, Tim. 2018. "Israeli Investors 'Will Invest in Portugal': Secretary of Industry." Portugalstartups.com, 11 September 2018. https://portugalstartups.com/2018/09/israel-invest-portugal.

FCT. 2019. "Cooperação Transnacional Portugal-Israel. 1º concurso para projectos bilaterais de investigação 2019-2021." https://www.fct.pt/apoios/cooptrans/israel/index.phtml.pt.

FCT. 2021. "Portugal e o Holocausto: investigação e memória. Apoio especial a projectos de I&D." https://www.fct.pt/apoios/programamemoriaholocausto/index.phtml.pt.

Idealista. 2020. "Israelitas investem 13,5 milhões em Lisboa num prédio com 18 apartamentos de luxo." 18 September 2020. https://www.idealista.pt/news/financas/investimentos/2020/09/17/44631-israelitas-investem-13-5-milhoes-em-lisboa-num-predio-com-18-apartamentos-de-luxo.

JTA. 2017. "2 Jewish Museums Open in Portugal, Amid Opposition to 3rd One in Lisbon." *Times of Israel*, 3 March 2017. https://www.timesofisrael.com/2-jewish-museums-open-in-portugal-amid-opposition-to-3rd-one-in-lisbon.
"Jewish Heritage." Paths of Faith. https://www.pathsoffaith.com/en/jewish-heritage.
Justo, Ana Rita. n.d. "Tecnologia israelita de visão artificial chega a Portugal." *PME Magazine*. https://pmemagazine.sapo.pt/tecnologia-israelita-de-visao-artificial-chega-a-portugal.
Kaneva, Nadia. 2016. "Nation Branding and Commercial Nationalism: Notes for a Materialist Critique." In *Commercial Nationalism. Selling the Nation and Nationalizing the Sell*, edited by Zala Volcic and Mark Andrejevic, 175–93. Basingstoke: Palgrave Macmillan.
Kaufman, Charles O. 2020. https://www.bnaibrith.org/uploads/1/1/6/9/116999275/portugal_letter.pdf.
Lidman, Melanie. 2019. "In Portugal, Israelis Search for a Little Slice of Rustic Paradise." *Times of Israel*, 20 August 2019. https://www.timesofisrael.com/in-portugal-israelis-search-for-a-little-slice-of-rustic-paradise.
Link to Leaders. 2020. "Plataforma israelita de equity crowdfunding OurCrowd chega a Portugal." 8 December. https://linktoleaders.com/plataforma-israelita-de-equity-crowdfunding-ourcrowd-chega-a-portugal.
Liphshiz, Cnaan. 2020. "Portugal's Ruling Party Looks to Limit Jewish Law of Return Policy." *Times of Israel*, 14 May 2020. https://www.timesofisrael.com/portugal-ruling-party-looks-to-limit-jewish-law-of-return-policy.
Lusa. 2019a. "Rede de Judiarias é mais-valia determinante para desenvolvimento da região Centro." *Observador*, 23 March 2019. https://observador.pt/2019/03/23/rede-de-judiarias-e-mais-valia-determinante-para-desenvolvimento-da-regiao-centro.
———. 2019b. "'Sefarad' estreou na Amazon Prime e fala da comunidade israelita no Porto desde 1496." *TSF*, 18 November 2019. https://www.tsf.pt/portugal/cultura/sefarad-estreou-na-amazon-prime-e-fala-da-comunidade-israelita-no-porto-desde-1496-11527830.html.
———. 2019c. "Hoje é o Dia da Memória das Vítimas da Inquisição." *Diário de Notícias*, 31 March 2019. https://www.dn.pt/lusa/hoje-e-o-dia-da-memoria-das-vitimas-da-inquisicao-10745150.html.
———. 2020a. "Parlamento aprova homenagem a Aristides de Sousa Mendes no Panteão Nacional." *Observador*, 3 July 2020. https://observador.pt/2020/07/03/parlamento-aprova-homenagem-a-aristides-de-sousa-mendes-no-panteao-nacional.
———. 2020b. "Marcelo reúne-se com o Presidente de Israel em Jerusalém." *Sábado*, 21 January 2020. https://www.sabado.pt/portugal/detalhe/marcelo-reune-se-com-o-presidente-de-israel-em-jerusalem.
Marketeer. 2017. "TAP Air Portugal fecha acordo com El Al Israel Airlines." 8 November. https://marketeer.sapo.pt/tap-air-portugal-fecha-acordo-com-el-al-israel-airlines.
Marques, João Filipe. 2008. "Racistas são os outros! Reflexão sobre as origens e efeitos do mito do 'não-racismo português." In *Estudos III*, 5–20. Algarve: Faculdade de Economia da Universidade do Algarve.
Mea, Elvira de Azevedo, and Inácio Steinhardt. 1997. Ben-Rosh. *Uma biografia do Capitão Barros Basto, o apóstolo dos marranos*. Porto: Edições Afrontamento.
Mesquita Nunes, Adolfo. 2020. Interview by Gabriela Anouck Côrte-Real Pinto and Isabel David. 2 October. Zoom, 41:00.
Mucznik, Esther. 2017. Interview by Gabriela Anouck Côrte-Real Pinto and Isabel David. 3 November. Telephone, 58:00.

———. 2020. "A árvore e a floresta." *Público*, 21 May 2020. https://www.publico.pt/2020/05/21/opiniao/opiniao/arvore-floresta-1917341.
Partido Socialista. 2020. "Proposta de alteração." https://app.parlamento.pt/webutils/docs/doc.pdf?path=6148523063446f764c324679626d56304c334e706447567a4c31684a566b786c5a793944543030764d554e425130524d527939456232 4e31625756756447397a5357357059326c6864476c3259554e7662576c7a 633246764c7a41304d6d6d6d59344e4441324c574a6a4e5467744e4455314e5331694f5331694f 4451334c5459785a5449784f5354457a5357457a5734975337757554574a47593d&fich=042f 8406-bc58-4555-b847-61e219a38275.pdf&Inline=true.
Pimentel, Irene Flunser. 2008. *Judeus em Portugal durante a II Guerra Mundial*. Lisbon: Esfera dos Livros.
Rede de judiarias de Portugal. http://www.redejudiariasportugal.com/index.php/pt.
Ribeiro e Castro, José. 2020. Interview by Gabriela Anouck Côrte-Real Pinto and Isabel David. 24 July. Zoom, 1:06:19.
Richards, David. 1996. "Elite Interviewing: Approaches and Pitfalls." *Politics* 16, no. 3: 199–204.
Rodrigues, Ricardo. 2018. "Judeus: estará em Portugal a nova terra prometida?" *Notícias Magazine*, 21 February 2018. https://www.noticiasmagazine.pt/2018/estara-em-portugal-a-nova-terra-prometida-dos-judeus/historias/219589.
Rothwell, Michael. 2017. Interview by Gabriela Anouck Côrte-Real Pinto and Isabel David. 31 October. Transcribed, 1:30:00.
———. 2020. "Efeitos positivos da lei dos sefarditas." *Expresso*, 8 June 2020. https://expresso.pt/opiniao/2020-06-08-Efeitos-positivos-da-lei-dos-sefarditas.
Rudee, Eliana. 2021. "Jews of Portugal and their recent rebirth." *Jewish News Syndicate*, 26 April 2021. https://www.jns.org/jews-of-portugal-and-their-recent-rebirth.
Sharon, Jeremy. 2020a. "New Restrictions Proposed for Citizenship for Jews of Portuguese Descent." *Jerusalem Post*, 13 May 2020. https://www.jpost.com/diaspora/new-restrictions-proposed-for-citizenship-for-jews-of-portuguese-descent-627893.
———. 2020b. "European Jewish Congress Calls on Portuguese Parliament not to Damage Jewish Citizenship Law." *Jerusalem Post*, 3 July 2020. https://www.pressreader.com/israel/jerusalem-post/20200703/281616717647925.
Silva, Catarina. 2020. "Sefarditas: Van Dunen quer limite de dez anos para pedir nacionalidade." *Jornal de Notícias*, 23 June 2020. https://www.jn.pt/nacional/sefarditas-van-dunem-quer-limite-de-dez-anos-para-pedir-nacionalidade-12345079.html.
Steemit. n.d. "Two Companies will Produce Cannabis Medicinal in Portugal—One Canadian and one Israeli." https://steemit.com/nature/@ak47balasbolin/two-companies-will-produce-cannabis-medicinal-in-portugal-one-canadian-and-one-israeli.
Stein, Sarah Abrevaya. 2016. *Extraterritorial Dreams. European Citizenship, Sephardi Jews, and the Ottoman Twentieth Century*. Chicago: University of Chicago Press.
Tansey, Oisín. 2007. "Process Tracing and Elite Interviewing: A Case for Non-Probability Sampling." *Political Science and Politics* 40, no. 4: 765–72.
Times of Israel. 2018. "Portugal says it wants Jews and Jewish investment in country." *Times of Israel*, 21 February 2018. https://www.timesofisrael.com/portugal-wants-jews-and-jewish-investment-in-country.
Urbano de Sousa, Constança. 2020. Interview by Gabriela Anouck Côrte-Real Pinto and Isabel David. 24 August. Skype, 46:08.
Van Ham, Peter. 2001. "The Rise of the Brand State." *Foreign Affairs*, 10 October 2001. https://www.globalpolicy.org/component/content/article/162-general/27557.html.

Varum, Celeste. 2020. Interview by Gabriela Anouck Côrte-Real Pinto and Isabel David. 13 October. Microsoft Teams, 45:00.

Volcic, Zala, and Mark Andrejevic. 2011. "Nation Branding in the Era of Commercial Nationalism." *International Journal of Communication* 5: 598–618.

Zorrinho, Carlos. 2020. Interview by Gabriela Anouck Côrte-Real Pinto and Isabel David. 2 October. Zoom, 35:04.

Chapter 3

Reparations in Spanish Parliamentary Debates about the 2015 Nationality Law for Descendants of Sephardi Jews

Davide Aliberti

Introduction

From the time of its first announcement in 2012, the Spanish nationality law for descendants of Sephardic Jews of 2015 received considerable media attention. With this law, the Spanish government apparently sought to repair the historical error of the 1492 Expulsion of the Jews from the newly consolidating state. But is "repair" the most appropriate word to describe such an initiative? In fact, as Alfons Aragoneses (chap. 1) and Elena Arigita and Laura Galián (chap. 8) also note in their contributions to this volume, the word "reparations" is never explicitly mentioned in the draft, the final text of the bill, or the law itself. On the contrary, the word in both the initial bill and the final law is "*reencuentro*," which refers to the reencounter between the Sephardic Jews and their ancestral homeland.[1] The same word was used by former Minister of Justice Alberto Ruiz-Gallardón on 22 November 2012, during the first official announcement of the initiative, at Centro Sefarad-Israel in Madrid (EFE 2012).

Looking back at the recent history of the relationship between Spain and the Sephardi Jews we can say that this word choice was neither neutral nor insignificant: the former Spanish king, Juan Carlos I, alluded to the word reencounter in his ceremonial speech at the Madrid synagogue on 31 March 1992, commemorating the quincentenary of the Expulsion. Everyone present, including the former president of Israel, Chaim Herzog, was waiting for an apology, but the king said only that they were celebrating the *"encounter* between the Spanish Jews and their kings" (Aliberti 2018, 282–83; emphasis added).

In 2014, two years after the announcement of the initiative, Rafael Catalá, the minister of justice who succeeded Gallardón and finally presented the proposed bill for discussion in parliament, stated that it was aimed at repairing *un agravio histórico* (a historical grievance) (Benarroch 2014). During the parliamentary sessions prior to the approval of the law (from 20 November 2014 to 11 June 2015), the concept of reparations was mentioned several times. However, Isaac Querub, former president of the Federation of Jewish Communities of Spain, the entity that initially proposed the law to Gallardón, said, "We never talked about reparations because legally this has other kinds of consequences. We talked about reparation of injustice from an ethical point of view, from a moral point of view" (Vega Toscano 2020, 36:55). Such divergences in the use (and nonuse) of the concept are striking and compel us to ask, what are the legal consequences of reparations? And what are the differences between ethical, moral, and legal reparations?

The concept of reparations has been widely used by the media and politicians referring to the 2015 law, but it has never been officially explained by its promoters. Scholars who have analyzed the law agree that it does not repair anything; rather they link the law to other dynamics such as the long-standing reproduction of philosephardic politics (Aliberti 2018; Aragoneses 2016), the improvement of Spain's international image, the strengthening of peninsular Jewish cultural tourism (Aliberti 2018; Flesler and Pérez Melgosa 2020), and the creation of new "legitimizing identities" shaped by institutional power (Ojeda-Mata 2018). If the reasons behind the law and its objectives are multiple, and if they are different from reasons behind the reparation of a historical injustice, it is still important to understand why this concept is mentioned so frequently and in which ways it is used. In this chapter I first analyze the different uses of the concept of reparations and briefly retrace the origins and meaning of reparations as well as its applications to ancestry-based naturalization laws. Second, I focus on the uses of this concept in the Spanish parliamentary debates around the 2015 law for descendants of Sephardi Jews. My analysis reveals the predominantly rhetorical use of the concept of reparations during the parliamentary debates. In fact, the different parliamentary groups seemed to agree to the idea of repairing a historical wrong, but their discussions (often ambivalent or ambiguous) were mainly speculative debates on the idea of reparations, and they did not really satisfy any of the practices of reparations politics described in the following section.

Reparations and Citizenship

Reparations and reparations politics are commonly referred to as a way to make amends and offer apologies for past injustices committed by the state against a segment of its population (Torpey 2003, 3). Some scholars refer to these retrospective practices as a politics of regret and consider these politics a necessary part of the modern rituals of human interaction (Olick 2013, 132).[2] The origin of the politics of regret is linked to the concept of universal human rights, as expressed in 1948 by the *Universal Declaration of Human Rights* (United Nations 1948). According to advocates of that concept, "Only gestures of reparation, apology, and acknowledgment can restore the dignity of history's victims and can deter new outbreaks of inhumanity" (Olick 2013, 126). Acknowledgment, apology, and reparations are essential elements within reparations politics, whose philosophical roots are embedded in Karl Jaspers's *Die Schuldfrage* (2000), originally published in 1947. As Olick points out (2013, 124): "Within a discussion about German collective responsibility for National Socialist crimes, Jaspers articulates four distinct varieties of guilt – criminal, political, moral, and metaphysical -- each of which entails a different form of responsibility" and, I would add, reparation.

The term "reparations politics" came into official usage in 1952 with the *Reparations Agreement between Israel and West Germany* (Torpey 2003, 95). However, the establishment of international laws and norms regarding reparations politics first appeared in the United Nations' resolution adopted by the General Assembly on 16 December 2005, entitled "Basic Principles and Guidelines on the Right to a Remedy and Reparation for Victims of Gross Violations of International Human Rights Law and Serious Violations of International Humanitarian Law" (United Nations 2005). The term "reparations politics" embraces a wide range of practices, including reparation itself, apologies, restitution, compensation, reconciliation, and transitional justice (Olick 2013, 138). "Reparations" refers to some form of material compensation—itself inherently symbolic—for what cannot be returned (Barkan 2000, xix), such as Jewish life in Spain before the 1492 Expulsion. "Apologies" refers to an essential element in reparations politics, but apologies are often delayed or refused by states. The reasons are multiple, such as when a government does not feel responsible for injustices committed in previous eras, refuses to accept responsibility for the event, or denies that the injustice even occurred. The term "restitution" refers to the return of material belongings confiscated or stolen, such as lands, properties, and ancestral remains. The term "compensation" refers to the refunding for damages or losses that can be quantified and repaid (Barkan 2000, 323–29). The term "reconciliation" acts primarily on a symbolic level and implies, for both the subject of the injustice and the state, the building of a new relationship that is not "haunted by the conflicts and hatreds of yesterday" (Hayner 2002, 161). In other words, without neglecting the conflicts of the past, political reconciliation should promise that the state will never again commit the same injustice and that the state and the former victims (or their descendants) are now members of the same community (Schaap 2005, 76, 82, 87).

Finally, the term "transitional justice," often considered a subset of reparations politics, focuses on the state's attempts to redress injustices committed by previous regimes (Teitel 2000, 5). Transitional justice is divided into five different categories: (1) criminal justice, characterized by trials and prosecutions; (2) historical justice, focused on the construction of a new shared collective memory, through truth commissions, written accounts, and open access to archived documentation; (3) reparatory justice, based on payments and monetary commitments for damages inflicted on the individual; (4) administrative justice, mainly aimed at corrective legislation and punishment of perpetrators; and (5) constitutional justice based on the creation or modification of a country's constitution to prevent recurrences. This categorization has been recently revised by Stephanie Wolfe, who combines the last two categories into one called "legislative justice" and adds a new fifth category of "symbolic justice" (Wolfe 2014, 62–63). Symbolic justice includes all those initiatives carried out by the state that have symbolic meaning—in other words, the creation of memorials, monuments, museums, or the issuance of official apologies and the establishment of days of remembrance (72–73).

In the case of Spain, the 2015 nationality law may be seen as a form of reparation—that is, a symbolic compensation for something that cannot be returned. Reparation is understood, in this sense, as "an act that cannot be undone but that cannot go unnoticed without compromising the current and future relationships of the parties, the legitimacy of the violated rule, and the wider social web in which the participants are enmeshed" (Tavuchis 1991, 13).

This is the only category within reparations politics applicable to the Spanish case. In fact, concerning apologies, the Spanish government and monarchy never officially apologized for the Expulsion. There could be several reasons for this, but the one provided most often is that the Spanish Constitution of 1869 (Constitución de la nación española) de facto abolished the Expulsion Decree. Article 21 of the 1869 Constitution states, "The public or private exercise of any other religion is guaranteed to all foreign residents in Spain, with no limitations other than the universal rules of morality and law."

This article did not abrogate de jure the Expulsion Decree but admitted the presence of non-Catholic citizens on Spanish soil. For this reason, there seemed to be no need or intention to apologize, not even symbolically, for something that was no longer in effect. The monarchs in particular have been deflecting official apologies since 1992, through statements made famous by the media, such as, "Sefarad is no longer nostalgia, but home," asserted by King Juan Carlos I at the Madrid synagogue (Rey de España 1992). More recently, his son, King Felipe VI, affirmed this sentiment, saying to the Sephardi people, "How we have missed you!" during the ceremony at the Zarzuela Palace on 30 November 2015, celebrating the new law (EP 2014).

Concerning restitution—one of the features of reparations politics—a recent case is illustrative. Spanish Jewish representatives have asked for the symbolic restitution of the medieval synagogue of Santa María la Blanca in Toledo, a space of beautiful Moorish arches that currently stands empty and is in the possession of the archdiocese of Toledo. The archdiocese has refused to relinquish its hold on the historic space (ABC 2017, 2018). In fact, Spain is filled with Jewish material heritage that could be symbolically restituted as a form of reparation. Yet requests made thus far have resulted only in refusals. Moreover, the argument is made that it would be impossible to quantify compensation for an injustice that was perpetrated five centuries ago.

Finally, reconciliation, another key aspect of the law, is mentioned several times in the 2015 parliamentary debates as well as by the press after Juan Carlos I's 1992 speech. In the framework of reparations politics, the king's speech could have been seen as a partial reconciliation, in statements like, "Never again should hatred or intolerance lead to desolation or exile," and "May we be able to build together a prosperous Spain based on harmony and mutual respect" (Rey de España 1992). The speech does not make any reference to the conflictual past. The 2015 nationality law would represent, according to its preamble, the final reconciliation between Spain and Sephardic communities (Law 12/2015, 52557).[3] But can the granting of citizenship be considered a reconciliation?

Citizenship per se is usually described as a special link between individuals and the state (Dumbrava 2014, 2342). Citizenship laws often facilitate the acquisition of nationality for certain categories of foreigners. These laws simplify access to citizenship, and often consist in the exemption from a minimum residency requirement. They are based on the existence of ethnonational ties between the foreigners and the state (2340). Several countries use these special dispensations in order to repair historical wrongs related to political persecutions, expulsions, citizenship withdrawals, or forced exiles. In Spain the Ley de memoria histórica (Historical Memory Law) for the descendants of refugees of the Spanish Civil War is a relevant example. The Greek government also offers the reacquisition of citizenship for its civil war refugees and to descendants of Greek Holocaust survivors. Austrian law extends reacquisition of citizenship to Holocaust survivors and political emigrants of the Third Reich; in addition, Germany's Basic Law, Article 116, enables the naturalization of Jews persecuted between 1933 and 1945 by the Nazi regime (see also Aragoneses, chap. 1 in this volume). However, this kind of reparative citizenship is often contested (Dumbrava 2014, 2355). Some scholars, for example, question how these naturalizations could be compatible with the idea that citizenship should be based on the existence of a genuine link with the home culture. Genuine link is still a vague concept introduced within the judgment of the International Court of Justice and based on "a genuine connection of existence, interests, and sentiments, together with the existence of reciprocal rights and duties" (2342; see also Bauböck 2018, 1019). Moreover, preferential citizenship-acquisition based on ethnonational ties is problematic because it generates multiple discriminations. According to Bauböck, for example, "Inherited external citizenship is a morally arbitrary criterion for allocating opportunities among the pool of potential immigrants" (2009, 484). Distinctions between noncitizens, in fact, can generate discrimination against particular groups, as was the case of the 2015 nationality law for Sephardi Jews and the descendants of Moriscos—that is, the descendants of Spanish Muslims forced to convert to Catholicism at the beginning of the sixteenth century (see Bolorinos Allard [chap. 6] and Arigita and Galián [chap. 8] in this volume).

Generally, the function of citizenship laws is one of gatekeeping, to include the desirable and exclude the undesirable (Orgad 2019, 524–25). In other words, they serve as an apparatus aimed at shaping new citizens. The concept of "apparatus" is here used in the sense of the Foucauldian concept of dispositive—that is, "anything that has the capacity to capture, orient, determine, intercept, model, control, or secure the gestures, behaviors, opinions, or discourses of living beings" (Agamben 2009, 9) The product of this apparatus is very similar to the consequence of the aforementioned "legitimizing identities" (Ojeda-Mata 2018, xviii), a concept originally formulated by Manuel Castells referring to those identities created by institutions of power in order "to extend and rationalize their domination vis à vis social actors" (Castells 2010, 8). The 2015 nationality law is therefore one of those controversial laws that facilitates the granting of citizenship to certain categories of people, with the aim of repairing a historical wrong. However, the conditions imposed by the law, such as expiration of the offer after a four-year window, the passing of language and culture exams, and the establishing of a "special connection" to Spain, make it an "apparatus" that shapes the recipients according to the needs of the state. As a result, the identity of these "new citizens" is "legitimized" by the state, reproducing "the sources of structural domination" (9).

Focusing again on the issue of whether the law represents a reconciliation (as stated in its preamble) or a reparation, we could argue that the law seems to better meet the criteria of reparations, albeit partially. However, as I already mentioned, the concept of reparations referred to in the 2015 law has never been officially explained. It has been a constant presence within the parliamentary debates. But has it really been discussed from the perspective of reparations politics, or has it only ever served a rhetorical function?

Reparations in the Spanish Parliamentary Debates

The concept of reparations was first mentioned during the parliamentary session of 20 November 2014. It was raised by the Grupo Parlamentario Mixto (Mixed Parliamentary Group) deputy, Sabino Cuadra Lasarte, who argued that the nationality law for Sephardi Jews would repair an injustice committed five centuries earlier against the Spanish Jewish community: "We are attempting to repair the injustice committed toward one of those communities" (Diario de Sesiones de los Diputados 2014 [Nov.]), 63). Cuadra Lasarte also asserted that through this law, addressed to the Sephardi Jews, Spain was claiming "truth, justice and reparation" for all the peoples who suffered expulsion: "We want to demand and vindicate, as with other issues, truth, justice and reparation for all peoples, for all populations that have been the object of plunder and expulsion. And, since we are on the topic, also truth, justice and reparations here and now for the Sephardic population that is demanding the recovery of part of those rights that were taken away from them" (63). Seen from the framework of reparations politics, naturalization could be considered a form of reparation, specifically a kind of symbolic com-

Timeline	
February 7, 2014	Draft bill submitted to the Council of Ministers.
June 23, 2014	Bill submitted to the Congress of Deputies.
November 20, 2014	Two amendments presented: Gaspar Llamazares Trigo of *Izquierda Plural*; and Joan Tardá I Coma of the Mixed Parliamentary Group.
February 19, 2015	The amendments were published in the *Boletín de las Cortes Generales*, there were 67 amendments in total, 18 of which were from the Partido Popular itself.
March 20, 2015	Amended bill submitted to the Congress of Deputies. Amendment nos. 49, 50, 51, 55, 56, 56, 58, 59, 59, 60, 61, 62, 62, 63, 64, 65, 66 and 67 by the Popular Parliamentary Group, and amendment no. 40 by the Mixed Parliamentary Group and no. 47 by the Socialist Parliamentary Group accepted.
March 25, 2015	Amended bill voted on, only Llamazares Trigo of Izquierda Plural voted against.
April 24, 2015	Bill submitted to the Senate, 4 veto proposals and 92 amendments presented.
May 5 and 27, 2015	Bill debated in the Senate. Only four amendments approved.
June 3, 2015	Final changes made to bill.
June 11, 2015	The modified bill debated in the Congress of Deputies.
June 19, 2015	Law approved in the Congress of Deputies.
June 25, 2015	The law published in the *Boletín Oficial del Estado* [Official Bulletin of the State].

Figure 3.1. Timeline. Created by Davide Aliberti

pensation for something that cannot be returned. However, the concepts of "truth and justice" are related to the "transitional justice" semantic field, or to what Wolfe calls "legislative justice" (Wolfe 2014, 72). Transitional justice intends to repair past injustices committed by previous regimes soon after the injustice was committed. The most obvious example in Spain is the Ley de memoria histórica, passed in 2007. Among the various measures favoring the victims of the Spanish Civil War and the Franco dictatorship, the law introduced the possibility for children and grandchildren of exiled Republicans to acquire Spanish nationality. However, transitional justice would not be applicable to the Sephardi Jews, principally because more than five centuries have passed since the Expulsion.

Just after the intervention of Cuadra Lasarte, a left coalition deputy, Gaspar Llamazares Trigo, representing the Izquierda Plural (The Plural Left), asked the conservative Partido Popular (People's Party) deputies if the initiative was about reparation, restitution, or compensation. "This is an initiative of reparation and restitution, however, Mr. Minister, is it the one thing or the other, or something different, like a compensation? Which of the three? Your Ministry has used all the arguments.... In our opinion, this is a partial reparation and an even more partial restitution" (Diario de Sesiones de los Diputados 2014 [Nov.], 64)[4]

Llamazares Trigo accused the People's Party of indistinctly invoking reparation, restitution, and compensation, affirming that, in his opinion, the draft law constituted both a partial reparation and a partial restitution. First, because of the 75-euro fee (later increased to 100 euros) that applicants had to pay upon submitting their documentation; and second, because the draft omits from consideration or inclusion the most recent injustices committed against the Sahrawis and the descendants of Spanish Civil War refugees (Diario de Sesiones de los Diputados 2014 [Nov.], 74–75.[5] In order to write a common narrative of the nation, Llamazares Trigo argued, "Memory cannot be and should not be partial, especially if we are striving for a common narrative of a people. The common narrative should include the injustice committed against the Sephardi Jews but other injustices as well. It is not good enough to include some and not others; it has to be all" (64). However, Llamazares Trigo's comparison to the Sahrawis and civil war refugees was inappropriate, since they constitute different categories that would require different types of reparations. Despite that, the Grupo Parlamentario Socialista (Socialist Parliamentary Group) senator, María del Carmen Silva Rego, claimed that reparations for the groups mentioned by Llamazares Trigo was a way for Spain to redress all its historical injustices: "[We] want to process this law of recognition of nationality for the Sephardi Jews to solve a historical injustice.... But we also want other groups to be included and be eligible to obtain Spanish nationality.... Do it so that we can reward all those who, for unjust reasons, were forced to lose their Spanish identity ... and we can finally say that we have settled accounts with events and decisions in the past that should not have never happened in the first place" (67, 71–72). Additionally, the Unión Progreso y Democracia (Progress and Democracy Union) deputy, Rosa María Díez González, affirmed that the proposed law would represent a moral reparation as well as a reconciliation and the acknowledgment of a historical error: "The law that returns Spanish nationality to its descendants is a moral reparation, a recognition of the harmful and grave historical error that still exists—antisemitism, because it continues to exist in our country today. This law is a symbol of reconciliation by a largely plural society, the Spain of today, democratic Spain, constitutional Spain. For these reasons it is our duty in this moment to do this" (68).

A moral reparation would signify a "process of moving from the situation of loss and damage to a situation where some degree of stability in moral relations is regained" (Walker 2006, 6). This process is not always possible, but, if it were, the price the Spanish state would have to pay would be, at minimum, the acknowledgment of the historical wrong and assignation of responsibility.

However, the Grupo Parlamentario Vasco (Basque Parliamentary Group) deputy, Emilio Olabarría Muñoz, countered that his group did not share the opinion of Llamazares Trigo about the inclusion of other groups like the Moriscos, Sahrawis and civil war refugee descendants, because of the specificity of the Sephardi condition: "We will abstain out of respect for these other mentioned groups . . . , given their constancy, their identity, and their importance. At the same time, if other laws are proposed . . . that seek similar legal effect as this proposed law, we would not hesitate to entertain those legislative initiatives" (Diario de Sesiones de los Diputados 2014 [Nov.], 68). Furthermore, Olabarría Muñoz stated that, for him, reparation, compensation and restitution were synonymous, because they had the same aim: the restitution of those rights illegitimately expropriated from the Sephardi Jews: "From this perspective, we are dealing with a process regarding an historical injustice that we can repair, that we can make up for, and we can use any of Mr. Llamazares's notions, which in legal terms are synonymous and mean the same thing: the recuperation of certain rights that were illegitimately plundered and expropriated" (68).

While Olabarría is right in asserting that the condition of the Sephardi Jews differs from that of the Sahrawis, Moriscos, and the descendants of civil war refugees, he is wrong in asserting that reparation, compensation, and restitution are synonymous concepts. In fact, as explained above, restitution refers to material possessions, like tangible heritage, which nobody seems interested in giving back to Sephardi Jews, while compensation refers to some kind of reimbursement for damages.

Complicating the discussion even further, a statement by the Convergència i Unió (Convergence and Union) deputy, Jordi Jané i Guasch, affirmed that the aim of the law was to repair a historical injustice through reencounter: "What today's bill seeks to do is repair an historical injustice through a process of reencounter" (Diario de Sesiones de los Diputados 2014 [Nov.], 69). Jané i Guasch used the concept of reencounter generally. In fact, there is no concept of reencounter within reparations politics. Moreover, it needs specification: What kind of reencounter? Between the descendants of victims and persecutors? Or between the descendants of victims and their ancient homeland? As I have argued, the issue was resolved in the final text of the law, affirming that the aim of the law was "sellar el reencuentro de la definitiva reconciliación" (to seal the reencounter with the definitive reconciliation) between Spain and the Sephardi Jews. Finally, the last speaker in the session, the People's Party deputy, Gabriel Elorriaga Pisarik, made a very general statement to the effect that the law was "without a doubt a historic reparation that was due" (68).

On 19 February 2015 the amendments to the bill were published in the *Boletín de las Cortes Generales* (Congressional bulletin). A total of sixty-seven amendments were submitted, eighteen of which were by the Popular Party itself. On 20 March 2015, the text of the amended bill was presented.[6] All other amendments were rejected. On 25 March 2015 the text of the amended bill was voted on, and only Llamazares Trigo of Izquierda Plural voted against it.

Among the amendments that made it into the bill on 19 February 2015, the Basque Parliamentary Group proposed inserting that the intention of the law was to achieve a definitive reconciliation and reparation of a historical wrong (*Boletín Oficial de las Cortes Generales* [Congreso de los Diputados] 2015, 17). The Basque party argued that:

> The current law attempts to heal the still open wounds and to give satisfaction to the citizens who suffered, through their relatives, the consequences of the repression and tragedy of the 1492 expulsion. As the expression of the right of the Sephardi people to moral reparations and the recovery of personal and family memory, it is the legislator's duty to recognize and declare the unjust nature of all the condemnations, sanctions and whatever form of personal violence committed for political, ideological, or religious reasons in the years leading up to 1492, as well as the violence suffered during the expulsion decreed by the Catholic King and Queen on March 31, 1492. (*Boletín Oficial de las Cortes Generales* [Congreso de los Diputados] 2015, 17)

In its amendment, the Basque Parliamentary Group mentions reconciliation and reparation, but also expresses the intention to "bring satisfaction to the citizens whose ancestors suffered the consequences of the repression and tragedy of the Expulsion of 1492" (17). These concepts would have meant to applicants the symbolic closure of a genealogical circle through the restitution of what had been unjustly wrested from their ancestors. Moreover, the Basque Parliamentary Group also included the need for an official apology for the Expulsion (*Boletín Oficial de las Cortes Generales* [Congreso de los Diputados] 2015, 17).

Both the Basque Parliamentary Group and the Catalan Parliamentary Group proposed the inclusion in the text of the law of a mention of the right of Sephardi Jews to moral reparation and recovery of their personal and familial memory (*Boletín Oficial de las Cortes Generales* [Congreso de los Diputados] 2015, 31). These two groups were the only parties that presented very similar amendments based on the insertion in the law's text of a reference to the recovery of familial memory as a form of apology.

On 25 March 2015 the Grupo Parlamentario Mixto deputy, Joan Tardà i Coma, pointed out that with this law, the government should not miss the opportunity to repair the injustice committed against the Sahrawis: "Note the satisfaction that we would all feel if we repair the historical injustice done to the Sephardi people and how proudly we could approve a law that also would register or resolve an injustice, that is much closer to us, if not graver, as with the situation of the Sahrawi people" (Diario de Sesiones de los Diputados 2015a [Mar.], 4). Moreover, as Llamazares Trigo did on 20 November 2014, Tardà i Coma also tried to liken the situation of Sephardi Jews to the Sahrawis, Moriscos, and civil war refugees.

Upon the refusal by the People's Party to consider these possibilities, Emilio Olabarría Muñoz, the Basque Parliamentary Group deputy, seized in the same session the opportunity to highlight the shortcomings in the law's preamble. Rather than explaining the inspiring principles behind historical reparation, he claimed that the preamble was full of nationalistic rhetoric and historical incongruities: "In the first place, we have some amendments related to the Preamble . . . in our opinion, jingoistic and patriotic rhetoric should be avoided, and certain historical imbalances be considered" (Diario de Sesiones de los Diputados 2015a [Mar.], 5). Also, according to Convergence and Union deputy, Jané I Guasch, the law was too complicated, so he exhorted the People's Party deputy, Gabriel Elorriaga Pisarik, to be more generous because there were many historical injustices that Spain needed to repair: "There are . . . many historical injustices that we must repair, above all, the language of the bill that seems to be restorative [and yet] sometimes establishes procedures that are difficult to meet. . . . Today we want to repair injustices. Let's do it if we can, Mr. Elorriaga and members of the Popular Parliamentary Group, with utmost generosity" (8–10). The bill was introduced in the Senate on 24 April 2015 and received four veto proposals and ninety-two amendments. In the Senate the bill was debated on 5 and 27 May 2015. Only four amendments were approved. On 24 April 2015 the Catalan Parliamentary Group presented an amendment asking the People's Party to clearly state the aims of the law: "Five hundred and twenty-two years later, recognizing and declaring the injustice of the exile of thousands of Sephardi Jews, this law aims to seal the definitive reconciliation with the Sephardi Jews and to repair an important historical error" (*Boletín Oficial de las Cortes Generales* [Senado] 2015, 57). The petition was not officially accepted, but one month later, on 27 May 2015, the People's Party senator, María del Carmen Dueñas Martínez, affirmed that the aim of all the parliamentary groups was to "approve a law focused on the reparation of a historical debt that we had to the Sephardi community" (Diario de Sesiones del Senado 2015 (May), 15289).

During the session on 11 June 2015, after the law was finally approved, the Mixed Parliamentary Group deputy, Jon Iñarritu García, said that he was disappointed because the reparative aim of the law had not been respected: "We want to also demonstrate our disappointment since this law, which was intended to be for reparation and justice, has taken an increasingly difficult path" (Diario de Sesiones del Congreso de los Diputados 2015b (June), 11). In his opinion, the law was too complicated and too expensive, and was valid for too short a period. For these reasons, Iñarritu García affirmed that the law was not a reparation, but just a symbol: "We believe that we cannot speak of reparation; this law is more of a symbol, a first step, but not one that satisfies the wishes of the majority of Sephardi Jews who would like to attain Spanish nationality" (11). However, in the same session, the Progress and Democracy Union deputy, Rosa María Díez González, confirmed that the law was both a moral and historical reparation, as we saw above. Moreover, she observed, "The objective . . . is to repair a historical injustice, to recognize the right to a homeland for those that the bill itself calls 'Spaniards without a homeland,' and to recognize their full citizenship rights. This law should—and will contribute, I am sure, to healing the wounds and repairing, for the descendants, the consequences of the oppression and persecution that they suffered" (13). The Plural Left deputy, Llamazares Trigo, said that the law was neither a historical reparation nor a partial reparation, because it was discriminatory toward other groups: "Today we would have had the opportunity to make history and to make this an act of reparation, but I do not believe that it is, or it is insufficiently so. This is a political gesture. We can also say that it is a miserly act because far from recognizing nationality as an historical reparation, [this law] adds new, tortuous, and greedy procedures to the existent ones for acquiring citizenship. . . . An act of partial reparation is not reparative if that political gesture provokes grievances and injustices to others" (15).

Conversely, the Convèrgencia I Unió deputy, Jané i Guasch, affirmed that, despite all the complexities, the law was an important historical rep-

Figure 3.2. Summary of Legislative Activity. Created by Davide Aliberti.

Congress of Deputies			
Position on the political spectrum	Group and party	Name of deputy	Position on the issue/ demands
Center-left	Grupo Parlamentario Mixto [Mixed Parliamentary Group]	Joan Tardá I Coma	Asks for the inclusion of Sahrawis.
Center-left	Grupo Parlamentario Mixto	Sabino Cuadra Lasarte	Asks for "truth justice and reparation for all the peoples who suffered expulsion".
Center-left	Grupo Parlamentario Vasco [Basque Parliamentary Group]	Emilio Olabarría Muñoz	Supports the initiative, but criticizes the rhetoric employed and proposes improvements to make the process easier.
Center-left	Unión Progreso y Democracia [Progress and Democracy Union]	Rosa María Díez González	Supports the citizenship initiative.
Centre-right	Grupo Parlamentario Catalán Convergència i Unió [Catalan Parliamentary Group Convergence and Union]	Jordi Jané I Guasch	Supports the initiative but asks for improvements to make the process easier.
Left	Grupo Parlamentario Socialista [Socialist Parliamentary Group]	María del Carmen Silva Rego	Supports the initiative but asks for the inclusion of Sahrawis, Moriscos, and descendants of Civil War exiles.
Left	Izquierda Plural [Plural Left]	Gaspar Llamazares Trigo	Opposes the initiative, asking for a comprehensive reform of the nationality law in order to repair all the injustices: Sahrawis, Moriscos, and descendants of Civil War exiles.
Center-right and right-wing	Grupo Parlamentario Popular [Popular Parliamentary Group]	Gabriel Elorriaga Pisarik	Proposer.
Center-right and right-wing	Grupo Parlamentario Popular	Rafael Catalá Polo	Proposer.

\multicolumn{4}{c}{Senate}			
Position on the political spectrum	Group and party	Name of deputy	Position on the issue/ demands
Center-left	Grupo Parlamentario Mixto	Jesús Enriquez Iglesias Fernández	He opposes the initiative, asking for a comprehensive reform of the Nationality Law.
Center-left	Grupo Parlamentario Mixto	Ester Capella i Farré	Asks for the inclusion of Sahrawis.
Center-left	Grupo Parlamentario Vasco	Jokin Bildarratz Sorron	Supports the initiative but proposes improvements to make the process easier.
Left	Grupo Parlamentario Socialista	Arcadio Díaz Tejera	Supports the initiative, but asks for the inclusion of Sahrawis, Moriscos, and descendants of Civil War exiled.
Left	Grupo Parlamentario Entesa pel Progrés de Catalunya	Rafael Bruguera Batalla	Supports the initiative, but asks for the inclusion of Sahrawis, Moriscos, and descendants of Civil War exiled.
Left	Grupo Parlamentario Socialista	José Vicente González Bethencourt	Supports the initiative but proposes improvements to make the process easier.
Center-right	Grupo Parlamentario Catalán Convergència i Unió	María Rieradevall Tarrés	Supports the initiative but asks for improvements in order to make the process easier and to apologize for the expulsion.
Center-right and right-wing	Grupo Parlamentario Popular	Silvia Franco González	Proposer.
Center-right and right-wing	Grupo Parlamentario Popular	María del Carmen Dueñas Martínez	Proposer.

aration (Diario de Sesiones del Congreso de los Diputados 2015b (June), 15-16), also affirmed by Socialist deputy Silva Rego: "It is five hundred years late, but today we have the honor of participating in this historical reparation" (16–17). Finally, José Manuel García Margallo, then minister of foreign affairs of the People's Party, said that the law repaired a historical debt: "Estamos aquí reparando una deuda histórica" (We are here repairing a historical debt) (20).

Overall, the parliamentary debates highlighted two different positions about whether the law constituted a reparation. The first position complained about the exclusion from the law of other groups such as Sahrawis, Moriscos, and descendants of Spanish Civil War refugees. The second, supported mainly by the Basque and Catalan representatives, criticized the lack of explicit references in the final text to the main aims of the law—that is, to apologize for a historical error and to facilitate the recovery of familial memory through the granting of citizenship. More specifically, the majority of the participants in the parliamentary debates, despite the numerous limitations of the law, considered this initiative a reparation (Díez González, Jané i Guasch, Silva Rego), while only Iñarritu García of the Mixed Parliamentary Group and Llamazares Trigo of Plural Left affirmed that the law was not a reparation at all.

Conclusion

The People's Party decided to repair the historical error of expulsion through the granting of citizenship. However, since the text of the law never openly mentioned the concept of reparations, this decision generated confusion. In fact, some members of parliament interpreted the law as clearly discriminatory to other groups that have waited a long time to claim Spanish citizenship. However, an interesting proposition emerged from these debates, presented both by the Basque and Catalan parliamentary representatives: they recommended mentioning in the final text of the law that, through this initiative, Spain was giving to the Sephardi Jews the opportunity to recover their familial memory. This would have signified, they contended, the symbolic closure of a circle for Sephardi Jews, and a way for Spain to make amends for its past. Yet the vast majority of the proposed amendments were ultimately rejected or withdrawn by the proposers themselves. At first sight, it might be said that all the parliamentarians stepped back from their initial positions for the sake of a common idea: the restitution of Spanish nationality to the Sephardi Jews. Although for many parties, in terms of reparations, the law remained unfinished because of the exclusion of other collectives mentioned during the debates, symbolically it still constituted a reparation that everyone perceived as necessary. It is a reparation that, as I have shown, was never conceived under the terms expressed by reparations politics, but, as Aragoneses also explains in this volume [chap. 1], was always only conceived in symbolic terms.

But that is not all. On 27 May 2015, Senator Rafael Bruguera Batalla of the Entesa pel Progrés de Catalunya (Agreement for the Progress of Catalonia) parliamentary group, denounced an improper procedure led by the People's Party:

> In the Congress of Deputies, the PPG presents in practice an amendment to the bill as a whole that contains only two articles. It completely changes the bill . . . , sidestepping the procedural reports that should be produced by the official bodies and avoiding amendments that different parliamentary groups might present as well as their respective debates. This bill, completely changed, is sent to the Senate . . . and the PPG vetoes its own bill and changes it again completely, returning more or less to the original text that was approved by the Government and submitted to the Congress of Deputies. (Diario de Sesiones del Senado 2015 [May], 15263–64)

According to Bruguera Batalla, the Partido Popular amended its own bill after submitting it to the Congress of Deputies in order to circumvent the amendments by the other parties. Later, the People's Party repeated the same procedure in the Senate, taking the bill back to its original form. This procedure was also denounced by the leftist senators María del Carmen Silva Rego (Socialist Parliamentary Group) and Gaspar Llamazares Trigo (Izquierda Plural) on 11 June 2015. What would have happened if the People's Party had not carried out this misleading procedure? Would the law still have been passed for the sake of a common idea? Probably so, but it is difficult to tell.

In the course of this chapter, we saw how the framework of reparations politics offers different approaches for states to come to terms with their own traumatic pasts. Despite several attempts, the Spanish government partially entertained only two of them—that is, reparations and reconciliation. Nevertheless, the 2015 law represents neither a reparation nor a reconciliation. In order to determine the success or the failure of a political reconciliation, apologies are extremely important (Wolfe 2014, 74). The absence of apologies in all the Spanish initiatives signaled their failure to fully reconcile and repair. That said, the parliamentary debates about reparations, the different positions put forward in that context, and the reflections that were generated could constitute a fruitful starting point for planning a true reparation.

In a broader perspective, Spain joined the list of countries that offer (or have offered) a privileged ancestry-based way to access nationality. However, unlike the other countries, Spain is the first (and still the only) state that offered this opportunity as a result of an injustice that happened five centuries ago. Since October 2019 the Spanish law is no longer in force. The exact number of naturalized people is still unclear, as is the number of Sephardi Jews who for different reasons have been excluded. Also, we cannot yet say whether the law might have served as a test case for a future initiative that would include not only Sephardi Jews, but also all other excluded collectives. In fact, it would be interesting to keep track of whether, in the long run, the Spanish initiative may prove to be an example for other states to make genuine reparations or, conversely, to attract political consensus abroad. Either way, such a preferential access to European nationality could raise controversy at the time of a more comprehensive reform of European citizenship. In this scenario, the Spanish law may turn out to be not only a partial reparation for its recipients, but also a new injustice for Spain to repair.

Davide Aliberti is an Assistant Professor at the University of Messina. He holds a PhD in Hispanic studies from the University of Naples L'Orientale and from the University of Aix-Marseille. He has held postdoctoral research positions at both of the above institutions and was seconded as a Research Associate at Casa de Velásquez in Madrid. His latest book is titled: *Sefarad: una comunidad imaginada (1924–2015)*, Marcial Pons, 2018.

Notes

1. The bill states, "It was a decision animated by the desire to contribute, after five centuries of estrangement, to the process of concord that has already begun, which summons the Sephardic communities to reencounter their origins, permanently opening the doors of their ancient homeland" (Ministerio de Justicia 2014). And "reencounter" is also used in the wording of the 2015 law: "With this Law, today's Spain intends to take a firm step to achieve the reencounter of the definitive *reconciliation* with the Sephardic communities" (Law 12/2015, emphasis added)." All translations in this chapter are by the author or the coeditors.
2. Referring to the works of Norbert Elias, Olick observes that "the complexly stylized ritual" of court societies "is the paradigm of contemporary civilization," which also applies to the more recent context. An apology, Olick concludes, "becomes a necessary part of the modern interaction ritual" (Olick 2013, 132).
3. See the reference to reconciliation in the second quotation of note 1.
4. Llamazares Trigo does not specify who, when, and in which context the three arguments were used.
5. The Sahrawi are the people living in the western part of the Sahara Desert, which was occupied and ruled by Spain from 1884 to 1976. As a result of the decolonization process begun in 1975, all Sahrawis who could not meet the requirements of the

Royal Decree 2258/1976 were deprived of their Spanish citizenship. Concerning the Historical Memory Law, the following categories were excluded: children of Spanish mothers (until the 1978 Constitution, Spanish women could not transmit nationality to their children); descendants of those who had renounced to their Spanish nationality; and adult children of naturalized parents.
6. See the 20 March 2015 amendments entry in figure 3.1 for specifics on the amendments. Figure 3.2 also provides further detail on the party positions regarding the proposed amendments in both the Congress of Deputies and the Senate.

References

ABC. 2017. "El arzobispado defiende la propiedad de Santa María la Blanca que reclama la comunidad judía." *ABC*, 23 February 2017. https://www.abc.es/espana/castil la-la-mancha/toledo/abci-arzobispado-defiende-propiedad-santa-maria-blanca-re clama-comunidad-judia-201702231944_noticia.html.
———. 2018. "Los judíos de España piden restituir Santa María la Blanca como sinagoga mayor de Toledo." *ABC*, 30 December 2018. https://www.abc.es/espana/castil la-la-mancha/toledo/ciudad/abci-judios-espana-piden-restituir-santa-maria-blan ca-como-sinagoga-mayor-toledo-201812301511_noticia.html.
Agamben, Giorgio. 2009. *What Is an Apparatus? and Other Essays*. Translated by David Kishik and Stefan Pedatella. Stanford, CA: Stanford University Press.
Aliberti, Davide. 2018. *Sefarad: una comunidad imaginada (1924–2015)*. Madrid: Marcial Pons.
Aragoneses, Alfons. 2016. "Convivencia and Filosefardismo in Spanish Nation-Building." *Max Planck Institute for European Legal History Research Paper Series*, no. 5: 1–34.
Barkan, Elazar. 2000. *The Guilt of Nations: Restitution and Negotiating Historical Injustices*. Baltimore: JHU Press.
Bauböck, Rainer. 2009. "The Rights and Duties of External Citizenship." *Citizenship Studies* 13, no. 5: 475–99.
———. 2018. "Genuine Links and Useful Passports: Evaluating Strategic Uses of Citizenship." *Journal of Ethnic and Migration Studies* 45, no. 6: 1015–26.
Benarroch, Elías L. 2014. "La ley que dará la nacionalidad española a los sefardíes pasa su primer examen en el congreso." *20minutos*. 20 November 2014. https://www .20minutos.es/noticia/2302515/0/ley-congreso/nacionalidad-espanola/sefardies.
Boletín Oficial de las Cortes Generales. Congreso de los Diputados. N. 99-2. 19 February 2015.
———. Senado. N. 509. 24 April 2015.
Castells, Manuel. 2010. *The Power of Identity. The Information Age: Economy, Society, and Culture*, vol. 2, with a new preface. 2 vols. Malden: Wiley-Blackwell.
Constitución de la nación española. June 6, 1869. https://www.congreso.es/docu/constituc iones/1869/1869_cd.pdf.
Diario de Sesiones del Congreso de los Diputados. 2014. Pleno y Diputación Permanente. N. 242, 20 November 2014.
———. 2015a. Comisiones. N. 773. 25 March 2015.
———. 2015b. Pleno y Diputación Permanente. N. 287. 11 June 2015.

Diario de Sesiones del Senado. X Legislatura. 27 May 2015.
Dumbrava, Costica. 2014. "External Citizenship in EU Countries." *Ethnic and Racial Studies* 37, no. 13: 2340–60.
EFE. 2012. "La condición de sefardí dará derecho automático a la nacionalidad española." *El País*, 22 November 2012. https://elpais.com/politica/2012/11/22/actualidad/1353599231_756068.html.
EP. 2014. "El rey expresa la voluntad de España de estrechar lazos con sefardíes y organizaciones judías." *ABC*, 14 February 2014. http://www.abc.es/espana/20140213/abci-sefardies-201402131632.html.
Flesler, Daniela, and Adrian Pérez Melgosa. 2020. *The Memory Work of Jewish Spain*. Bloomington: Indiana University Press.
Hayner, Priscilla B. 2002. *Unspeakable Truths: Facing the Challenge of Truth Commissions*. New York: Routledge.
Jaspers, Karl. 2000. *The Question of German Guilt*. Translated by E. B. Ashton. New York: Fordham University Press.
Law 12/2015. 2015. "Ley 12/2015 de 24 de junio, en materia de concesión de la nacionalidad española a los sefardíes originarios de España" [Law 12/2015 of 24 June, granting Spanish nationality to Sephardi Jews originating from Spain]. *Boletín Oficial del Estado*, 25 June 2015, no. 151.
Ministerio de Justicia. 2014. "Anteproyecto de ley en materia de concesión de la nacionalidad española a los sefardíes que justifiquen tal condición y su especial vinculación con España y por el que se modifica el artículo 23 del código civil." 7 February. Ministerio de Asuntos Exteriores y de Cooperación.
Ojeda-Mata, Maite. 2018. *Modern Spain and the Sephardim: Legitimizing Identities*. Lanham, MD: Lexington Books.
Olick, Jeffrey K. 2013. *The Politics of Regret: On Collective Memory and Historical Responsibility*. Hoboken, NJ: Taylor and Francis.
Orgad, Liav. 2019. "The Citizen-makers: Ethical Dilemmas in Immigrant Integration." *European Law Journal* 25, no. 6: 524–43.
Rey de España, Juan Carlos I. 1992. "Palabras de su majestad el rey a la comunidad israelita." Speech presented at the commemoration of the fifth centenary of the expulsion of the Jews from Spain, Madrid, 31 March 1992. https://www.casareal.es/GL/actividades/Paginas/actividades_discursos_detalle.aspx?data=4131.
Schaap, Andrew. 2005. *Political Reconciliation*. New York: Routledge.
Tavuchis, Nicholas. 1991. *Mea Culpa: A Sociology of Apology and Reconciliation*. Stanford, CA: Stanford University Press.
Teitel, Ruti G. 2000. *Transitional Justice*. Oxford: Oxford University Press.
Torpey, John C. 2003. *Politics and the Past: On Repairing Historical Injustices*. Lanham, MD: Rowman & Littlefield.
United Nations. 1948. "Universal Declaration of Human Rights." General Assembly Resolution 217 A. Accessed 10 November 2020 from https://www.un.org/en/universal-declaration-human-rights.
———. 2005. "Basic Principles and Guidelines on the Right to a Remedy and Reparation for Victims of Gross Violations of International Human Rights Law and Serious Violations of International Humanitarian Law." General Assembly Resolution 60/147. Accessed 10 November 2020 from https://www.ohchr.org/en/professionalinterest/pages/remedyandreparation.aspx.
Vega Toscano, Ana. 2020. "Reencuentro en Sefarad." *Documentos RNE*. Radio Exterior de España. https://www.rtve.es/radio/20200305/reencuentro-sefarad/2005520.shtml.

Walker, Margaret Urban. 2006. *Moral Repair: Reconstructing Moral Relations after Wrongdoing*. New York: Cambridge University Press.
Wolfe, Stephanie. 2014. *Politics of Reparations and Apologies*. New York: Springer Science + Business Media.

Chapter 4

Personal Essay
Passport to the Past, Passport to the Future

Colette Capriles

> To my grandfather, Elías Manuel "Manchi" Capriles Capriles

Now I have a Spanish passport.[1] Passports are used to move through space, but for me they serve to move through time. I do not know if this is the case for all those who responded to the Spanish or Portuguese nationality laws for Sephardi Jews. For me, the process involved a legitimization of a part of my identity that lacked support and drifted around other possible identity choices.

I am a Venezuelan born in France, with one German grandfather and one Jewish grandfather. To acquire this passport, I had to put together a narrative of my family origins that shed light on the history of a particular Sephardi community, the Curaçaoan, the first one established in the New World. Though my paternal ancestors came to the Americas from Portugal, I was unaware of its offer of citizenship when I applied to Spain. Somehow, gathering family birth certificates, establishing the genealogical lines, and going through a dry bureaucratic process led me to what I call an *effet de mémoire*, memories I can relate to just because I needed to make sense of where I come from.

At the same time, as a Venezuelan, I see this passport pointing to another diaspora, the one endured by my fellow nationals today, exhausted under a regime that every day becomes more authoritarian and indifferent to the suffering of the people in whose name it supposedly speaks. Five million Venezuelans have fled in the past few years. For some of them, the nationality laws for Sephardi Jews means the prospect of a passport to a future not possible anymore in their country. In becoming Spanish or Portuguese citizens, we repeat the journey that once brought our ancestors to America, this time in the other direction.

A Menu of Identities

When my father died, one of his old friends, a colleague from the Universidad Central de Venezuela, told me, "During an academic trip your father and I visited Amsterdam, and I was impressed by his deep knowledge of the history of the Sephardi communities established there." I do not have a systematic memory of such knowledge. In my family there were some anecdotal narrative fragments that made up a kind of *basso continuo* but never became the dominant family history.

I think my father had an ambiguous relation with his Jewish origins, based not in religious practice but rather in the idea of belonging to a community imagined as enlightened and historically complex, led by wise Sephardi men. Knowledge and erudition are fundamental elements in the identity of the "Portuguese Nation," as the Portuguese Jews of Spanish origin were referred to when they dispersed from Iberia and settled, as in my family's case, in Curaçao. This aspect of Jewish life somehow ran through our family while religious practice was categorically erased. Unquestionably, this "Sephardi imagination" was also construed to mark a difference from the Ashkenazi, who were portrayed as less cosmopolitan, less educated, and resistant to the wider cultural environment. Hence, in the family, any mention of "Jewishness" was humorous, reproducing the tradition of Jewish humor nurtured by a certain benevolent and fatalistic embrace of self-stereotyping.

Undoubtedly, the loss of the religious dimension, which took place in the generation before that of my father, was part of a process of assimilation to Venezuelan society, separating us from the original community. My paternal grandfather, Elías Capriles Capriles, never converted to Catholicism, but when he married my grandmother, a devout Catholic and sister of a prominent prelate of the Venezuelan Catholic Church, he allowed his children to be raised in that faith and abandoned all religious practice himself. His brothers did the same, although his eldest sister was buried according to Jewish rites. On the eve of World War II, she made a critical contribution on behalf of the Venezuelan government, receiving Jewish refugees on land lots that belonged to her husband. However, although I have no clear memory of this, I know that the five siblings used to get together every Friday evening in what was, perhaps, a kind of substitute rite for Shabbat. What kept them together more than anything else was their identity as Curaçaoans, within which their Jewish identity was embedded. That identity was related also to a secondary aspect of having been raised between Willemstad, the island's capital, and Coro, the closest Venezuelan city, where part of the Capriles family along with other families (the Seniors, the Curiels) started businesses in the last quarter of the nineteenth century.

I said that the loss of religious observances separated us from Judaism, but in a certain way that was not exactly true. My father reacted strongly to his Catholic education and embraced an active atheism. My mother, on the other hand, was the child of a Lutheran German and a Catholic Venezuelan. My maternal grandparents married without religious rites because my grandfather Friedrich refused to abandon his Lutheran faith. My father and mother built an atheist home. Paradoxically, this put a narrative of antireligious arguments at the center of the family and, as a consequence, religion was a permanent piece of conversation.

Despite the atheism, my sisters and I were baptized, yielding to the pressure of relatives to continue the tradition of *compadrazgo* (godfatherhood). But the resistance to raising us in the Catholic faith generated tensions. When I started attending primary school, following my parents' instructions, the teacher would send me to the school library during religion lessons. I did not much understand the reason why, but at some point I started attending catechism classes. I found the stories of the Old Testament incredibly fascinating. The young priest who taught the class made complex drawings on the blackboard in his attempt to represent the Tree of Good and Evil, and probably of Adam and Eve as well. He used to throw pieces of chalk at noisy students. Curiosity led me to find a Bible among our family books, a complete version that I read as an epic story when I was eight years old. Perhaps it was around that time that I discovered that my grandfather was Jewish and that, had we been in Hitler's Germany, we would have ended up in Auschwitz. But it could also be that I learned this a little bit earlier, at age five or six, when we went to visit a family living in the apartment above us. The neighbor's daughter was a medical student, and more than once she came to help my parents concerning childhood illnesses or domestic accidents. Her mother had *the* number tattooed on her left forearm. And I, without any doubt, must have asked why, thus starting my endless curiosity about the subject.

The Two Sides of Silence

I remember clearly asking my parents about how to manage our German maternal identity and our Jewish paternal one. My maternal grandfather was German. He was sent to Venezuela by the government in 1912, as an cooperant teacher. After marrying my Venezuelan grandmother, the family went back in the early 1930s, and lived in Hitler's Germany. My mother was born in Dresden just before the war, and she was a toddler when the family returned, but her elder brothers and her sister went to school in Germany and witnessed the establishment of Nazism. Fortunately, the family managed to return to Venezuela in September 1939. The return trip was in truth a flight, disguised as a family vacation. My grandfather, born into a Saxon family with a military tradition, a professor in a *gymnasium* in Dresden, had already been warned, that his lack of enthusiasm for the Nazi party was putting his job—and more—at risk. His Venezuelan wife could also be the object of persecution even though she had obtained from the bishop of her birthplace a certification that she possessed "neither Jewish nor Black blood."

That German part of my history is, paradoxically, the one that brings me closer to the trauma of the Holocaust. From my mother's eldest sister, I heard a chilling account of the *Kristallnacht*, which she remembered vividly. For her, it was clear that such a pogrom was carefully prepared and that school children received instructions two days before to ransack Jewish stores. She told me about the last visit the family paid to a Jewish family friend, how they said goodbyes while the lady of the house told them in tears, "We shall not meet again. Don't come back, it is so dangerous." Or the story of a neighbor or a friend of my grandfather who was forced to carry a sign saying, "Spit on me. I'm a friend of Jewish people." She also told me about how she raised suspicions when she skipped the *Hitlerjüngend* activities, claiming to be sick. But perhaps the scariest part was the atmosphere of normalcy and optimism in daily life while these things were taking place. The apartments belonging to Jewish families appeared one day, without notice, closed or left empty. Neighbors would look at each other for a few seconds and then willingly produced a rationale: Jews were "emigrating" rather than disappearing. The entire society was seeking a way to blur suspicions of the horror taking place, seeking an alternative story to protect themselves from the unthinkable, something that would block the signs that every day ripped open the dreadful veil of Nazi normality.

On the other hand, I do not remember my Jewish grandfather Elías Capriles ever speaking about the Holocaust. I regret not having had this conversation with him. I do not know if the German origin of his daughter-in-law (my mother) stopped us from talking about the Holocaust. I have only a single recollection from my father: When he was a child, he found that my grandfather jealously guarded a book containing horrible photos of the extermination camps. Elías did not want his children to see it, and I can only guess that behind the intention of hiding such atrocity there was some survivor's guilt or victim's shame, the same shame felt by my German grandfather Friedrich, who never went back to Germany and never again visited his hometown, Dresden, which was almost totally destroyed by the air raids of 1945. Between those two different silences are two experiences of the same catastrophe, and both are within me.

My parents, I figure, solved this tension by clinging to a Venezuelan cosmopolitanism. It sounds like an oxymoron, but it is not. Since the second half of the twentieth century, Venezuela has undergone an accelerated economic and political modernization process that fostered the coexistence of cultural diversities. The traditional and the new, the local and the foreign, the national and the regional, everything merged in a country that looked outward, built highways and skyscrapers, received immigrants, and celebrated its oil wealth. I was born in Paris, where my parents studied, and our home culture turned, of course, toward our own Francophile version that excluded questioning the past.

But the past came back. To apply for the Spanish citizenship meant, for me, taking the past seriously. In fact, when asked, I always state that I have a Sephardi passport, not a Spanish one. That could be more or less idiosyncratic, as most Venezuelans seem to value the Spanish citizenship as a ticket to a better life without special regard to Jewishness. It would be interesting to explore more systematically whether their new status has had any impact on the identity of those Venezuelans, considering that at least a part of them descends from *cristianos nuevos*, many of whom erased their Jewish roots. For me, as I said, it is the feeling of belonging to a community that carries a very specific historical weight.

Genealogy as History

The Sephardi community was imagined in our family almost like a proud mythical past. Obviously, this is a metonymy: the Sephardi world cannot be reduced to the Portuguese Nation that flourished in the Netherlands from the seventeenth century, but that is where our imagination is fixed. The Capriles family is related to the traditional names of the Sephardi diaspora that came to Curaçao: Senior, Ricardo, De Sola, Penso, Curiel, Henriques. In Amsterdam, the Capriles name is related to the Teixeiras and the Belmontes. Thus, there is a twofold story of belonging: On the one hand, the history of the Sephardi diaspora, culturally distinct from the Ashkenazi; and on the other, the sense of belonging to a particular elite, a Sephardi elite, that, once established in the Netherlands, took part in the construction of an enlightened modern order and in the transnational spirit of early capitalism (Israel 1998). Jews from Curaçao were a node in this transatlantic network. They formed a powerful community, united under the pious and permanent supervision of the Portuguese community of Amsterdam and that acted as a focus for the radiation of modernity to the American continent, as if that desertic rock in the shape of a heart were not an island but a bridge. My family history reproduced this community dynamism; bridges and links between the metropole and the Caribbean Sephardi communities are interestingly interwoven in the biographies of some ancestors, whose lives show also the cultural and economic importance of Jews in certain moments of Venezuelan history. This was, I think, one of the intended effects of the Spanish and Portuguese citizenship laws: to recall and highlight this rich historical past.

The Doctor of the Sword

The history of Joseph Capriles Teixeira, the founder of the clan in Curaçao, is legendary. Most probably he was born in Udine, in the Veneto, in 1723. The Italian scholar Ioly Zarattini (2016) claims that the family was originally an Ashkenazi one that settled in Udine during the fourteenth century as bankers and businesspeople, and that they became part of the network between the Levantines and the communities in the Netherlands. At least three generations before Joseph's, the family seemed to be already integrated into the Amsterdam community. His grandfather, Moisés Capriles Belmonte, was born in Amsterdam and is buried in Beth Haim near there.

Joseph was a medical doctor who studied at the University of Padova, one of the few universities that Jews were then allowed to attend. We know he arrived in Curaçao before 1762, the registered date of his first marriage. Perhaps, as a medical doctor, he was sent to Curaçao as part of the consistent assistance provided by the mother community of Amsterdam (Oliel-Grausz 2008, 164), although his former life was apparently quite adventurous. I heard many times the family legend of Joseph having received from a high Ottoman officer a scimitar adorned with precious stones as thanks for saving the life of his daughter. He was from then on known as the Doctor of the Sword.

But facts set the record straight. After graduating from the University of Padova, Joseph moved to Trieste where he converted to Catholicism. Several years later, we find him in Tunisia, as the doctor in the court of a bey, who kindly suggested that he convert to Islam, which he did, adopting the name of Suleiman. In 1757 he appeared before the Inquisition in Malta, where he proclaimed his Catholic faith. A couple of years later, he arrived in Curaçao, where he entered with distinction into the Mikveh Israel community (Ioly Zorattini 2016, 81).

This life story seems an almost archetypal biography of the predicaments of a modern and cosmopolitan Sephardi Jew who takes on multiple identities but who finally gets back to his original Judaism. These accidental identities are possible precisely because of the certainty that, at the end, there is a community that forever acknowledges its children and reconnects them with its traditions, *resisting* the particular wanderings experienced by each one, thereby persevering over time.

The Plantation

Doctor Capriles did not dedicate himself exclusively to medical practice. He got involved in several businesses as well and in 1795 he bought the Ronde Klip plantation from the De Jongh family, whose house still stands today as a hotel. It was a productive property with cattle, sheep, and more than fifty slaves. In 1807 Joseph granted in his will freedom to his slaves. Although in Curaçao there seemed to be certain ad hoc rules to deal with the complicated matters of including slaves and mulatto children in the Jewish community (Schorsch 2019), it is difficult to trace the genealogical records of descendants of freed slaves or of children born outside of wedlock. In Venezuela, the 1982 reform of the civil code established legal equality for all children, regardless of the marriage bond of their parents. This could pose a problem for potential beneficiaries of the Spanish or Portuguese citizenship laws who may be unable to document legal proof of kinship in the filiation chain prior to 1982.

The Man of the Statue

In the same manner that Joseph's life reminds us of the wanderings of the Sephardim during the early-modern period, the life of Manasés, his great-grandson and my great-grandfather, embodies the history of the entrepreneurs of the nineteenth century in the context of the first industries in Venezuela. Joseph's mother, Bethsabé Ricardo, was the daughter of Mordechai Ricardo, a lawyer born in Amsterdam, cousin of the economist David Ricardo. Mordechai was a friend and protector of Simón Bolívar, who, after the fall of the First Republic in 1812 took refuge in Curaçao. It was in Mordechai's library that Bolívar wrote the *Manifiesto de Cartagena*, his first political writing. That friendship later led to a financial and logistical support of the Curaçao Jewish people for the cause of independence.

Manasés married Sara Cecilia Senior, whose family was part of the Curaçao Jewish community that had established itself in 1831 in Coro. Around 1878 Manasés took part in several industrial enterprises and in the construction of the railway connecting Coro to its port, La Vela de Coro. He belonged to that small community with a vision of modernity that took root in Venezuela, bringing capital for investments and purchasing properties (De Lima and Jaber 2016). There is a certain romantic story that presents this process as an optimistic and fluid integration, especially when one stops to admire the so-called House of the Windows in Coro, bought by Senior family in 1840; or when in 2013 a unique *mikveh* (bath for ritual purification) was discovered in that house. The creation of cultural associations, Alegría and Armonía (Joy and Harmony), by Jewish and Catholic women around 1895 also showed the aspiration of practicing a modern and tolerant sociability (Galindo 2004, 189). However, this was in reality a complex process, at times a traumatic one. Antisemitic libels and assaults to the houses of Jewish merchants took place in 1831, 1855, and 1884. In one case, the attack came directly from the pulpit of Presbyter T. A. Navarrete, during a Holy Week sermon. Manasés Capriles replied to him in an open letter: "What sentiments have allowed you to pronounce such words against a race that far from hostile to your Church, tries to fraternize with Her? Which sentiment has induced you to insult a harmless people with the utmost injuring epithets? In the present age, when all races try to forget mutual injuries and look to unite in an embrace of charity and tolerance, your sermon was inopportune, Reverend Father" (Aizenberg 1983, 139–40).

Manasés had the privilege of belonging to the notables of the city. He had been made vice-consul of the Spanish Crown in La Vela de Coro and a knight of the Order of Queen Isabel, the Catholic, in 1878. This brings to mind the relationship between the Spanish power and the Sephardi Jews of the Netherlands who were involved in commerce and diplomacy between European powers in the seventeenth century. Manasés was awarded the Orden del Libertador (Order of the liberator) from the Venezuelan government in 1884, the same year of the Navarrete incident (Aizenberg 1983, 139–40). In the Willemstad cemetery, Beit Haim Blenheim, his tombstone is adorned with an imposing bust of himself, something rather uncommon, that evokes the angel sculptures found in the Jewish cemetery of Coro.

The antisemitic tensions could have influenced the next generations of Coro Jewish families to move to the capital, Caracas. They also settled in other Venezuelan cities, and in Colombia, Panama, and Bolivia, which encouraged their total assimilation, including the abandoning of the religion, into a society rapidly changing its economic structure due to the exploitation of oil. The Capriles family entered the commercial and industrial circles, the media business, and then the liberal professions and politics. Most members of the family were already living and investing in Spain, which recalls the beneficial effects of the Spanish citizenship law in terms of welcoming capital and an educated workforce in Spain. The specific Venezuelan political context highlights the humanitarian impact that the law is having for thousands of Venezuelans whose human rights are now protected. For me, indeed, it also means the protection of my work as political scholar and consultant to humanitarian nongovernmental organizations and political parties.

Passport to the Future

In his book *Fantasmas precursores*, Fernando Yurman (2010) explores the relationship between historical memory and history through psychoanalytic experience. Historical trauma marks experience, leaving an ineffable trace impossible to articulate, without resolution in the historical consciousness. Yurman examines historical memory to articulate the case concerning the Sephardi diaspora and its impact in the historical imagination of the New World.

I think the trauma is doubly relevant in the current circumstances of the Venezuelan diaspora, a phenomenon estimated to be one of the largest migrations of this century, along with the Syrian. What Venezuelan migrants are suffering is the trauma of the loss of their dreams of modernity, of that set of modern aspirations that were embedded in the collective imagination as the hallmark of Venezuelan identity.

The Spanish citizenship law means for many Venezuelans a return—not to a Sephardi identity, but to the possibility of a normal way of life, as was the promise of an oil-rich and democratic Venezuela of the twentieth century, and that now seems lost. The goal of the movement led by Hugo Chávez was to install *a revolution of the past*, to erase history and to return to the imaginary nation established by Bolívar in 1830. The consequent loss of the modern country affects us all. This Spanish passport means much about the past for me, but for many it signifies the future that they feel has been stolen from them. Perhaps. And, I hope that it will be instrumental in our reconciliation with this present and in the reconstruction of a shared future for our country.

Colette Capriles is a professor of political philosophy and social sciences at Universidad Simón Bolívar, Caracas. She is general editor of *Argos,* a peer-reviewed humanities journal. She combines her academic activity with opinion journalism and political consulting. She has authored two books of political chronicles: *La revolución como espectáculo* [Revolution as spectacle] (Caracas, Random House Mondadori

2004) and *La máquina de impedir* [The machine to impede] (Caracas, Alfa Editorial 2010); and articles in academic journals. Her work *The Wealth of Passions: The Moral Philosophy of Adam Smith*, received the 2001 national prize for philosophical research. Her current academic interests center on the philosophy of tyranny, new authoritarianisms, and ethics and politics in digital culture.

Note

1. Translated by Dr. Carolina Iribarren, to whom I owe a great debt of gratitude, as I do to Rina Benmayor and Dalia Kandiyoti for their careful editing and insightful suggestions. My special acknowledgment goes to Dr. Alberto Levi, from the Asociación Israelita de Venezuela, for his unending work supporting the citizenship application process for so many Venezuelans.

References

Aizenberg, Isidoro. 1983. *La comunidad judía de Coro 1824–1900. Una historia.* Caracas: Asociación Israelita de Venezuela.
De Lima, Blanca, and Jorge Jaber. 2016. "Los sefarditas corianos: el apellido Senior de Curaçao a Coro." *Presente y Pasado, Revista de Historia* 21, no. 41: 80–100.
Galindo, Dunia. 2004. "Espacio público y poder político en Armonía y Alegría: Dos sociedades culturales de mujeres en el siglo XIX." *Revista Iberoamericana* 70, no. 206: 183–96.
Ioly Zorattini, Pier. 2016. "Joseph Capriles, un medico ebreo del Settecento tra Chiavris, Udine e Curaçao." In *Ebrei nella storia del Friuli Venezia Giulia: Una vicenda di longa durata*, 77–85. Florence: La Giuntina.
Israel, Jonathan I. 1998. *European Jewry in the Age of Mercantilism.* 3rd ed. Oxford: The Littman Library of Jewish Civilization.
Oliel-Grausz, Evelyne. 2008. "*Patrocinio* and Authority: Assessing the Metropolitan Role of the Portuguese Nation of Amsterdam in the Eighteenth Century." In *The Dutch Intersection: The Jews and the Netherlands in Modern History*, edited by Yosef Kaplan, 149–72. Leiden: Brill.
Schorsch, Jonathan. 2019. "Revisiting Blackness, Slavery, and Jewishness in the Early Modern Sephardi Atlantic." In *Religious Changes and Cultural Transformations in the Early Modern Western Sephardi Communities*, edited by Yosef Kaplan, 512–40. Leiden: Brill.
Yurman, Fernando. 2010. *Fantasmas precursores. La función histórica del trauma.* Caracas: Editorial Debate, Random House-Mondadori.

Part II.

Roots of "Returns"

Early Uses of Jewish and Muslim History

Chapter 5

"Spaniards We Were, Spaniards We Are, and Spaniards We Will Be"

Salonica's Sephardic Jews and the Instrumentalization of the Spanish Past, 1898–1944

Devin E. Naar

A ceremony in Athens in the summer of 2020 marked the establishment of a new agreement between the Cervantes Institute and the Jewish Community of Salonica that aims to enhance opportunities for Salonican Jewish youth to reconnect with their purported linguistic and cultural patrimony. At the ceremony, presided over by the Jewish Community's president, David Saltiel, who had recently acquired Spanish citizenship through the 2015 law, the Spanish foreign minister Arancha González Laya proclaimed, "I believe that one of the last Sephardic Jews who was expelled from Spain said, 'Spaniards we were, Spaniards we are and Spaniards we will be' [*españoles fuimos, españoles somos y españoles seremos*], and I believe that the same can be said for the language: the Spanish that we once spoke, the Spanish we speak today, and the Spanish we will speak." The initiative imagines that by teaching Salonican Jews Castilian they might reconnect with their "language of origin, Judeo-Spanish" (Segura 2020).

The foreign minister's claims form part of a broader discourse that legitimizes and values Sephardic culture only when it is conceptualized as a historical vestige of "the beautiful mediaeval Spanish of Cervantes" (Gibbons 2003). Ladino songs such as the genre of Romansas (ballads), and even late twentieth century compositions such as Flory Jagoda's

A MI MADRE,
FLOR DE MI VIDA!

Aquí me oí llamar de un modo tal,
Que al apellido añadí el maternal.
¡ Para mí el mayor título de nobleza.
Que tu hijo tuvo sobre su cabeza!
Tu sabes cuánto yo amo nuestro Sión!
Así, por ti, mi Flor, arde mi corazón:
Tus palabras dicen: "Paz, Justicia, Bondad".
También: "Libertad, Igualdad, Fraternidad."
Y, lejos de ti, lo que más me conorta
Mâ! (1) es firmar

Isaac Alcheh y Saporta

Madrid, mayo 1917.

(1) Abreviación cariñosa de "mamá" usada en Oriente.

Figure 5.1. Photograph of Isaac Alcheh y Saporta published in his pamphlet, *Los españoles sin patria de Salónica* (1917), accompanied by a poem in honor of his mother in which he explains that he added her surname to that of his father's in line with Spanish custom. He also alludes to Spain as *nuestro Sión* (our Zion)—or, in other words, as the Sephardic homeland. Public domain.

"Ocho Candelikas," are celebrated as relics of medieval Spain and as signs of the allegedly unmitigated affection and fidelity among Sephardic Jews for Spain over the centuries. But, at the Athens ceremony in 2020, the foreign minister added a new myth to the repertoire: the quote above attributed to one of the last Sephardic Jews expelled in 1492 is, in fact, a line from a speech delivered by Isaac Alcheh, a Salonican Jewish leader, during his visit to Madrid more than four hundred years later, in 1916. Alcheh articulated a relatively new sentiment about the allegedly unbroken identification of Sephardic Jews with Spain since 1492. Amidst World War I, Alcheh hoped that his claim, "Spaniards we were, Spaniards we are, and Spaniards we will be," would facilitate the goal of his visit: to secure Spanish nationality and attendant privileges and protections for thirty Jewish merchant families in Salonica (Alcheh y Saporta 1917; for names of those families, see Muñoz Solla 2021). The foreign minister's instrumentalization of Alcheh's statement embodies the mythologizing tactics that both Spaniards and Jews have deployed in the production of a useable past over the last 120 years in the service of rapprochement, political advantage, and profit.

Much has been written about the philosephardic campaigns initiated by Spanish senator Ángel Pulido in the early twentieth century to achieve rapprochement between Spain and the "Spaniards without a homeland," as he designated the descendants of those Jews expelled from Spain in 1492 (inter alia, Alpert 2005; Ginio 2007, 2008; Rohr 2005; Goode 2009; Bolorinos Allard's chapter in this volume). Based on archives, newspapers, and other publications in Judeo-Spanish, Spanish, French, and English, this chapter reframes the historical narrative by emphasizing that Spain's philosephardic campaigns emerged partly due to the desire for reparation for historical injustices (such as the Inquisition and the Expulsion of 1492); romantic notions of shared language, culture, and immutable loyalties among Sephardic Jews and Spain; and as a result of Spain's effort to transform Sephardic Jews into commercial agents in the eastern Mediterranean in a bid to revive the Spanish Empire following the losses of its American colonies in 1898. (The practice of European countries recruiting Jews due to perceptions of their economic utility—a policy known as mercantilism—was by no means new, but rather motived the (re)entry of Jews into the Netherlands and England since the seventeenth century [Israel 1998]. In 1797 the Spanish secretary of finance unsuccessfully advocated for the abolition of the 1492 Expulsion decree to recruit so-called rich Jews to the country [Asuero 2007].) Significantly, the discourse of race science—ubiquitous in Europe and the United States at the turn of the twentieth century—shaped the underlying terms of engagement for *philosefardismo* (philosephardism) as a distinctly modern discourse articulated in the language of national degeneration and regeneration, on which all the previously mentioned factors were refracted. Perceptions of presumed scientific blood ties underpinned conceptions of shared culture, language, and physiognomy, and justified aspirations for economic ties.

Expanding on recent scholarship that conceptualizes philosephardism (like philosemitism) as a modern dehumanizing logic that views Jews, through an antisemitic lens, as allegorical figures representing the quintessential Other, or as political and economic instruments, this chapter explores how Sephardic Jews themselves also instrumentalized philosephardism to their own advantage—and the limits of the enterprise (Álvarez Chillida 2020; McDonald 2021). The embrace and manipulation of philosephardism by Sephardic Jews forms part of a broader dynamic through which they harnessed various Western gazes for their own benefit, including orientalism (Cohen 2014b; Friedman 2019). The multiple iterations of philosephardism should not be conceptualized as a dialogue of equal partners, but rather as the product of ongoing negotiation, contestation, and exploitation among Spanish actors (such as Pulido), Sephardic Jews in the eastern Mediterranean (such as Alcheh), and European Jews more broadly, such as Zionists (such as Max Nordau, cofounder of the World Zionist Organization). These figures engaged with the rhetoric of "race science," developed their own mythologies about Sephardic grandeur, and, in the case of European Jews (such as Nordau), served as intermediaries, and sometimes adversaries, in exchanges between Spain and Sephardic Jews (compare to Ben-Ur 2016).

This chapter further elaborates on the mixed reception of and engagement with philosephardism among Sephardic Jews from (former) Ottoman territories, especially from Salonica, which was once home to the largest Jewish community in the eastern Mediterranean. Salonican Jewish merchants expressed divergent attitudes toward Spain as they debated extraterritorial status—afforded by European consular protection and later citizenship—especially as the city shifted from Ottoman to Greek sovereignty. No Sephardic Jew reflected the blood logic of philosephardism back to Spanish elite as fully as Alcheh did in his quest for Spanish nationality as an emissary representing Jewish merchants in Salonica during World War I. Those Salonican Jews of more modest means, however, who simultaneously sought refuge in neutral Spain during the war, encountered misery, rejection, and even violence; most returned, revealing the limit of the status of Spain as homeland. During the interwar years, figures like Alcheh harnessed philosephardism in Salonica to develop a creative narrative emphasizing the Byzantine roots of that city's first Sephardic Jews that insinuated them into the Greek nationalist narrative. At the same time, the Spanish connection became a liability and an excuse for Greek ultranationalists to accuse Jews of disloyalty and to perpetrate violence against them during the Great Depression. Finally, the tensions inherent in philosephardism played out most dramatically during World War II when the claim that Sephardic Jews shared Spanish blood barely saved the lives of a group of Salonican Jews with Spanish nationality—but only on the condition that they not repatriate to Spain and undo the 1492 Expulsion decree.

Philosephardisms and Fantasies of Racial Regeneration

Liberal senator, physician, criminologist, and "race scientist" Ángel Pulido (1852–1932) famously publicized his so-called rediscovery of the descendants of the Jews exiled from Spain who dwelt throughout the Mediterranean through his campaigns of philosephardism during the first decades of the twentieth century. In essence, Pulido reversed the blood logic of the Spanish Inquisition according to which Jewishness (like Muslimness) constituted a defect or stain on the blood—one of the earliest meanings of the Spanish term *raza* ("race"; Gómez-Bravo 2020)—that had to be removed in the name of Spanish and Catholic unity and purity. By repudiating the goals of the Inquisition, but retaining its blood logic, Pulido viewed the reintroduction of Jewish blood into the Spanish nation as an antidote to the country's decline. He argued that the descendants of the Jews expelled from Spain in 1492 preserved their Spanish essence—including Sephardic women who maintained their Spanish beauty and physiognomy (del Pozo 2013; see Díaz-Mas 2020)—despite their temporal and geographic distance from Spain and thereby constituted Spaniards without a homeland (*Españoles sin patria*), as he entitled one of his books (Pulido 1905).

Pulido traced the decline of the Spanish Empire—culminating in 1898—and the concomitant degeneration of the Spanish nation back to the expulsion of the Jews in 1492, which resulted in an "excision from the Spanish national body" (Goode 2009, 193). At the core of his thought was a distinctive concept of racial heterogeneity that distinguished Spain's national character. Jews had provided strength to the Spanish nation, and now, more than four hundred years later, they could contribute to Spain's national regeneration—insofar as they represented an untapped commercial market in the Levant that could be transformed into a Spanish colony to benefit the metropole. He even assigned metaphysical, curative power to Jewish blood. "The Hebrew race," he wrote in *Españoles sin patria y la raza sefardí*, contains "an energetic substance, a medical condition [that induces] strong action [*medicamento de acción fuerte*]" (Puldio 1905, 538). Those Sephardic Jews who demonstrated the best potential with their active "blood" and commercial instincts offered the "key to Spanish modernization" (Goode 2009, 197). The mutual benefit of the return of Jews to the Spanish orbit nonetheless had a limit: he was very clear that Spain could only afford to admit into its neo-imperium elite Jews.

Among the key texts that informed Pulido's racial theories was Max Nordau's *Degeneration* (1892), which influenced race scientists, nationalists, and white supremacists across Europe and the United States (Burgers 2011; Davis 1977; Harrison and Hoyle 2000; Penslar 1996). Pulido described *Degeneration* as a "notable study" in writings on criminology already in the 1890s (Pulido 1897, 73). In turn, Nordau befriended Pulido in Paris in 1904, and stayed with him while Nordau was exiled in Madrid during World War I. Nordau also translated Pulido's work into French as *Le Peuple judéo-espagnol*, which included a provocative subtitle—*première base mondiale de l'Espagne* (Spain's first world base)—that viewed the dispersion of Sephardic Jews as the foundation of a global Spanish Empire; the book also referenced Alcheh's visit to Spain as evidence of Sephardic Jews' embrace of philosephardism and the Spanish imperium (Pulido 1923, 153). Pulido referred to Nordau not only as a "sage and publicist of universal fame," but also as "an eminent Jewish publicist *of Spanish origin*" (Pulido 1905, 46, 181; emphasis added). Feted by Spain's liberal elite and invited to speak at the Ateneo, the most prestigious literary society in Madrid, Nordau saw Spain as the land that gave rise to his own sense of racial identity: "Traits of both his mind and his physique could without undue exaggeration be attributed to his Mediterranean and Hispano-Judaic ancestry" (Nordau and Nordau 1943, 221–22). Although born in Budapest, Nordau claimed family origins in Segovia and descent from the Abravanel rabbinical dynasty that settled in Salonica after 1492 and later in the Habsburg Empire (Nordau and Nordau 1943, 12; Pulido 1905, 47). Like many Zionist and European (especially German) Jewish leaders, Nordau claimed Sephardic roots to assert his superiority, cast in racialized language, over the alleged degenerate, shtetl Jews of Eastern Europe (Efron 2016; Schapkow 2020). The discourse of Sephardic superiority, which emerged in dialogue with antisemitic thought, does not seem to have been familiar to Ottoman Jews themselves until the late nineteenth or early twentieth centuries.

Yet Nordau expressed skepticism over whether Sephardic Jews would respond positively to Spain's overtures. "Very few individuals of my blood and my race," wrote Nordau, "would be interested in returning to Spain in the present era." He argued that Sephardic Jews did not speak Castilian but rather a corrupt jargon of which his own father allegedly taught him the basics (quote at Nordau and Nordau 1943, 12; see also 67; Pulido 1905, 88–89, 179, 330). Pulido responded that Sephardic Jews—including Nordau—felt little affinity to Spain and the Spanish language due to Spain's degenerate status: "Today it is less powerful, less wealthy, less intelligent, more unhappy and less advanced than the glorious nation of which the intellectuals of the world, like Voltaire, once spoke" (181). Sephardic Jews and Spain thus needed each other for their mutual regeneration.

Despite their shared racial logic, Pulido and Nordau disagreed on the redeeming qualities of Sephardic Jews. Less concerned with their finances, Nordau exoticized the physically fit bodies of Sephardic Jews of the Orient whom he deemed worthy of emulation. As one of Nordau's most enduring contributions to Zionism, his gendered concept of "muscular Judaism" imagined that if Jews could be liberated from their ghetto-like conditions in Europe they could reclaim their ancient status as a physically fit people, "deep chested, sturdy, sharp eyed men" (Nordau 1903, 547–48)—prepared for sports, war, and self-government on their own land. "Specimens" of the rare physically fit Jew could already be found in Salonica: "Pay a visit to Salonica, in Turkey, you will find ready to carry your luggage as fine a body of men as the world has ever harbored—athletes of wonderful development body and limb. You could not tell them for Jews if you wanted to; and yet they are Jews; they are the descendants of the refugees from Spain. They are working men, porters, hod-carriers, etc. This open air occupation has left its impress on them" (Hirsch 1902, 279).

In contrast to Pulido, who courted Salonica's Jewish merchants, Nordau, like other Zionists, fetishized the bodies of the city's poorest Jews. Nordau's doubts about whether Salonican Jews would be drawn to Pulido's overtures would soon be tested as war engulfed the Balkans and the Ottoman Empire unraveled. As a philhellene, Nordau encouraged Salonica's Jews to remain in place, to learn Greek like Athenians as they awaited the formation of a Jewish state in Palestine, and, in short, to ignore Spain's overtures (Nordau 1913–14).

The Allure of Extraterritoriality

As Ottoman rule ended in Salonica during the Balkan Wars (1912–13), local merchants feared the detrimental economic consequences that would emerge from being cut off from the Balkan markets and confined to a small nation-state like Greece. As an alternative, merchants advocated for Salonica to be transformed into an international city or a Jewish city-state (Naar 2016, 1–4). Recognizing the unlikelihood of either option, some Jewish merchants clamored for other privileges—namely, consular protection or nationality from whichever European power offered the best arrangement (Morcillo-Rosillio 1997, 2008b). The benefits of extraterritorial status acquired through foreign protection without leaving home proved attractive for Jewish elites for strategic purposes. Some embraced philosephardism if it could secure them coveted privileges. Other elites expressed resentment for their ancestors' expulsion from Spain, emphasized their feelings of loyalty to the Ottoman Empire, or even advocated for the fall of the Spanish Empire by supporting Filipino independence (Bayona 2021; Cohen 2014a; Díaz-Mas 2000). Even in the arena of consular protection, Spain did not play the dominant role for most Ottoman Jews. Notably, Spain's consular representatives in Salonica until the early twentieth century were British Levantines and a local Muslim (Dönme) merchant (Kaya 2020, 273–74).

The prospect of residents of the eastern Mediterranean gaining foreign protection had longstanding roots. The Capitulations—trading privileges granted by the Ottoman authorities since the sixteenth century—permitted European powers to protect their own agents, often non-Muslim merchants, including *francos* (Jews from Italy; often merchants). Dispensations via the *berat* (special patent) exempted them from Ottoman and communal taxes and granted them immunity from prosecution by local courts. The Capitulations, however, came to represent the weakness of the Ottoman Empire and the detrimental penetration of European influence. With the new primacy of the rule of equal law for all citizens in the nineteenth century, foreign protégés became legal misfits—they were even viewed as threats to national integrity (Ginio 2006–7, 2014; Rozen 1992; Stein 2016; Vlami 2009).

Some Ottoman Jews demonstrated their eligibility for European protection through economic prowess. Those wealthy enough could purchase the *berat* regardless of ancestral ties to the given country. In his memoir, Leon Sciaky recalled "'Italians' who knew nothing of Italy, 'Danish,' 'Norwegian' and 'British' subjects whose purely nominal nationality rid them of any obligation toward any country. We had a host of 'Austro-Hungarians,' native-born [in Salonica] for many generations, speaking the languages of Macedonia and living its life, but privileged to fly the flag of their fatherland and seek its protection in time of political crisis" (2003, 161).

Some Salonican Jewish merchants engaged in legal "forum shopping" to procure consular protection from whichever European state provided the best privileges, sometimes switching between nationalities (Clancy-Smith 2011; Morcillo-Rosillo 1992). In contrast, owners of a tobacco business in Salonica, the Saportas, claimed descent from Cataluña and submitted to the Spanish consul in 1852 a family tree to justify their claim to Spanish protection (notably, they penned the document in Italian) ("Rams di discendenza" 1852; Sariyannis 1997). But the submission of documentation purporting genealogical or blood links to the country in question seems to have been uncommon.

A series of wars tested the extent to which individuals with foreign protection would be permitted to reside in the (former) Ottoman realms. Due to the Italo-Ottoman war over Libya (1911–12), the Ottoman authorities expelled Italian nationals, including prominent Jewish families, like the Allatinis, whose absence destabilized communal leadership (Rozen 2005, 1:169). Amidst the Balkan Wars (1912–13), Jewish merchants appealed to European consuls to acquire foreign protection to avoid becoming Greek citizens and to gain the benefits of extraterritoriality, including exemption from military service. Not only Spain, but also Portugal, which developed a narrative about the "Oriental Jews of Portuguese Origin" (Franco 2011), and Austria-Hungary, which sought Mediterranean commercial connections, extended protection to several thousand Salonican Jews. While the *New York Times* reported on 10 April 1913 ("Turkish Jews" 1913) that eight thousand Jews from former Ottoman territories appealed to the Spanish government for protection, local Jewish communal leader Joseph Nehama estimated that Spain registered only 850 Salonican Jews, while Austro-Hungary registered 1,000 and Portugal registered 1,200 (Stein 2016, 151n9).

Foreign protégés constituted a demographic minority of the Jewish population (no more than 5 percent), yet one that received disproportionate attention because their presence heightened the association of Jews with foreign interests. While Nehama had numbered among Pulido's correspondents and began to refer to Salonica's Jews as "Spanish" after 1903, he initially opposed the acquisition of foreign protection because he feared accusations of disloyalty; he also feared that communal coffers would be damaged by those exempted from communal taxes (Naar 2016, 211–13; Stein 2016, 38–39). The association of Jews with foreign powers was aggravated due to the overrepresentation of Jews at consuls: Spain, Belgium, Britain, Denmark, France, Germany, Italy, Japan, the Netherlands, Persia, Poland, Portugal, and the United States (Almanach National 1915, 56–59). The connection with Spain finally emerged as noteworthy: Salomon Ezratty served as vice-consul, processed applications of those applying for Spanish nationality, and, in recognition of his dedication, was knighted by the Spanish crown with the order of Queen Isabel—the same monarch who had expelled his ancestors in 1492 (Morcillo-Rosillo 2014b, 124–25).

The instability provoked by ongoing war and lingering uncertainty over whether Greece would retain control of Salonica jeopardized the citizenship status of those who ostensibly had acquired foreign nationality. The Prefecture of Salonica even issued a decree in 1916 offering residents of territories recently incorporated into Greece the possibility of reverting to Ottoman nationality. While more than eight thousand Muslims from the area embraced the offer, it remains unclear how many Jews did ("El derito de eskojer" 1916). At that time, in 1916, the Spanish consulate in Salonica formally registered a total of 230 Jewish families (approximately 900 individuals) (Morcillo-Rosillo 2004, 2008b,

48). But the Spanish consul, Fernando del Pulgar, also rejected petitions from certain families who claimed to have benefitted from Spanish nationality previously, provoking indignation and petitions to Madrid requesting that their grievances be addressed. Isaac Alcheh even accused Spanish consular officials—including the aforementioned Ezratty and Paul (Pablo) Abravanel, both Salonican Jews—of abusing their authority by demanding vast sums of money and prioritizing requests from their relatives (Muñoz Solla 2021). As Spain again came to the fore, the unresolved nationality question in the context of the war provoked Alcheh to journey across the Mediterranean in the hope of securing Spanish protection for his constituents back home.

Reflecting Philosephardism back to Spain

While Sephardic Jews had engaged with philosephardism since the turn-of-the-century, during his visit to Spain in 1916, Isaac Alcheh most elaborately reflected Pulido's rhetoric back to Spanish elite. The director of Salonica's most prestigious Jewish private school, Alcheh also numbered among the members of Preseverancia, Lodge 292 of the Spanish freemason order Grande Oriente Español (est. 1907) (del Arbol 1993). Drawing on support from Spanish intelligentsia, including Carmen de Burgos, the country's first female professional journalist, Alcheh delivered the lecture at Madrid's most prestigious literary and cultural society, the Ateneo, during which he claimed to represent "Spaniards without a homeland of Salonica" (quote at Alcheh y Saporta 1917, 59; Díaz-Mas 2018; Hernández Gonzalez 2019, 134–35; Naar 2016, 166). Alcheh hoped that his proclamation of the immutable Spanish essence and fidelity of Salonica's Jews would prompt the Spanish government to grant Spanish nationality to those Salonican merchant families he represented, himself included; he had argued unsuccessfully to Salonica's Spanish consul that he deserved Spanish nationality because his father previously held Spanish papers and he himself had received a Spanish passport just two years earlier (Muñoz Solla 2021, 101). His declaration nonetheless made an indelible imprint in the annals of Spanish history—a sign that Sephardic Jews themselves validated philosephardism (Alvarez Chillida 2002, 266; Avni 1982, 28; Estrugo 1933, 25; Corcoll and Siguán 1987, 23; Díaz and Leseduarte 2007, 574; Díaz-Mas 1992, 170; Pérez 2005, 304). As much as Spain viewed Salonican Jews as "useful instruments" (quoted in Rohr 2005, 381), as a Spanish decree in 1924 declared, so, too, did Salonican Jews view Spain's overtures through a utilitarian lens.

Alcheh's visit to Spain was risky not only due to the submarine warfare plaguing the Mediterranean Sea during the war, but also because the Greek state already questioned the loyalty of Salonica's Jews. Tensions escalated in the context of the National Schism in 1916 that divided Greece over whether to enter the war. Intra-Jewish disputes erupted between pro-French representatives of the Alliance Israélite Universelle and pro-German Zionists that provoked a local Jewish schism mirroring the broader conflicts (Papamichos Chronakis 2017). Spain's neutrality—and the country's absence from the local scene—rendered Alcheh's overture to Spain less provocative. Aboard the ship to Spain, Alcheh read Cervantes' *Don Quixote* and refashioned himself as Isaac Alcheh y Saporta, adding his mother's surname in line with Spanish custom (introduced in the eighteenth century).

As a member of Salonica's Katalan Hadash congregation—one of several dozen congregation in Salonica named after the ostensible places of origin of their founders—Alcheh viewed Barcelona as his true native city and as Salonica's sister city (16, 44–45). He described the familiarity of the faces, the names of places and people, and the customs that reminded him of Salonica. He (like Pulido) attributed Spanish origins to the beauty of Salonica's Jewish women. It remains unclear whether the Spanish public or Alcheh himself recognized the potential irony in his claim that his Catalan ancestry proved his Spanish bona fides as the Catalan independence movement emerged (formalized with the creation of the Estat Català political party in 1922).

From Barcelona, Alcheh continued to Madrid where he emphasized the bonds of shared blood that united Spaniards, the Jewish sages of medieval Spain, and contemporary Sephardic luminaries. He was a guest in the home of Max Nordau, then in exile in Madrid, where he first met Pulido and also befriended Abraham S. Yahuda, a Jerusalem-born, Baghdadi-origin professor at the University of Madrid and one of the first Jewish scholars to hold a chair of Jewish studies at a European university—the position itself an outgrowth of Pulido's campaigns (Gonzalez 2019). Alcheh referred to Nordau as his "venerated teacher and illustrious doctor" who was a "noble descendant" of the Abravanels; and to Yahuda, who served as his principal intermediary with officials in Madrid, as his "distinguished friend" with a lineage "stamped with glory in the History of immortals!" The living genius that he saw in Nordau and Yahuda provided, so he argued, irrefutable evidence of the continued glory of medieval Spanish Jews transmitted to the present, from Judah Ha-Levi and Maimonides to Joseph Caro and Moses Almosnino, "through whose veins course a plethora of ardent Spanish blood" (Alcheh y Saporta 27–28). At Yahuda's initiative, Alcheh also participated in a milestone in

Spain's Jewish history by helping to organize the first Jewish community in Madrid since 1492 and thus returning Jewish glory to Spain. For the High Holidays in 1916, he served as one of the principal prayer leaders. Shortly thereafter, the first official synagogue since 1492 opened in Madrid and was recognized in New York as "one of the most notable events in recent Jewish history" ("Spain as a Jewish Center" 1917).

The highpoint of Alcheh's visit came with his lecture, "The Spaniards without a Homeland of Salonica," through which he hoped to convince the Spanish elite that their government should recognize Salonica's Jews as loyal representatives of their interests in the eastern Mediterranean; to amplify commercial and cultural initiatives in partnership with Salonican Jews; and to grant Spanish nationality to the select group of Salonican Jews for whom we was advocating in recognition of their roles as Spanish "ambassadors" in the Levant. He further proposed establishing Spanish classes for Salonican Jews to restore their allegedly bastardized Judeo-Spanish to the language of Cervantes. He even suggested establishing a Sephardic consul to work with the Spanish consul in Salonica (Alcheh y Saporta 1917, 27 ff). In this city, he claimed, "all the *sefardíes*, without distinction of class, yearn for her [Spain] in their hearts" (34). Remembered as a "big burly man" with a "fearsome, booming voice," Alcheh no doubt drew on these attributes during his lecture (Saporta 2009, 48).

The impact of Alcheh's visit remains difficult to gauge. Despite efforts to gain an audience with King Alfonso XIII—by writing to him directly and by relying on intermediaries including Spanish philosopher Gumersindo de Azcárate—Alcheh did not succeed. Moreover, the Spanish press reported varyingly on his visit with fascination, exoticism, even disinterest (Díaz-Mas 2018). In Salonica, Spanish official Pedro de Prat even accused Alcheh, who had criticized the consul's approach to the nationality question, of "bad faith" and of "dishonoring our colony"; he also opposed Alcheh's proposal for a "Sephardic consul." Abraham S. Yahuda, in Madrid, even intervened at Alcheh's request although to no avail (Muñoz Solla 2021, 98–100). Yet as Alcheh had hoped, as part of an effort to spread Spanish influence in the eastern Mediterranean, the Spanish government established a short-lived Castilian journal, *Hispania*, in Salonica (1919) (Morcillo-Rosillo 1991). But some Salonican Jews complained about the difficulty of learning Castilian orthography (Naar 2016, 227).

Most importantly, Alcheh's visit likely contributed to the philosephardic momentum that culminated in a Spanish royal decree in 1924 offering Spanish citizenship to Sephardic Jews. Even Pedro de Prat, who criticized Alcheh personally, agreed that granting Spanish nationality to well-to-do Salonican Jews, who would be obligated to pay an annual tax, would be worthwhile; he communicated his position to King Alfonso XIII (Muñoz Solla 2021, 109). With the collapse of the Ottoman Empire and the end of the Capitulations, the government of General Primo de Rivera issued a royal decree, under the aegis of King Alfonso XIII, granting Spanish citizenship to the "former subjects of Spain or their descendants," a veiled reference to Sephardic Jews. The decree specified that naturalization would be available for only six years, and included other restrictions (Berthelot 1995, 82). The decree indicated that the repatriation of Sephardic Jews was *not* an objective. To the contrary, the decree justified the offer "in deference to the realization that these elements in general know our language and that naturalization makes them *useful instruments* in the service of our cultural relations in distant lands where they form colonies which can be *useful* to Spain" (quoted in Rohr 2005, 381; emphasis added). In short, by embracing philosephardism, Alcheh helped to achieve the instrumental goal of his visit—not repatriation to Spain, but rather extraterritoriality in Salonica.

Return to Spain, Land of Misery

Simultaneous with Alcheh's visit to Spain in 1916, other Salonican Jews pursued an additional avenue to secure their future—by migrating. Wartime conditions, economic downturn, and Greek military conscription provoked a wave of emigration, especially among Salonican Jewish men. Many sought refuge in neutral countries, including the United States (which did not enter the war until 1917)—and Spain. Other Salonican and Ottoman Jews already residing in France and Britain found themselves classified as enemy aliens (Ben-Ur 2015; Stein 2015). Those thousands who sought refuge in Spain tested the extent to which Spain would accept them and called into question the efficacy of philosephardism and its undergirding blood logic.

In the autumn of 1916 an anonymous letter published under the pseudonym *un selanikli* ("a Salonican") in Salonica's Judeo-Spanish newspaper, *El Liberal*, argued passionately *against* migration to Spain. The letter described the human torrent fleeing the city in the context of the war and in search of new opportunities abroad. Due to their proficiency in French, many of the migrants initially sought to disembark in France, but likely because of their Ottoman nationality and potential status as enemy aliens, continued to Barcelona. They held out high hopes albeit based on "false information" spread in Salonica about Spain as a "prosperous country" where "life is easy and cheap." But "nothing is falser," the letter continued, describing Spain's high cost of living, limited natural resources, and negligible commerce and industry. Salonican Jews who had recently arrived in Spain "lost all hope" and set their sights on the Americas, but encountered obstacles—few ships, high costs, and priorities for Spanish nationals. The article concluded that "the misery is even worse" in Spain than in Salonica and discouraged readers from setting foot in Spain (Un Selanikli 1916).

Completely bereft of any of the sentimentality deployed by Alcheh, the letter in *El Liberal* did not comment on Spain as the ancestral homeland of Salonica's Jews or on racial affinities between Spaniards and Sephardic Jews. That kind of rhetoric was irrelevant in the face of the harsh material reality that Salonican and other (former) Ottoman Jewish migrants encountered in Spain, but nonetheless did not halt migration to Barcelona (Ojeda-Mata 2015). To the contrary, a group of Salonican Jews in the United States resettled in Spain during World War I, drawn less by romantic notions and more by the desire to avoid the American military in 1917. Among them were the memoirist Leon Sciaky and founders of New York's Salonician Brotherhood of America, all of whom returned to the United States after the war (Sciaky 2003). The most famous Salonican Jew to migrate to Barcelona during the war was Isaac Carasso, who eventually came to the United States as a Spanish citizen and introduced his yogurt brand Danone (Dannon) (Candil 2015).

The new arrivals in Barcelona in 1916 benefitted from limited support, but largely confronted indifference, even violence, and the limits of philosephardism. In Madrid's republican newspaper, *El Liberal*, Rafael Cansinos Assens, who mentored Jorge Luis Borges and befriended Max Nordau, advocated that the Spanish government aid the Sephardic refugees because they were "blood of our Hispanic blood"—and thus deserved special consideration (Díaz-Mas 2019, 48–83; full text 486–88). But the Spanish government did not support the newcomers, in part because, in a repudiation of philosephardism, it viewed them as "Turks." Instead, the German consulate took the Ottoman nationals under its protection and offered modest aid. But when that aid ended—because, as the Spanish press alleged, the German consulate came to view the refugees as Jews rather than Turks—a revolt ensued as the refugees, women and children included, cried out in hunger. The Spanish police put down the cries with brutal violence; several people were injured (Díaz-Mas 2017a, 130–31). *El Imparcial* lamented the sad irony of the situation: "Because they were Turkish Jews, the most part from Salonica, speakers of archaic Spanish, of ancient Spanish stock, they have returned to their former ancestral land once again only to suffer inclemency through Destiny's new decree" (Díaz-Mas 2019, 484–85, 489–92). The article concluded that Salonican

Jews did not find their promised land in Spain, but rather wandered the streets of Barcelona, wondering where their Canaan would be, begging in broken Castilian to be taken to America (Díaz-Mas 2017a, 2019).

Although Salonican Jewish refugees in Barcelona largely did not travel to America, aid from the United States helped them to survive and to establish an organized community. Nordau, Pulido, and Yahuda convinced the American Joint Distribution Committee in New York to wire $4,000 of support, but they could not prevent another ship full of Ottoman Jewish refugees from being denied landing privileges at Barcelona (Nordau and Nordau 1943, 242; "Refugees in Spain" 1917). By 1918 ten Ottoman Jews, two Moroccan Jews, and three Ashkenazi Jews formed the Comunidad Israelita de Barcelona. Many Ottoman-born Jews—perhaps as many as half of the estimated thousand Jews in the city after World War I—found work as street traders, especially in clothing, at Barcelona's San Antonio Market (Ojeda-Mata 2015). The strife of the Spanish Civil War inspired a few Ottoman-origin Jews in the United States to volunteer in the Lincoln Brigade (Victor Franco was killed in action whereas Samuel Nahman [aka Manny Harriman] led the effort to collect oral histories of fellow Lincoln Brigade veterans). Many others already established in Barcelona fled the conflict ("Famiyas Tesaloniklias de Barselona" 1938). The Italian and German airstrikes (1937–38) in support of Franco's nationalist rebel army resulted in more than a thousand civilian casualties, including five Salonican Jews ("Las orrores de la gerra" 1938; "Letra de Barselona" 1937). *La Aksion*, Salonica's Judeo-Spanish daily, published a front-page story about a group of Jews from Kavala, near Salonica, who had "escaped the inferno of Barcelona" ("Los ke fuyen del inferno" 1938; see also Gruss 2021). Their return to their *patria*—Greece—aboard a Greek ship that was orchestrated and funded by the Greek consuls in Spain and France, revealed once again the sense that, despite the lofty rhetoric, the Spanish state was not prepared to embrace and protect those Sephardic Jews who had sought refuge on Spanish shores.

The Leverage and Liabilities of the Spanish Connection in Interwar Greece

The racial language underpinning philosephardism helped to justify the granting of Spanish nationality to Sephardic Jews abroad while simultaneously proving largely incapable of securing their entry into, or protection from, Spain itself. Back in Greece, however, race science thinking developed later, during the interwar years. By 1937 the German Foreign Office praised the Greek state for maintaining the Ottoman prohibition against intermarriage between Jews and Christians but expressed disappointment that conversion remained possible—a sign that Greece had not embraced the principles of modern "race hygiene" and instead remained a "primitive" civilization (Dublon-Knebel 2007, 73–75). Discussion of religion, language, and culture predominated in the Greek public sphere but nonetheless served as cyphers for perceived racial essence. The slippage was particularly pronounced because the same Greek word, "*fili*," signified both nation and race (Trubeta 2013). Within this framework, Salonican Jewish elite like Isaac Alcheh leveraged the discourse of philosephardism, largely stripped of overt racial language, to develop Spanish genealogies that paradoxically sought to legitimize the status of Jews as Hellenes. An emphasis on Jews' Spanish identity also became a liability, a sign of their allegedly irremediable disloyalty to Greece, and a pretext for anti-Jewish violence.

Shortly after Alcheh returned from Spain, a devastating fire that destroyed the downtown of Salonica in 1917 provided an opportunity for the new Greek sovereigns to implement an urban plan to transform the Ottoman and Jewish city into a Hellenic metropolis. The plan to Hellenize Salonica's cityscape—which Jews benefitting from Spanish nationality protested (Morcillo-Rosillo 1999)—formed one of several policies implemented by the Greek state to limit Jews' economic and cultural position while also seeking to Hellenize them. Jews responded in numerous ways, including through concerted efforts to publicize their deep roots in the city and to integrate themselves into the emerging Greek nationalist narrative stretching from ancient Greece through Byzantium to the Hellenic Republic (est. 1924). Alcheh and other members of the Katalan Hadash congregation, one of thirty-two synagogues destroyed by the fire of 1917, constructed a particularly creative useable past for their congregation by claiming that as Catalan Jews, their forebears had fled Spain in 1391 in response to the anti-Jewish violence in Barcelona of that year and settled in Salonica while the city remained under Byzantine rule. They thus claimed the mantle as the first "Greek" Sephardic Jews in the city and as those best prepared to lead Salonica's Jews in the Hellenic Republic (Naar 2011, 123–39; Perez 2019; Shaltiel-Gracian 2005, 81–83).

As part of the rising interest in history and folklore in interwar Greece, the Judeo-Spanish press published articles about local customs and family names linked to synagogues destroyed during the fire to offer a sense of continuity during a period of rupture. Joined by Shemtov Saltiel, a merchant and officer of Catalan Hadash who had acquired Spanish nationality, Alcheh republished their congregation's 1527 High Holiday prayerbook "according to the customs of Barcelona." (Saltiel 1927, title page). They hoped that the new

Figure 5.2. Cadastral document for the Katalan Hadash (New Catalan) synagogue issued to the Jewish Community of Salonica in 1922, after the synagogue, along with thirty-one others, had been destroyed by the fire of 1917. Source: The Jewish Museum of Thessaloniki, used with permission.

prayerbook would publicize the famed past of the congregation—founded by the city's first Greek Sephardic Jews whose grand tradition passed through sixteenth-century rabbi Moses Almosnino to the present—and also celebrate the advent of the printing press in Salonica. The writer Baruch Ben-Jacob claimed that the 1527 edition was the first book published in Greek Macedonia on the region's first printing press—the Jews' greatest contribution to Hellenic civilization (Covo 1931; Saltiel and Ben-Jacob 1927, 3–6; "La prima estamparia djudia en Saloniko" 1931). Trying to prove their worthiness for inclusion in the Greek nation, Ben-Jacob, Alcheh, and Saltiel ironically harnessed narratives about their Iberian roots to stake a claim on their belonging—indeed, their indispensability—to Greek society during a period in which the Greek state challenged their position.

By the 1930s the past and present accomplishments of members of the Katalan congregations (both Yashan [old] and Hadash [new]) were construed as an expression of their essential characteristics. Joseph Nehama codified the image:

Figure 5.3. Title page of the *Mahzor Katalan*, a high holiday prayer book published by the Katalan Hadash congregation in Salonica in 1927 in honor of the four-hundredth anniversary of its first printing in 1527 and with the hope that the new prayer book would inspire the congregation's members to rebuild their synagogue. Source: New York Public Library, used with permission.

> The Catalonians . . . were a people from the seacoast, alert and mobile, friends of novelty, gay, communicative, of smooth and polished manners, of vivid intelligence, penetrating in their enterprises, self-willed in their projects; the Catalonians were all activity, exuberant in their vitality. Skillful in their work, the Jews hailing from Barcelona, Gerona, from Tarragona, and from the Valencian coasts, were had workers, unrelenting in their industry. *Los Catalanes de las piedras sacan panes*, the Catalonians are capable of turning stones into bread. And, as they were, despite all that, refined people, cultured conversationalists, good dialecticians, they were not wrong in recalling on their behalf the praising proverb current among Spaniards: *El aire de Cataluña agudece*, the air of Cataluña makes one nimble-minded. (Nehama 1935–78, 2: 26–27; tr. by Benardete 1952, 62–63)

The Judeo-Spanish press similarly invoked proverbs to explain the prominence and prosperity of the Catalan congregations' members, who rose to key positions in the Jewish Community: as president (Leon Gattegno), head of the rabbinical court (Isaac Broudo), and head of the burial society (David Saadi Saltiel) (Naar 2011, 136–38). While the language of race was not explicit, the conceptualization of certain characteristics as part of an inborn essence resonated with the racialized underpinnings of philosephardism and European nationalisms, more generally.

As much as the Catalan and Spanish connections could serve as leverage for Salonican Jews to achieve influential communal positions, those same affiliations became liabilities vis-à-vis the Greek public and state. During the Great Depression, in 1930, representatives of the Jewish community of Salonica worked with the Spanish Embassy in Athens to propose to the Greek government the establishment of a Spanish chair at the University of Salonica to "satisfy the needs of the seventy thousand Spanish-speaking Sephardim in the city" (quote at Naar 2016, 171–73; see also Philippēs 2010, 199–201). That Salonica's Jews were described as speaking Spanish reveals the influence of philosephardism and other discourses that erased any sense of the Jewish distinctiveness of the language. The Spanish Embassy saw the proposal as an act of diplomatic reciprocity in acknowledgment of the creation of a chair of Hellenic studies at the University of Barcelona in 1928. But the University of Salonica rejected the overture by arguing that the creation of the new chair would "perniciously counter the work of Hellenizing the Jewish element in the city" (quoted in Naar 2016, 172; Naar 2016, 171–73; see also Philippēs 2010, 199–201)

Similar anxieties provoked unprecedented anti-Jewish violence in 1931. Ultranationalist Greek Orthodox Christians, many of them refugees from Turkey, perpetrated the first major anti-Jewish attack in the city's history, burning down the Campbell district, a poor Jewish neighborhood established for the victims of the fire of 1917. The Greek nationalist newspaper, *Makedonia*, provoked the violence with diatribes against the Jews that enumerated dozens of reasons for their perfidy, including the false claim that "three-quarters" held foreign nationality; and because "they refuse with impudence and obstinacy to speak the Greek language and prefer Spanish, which does not remind them of anything but a very bad period of their life" (Vassilikou 2000, 99–101) Notably, considerable strides had been made in the acquisition of the Greek language, especially among Jewish youth attending Jewish and state schools; in contrast, Judeo-Spanish had been reduced in Jewish schools to only one hour per week by 1927 and was essentially removed from the curriculum in the 1930s (Naar 2016, ch. 3).

Salonican Jewish elite, including Katalan Hadash leaders, instrumentalized their Spanish Jewish past not only in response to Spanish overtures, but also as a strategy to secure their position in their community, their city, and their new state. Like those who sought Spanish nationality, the goal rarely involved return to the purported ancestral *patria* but rather a desire to strengthen their position in their local context. Those same overtures toward Spain, however, proved dangerous when they confirmed the prejudices of antisemites and Greek nationalists who viewed Jews' continuing identification with Spain as national betrayal.

Repatriation Ultimatum: Limiting and Lifesaving Factors during the Holocaust

By the time of the Nazi occupation of Salonica in 1941, the number of Jews benefitting from foreign nationality had decreased considerably since the city's incorporation into Greece in 1912–13—from at least three thousand to fewer than a thousand. Despite pressures from the Greek state, some Jews retained whereas others acquired foreign nationality (the Spanish government confirmed nationality for 249 Salonican Jewish families in 1933) ("Le retour des Sepharadim" 1933). Even Joseph Nehama, who initially had discouraged the acquisition of foreign nationality and founded the Association of Assimilationists (1928) to advance Jewish integration into Greece, ultimately acquired Spanish citizenship on the eve of World War II (Stein 2016, 121). The German Foreign Ministry reported in 1943 that 864 individuals—fewer than 2 percent of the city's Jews— held foreign citizenship, including 511 Spanish nationals, down from 900 in 1916, 800 in 1931, and 734 in 1935 (Dublon-Knebel 2007, 298–319; Morcillo-Rosillo 2014a). The fate of those remaining Spanish nationals became the ultimate test of philosephardism that confirmed the previous conflictual pattern: Spain interceded on behalf of Sephardic Jews from a distance, principally when useful for state interests, but opposed their permanent repatriation even in life-or-death circumstances.

The possession of Spanish nationality nonetheless proved to be lifesaving for Joseph Nehama and the other Salonican Jews who succeeded in being classified as privileged, as nationals of a neutral country. In late 1942 and early 1943, Nazi authorities issued a repatriation ultimatum to Spain and nine other neutral countries, demanding that said countries admit "their" Jews or permit them to be treated as enemy nationals and deported to the East—namely to death camps. Spanish officials offered conflicting responses (Fragkou 2020; Hagouel 2013, 20–31; Rother 2001, 2002; Sáenz-Francés San Baldomero 2009; Schulze 2012). They did not wish to undo the Expulsion edict of 1492 and invite a permanent influx of Jews; some officials expressed old-style Catholic anti-Judaism whereas others feared Jewish Bolshevism. Such officials prevented some

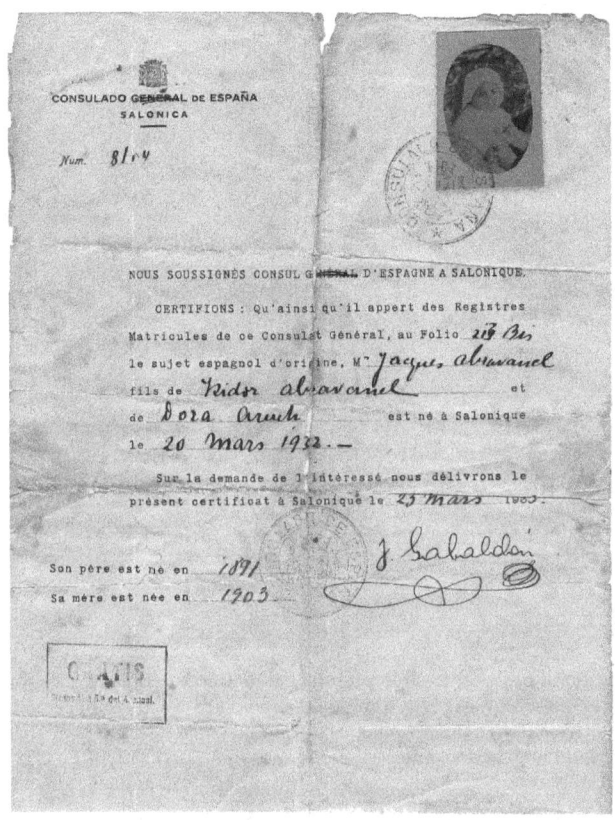

Figure 5.4. Birth registration issued by the Spanish consul of Salonica for Jacques, son of Isidor Abravanel and Dora née Aruch, 1932. Jacques's grandfather Yakov (d. 1939), after whom he was named, was a prominent merchant and notable in the Jewish community of Salonica. Jacques, his parents, and his brother numbered among the 511 Salonican Jews recognized as Spanish nationals at the onset of the Nazi occupation in 1943. Source: Abravanel's granddaughter, Makena Mezistrano, used with permission.

Jews holding Spanish papers from entering the country at the border with France. But they also sought to defend Spain's reputation, sovereignty, and neutrality, and, due to economic rather than humanitarian interests, expressed concerns about the fate of the properties of Spanish nationals.

As during World War I, philosephardism reached its limit with repatriation to Spain. Replicating and intensifying bureaucratic debates over eligibility for Spanish protection that had preoccupied figures like Isaac Alcheh in 1916, this time the Spanish government required more documentation than Nazi officials did for Salonican Jews to prove their Spanish nationality. The German Foreign Ministry was also willing to grant special treatment to those Jews of Spanish and other neutral nationalities—exempt from forced labor, wearing the yellow star, and

Figure 5.5. Spanish passport for Salonican Bergen Belson survivor Jacques Abravanel (1932–2012). After the war, Abravanel returned to Salonica where he became a star soccer player for Iraklis (Hercules) before eventually settling in Seattle, Washington State. Source: Abravanel's granddaughter, Makena Mezistrano, used with permission.

ghettoization (Abravanel 2005)—to protect German economic interests: Spain, for example, supplied wolfram (tungsten ore) to Germany to produce machine tools and armaments (Schulze 2012, 56). But, due to the unwillingness of the Spanish Foreign Ministry to respond to the repatriation ultimatum in a timely manner, the German authorities deported 367 Spanish nationals from Salonica, along with other privileged Jews, namely the Judenrat, on the penultimate of nineteen transports of Jews from the city—not to Auschwitz but rather this time to Bergen Belson, in August 1943. An additional transport of 155 Spanish nationals from Athens to Bergen Belson benefitted from additional privileges of not having the windows on their cattle cars sealed and also received permission for the Spanish consul to provide some food for the treacherous journey (Fragkou 2020, 141).

It remains unknown how many Salonican Jews sought to be recognized as Spanish nationals during the occupation but failed to do so due to the stringency of the Spanish bureaucracy. Because Spanish authorities did not wish to repatriate Jews holding Spanish nationality—a position that angered the British foreign office and that Spanish bureaucrats feared would also harm Spain's image in the United States—the 367 Salonican Jews in Bergen Belson remained there for several months, although they were largely exempt from forced labor and were permitted to contribute to the camp's cultural life; Joseph Nehama gave lectures (Benosiglio 1998, 213). Finally, the American Joint Distribution Committee intervened in 1944, paid for the group to be transferred, piecemeal, to Barcelona and then as rapidly as possible to a refugee camp in Casablanca, where some composed French poetry for the refugee newspaper (Hantzaroula 2021, 142). Only once the first group left Spain was the second group permitted to enter; the third group of 155 Spanish nationals from Athens remained in Bergen Belson until the end of the war. From Casablanca, the American Joint Distribution Committee transferred the Salonican Jews to Gaza, Palestine. Most returned to Greece after the war. Only Salonica's former Spanish vice-consul, Salomon Ezratty, was permitted to remain in Spain (Revah 2014).

Those privileged Jews with Spanish nationality confronted resentment from those Jews who survived Auschwitz-Birkenau and returned to Salonica. A movement even emerged that suspected them of collaboration and sought to exclude them from certain roles in the reconstituted Jewish community (Benveniste 2014, 294–343; Minutes of the General Assembly 1951, Book 2, 4 February 1951, p. 54). In contrast, Spanish nationals themselves expressed gratitude to their saviors. Joseph Nehama's nephew, Princeton University philosopher Alexander Nehamas, born after his father survived the war hidden in the basement of the Spanish Embassy in Athens, retains Spanish nationality today as a sign of gratitude (Nehamas 2020). A child during his internment in Bergen Belson, Isaac Revah successfully petitioned Yad Vashem, the Israeli Holocaust Museum, to recognize Sebastian Romero de Radigales, the Spanish consul general in Athens, as Righteous Among the Nations for ensuring the survival of Greece's Spanish nationals—despite the obstacles posed by the Spanish government (Morcillo-Rosillo 2008a; Revah 2014).

The most creative effort to save Salonican Jews from the death camps extended the racial argument underpinning philosephardism to an extreme. Writing to the German Embassy in Paris in 1942, Sam Lévy, a prominent Salonican journalist who had been an early correspondent of Pulido's and a defender of Judeo-Spanish, argued that as Sephardim, Salonican Jews constituted "Ario-Latins of the Mosaic faith" and that, in effect, they were not racially Jewish and should be exempted from anti-Jewish measures. The German Embassy took the inquiry seriously, commissioned research into the question, and received a reply declaring the claim "completely untenable" and "merely a noteworthy Jewish attempt to use this thesis in order to save themselves from the fate that awaits European Jewry in its entirely" (quotes at Dublon-Knebel 2007, 84–87; Rother 2001).

Those Salonican Jew benefitting from Spanish nationality comprised about 1 percent of the city's total Jewish population on the eve of the German occupation—even though nearly all could have claimed Spanish "blood." But the principal prerequisite for eligibility for Spanish protection did not involve demonstrating descent from Spain, but rather one's economic status and utility for advancing the regeneration of the Spanish nation and enriching the Spanish state. Even though the underpinning philosephardic movement emerged from eugenic thinking and racial fantasies in the work of Pulido and Nordau, the redemptive potential of Sephardic Jews' Spanish blood dissolved in the face of Nazi Germany and a racist Spanish bureaucracy. Nearly all the main figures involved in the Catalan prayerbook project in interwar Salonica who promoted their Spanish heritage as inspiration and justification for their own leadership roles in Greek Salonica—Isaac Alcheh, David Saadi Saltiel, Baruch Ben-Jacob, Leon Gattegno, Isaac Broudo—perished in Auschwitz-Birkenau.

The potent claim about Salonica's Sephardic Jews—"Spaniards we were, Spaniards we are, and Spaniards we will be"—still invoked today by Spanish officials as a sign of Sephardic fidelity to Spain, takes on darker meaning because its author, Isaac Alcheh, one of the most fervent Sephardic advocates of philosephardism, could not count on the Spanish government to save him from extermination. Although blood logic underpinned the rhetoric of philosephardism, perceptions of consanguinity did not trump Spanish nationalist objectives and raison d'état. Just as philosephardism came to be exploited and instrumentalized by both Spanish officials and Sephardic Jews themselves, even the rupture of the Holocaust did not render the rhetoric obsolete. Sephardic Jews continued to draw on philosephardism when useful. The New York–based Salonican-born intellectual, Henry Besso, invoked both Pulido's campaigns and Alcheh's famous quote to justify the establishment of the first Sephardic studies initiative at an American university—at Columbia University, within the Hispanic Institute—when marginalized by the emergent field of Jewish studies in the 1930s and 1940s (Ben-Ur 2009, 161–73; Besso 1981; Díaz-Mas 2017b, 245–47). The paradoxes of philosephardism, its interconnections with antisemitic discourses, and its mutual instrumentalization by Sephardic Jews and Spaniards alike over the first half of the twentieth century—which also shaped the fate of Salonica's Jews with Spanish nationality during World War II—all presaged and make much more intelligible the debates, aspirations, and cynicism around the 2015 Spanish nationality law.

Devin E. Naar is the Isaac Alhadeff Professor in Sephardic Studies, associate professor of history, and faculty at the Stroum Center for Jewish Studies, University of Washington. He is founder and chair of the Sephardic Studies Program, transforming the University of Washington into a major center in the field and the world's largest digital repository of Ladino texts. His book, *Jewish Salonica: Between the Ottoman Empire and Modern Greece*, received the National Jewish Book Award and the Modern Greek Studies Association Award. His current project investigates the multifaceted experiences of Sephardic Jews regarding race, class, and politics in the United States.

References

Abravanel, Eugenia. 2005. Interview by Valia Kravva. Centropa. https://www.centropa.org/biography/eugenia-abravenel.

Alcheh y Saporta, Isaac. 1917. *Los españoles sin patria de Salónica.* Madrid: Rev. de Arch., Bibl., y Museos.

Almanach National. 1915. Salonica: Hôpital de Hirsch.

Alpert, Michael. 2005. "Dr. Angel Pulido and philo-Sephardism in Spain." *Jewish Historical Studies* 40: 105–19.

Álvarez Chillida, Gonzalo. 2002. *El antisemitismo en España: La imagen del judío (1812–2002).* Madrid: Marcial Pons.

———. 2020. "Antisemitism and Philosephardism in Spain, 1880–1945." In *Spain, the Second World War, and the Holocaust*, edited by Sara J. Brenneis and Gina Herrmann, 65–80. Toronto: University of Toronto Press.

Asuero, Pablo Martin. 2007. "The Spanish Consulate in Istanbul and the Protection of the Sephardim (1804–1913)." *Quaderns de la Mediterrania* 88:169–78.

Avni, Haim. 1982. *Spain, the Jews, and Franco.* Philadelphia: Jewish Publication Society of America.

Bayona, Jorge. 2021. "'The Population Wants to Be Completely Free from the Spanish Yoke': A Case of Sephardic Jewish Anticolonial Solidarity from the Ottoman Empire During the Wars of Philippine Independence (1896–1899)." *World History Bulletin* 37, no. 1: 13–16.

Benardete, Mair José. 1952. *Hispanic Culture and Character of the Sephardic Jews.* New York: Hispanic Institute in the United States.

Benosiglio, Maurice. 1998. "Hommage à Joseph Nehama." In *Salonique: Raconte-nous tes histoires*, edited by Jacques Aelion, 209–16. Tarascan: Cousins de Salonique.

Ben-Ur, Aviva. 2009. *Sephardic Jews in America: A Diasporic History.* New York: New York University Press.

———. 2015. "Identity Imperative: Ottoman Jews in Wartime and Interwar Britain." *Immigrants & Minorities* 33: 165–95.

———. 2016. "The 'Spanish Jewish Project:' Reciprocity in an Age of Westernization." In *Languages of Modern Jewish Cultures; Comparative Perspectives*, edited by Joshua L. Miller and Anita Norich, 174–203. Ann Arbor, MI: University of Michigan Press.

Benveniste, Rika. 2014. *Those who Survived: Resistance, Displacement, Return: Jews of Thessaloniki in the 1940s.* Athens: Polis (Greek).

Berthelot, Martine. 1995. *Cien años de presencia judía en la España contemporánea*. Barcelona: KFM Editorial.
Besso, Henry. 1981. "Los sefardíes: españoles sin patria y su lengua." *Nueva Revista de Filología Hispánica* 30, no. 2: 648–65.
Burgers, J. H. 2011. "Max Nordau, Madison Grant, and Racialized Theories of Ideology." *Journal of the History of Ideas* 72, no. 1: 119–40.
Candil, Manuel Mira. 2015. *El olivo que no ardió en Salónica: La historia épica de los Carasso, la saga de sefardíes españoles que sobrevivió a seis guerra y construyó EL IMPERIO DANONE*. Madrid: La Esfera.
Clancy-Smith, Julia. 2011. *Mediterraneans: North Africa and Europe in an Age of Migration, c. 1800–1900*. Berkeley: University of California Press.
Cohen, Julia Phillips. 2014a. *Becoming Ottomans: Sephardi Jews and Imperial Citizenship in the Modern Era*. New York: Oxford University Press.
———. 2014b. "Oriental by Design: Ottoman Jews, Imperial Style, and the Performance of Heritage." *American Historical Review* 119, no. 2: 364–98.
Corcoll, Roberto and Marisa Siguán, eds. 1987. *Homenaje a Elias Canetti*. Barcelona: Promociones y Publicaciones Universitarias.
Covo, Mercado, 1931. "Nuevos detayos sobre las primas estamparias de Saloniko." *El Puevlo*, 20 September 1931.
Davis, Lisa. 1977. "Max Nordau, 'Degeneration' y la decadencia de España." *Cuadernos hispanoamericanos* 326/327: 307–23.
del Arbol, Eduardo Enríquez. 1993. "Masonería y diáspora sefardí en siglo XX: El origen de las logias otomanas (1907–1909)." In *Masonería española y América*, edited by José Antonio Ferrer Benimeli, 551–90. Cáceres: CEHME.
del Pozo, Alba. 2013. "Degeneración, tienes nombre de mujer: género y enfermedad en la cultura del fin del siglo XIX–XX." *Lectora* 19: 137–51.
Díaz, José Belmonte, and Pilar Leseduarte. 2007. *La expulsión de los judíos: auge y ocaso del judaísmo en Sefarad*. Bilbao: Ediciones Beta.
Díaz-Mas, Paloma. 1992. *Sephardim: The Jews from Spain*. Chicago: The University of Chicago Press.
———. 2000. "Repercusión de la campaña de Ángel Pulido en la opinión pública de su época: la respuesta sefardí." In *España y la cultura hispánica en el sureste europeo*, edited by Juan González-Barba. Athens.
———. 2017a. "Sephardim in the Spanish Newspapers during World War I." *El Prezente* 11: 117–32.
———. 2017b. "The Hispanic Legacy and Sephardic Culture: Sephardim and Hispanists in the First Half of the 20th Century." In *Sepharad as Imagined Community: Language, History and Religion from the Early Modern Period to the 21st Century*, edited by Mahir Saul and José Ignacio Hualde, 231–54. New York: Peter Lang.
———. 2018. "La visita a España de Isaac Alcheh y Saporta (1916) y su repercusión en la prensa española." In *Caminos de leche y miel. Jubilee Volume in Honor of Michael Studemund-Halévy*, vol. 2, *Language and Literature*, edited by David M. Bunis, Ivana Vucina Simovic y Corinna Deppner, 315–33. Barcelona, Tirocinio.
———. 2019. "Refugiados sefardíes en Barcelona en 1916." In *Et amicorum: estudios en honor al profesor Carlos Carrete Parrondo*, edited by Efrem Yildiz, 479–92. Salamanca: University of Salamanca.
———. 2020. "Sephardi Women in Ángel Pulido's Correspondence." *Quest* 18: 1–33.
Dublon-Knebel, Irith. 2007. *German Foreign Office Documents on the Holocaust in Greece, 1937–1944*. Tel Aviv: Goldstein-Goren Diaspora Research Center.

Efron, John. 2016. *German Jewry and the Allure of the Sephardic*. Princeton: Princeton University Press.
"El derito de eskojer la nasionalidad." 1916. *El Liberal*, 8 November 1916.
Estrugo, José. 1933. *El retorno a Sefard* [sic]*: un siglo después de la inquisición*. Madrid: Imprenta "Europa."
"Famiyas Tesaloniklias de Barselona tornaron ayer en nuestra sivdad." 1938. *El Mesajero*, 1 June 1938.
Fragkou, Maria. 2020. "Spanish Jews in Bergen-Belsen Camp, 1943–1944: Primary Evidence of Spanish Diplomacy." In *Spain, the Second World War, and the Holocaust*, edited by Sara J. Brenneis and Gina Herrmann, 138–52. Toronto: University of Toronto Press.
Franco, Manuel. 2011. "The Twentieth-Century Portuguese Jews from Salonika: 'Oriental Jews of Portuguese Origin.'" In *Borders and Boundaries in and around Dutch Jewish History*, edited by J. Frishman, D. Wertheim, I. de Haan, and J. Cahen, 111–23. Amsterdam: Askant.
Friedman, Michael. 2019. "Orientalism between Empires: Abraham Shalom Yahuda at the Intersection of Sepharad, Zionism, and Imperialism." *Jewish Quarterly Review*. 109, 3: 435–51.
Gibbons, Fiachra. 2003. "The Attack on Istanbul Jews Is An Attack on Hope Itself." *The Guardian*, 16 November 2003. https://www.theguardian.com/world/2003/nov/17/turkey.comment.
Ginio, Alisa Meyuhas. 2007. "Reencuentro despedida: Dr. Ángel Pulido Fernández y la diáspora sefardí." In *España e Israel. Veinte años después*, edited by Raanan Rein, 57–66. Sevilla: Fundación Tres Culturas del Mediterráneo.
———. 2008. "The Sephardic Diaspora Revisited: Dr. Ángel Pulido Fernández (1852–1932) and His Campaign." In *Identities in an Era of Globalization and Multiculturalism: Latin America in the Jewish World*, edited by Judit Bosker Liwerant, Eliezer Ben-Rafael, Yosef Gorney, and Raanan Rein, 287–96. Leiden: Brill.
Ginio, Eyal. 2006–7. "Perceiving French Presence in the Levant: French Subjects in the Sicily of 18th Century Ottoman Salonica." *South-East Studies* 65–66: 137–64.
———. 2014. "Jews and European Subjects in Eighteenth-Century Salonica: The Ottoman Perspective." *Jewish History* 28, no. 3–4: 289–312.
Gómez-Bravo, Ana. 2020. "The Origins of *Raza*: Racializing Difference in Early Spanish." *Interfaces* 7: 64–114.
Gonzalez, Allyson. 2019. "Abraham S. Yahuda (1877–1951) and the Politics of Modern Jewish Scholarship." *Jewish Quarterly Review* 109, no. 3: 406–33.
Goode, Joshua. 2009. *Impurity of Blood: Defining Race in Spain, 1870–1930*. Baton Rouge: Louisiana State University Press.
Gruss, Susy. 2021. "La guerra civil española en la prensa en judeoespañol de Salónica." In *Ovras son onores. Estudios sefardíes en homenaje a Paloma Díaz-Mas*, edited by Zeljko Jovanovic and María Sánchez Pérez, 121–42. Leioa: Universidad del Pais Vasco.
Hagouel, Paul. 2013. "The History of the Jews of Salonika and the Holocaust: An Exposé." *Sephardic Horizons* 3, no. 3. https://www.sephardichorizons.org/Volume3/Issue3/hagouel.html.
Hantzaroula, Pothiti. 2021. *Child Survivors of the Holocaust in Greece: Memory, Testimony and Subjectivity*. New York: Routledge.
Harrison, Joseph, and Alan Hoyle. 2000. *Spain's 1898 Crisis: Regenerationism, Modernism, Postcolonialism*. Manchester: Manchester University Press.

Hernández Gonzalez, and Maria Belén. 2019. "Carmen de Burgos, Defensora de la Comunidad Sefardita Internacional." *Revista Internacional de Culturas y Literaturas* 22: 122–38.

Hirsch, Emile. 1902. "Prejudice against the Jews." *Reform Advocate*, 12 April 1902, 276–81.

Israel, Jonathan I. 1998. *European Jewry in the Age of Mercantilism, 1550–1750*. Oxford: Littman Library of Jewish Civilization.

Kaya, Dilek Akyakçin. 2020. "Entrepreneurial Networks in the Ottoman Empire: The Case of Osman Inayet." *Proceedings of the Centre for Economic History Research* 5: 265–79.

"La prima estamparia djudia en Saloniko. Eya data de mas de 400 anyos antes. Detayos deskonosidos sovre la estoria de los djidios de Saloniko." 1931. *El Puevlo*, 27 September 1931.

"Las orrores dela gerra sivil en Espanya: loke kontan los 6 djidios suditos elenos, arivados antiyer en Pireo." 1938. *El Mesajero*, 8 April 1938.

"Le retour des Sepharadim." 1933. *L'Avenir Illustré*, 15 January 1933.

"Letra de Barselona: Los djidios en Espanya." 1937. *El Mesajero*, 3 March 1937.

"Los ke fuyen del inferno." 1938. *La Askion*, 8 April 1938.

McDonald, Charles A. 2021. "Rancor: Sephardi Jews, Spanish Citizenship, and the Politics of Sentiment." *Comparative Studies in Society and History* 63, no. 3: 722–51.

Minutes of the General Assembly of Jewish Community of Salonica. 1951. Archive of the Jewish Community of Thessaloniki.

Morcillo-Rosillo, Matilde. 1991. "'Hispania,' Primer revista española en Oriente (1919)." *Ensayos: Revista de la Facultad de Educación de Albacete* 5: 71–77.

———. 1992. "Aproximación al pensamiento del sefardita salonicens. Alberto Samuel Asseo (1912)." *Revista de la Facultad de Humanidades de Jaén* 1, no. 2: 81–92.

———. 1997. "La comunidad sefardí de Salónica después de las guerras balcánicas (1912–1913)." *Sefarad* 57, no. 2: 307–31.

———. 1999. "España y los sefarditas de Salónica durante el incendio de 1917." *Sefarad* 59, no. 2: 353–69.

———. 2004. "Gestión de los diplomáticos Españoles en favor de la Comunidad Sefardita de Grecia durante la primera guerra mundial. Papel desempeñado por el encargado de negocios, Pedro de Prat." In *Proceedings of the Twelfth British Conference on Judeo-Spanish Studies (2001): Sephardic Language, Literature and History*, edited by Hilary Pomeroy and Michael Alpert, 181–90. Leiden: Brill.

———. 2008a. *Sebastián de Romero Radigales y los sefardíes españoles de Grecia durante el holocausto a través de la correspondencia diplomática*. Madrid: Metáfora Ediciones.

———. 2008b. "La communidad sefardita de Salónica: cuestíon del reconocimiento de la nacionalidad española. Desde el final de las gueras balcánicas hasta la segunda gerra mondial." *Sefárdica* 17: 47–56.

———. 2014a. "Política cultural de España en los Balcanes: inventarios de los intereses de España en las comunidades sefardíes de Grecia (1931–1936)." *Miscelánea de Estudios Árabes y Hebraicos. Sección Hebreo* 63: 179–223.

———. 2014b "La diplomacia española y las comunidades sefardíes de Grecia durante el primer tercio del siglo XX." *Cuadernos Judaicos* 31: 116–41.

Muñoz Solla, Ricardo. 2021. "Notas sobre la misión de Isaac Alcheh para la nacionalización española de sefardíes en Salónica (1916–1917)." In *Ovras son onores. Estudios sefardíes en homenaje a Paloma Díaz-Mas*, edited by Zeljko Jovanovic and María Sánchez Pérez, 95–120. Leioa: Universidad del Pais Vasco.

Naar, Devin E. 2011. "Jewish Salonica and the Making of the 'Jerusalem of the Balkans,' 1890–1943." PhD dissertation, Stanford University, Stanford, CA.
———. 2016. *Jewish Salonica: Between the Ottoman Empire and Modern Greece*. Palo Alto: Stanford University Press.
Nehama, Joseph. 1935–78. *Histoire des Israélites de Salonique*. Thessalonique: Communauté Israelite de Thessalonique. 7 vols.
Nehamas, Alexander. 2020. "The Lost Voices of Salonica." *Jewish Review of Books* (Spring).
Nordau, Anna, and Max Nordau. 1943. *Max Nordau: A Biography*. New York: Nordau Committee.
Nordau, Max. 1995 [originally 1903]. "Jewry of Muscles." In *The Jew in the Modern World*, edited by Paul Mendes Flohr, 547–48. New York: Oxford University Press.
———. 1913–14. "Les Israélites de Salonique." *Graecia* 5, no. 38–39: 363–70.
———. 1892. *Degeneration*.
Ojeda-Mata, Maite. 2015. "The Turkish Sephardim of San Antonio Market, Barcelona, 1900–1945." *Journal of Modern Jewish Studies* 14, no. 3: 465–81.
Papamichos Chronakis, Paris. 2017. "Global Conflict, Local Politics. The Jews of Salonica and World War I." In *World War I and the Jews: Conflict and Transformation in Europe, the Middle East, and America*, edited by Jonathan Karp and Marsha Rozenblit, 175–200. New York: Berghahn.
Penslar, Derek. 1996. "From 'Conventional Lies' to Conventional Myths: Max Nordau's Approach to Zionism." *History of European Ideas* 22, no. 3: 217–26.
Perez, Idan. 2019. *Sidur Katalunya ke-minhag K. K. Katalunya*. Jerusalem: Sidur Katalunya.
Pérez, Joseph. 2005. *Los Judíos de España*. Madrid: Marcial Pons.
Philippēs, Dēmētrēs. 2010. *Prophasismos, ekphasismos, pseudophasismos: Hellada, Italia kai Hispania sto mesopolemo*. Thessaloniki: University Studio Press.
Pulido, Angel Fernandez. 1897. *La Pena Capital en España*. Madrid: Enrique Teodoro.
———. 1905. *Españoles sin patria y la raza sefardi*. Madrid.
———. 1923. *Le peuple judéo-espagnol: première base mondiale de l'Espagne*. Trans by Max Nordau. Paris: Le Revue Mondiale.
"Rams di discendenza della famiglia Saporta." 1852. from the Consulato di Spagna en Salonicco, 21 July 1852, donated to the Jewish Museum of Greece, Athens, by Alberto Saporta Beraha.
"Refugees in Spain." 1917. *The Bulletin of the Joint Distribution Committee Representing American Jewish Relief Committee* 1: 66.
Revah, Isaac. 2014. "Testimony of Isaac Revah, on the actions of the Spanish consul in Athens in 1943, Sebastian de Romero Radigales, who obtained the release from Bergen Belson of a group of Spanish Jews." https://esefarad.com/?p=35916.
Rohr, Isabelle. 2005. "Philosephardism and Antisemitism in Turn-of-the-Century Spain." *Historical Reflections / Réflexions Historiques* 31, no. 3: 373–92.
Rother, Bernd. 2001. "Did the Nazis Think the Sephardim Were Jews?" In *Proceedings of the World Congress of Jewish Studies*, 105–13. Jerusalem: World Union of Jewish Studies.
———. 2002. "Spanish Attempts to Rescue Jews from the Holocaust: Lost Opportunities." *Mediterranean Historical Review*, 12, no. 2: 47–68.
Rozen, Minna. 1992. "Strangers in a Strange Land: The Extraterritorial Status of Jews in Italy and the Ottoman Empire in the Sixteenth to Eighteenth Centuries." In *Ottoman and Turkish Jewry; Community and Leadership*, edited by Aron Rodrigue, 123–66. Bloomington: Indiana University Press.

———. 2005. *The Last Ottoman Century and Beyond: The Jews in Turkey and the Balkans, 1808–1945*. 2 vols. Tel Aviv: Tel Aviv University Press.
Sáenz-Francés San Baldomero, Emilio, 2009. "'Not to Be Shown to Researchers': Spanish Foreign Policy towards the Deportation of the Spanish Sephardic Community of Salonica in 1943." In *European Migrants, Diasporas and Indigenous Ethnic Minorities*, edited by Matjaz Klemencic and Mary N. Harris, 211–33. Pisa: Plus-Pisa University Press.
Saltiel, David Saadi and Baruch Ben-Jacob, eds. 1927. *Tefilat Shemuel. Mahzor le-Rosh a-Shana kefi minhag*. Salonica: Asher Mordehai Brudo.
Saporta, Alberto Benandón. 2009. *Live*. Madrid: Cultivalibros.
Sariyannis, Georgios M. 1997. "From Catalonia and Aragon to Greece: The Saporta Family's Relations with Romaniotes and Sephardim on Hellenic Territory." In *The Jewish Communities of Southeastern Europe from the Fifteenth Century to the End of World War II*, edited by I. K. Hassiotis, 473–92. Thessaloniki: Institute for Balkan Studies.
Schapkow, Carsten. 2020. "Max Nordau's View on Sephardic Judaism and the Emergence of Political Zionism." In *Sephardim and Ashkenazim*, edited by Sina Rauschenbach, 209–28. Berlin: De Gruyter Oldenbourg.
Schulze, Rainer. 2012. "The *Heimschaffungsaktion* of 1942–1943: Turkey, Spain and Portugal and Their Responses to the German Offer of Repatriation of their Jewish Citizens." *Holocaust Studies* 18, 2–3: 49–72.
Sciaky, Leon. 2003. *Farewell to Salonica*. Philadelphia: Paul Dry Books.
Segura, Ana Mora. 2020. "El Cervantes llega a Salónica para insuflar vida a la cultura sefardí." *La Vanguardia*, 28 July 2020. https://www.lavanguardia.com/politica/20200728/482572389718/el-cervantes-llega-a-salonica-para-insuflar-vida-a-la-cultura-sefardi.html.
Shaltiel-Gracian, Moshe. 2005. *Shaltiel: One Family's Journey through History*. Chicago: Academy Chicago Publishers.
"Spain as a Jewish Center." 1917. *The American Jewish Chronicle*, 9 March 1917.
Stein, Sarah Abrevaya. 2015. "Citizens of a Fictional Nation: Ottoman-born Jews in France during the First World War." *Past & Present* 226: 227–54.
———. 2016. *Extraterritorial Dreams: European Citizenship, Sephardi Jews, and the Ottoman Twentieth Century*. Chicago: University of Chicago Press.
Trubeta, Sevasti. 2013. *Physical Anthropology, Race and Eugenics in Greece (1880s–1970s)*. Leiden: Brill.
"Turkish Jews Appeal to Spain." 1913. *New York Times*, 10 April 1913.
Un Selanikli. 1916. "La emigrasion en Espanya." *El Liberal*, 14 November 1916.
Vassilikou, Maria. 2000. "Politics of the Jewish Community of Salonika in the Inter-War Years: Party Ideologies and Party Competition." PhD dissertation, University of London, London.
Vlami, Despina. 2009. "Entrepreneurship and Relational Capital in a Levantine Context: Bartolomew Edward Abbott, the 'Father of the Levant Company' in Thessaloniki (Eighteenth–Nineteenth Centuries)." *Historical Review* 6: 129–164.

Chapter 6

"Spanish Jews" and "Friendly Muslims"

The Historical Absence of a Citizenship Campaign for Muslims of Iberian Descent

Elisabeth Bolorinos Allard

When the Spanish reparative citizenship law was passed in 2015, it was framed as an effort not only to reconcile with the descendants of the Jews who were expelled in 1492 but also more widely to reconcile Spain's past with its present vocation to be an open society, in the words of the then Spanish minister of justice. This gesture of atonement for a history of religious intolerance and desire to recuperate the medieval Iberian legacy of multiculturalism, while commendable, made a striking omission (for a discussion of parliamentary debates on this issue, see Aliberti, chap. 3 in this volume). What of the descendants of the Moriscos, Muslim converts to Christianity who were forced to leave Spain under Philip III's Expulsion decree of 1609? The expulsion of 40,000 to 100,000 Jews from the Iberian Peninsula in 1492 was part of Queen Isabel and King Ferdinand's attempt to create a hegemonic Christian identity and erase any traces of Muslim and Jewish influences on the newly unified territories of Spain. Connections between Muslims, Jews, and Christians were deeply intertwined and constantly being reconfigured through intermarriage, frequent conversions and borrowings across faiths, and the continuity of cultural practices associated with Islam and Judaism even after conversion to Christianity (de la Serna 2001; Fletcher 1992; García Arenal 2014; Menocal 2002). Consequently, the impossibility of erasure is evident in the fact that it remained a contentious, ongoing process 115 years later. The Morisco expulsions, which took place between 1609 and 1614, involved the forcible displacement of around 275,000 people (Kassam 2014), many of whom settled in the same coastal regions of North Africa as some of the Sephardi exiles.

While an abundance of scholarship exists on the Sephardi diaspora and the cultural ties that Sephardi communities maintained with Spain, the diasporic framework has rarely been applied to the history of the Moriscos so that much less is known of the group's relationship to Spanish culture after their exile (García-Arenal et al. 2014, 413–41). Currently there are at least five hundred families in Morocco who can trace their origins to the Iberian Peninsula (Kassam, 2014). Although by the nineteenth century they had definitively lost their linguistic ties to Spain and were indistinguishable from their coreligionists, historical documents affirm that the Moriscos who settled in North Africa continued to speak Spanish and Catalan until the mid-eighteenth century, used religious texts written in Spanish, and did not intermarry outside their communities (García Arenal 2014, 286). Natalia Muchnik (2014) has highlighted the commonalities between exiled Morisco and Sephardi populations; both groups maintained cultural and social practices associated with their Iberian heritage, formed a distinct group within the societies that received them, and in later centuries frequently acted as interpreters and diplomats for the Spanish. Both populations were displaced as a result of a discourse of ethno-religious exclusion that some scholars regard as the precursor to modern racism (Anidjar 2014; Carr 2009; Contreras 1997; Yerushalmi 1982). If Spain desired to make amends for this legacy and recover the ideal of *convivencia* (peaceful coexistence) associated with medieval al-Andalus, why has the offer of citizenship not been extended to the descendants of the Moriscos?

In order to answer this question, I will turn to the origins of the Sephardic citizenship campaign, which emerged as part of the philosephardic movement promoted by the Spanish physician and senator Ángel Pulido (1852–1932) in the early twentieth century. Spanish philosephardism, which sought to recover Spain's Jewish legacy and emphasized the bond between the Spanish nation and Sephardi communities worldwide, developed alongside a movement known as Africanism, which sought to recover Spain's Islamic heritage and emphasized the ties between Spain and the Islamic cultures of North Africa, where Spain had colonial aspirations. In what follows I compare the notions of historical, cultural, and biological belonging that underpinned both of these movements and their intersection with colonialist ideology, pan-Hispanism, proto-fascism, and ethno-nationalism in order to explain why a movement to reintegrate Sephardi Jews into the Spanish nation did develop in this historical context, while a movement to reintegrate Muslims of Iberian descent did not.

The Origins of Philosephardism and Africanism

When Islamic and Jewish studies emerged in Spain in the nineteenth century, they formed part of a wider Orientalist cultural movement closely tied up in the liberal nationalist project. This project was to redefine Spanish identity by framing the tolerance and cosmopolitanism of medieval Iberia as essential Spanish values, while the rise of militant Catholicism, the expulsion of the Jews and Moriscos, and the Inquisition were presented as the primary causes of the decline of Spain. Michal Friedman (2011a; 2011b) and Manuela Marín (2009) have shown how Iberian Jewish and Muslim cultures were nationalized in this context, becoming the Jews of Spain and Spanish Islam. Spain's colonial incursions in North Africa, which began in 1859, gave further impetus to this process and extended the interest in recovering the Spanish Islamic and Jewish past beyond the academy and the liberal identity-building agenda into the realms of commerce, industry, and colonial domination. It was the colonization of northern Morocco, which became a protectorate of Spain from 1912 until Moroccan independence in 1956, that consolidated the power structures by which Spain would relate differently to the descendants of the Sephardi and the Moriscos.

Angel Pulido's book, *Españoles sin patria y la raza sefardí* (1905a), played a fundamental role in igniting the interest of prominent politicians and intellectuals from across the political spectrum in reconnecting with the descendants of exiled Iberian Jews. The title of the study reveals the level of belonging that Pulido assigns to the Sephardi; because of their faithful adherence to the Castilian language and cultural traditions for centuries since their expulsion, he argues, these so-called stateless Spaniards should be reintegrated into the Spanish nation as citizens. In fact, he suggests that the Sephardi are more Spanish than many inhabitants of the Iberian Peninsula such as the Basques and Catalans, who do not have as powerful an attachment to the Spanish language or who do not even speak it, a criticism that Pulido directs toward Catalonia in the introduction to the book (5). The senator and philologist Rodolfo Gil, a scholar of both Hebrew and Arabic, makes a similar lament when he writes that the Sephardi "preserve the language that they learned from us like a precious jewel" while in Spain the language is in a state of decline (Revenga 1911, 3). Judeo-Spanish is a dialect that was shaped by exile and belongs to Sephardi culture, not to Spain, but Spanish commentators invariably claimed it as their own. Philosephardic scholars like Gil, the writer and philosopher Miguel de Unamuno, and the philologist Ramón Menéndez Pidal were drawn to the Sephardi in particular because of their preservation of the *romancero viejo* (medieval Castilian ballad) tradition, which had been all but lost in Spain by the twentieth century. The recovery of the Sephardi ballads by Spanish scholars from Jewish communities in northern Morocco formed part of a wider cultural project that sought to achieve national regeneration through a return to traditional or essential values, which were believed to be revealed in their purest form in the classic canon of Castilian literature. The *romancero* was, in the words of the philosopher Ángel Ganivet, "The poetry of the people from which the defining characteristics of the Spanish spirit were born" (1897, 13). Thus, the philosephardic campaign was tied to Castilian nationalism and the ideal of *la hispanidad* (Hispanism) that emerged in the wake of the loss of Spain's last American colonies in the war of 1898 as a vision for Spain's postcolonial cultural hegemony in the Spanish-speaking world, one that posited language as the key form of expression of national and pan-national identities. Unamuno, who devoted himself to theorizing the pan-Hispanic community perhaps more than any other intellectual of this period, expressed this ideal of belonging as follows: "The blood of my spirit is my language, and my homeland is wherever its word resounds" (1911, 144).

If philosephardists focused on language rather than blood as the cord of tradition that connected Spain to the Sephardi,[1] Africanists emphasized the biological ties between Spaniards and North Africans. Joaquin Costa, a prominent fin-de-siècle politician and regenerationalist[2] who was central to the development of Spanish Africanism, coined the term "blood brotherhood" to describe the cultural and ethnic relationship between Spain and Morocco: "We will not find a single fiber in our bodies, nor a sentiment in our souls, nor an idea in our minds . . . which doesn't bear the mark of those Berber and Oriental races that made of the Peninsula a shining beacon in the middle of the Dark Ages . . . the Spanish people, because of their psychology and culture, must seek out the birth of civilization and the elevation of their spirit on the other side of the Strait rather than on the other side of the Pyrenees" (Costa in Martín-Márquez, 2008, 59).

Costa's statement illustrates how vague concepts of biology, culture, and sentiment are conflated in Spanish ethnic nationalism during this period, which developed around the idea that Spain was racially hybrid because of the medieval Iberian past and that this was a national strength rather than a weakness (Goode 2009). The idea that the blood of Africans still flowed through the bodies of Spaniards, where the word "African" actually meant Islamic Maghrebi, was articulated not just by ethnologists but also by public intellectuals and writers, many of whom were also associated with philosephardism. For example, Unamuno asks, "If we are Berbers, why shouldn't we embrace this identity?" (1918, 184-

85) Ernesto Giménez Caballero, a prominent philosephardist and pan-Hispanist and the first ideologue of Spanish fascism, claimed in his memoirs to have discovered his Euro-Moorish spirit in Morocco (1979, 23). It is worth noting that, although Pulido and Giménez Caballero made explicit references to the ethnic ties between Spaniards and the Sephardi, most philosephardic intellectuals at this time omit any mention to ethnic ties with the Sephardi, revealing the ambivalence of Spaniards toward a group that they viewed on the one hand as having profound ties to Spain but on the other hand as ethnically distinct from them.

The medieval Iberian past is a focal point in Africanist discourse just as it is in philosephardic discourse, and the traces of Islamic Iberian culture in Morocco, particularly in its architecture and musical traditions, are used to highlight the brotherhood between Spain and Moroccan Muslims (see Bolorinos Allard 2017; Calderwood 2018). But there is an important divergence between philosephardism and Africanism here: Whereas the Sephardi are posited as faithful guardians of a medieval Castilian culture that has been lost in the Peninsula, albeit with some linguistic corruption of Spanish, Moroccan Muslims are presented as inadequate stewards of an Islamic Iberian cultural heritage that is now in decline and in need of being rescued by Spain, the true guardian of the literature, art, and civilization of "those people who returned to Africa" [the Moriscos] (García Figueras 1928, 20).[3] It might seem that this difference derives from the fact that the Sephardi had preserved their linguistic and cultural ties to Spain, so exalted in pan-Hispanism, while the descendants of the Morisco exiles were virtually indistinguishable within Islamic Maghrebi culture in the early twentieth century. However, in my view the underlying reason for this distinction is that, while philosephardism played an instrumental role within Spanish nationalist and colonialist ideologies, Africanist discourse served the fundamental purpose of justifying Spain's colonial aspirations in Morocco.

Ángel Pulido and Ernesto Giménez Caballero helped give shape to Spanish nationalism through their desire to strengthen connections between Spanish-speaking cultures across the world, which pan-Hispanists soon began to refer to as *la hispanidad*. This concept sought to articulate Spain's cultural influence in a postcolonial context, presenting Spain as the spiritual head of the pan-Hispanic world, and would become integral to Spanish fascism and Francoism. One of its key aims was to protect the Spanish language. Pulido became interested in the Sephardic Jews after meeting Enrique Bejarano, the director of a Sephardic school in Bucharest, during a trip in the Balkans in 1903. As a result of this encounter, he presented a petition to the Spanish government for funding to protect the Spanish (Castilian) language of the Jews in Eastern Europe and the Eastern Mediterranean (Pulido Fernández 1905, 6). Both Pulido and Giménez Caballero believed that national regeneration would be achieved through renewed contact with Sephardic communities across the world. For example, one result of Pulido's campaign was the creation in 1920 of the *Casa universal de los sefardíes* (Universal Sephardi center) to connect prominent individuals in business and culture in Sephardic communities across the world. King Alfonso XIII gave his support to the institution for promoting *la hispanidad* (Ojeda Mata 2012, 64).

Africanism developed parallel to pan-Hispanism and philosephardism within Spanish nationalism. However, unlike these movements it did not focus on restoring cultural ties with Islamic societies in North Africa that had historical links to medieval Iberia, but rather on justifying its colonial conquest of the territory. As colonial administrator and Arabist scholar Tomás García Figueras (1928, 20) writes, "This fruitful period of coexistence between Africans and Andalusians which gives us the ability, unrivalled by any other nation, to serve as [their] true spiritual guide." Costa's famous speech cited earlier on the blood brotherhood of Spain and Morocco was delivered at an event organized in Madrid in 1884 by the newly formed Spanish Society of Africanists and Colonialists to mobilize support for the colonization of North Africa (cited in Martín Márquez 2008, 57). The Arabist scholar, architect, and founder of the Spanish Royal Geographical Society, Eduardo de Saavedra, inaugurated the first Hispano-Moroccan cultural center in 1907 with the following statement: "Our purpose has been the peaceful penetration of Morocco, the civilization of our brothers, our neighbors. . . . Our objective has been merely to protect them and lift them out of their state of backwardness" (Mateo Dieste 1997, 80–81). After the Spanish Civil War, Hispano-Arab culture became a Francoist imperialist discourse that traced the genealogical origins of Spanish colonialism back to Al-Andalus and projected Spain's cultural influence towards the Arab and Muslim world (Calderwood 2019, 100). In contrast, Calderwood notes, philosephardism was a discourse of colonial expansion, but it was one that brought Sephardi communities into its fold (92).

"Spanish Jews" and "Friendly Muslims"

The difference in the power structures established between Spain and the Sephardi Jews and Spain and the descendants of the Moriscos fundamentally shaped its cultural relationship with these two groups. The narrative of cultural commonality with Islamic Maghrebi society was underpinned by an intention to dominate and colonize that society. The narrative of commonality with the Sephardi was underpinned by a desire to benefit culturally and economically from stronger ties with communities that were regarded as an elite class by the Spanish, especially in Morocco, where the Judeo-Spanish speaking Sephardi Jews were viewed as potential commercial intermediaries, informers, and allies in the Spanish colonial enterprise. Pulido and others describe the Sephardi Jews as an aristocracy, "distinguished by their Iberian cultural heritage, wealth, and superior 'character,'" (Salaverría 1929, 1) qualities that could help regenerate Spanish culture and revive its economy (see also Pulido Fernández, 1905). Philosephardism reached its height during the Primo de Rivera dictatorship in 1924 when Spain offered Spanish citizenship to Sephardi Jews in the Balkans who found themselves stateless after the disintegration of the Ottoman Empire following World War I. Many Spanish intellectuals at the time supported the extension of this offer of citizenship to all Sephardi communities worldwide. The colonial newspaper *El Telegrama del Rif* urged in 1919 that Spain begin the reintegration of the Spanish Jews quickly "before other nations reach them first" (1919, 1), and the philosephardic journal *Revista de la raza* declared in 1923 (Cabrera, 21–22) that "any nation that welcomes [the Sephardi] is on the path to greatness." However, the 1924 citizenship law and Pulido's philosephardic campaign in general also generated significant opposition, in particular from Catholic traditionalists. One Franciscan missionary in Morocco who wrote a pamphlet during the Rif War on the so-called Jewish threat to Spain, warned of "the dark schemes of the nation without a state, who infiltrate themselves into Spanish life and lurk in its shadows" (Fernández 1918, 8). Interestingly, Pulido himself was not in favor of offering Spanish citizenship to the Sephardi. In 1924 he wrote, "[I never thought] that the Spanish Jews would come to Spain, creating waves of mass immigration. That is absurd. We do not want it, and they are not asking for it" (cited in Ginio 2014, 276). Regardless of these debates, the fact is that a parallel movement to offer citizenship to Moroccan Muslims of Iberian ancestry never emerged during this period. Nor did it emerge after the Spanish Civil War, when 80,000 Moroccan troops fought as part of Franco's rebel forces and were instrumental to their rapid advance through Spain in the first months of the war (see Madariaga 2002). *La Revista de la raza* clearly states the difference in Spain's position toward Muslims and Jews in Morocco under the Protectorate in an article in 1923 that again gives support to the Sephardic citizenship campaign in no uncertain terms: "The Moor can be and must be our friend, we will not have a moment's peace in the Rif and the Yebala if we do not practice this brotherhood, . . . but the Jew must be more than a brother, he must become a Spaniard" (1923, 15–16).

This comparison between the two cultural groups, lumped under the sweeping stereotypes of the Moor and the Jew, reveals a second fundamental reason why Spain related differently to Muslims of Iberian descent in the early twentieth century. Between 1909 and 1927 Spanish colonial rule in Morocco was characterized by a series of "pacification" campaigns known as the Rif War, which resulted in various military disasters and tremendous casualties for Spain, most notably in the Battles of Barranco del Lobo in 1909 and Annual in 1921. The most formidable resistance movement to both Spanish and French colonialism emerged from the Rif region, under the leadership of Muhamed Abd el-Krim from the Amazigh tribe of Beni Uriaghel. The Amazigh Islamic communities that resisted Spanish colonial penetration also had strong historical ties to Spain; the Islamic armies that conquered most of the Iberian Peninsula from the Visigoths in 711 led by Tariq ibn Ziyad were Amazigh, as were the two successive dynasties that subsequently ruled al-Andalus, the Almoravids (1042–47) and Almohads (1147–276). As a result, from the eighth century until the twentieth century the history of Iberian Muslims and their descendants in North Africa is intertwined in a history of military invasion and conflict with Spain.

Juan Goytisolo (1982), María Rosa de Madariaga (1988), Eloy Martín Corrales (1999, 2002a, 2002b, 2007), and Daniela Flesler (2008; Flesler and Melgosa, 2003), among others, have highlighted the ambivalence of the figure of the Moor, with which the Moriscos are associated in the Spanish collective imaginary. The parallel images of the fraternal, nostalgic, and noble Moor and the attacking or invading violent Moor continue to have a presence in Spanish society. Flesler (2008) in particular has argued that contemporary Moroccan immigrants have become conceptually collapsed into the category of the imaginary and threatening Moor as an invading Other. Yet Flesler also cites Sara Ahmed's theory on cultural encounters in which she argues that in order for a stranger to be constituted as such there needs to be a recognition, and that that recognition is dependent on a prior history of encounters (Ahmed 2000). The history of the encounters between Christian and Muslim Iberians and between Spaniards and Islamic North Africans is characterized by the historical myth of *convivencia*, but also by moments of violent conflict and shifting military alliances. When the large-scale migration of Granadan and Valencian Moriscos to North Africa began after the fall of Granada in 1492, many of these migrants became involved in piracy alongside Berber, Algerian, and Tunisian corsairs who threatened the coasts of the Iberian Peninsula for the next two centuries (Madariaga 1988, 580). Over the course of the sixteenth century, Morisco communities in both Spain and Morocco made various petitions to Ottoman and

Moroccan sultans to undertake a reconquest of the territory of the old kingdom of Granada (García Arenal 2014, 15). The Morisco rebellion in the Alpujarras (1568–71), a bitter conflict that is often described as a civil war, further solidified the view of the Moriscos as a military threat, rightly or wrongly. It is also a fact that many of the Moriscos expelled between 1609 and 1614 were fervent Catholics who were not considered an integral part of the populations in North Africa that received them for many years, suffered violent persecution for their faith, and tried to return to Spain.[4] But, in early modern Spain, the threat of an invasion of an Islamic army of Moriscos allied with the corsairs of North Africa or the powerful navies of the Ottoman Empire, though amplified in the climate of religious intolerance and ethnocultural prejudice of Inquisitorial Spain, was not altogether imaginary. From the nineteenth century on, as Spain began its colonial incursions in North Africa, it once again faced an Islamic attacker in the Moroccan resistance to colonial penetration in the African wars of 1859–60, 1893, and 1909–27. The encounter with the Amazigh insurgents on the battlefields of Morocco, especially at Annual, where 15,000 Spanish soldiers were killed in less than two weeks and Moroccan colonial troops turned their guns on their officers and joined the insurrectionary forces (Balfour 2002, 79), revived the stereotype of the threating Moor. In fact, Moroccan leaders of the resistance movement framed the conflict as a holy war against the European enemies of Islam (see Willis 2012). The colonial encounter was thus mediated by a series of past encounters that involved violent conflict and the fear of invasion or treason.

These encounters positioned Muslim Moroccans, including those with ancestral ties to the Iberian Peninsula, as enemies of the Spanish nation even as Spanish-Arab brotherhood was emphasized in Africanist discourse. The ambivalence of this discourse is captured in the distinction often made in the Spanish press during the Rif War between *moros amigos* (friendly Moors) and *moros enemigos* (enemy Moors). These two categories were constantly shifting because of the fluid structure of Riffian tribal alliances with each other and with the Spanish colonial authorities, which was further unbalanced by the Spanish policy of divide and rule (Balfour 2002, 22). All of this reinforced stereotypes of Moroccans as canny and untrustworthy. Even General Franco, the great proponent of Spanish-Arab brotherhood, was cited by one newspaper in 1926 as follows: "General Franco knows the Moors well and he has warned us that they can turn in a second from friendship to enmity, from submission to rebellion, from surrender to attack" (Mirabal 1926, 1).

In contrast to the Moriscos, the Jewish converso community in Inquisitorial Spain did not ever maintain ties with a foreign army, and there were no converso revolts, although it should be noted that exiled Iberian Jews on the North African Coast were involved in corsair activities and the trading of slaves alongside Moriscos (García Arenal 2014, 63). However, where the Moriscos were primarily seen as a military threat, Jewish conversos were regarded as a spiritual threat. Fears over crypto-Judaism possessed Spain to such a degree that they led to the Inquisition and the blood purity statutes of sixteenth century Spain and Spanish America, which prohibited individuals of Jewish descent from practicing certain professions or holding public office. However, when Spain attempted to colonize Morocco in the African wars of 1859–60 and 1893, the Sephardi minority welcomed them, hoping to escape the discrimination they had suffered under the Sultanate in recent decades (Ojeda Mata 2012, 63). In fact, Spanish accounts of the conquest of Tétouan in 1860 and later of Chefchauen in 1919 mythologized the image of the Jewish community emotively greeting the Spanish, weeping, and bringing out the keys to their ancestral homes in Spain (see, e.g., Núñez de Arce 1860). If the loyalty of Moroccan Muslims was constantly in question, the loyalty of the Sephardi to Spain was portrayed as unwavering, to the extent that the nostalgia for Sephardi Jews was conflated with nationalist, even protofascist ideals of patriotism (see Bolorinos Allard 2021). The preservation of cultural ties is offered as evidence of their devotion to Spain and described as "the highest patriotic ideal" and "living passion for the homeland" (Cabrera 1923, 22–23), "inextinguishable love for Spain" (Azorín 1929, 3), and "intense, traditional affection" (Yuste 1928, 20). However, it should be noted that Spain's relationship with the Sephardi under the Protectorate was also marked by ambivalence (see Calderwood 2019; Ojeda Mata 2012; Rohr 2007). The image of the Moroccan *juderías* (Jewish quarters) as places of disease and physical and moral corruption and other antisemitic stereotypes about Jewish avarice and usury appear across fictional and nonfictional accounts of the Spanish Protectorate in the early twentieth century, even in the writing of intellectuals associated with philosephardism such as Giménez Caballero and the novelist and feminist activist Carmen de Burgos (Bolorinos Allard 2021). Calderwood (2019) notes the continuation of philosephardic policies alongside the marked antisemitism of the Franco regime, which presented the worldwide Jewish community alongside communists, freemasons, and Protestants as members of an international conspiracy that threatened the Spanish nation. Spain has still not overcome this legacy of antisemitism; according to recent surveys by the Anti-Defamation League and the Pew Research Center, the Spanish public still harbors many antisemitic stereotypes, more than other Western European countries (Adato 2019).

Conclusion

Philosephardism and Africanism in early twentieth-century Spain nationalize both the Sephardi and the Morisco cultural legacy, but ultimately only the Sephardi come to be regarded as *judíos españoles* (Spanish Jews), a position that allows for the groundwork to be laid for the reparative citizenship movement or reconciliation, as it is referred to in Spain. The term "*judío español*" is used by early advocates of offering Spanish citizenship to the descendants of exiled Sephardi across the world, but it is also used more generally by nationalist, pan-Hispanist intellectuals to emphasize the closeness of Sephardi culture to Spain because of their preservation of the Castilian language and cultural traditions. The fact that Jewish communities in the Maghreb were not involved in the violent resistance movement to Spanish colonialism obviously resulted in them being portrayed then, and remembered now, in a more positive light. Moroccan Jews had suffered discrimination under the sultanate in the decades before the Spanish arrived (Ojeda Mata 2012, 63). Sources from the colonial period suggest that the relationship between Muslim and Jewish communities in the cities of the Protectorate was tense. For example, an article written by Franco in the *Revista de tropas coloniales* in 1926 describes a violent attack on the Jewish community of Chefchauen, who were seen as collaborators with the Spanish, after Spanish troops withdrew from the city in 1924 (Franco Bahamonde 1926, 6). Perhaps the protection of the Spanish against these types of attacks was a motive for prominent members of the Sephardi community to serve as go-betweens for the Spanish. During the Spanish Civil War, some Jewish communities in Morocco openly supported the nationalist cause (González García 2014, 269), but this may have been out of fear of persecution after the war, given the wide circulation of Francoist antisemitic propaganda that framed the Republic as a "Judeo-masonic conspiracy to destroy Spain."[5] In Spain, like in the rest of Europe in the modern period, antisemitic discourses fundamentally differed from colonialist discourses in the sense that they projected onto the Jews profound anxieties about modernity, secularism, and the ideologies it produced, especially Marxism, rather than portraying them as primitive or backward. The same association of the Jews with progress and modernity appears in philosephardic discourses, as I have shown, but in this case the association is positive and potentially regenerative rather than degenerative.

Although the idea of *Islam español* (Spanish Islam) is frequently invoked to describe the Islamic Iberian past and its cultural traces in Morocco, the term "Spanish Muslim" is never applied to Moroccan descendants of the Moriscos, nor are there any concerted attempts to draw out this group from within Maghrebi Islamic society as a whole. This recent history of colonial domination has profoundly shaped Spanish cultural attitudes toward North African Muslims, including the descendants of the Moriscos. Moroccan Muslims, in particular the Amazigh communities of the Rif, were regarded as primitive societies to be subjugated. The vestiges of this colonial relationship remain, I would argue, in an attitude of superiority towards North Africans and their culture that persists in Spain. Collective memory of the violent encounter with the Islamic Riffian resistance in Morocco further problematizes the narrative of cultural commonality with the descendants of the Moriscos. The rise of Islamic extremism in the twenty-first century and the radicalization of some European Muslims to the terrorist agenda of the Islamic State have exacerbated the deeply rooted cultural prejudice against Muslims as violent and duplicitous, as Eloy Martín Corrales writes: "The sense of mistrust and fear of Muslims remains a dominant cultural sentiment" (2004, 49). In particular, the image of the contemporary North African immigrant as an invading Other has been revived in light of the infamous call made by Osama bin Laden and later by the Islamic State (Daesh) to their followers to reclaim the lost territories of Al-Andalus. This image is integral to the anti-immigrant discourse of Santiago Abascal's far-right party Vox, the fastest-growing party in Spain in the second decade of the twentieth century, who portray illegal immigration as an invasion of terrorists.[6]

In contrast, Vox advocates the establishment of immigration quotas that would prioritize those nations that share the Spanish language and "important ties of friendship and culture" with Spain (Mayor Ortega 2019), which are essentially the criteria of the reparative citizenship law. The fact that there was broad consensus across the political spectrum for the 2015 Sephardi citizenship law suggests that Vox's ideas about which cultures are compatible with Spain and which are not may be much more widespread in Spanish society. The idea that Muslim immigrants, either of Iberian heritage or not, are culturally incompatible is not an explicit stance that has ever been taken by a Spanish government since 1975, but it is an underlying social attitude that the Spanish right has mobilized. In contrast, the narrative of cultural commonality with the Sephardi has survived. This is despite ambivalent cultural attitudes toward the Sephardi because of their lack of involvement in the colonial conflicts but also because, during the period of the Spanish colonization of Morocco, this cultural group was never constructed as backward and in need of civilizing, but rather as a group that had maintained a cultural identity that Spanish nationalists, both liberals and conservative, idealized and admired. The omission of the Moriscos from the 2015 citizenship law ultimately reveals how Spain continues to conceive of its relationship with

Islamic and Jewish societies in profoundly different ways and the extent to which these relationships continue to be mediated by encounters, both real and imagined, from the medieval Iberian past and the more recent colonial past.

Elisabeth Bolorinos Allard holds a permanent post in Peninsular Spanish Studies at the University of Bristol. Her book *Spanish National Identity, Colonial Power, and the Portrayal of Muslims and Jews during the Rif War (1909–27)* (Tamesis 2021), examines Spanish visual and textual discourses on Muslim and Jewish cultures in colonial Morocco in the early twentieth century, drawing out questions about Spain's own cultural identity that emerged as a result of its contact with North Africa.

Notes

1. The term "cord of tradition" was used by the High Commissioner of the colonial administration in Morocco, General Gómez Jordana, in an article on the Moroccan Jews ("Los hebreos en Marruecos" 1919, 1).
2. Regeneracionismo was a movement of intellectuals who sought to understand and propose social and political remedies for the decline of the Spanish nation.
3. "Habíamos quedado *nosotros* como depositarios de todos los valores espirituales del pueblo retornado a África (literatura, artes, civilización)."
4. For example, in 1631 the Morisco inhabitants of the Moroccan city of Salé negotiated with the Spanish authorities in an attempt to hand over control of the town's port in exchange for the right to return to their hometowns in Spain (García Arenal 2014, 326).
5. For an in-depth study of Spanish antisemitism during this period, see Álvarez Chillida (2002).
6. "¿Qué opina VOX sobre la inmigración?" (2018). The portrayal of immigrants as invaders is of course not limited to Spanish far-right nationalism. Donald Trump has repeatedly referred to immigrants at the US border as a "Hispanic invasion." See White House (2018).

References

Adato, Kiku. 2019. "Spain's Attempt to Atone for a 500-Year-Old Sin." *The Atlantic*, 21 September 2019. https://www.theatlantic.com/international/archive/2019/09/spain-offers-citizenship-sephardic-jews/598258.
Ahmed, Sarah. 2000. *Strange Encounters: Embodied Others in Post-Coloniality*. London: Routledge.
Álvarez Chillida, Gonzalo. 2002. *El antisemitismo en España: la imagen del judío, 1812–2002*. Madrid: Marcial Pons.
Anidjar, Gil. 2014. *Blood: A Critique of Christianity*. New York: Columbia University Press.
Azorín, 1929. "Hebreos españoles: patriotismo." *ABC*, 2 August: 3.

Balfour, Sebastian. 2002. *Deadly Embrace: Morocco and the Road to the Spanish Civil War*. Oxford: Oxford University Press.

Bolorinos Allard, Elisabeth. 2017. "Visualizing 'Moorish' Traces within Spain: Orientalism and Medievalist Nostalgia in Spanish Colonial Photojournalism 1909–33." *Art in Translation* 9, no. 1: 114–33.

———. 2021. *Spanish National Identity, Colonial Power, and the Portrayal of Muslims and Jews during the Rif War*. Woodbridge: Tamesis.

Cabrera, Francisco de A. 1923. "La acción de España: los hebreos." *Revista de la raza* (January): 21–22.

Calderwood, Eric. 2018. *Colonial al-Andalus: Spain and the Making of Modern Moroccan Culture*, Cambridge: Harvard University Press.

———. 2019. "Moroccan Jews and the Spanish Colonial Imaginary, 1903–1951." *Journal of North African Studies* 24, no. 1: 86–110.

Carr, Matthew. 2009. *Blood and Faith: The Purging of Muslim Spain*. London: Hurst.

Contreras, Jaime. 1997. "The Urban Conversos in Spain After the Expulsion." In *The Jews of Spain and the Expulsion of 1492*, edited by Moshe Lazar and Stephen Haliczer, 289–98. Lancaster: Labyrinthos.

Costa, Joaquin. 1949. "Los intereses de España en Marruecos." In *África a través del pensamiento español: (de Isabel la Católica a Franco)*, edited by Ángel Flores Morales, 141–84. Madrid: Consejo Superior de Investigaciones Científicas, Instituto de Estudios Africanos.

de la Serna, Alfonso. 2001. *Al Sur de Tarifa: Marruecos-España, Un malentendido histórico*. Madrid: Marcial Pons.

Fernández, Africano. 1918. *España en África y el problema judío: apuntes de un testigo desde 1915 a 1918*. Santiago de Compostela: El Eco Franciscano.

Flesler, Daniela. 2008. *The Return of the Moor: Spanish Responses to Contemporary Moroccan Immigration*. West Lafayette: Purdue University Press.

Flesler, Daniela, and Adrián Pérez Melgosa. 2003. "Battles of Identity, or Playing 'Guest' and 'Host': The Festivals of Moors and Christians in the Context of Moroccan Immigration in Spain." *Journal of Spanish Cultural Studies* 4, no. 2: 151–68.

Fletcher, Richard. 1992. *Moorish Spain*. Berkeley: University of California Press.

Flores Morales, Ángel. 1949. *África a través del pensamiento español: (de Isabel la Católica a Franco*. Madrid: Consejo Superior de Investigaciones Científicas, Instituto de Estudios Africanos.

Franco Bahamonde, Francisco. 1926. "Chefchaouen la Triste." *África* (July): 6.

Friedman, Michal. 2011. "Jewish History as 'Historia Patria': José Amador de los Ríos and the History of the Jews of Spain." *Jewish Social Studies: History, Culture, Society* 18, no. 1: 88–126.

———. 2011. "Reconquering 'Sepharad': Hispanism and Proto-Fascism in Giménez Caballero's Sephardist Crusade." *Journal of Spanish Cultural Studies* 12, no. 1: 35–60.

Ganivet, Ángel. 1897. *Idearium español*. Granada.

García Figueras, Tomás. 1928. "Recuerdos de la campaña." *África* (November): 20.

García-Arenal, Mercedes. 2014. "The Moriscos in Morocco: From Granadan Immigration to the Hornacheros of Salé." In *The Expulsion of the Moriscos from Spain: A Mediterranean Diaspora*. Edited by Mercedes García-Arenal and Gerard A. Wiegers. Leiden: Brill: 286–329.

García-Arenal, Mercedes and Gerard A. Wiegers, eds. 2014. *The Expulsion of the Moriscos from Spain: A Mediterranean Diaspora*. Translated by Consuelo López-Morillas and Martin Beagles. Leiden: Brill.

Giménez Caballero, Ernesto. 1979. *Memorias de un dictador.* Barcelona: Planeta.
Ginio, Alisa Meyuhas. 2014. *Between Sepharad and Jerusalem: History, Identity, and Memory of the Sephardim.* Leiden: Brill.
González García, Isidro. 2014. *Los judíos y España después de la expulsión. Desde 1492 hasta nuestros días.* Córdoba: Editorial Almuzara.
Goode, Joshua. 2009. *Impurity of Blood: Defining Race in Spain, 1870-1930.* Baton Rouge: Louisiana State University Press.
Goytisolo, Juan. 1982. *Crónicas sarracinas.* Barcelona: Ruedo Ibérico.
Kassam, Ashifa. 2014. "If Spain Welcomes Back Its Jews, Will Its Muslims Be Next?" *The Guardian*, 24 February 2014. https://www.theguardian.com/world/2014/feb/24/spain-sephardic-jews-islam-muslim.
"Los hebreos en Marruecos." *El Telegrama del Rif*, 27 October 1919.
Madariaga, Maria Rosa de. 1988. "Imagen del moro en la memoria colectiva del pueblo español y retorno del moro en la Guerra Civil de 1936." *Revista internacional de sociología* 46, no. 4: 575–600.
———. 2002. *Los moros que trajo Franco: la intervención de tropas coloniales en la guerra civil española.* Barcelona: Ediciones Martínez Roca.
Marín, Manuela. 2009. *Al-Andalus/ España: Historiografías En Contraste: Siglos XVII–XXI.* Madrid: Casa De Velázquez.
Martín Corrales, Eloy. 1999. "Imágenes del protectorado de Marruecos en la pintura, el grabado, el dibujo, la fotografía, y el cine". In *España en Marruecos (1912-1956). Discursos e intervención territorial*, edited by Joan Nogue and José Luis Villanova. Lleida: Milenio.
———. 2002a. "Entre el 'moro' violador y el 'moro' seductor: la imagen de los marroquíes en la guerra civil según las fuerzas republicanas." In *Antropología y antropólogos en Marruecos: Homenaje a David M. Hart*, edited by Ángeles Ramírez and Bernabé López García, 221–36. Barcelona: Bellatierra.
———. 2002b. *La Imagen Del Magrebí En España: Una Perspectiva Histórica, Siglos XVI–XX.* Barcelona: Bellaterra.
———. 2004. "Morophobia/Islamophobia and Morophilia/Islamophilia in 21st-Century Spain." *Revista CIDOB D'afers Internacionals* 66–67: 39–51.
———. 2007. *Marruecos y los marroquíes en la propaganda oficial del protectorado (1912–1956).* Madrid: Casa de Velázquez.
Martín Márquez, Susan. 2008. *Disorientations: Spanish Colonialism in Africa and the Performance of Identity.* New Haven, CT: Yale University Press.
Martínez Ruiz, José (Azorín). 1929. "Hebreos españoles: patriotismo." *ABC*, 2 August 1929: 3.
Mateo Dieste, Josep Lluís. 1997. *El moro entre los primitivos: el caso del protectorado español en Marruecos.* Barcelona: Fundación La Caixa.
Mayor Ortega, Leonor. 2019. "Vox quiere privilegiar la inmigración procedente de América Latina." *La Vanguardia*, 29 March 2019. https://www.lavanguardia.com/politica/20190329/461317050343/vox-santiago-abascal-inmigracion.html.
Menocal, María Rosa. 2002. *The Ornament of the World: How Muslims, Jews, and Christians Created a Culture of Tolerance in Medieval Spain.* New York: Little.
Mirabal. 1926. "La situación en Marruecos: la táctica de sentido común." *El siglo futuro*, 5 February 1926.
Muchnik, Natalia. 2014. "Judeoconversos and Moriscos in the Diaspora." In *The Expulsion of the Moriscos from Spain*, edited by Mercedes García-Arenal and Gerard A. Weigers. Leiden: Brill: 413–39.

Núñez de Arce, Gaspar. 1860. *Recuerdos de la campaña de África.* Madrid: Editorial José M. Rosés.

Ojeda Mata, Maite. 2012. *Identidades ambivalentes: Sefardíes en la España contemporánea.* Madrid: Sefarad Editores.

Pulido Fernández, Ángel. *Españoles sin patria y la raza sefardí.* Madrid: Establecimiento tipográfico de E. Teodoro.

"¿Qué opina VOX sobre la inmigración?" 2018. Video. YouTube. https://www.youtube.com/watch?v=ttVEDm1cr0E.

Revenga, Emilio Ferrez. 1911. "Romancero judeo-español." *El Heraldo de Madrid,* 29 August: 3.

Rohr, Isabelle. 2007. *The Spanish Right and the Jews, 1898–1945: Antisemitism and Opportunism.* Brighton: Sussex Academic.

Salaverría, José María. 1929. "Interpretaciones: los desterrados." *ABC,* 18 July 1929.

Unamuno, Miguel de. 1918. "Sobre la europeización." Publicaciones de la Residencia de Estudiantes. Madrid.

———. 1911. *Rosario de Sonetos Líricos.* Madrid: Imprenta Española.

White House. 2018. "Remarks by President Trump on the Illegal Immigration Crisis and Border Security." White House, Washington, DC. https://trumpwhitehouse.archives.gov/briefings-statements/remarks-president-trump-illegal-immigration-crisis-border-security.

Willis, Michael J. 2012. *Politics and Power in the Maghreb: Algeria, Tunisia and Morocco from Independence to the Arab Spring.* London: Hurst.

Yerushalmi, Yosef Hayim. 1982. *Assimilation and Racial Anti-Semitism: The Iberian and the German Models.* New York: Leo Baeck Memorial Lecture.

Yuste, Juan B. 1928. "La construcción de una iglesia española en Jerusalén." *ABC,* 6 April.

Chapter 7

Personal Essay
The Story of a Spanish Dönme

Uluç Özüyener

"Come, *chico*. I have a secret to tell you," said my youngest aunt. *Chico* was what my family used to call me when I was a child growing up in Turkey in the 1980s. Hesitant, she whispered in my ear, "We are Yahudi Dönmesi (Jewish converts), but this needs to remain a secret. Do not tell anybody, especially your mom. She would kill me if she found out that I told you this."

A secret? It was my first one. I was a tight-lipped kid by nature, with no compulsion to share anything with others. Yet I did not know how to handle this information, peculiarly labeled as a secret, and I ended up going straight to my mother and telling her what I had sworn to keep to myself: that we were Yahudi Dönmesi. I pronounced the freshly heard term in a completely rote way, because its connotation was unknown to me. In all likelihood, this was the reason for my short-lived discretion: nothing compelled me to keep it inside.

In our family, my mother was always known for being judicious and phlegmatic. She maintained her calm upon hearing my unexpected comment. Nevertheless, I could tell she was bothered. With a serious tone, she said, "Never use those words at home or outside."

I did not know the meaning of Yahudi. We were raised secular and distant from any belief system; we had no indication of any religion in our house. The word "Dönme" could imply the meaning of turning or turned, but most definitely for me it did not evoke anything religious. It was apparent that these two words together were troublesome, and on the few occasions they were spoken, they caused a baffling fluster in the family. I would spend years guarding them while mentally trying to riddle out the secret I was told in my youth. It was not until my early twenties, while studying at a college in Istanbul, that I dared invoke those two words together again.

Although I didn't know it then, my journey to becoming a Spanish Dönme began with this discrete puzzle piece. It was a tiny spark in the absence of any knowledge, but it helped me realize something important: my family was different from the bulk of society. In my youth, I continued to add more bits to my knowledge base as I listened to vague implications. But because nothing was explained clearly to me, I was unable to put the pieces together in a meaningful fashion.

Some mornings, my grandmother would shout, "Bonjour, petit. Tu as perdu ta mère?" (Good morning, little boy. Did you lose your mom?). She lived with us and had both Alzheimer's and Parkinson's diseases. I would find her, as usual, sitting on her single sofa with a piece of white cloth tied around her waist and fastened to the sofa to prevent her from falling. Even though she was not able to walk, she would sometimes attempt to stand up to visit with old friends, some of whom were not living in our town anymore and some who were no longer alive. Sadly, the Alzheimer's made it difficult for her to recognize her family members and friends.

Due to her illness, she randomly told old family stories, mostly from Salonica—or, as we referred to it, Selanik—the city from which she migrated during the Greek-Turkish Population Exchange of 1923. She was proud of the Turkish republic's founder, Mustafa Kemal Atatürk, who was also from Selanik. According to my grandmother, Atatürk knew our family and practiced French with my great-grandmother who was a French teacher at a school established by Dönmes.

One day, my grandmother told me a mysterious childhood story. Before departing from Selanik, she said, she had attended a relative's funeral with her family. They were in a building that looked to her like a small temple, but it was not a mosque or church. At a gathering there, probably a prayer room, everyone wore one type of dull-colored clothing that she had not seen before. Everyone started speaking a language that she had never heard before.

This was especially strange because my grandmother was fluent in French, Greek, and Turkish, and she also spoke some Italian. Coexisting cultures had flourished in the metropolitan city of Ottoman Selanik, and many Dönme families were multicultural and multilingual. Some Dönmes were business people, like those in my family, and they had commercial ties to Europe. Therefore, it was odd that my grandmother could not recognize this mysterious language in a family with such a wealth of culture. But in all probability, this was because it was used on special occasions and only among the adults. Looking back, I wonder if they were speaking Ladino, the language often used in our sect's hymns and prayers.

In my teenage years, when she was still well, my grandmother gave me an unusual piece of advice: "You should memorize the Muslim prayer "Āyat al-Kursī" (The throne verse), as it might be useful when you find yourself in a difficult situation." She added, "I know it: listen." A prayer? In a secular family? It was a strange request. Still, I listened to her recite it, and I memorized it without knowing the meaning of the Arabic words I mumbled. Strangely, to date, I still know the prayer by heart, and I still do not know the meaning.

During my college years, my grandmother's memory started deteriorating in a fast-paced fashion. Often, she gave random answers to my questions . . . except for one. When I asked her what she meant by the "difficult situation" regarding the prayer, she said, "You might find yourself in a group of Muslims where you need to prove that you are a Muslim, too." My grandmother departed this earth in 1995 and left me with corner pieces of the puzzle that I ended up shelving in my memory until I was more mature and could make sense out of them. Over the years, my eagerness to learn about our true identity led me to replace all the novels in my library with sources covering the pre- and post-Inquisition period, Sabetay Sevi and his movement, and the Dönmes. I also have been learning from the culturally and theologically engaged Dönmes, oral traditions, and the artifacts preserved to date such as prayers, hymns, and genealogical trees.

My Dönme History

The word "Dönme" means converted, and is commonly used to describe the subset group of Sabbateans, followers of Sabetay Sevi, living mostly in Turkey, who also refer to themselves as Maaminim (Hebrew for believers). In today's Turkey, Dönme means more than its original definition, since it has the derogatory connotation of turncoat. However, Dönme is also adopted internally within the family, as my aunt did when she said in a hushed voice, "We are Yahudi Dönmesi [Jewish converts]."

While my own journey started with this whisper, our story began many centuries ago in the medieval Spanish kingdom of Aragon. According to the papal *regesta* (register) of the pre-Inquisition period, one of my ancestors, Samuel Passarell, fled Zaragoza with other Jews due to the socioeconomic restrictions they faced, and became a resident of Morvedre, near Valencia. Samuel was a wealthy businessman and a moneylender who was compelled to lend money to King Alfonso and the community many times in the mid-1200s.

According to the surviving records of the Inquisition period, the descendants of the Passarells scattered and migrated to Murcia, Toledo, and Majorca around the beginning of the 1390s. Perhaps these were not coincidental migrations: the massacre of Jews in 1391 in Valencia caused my ancestors to flee and disperse to many Spanish and Portuguese cities. The Passarell families that were able to keep body and soul together were split into branches.

My ancestors' journey in the following years took them to Livorno, the port city of Italy. After living there for decades in the sixteenth century, they migrated to a welcoming Ottoman cosmopolitan city, Selanik, then, in the twentieth century, to beautiful Istanbul. They were among the Jews of Selanik who became devotees of Sevi and whose loyalty was sealed with their public acceptance of Islam following their messiah's conversion in 1666. This permanently changed the way they lived in their societies, from their appearance to the adoption of new Turkish names and public identity as Muslims; the continuation of Jewish customs in secret, including the use of the Ladino language; Sabbeatean belief and rituals; and endogamy, to name a few ways.

An important and recurring character in my grandmother's stories of Selanik was her great-uncle, Mehmed Esad Dede. He was known for frequently organizing feasts where his apprentices gathered. The many needy people from the neighborhood were also welcomed to join the feast with no question. After the supper, where there was plenty of food to eat and *rakı* to drink, Mehmed Esad Dede used to play his oud and sing his poems about loving people and Allah. The title "Dede" is granted to a spiritual teacher in the Mevlevi Order in mainstream Muslim Sufism. Mehmed Esad earned this title after six years of religious studies in Konya, the city of Mevlevis. Hüseyin Vassaf, a student and admirer of the Dede, wrote about him in his manuscript, *Esadnâme*. He reported that my great-grand-uncle was born in Selanik in 1843 to a Jewish family named Paşârals, who later converted to Islam. While this last name had various spellings, including Passarell as it was used in Spain, my family dropped it because Muslim Turks never used last names in the Ottoman era.

A person with a Jewish background becoming a Sufi Dede may seem odd. Yet, the Jewish mystical tradition, the Kabbalah, and its central text, the Zohar[1], have always been at the center of Dönme theology. The Kabbalah and Sufism share a common goal of understanding the unity of existence and helping to enlighten humanity to ultimately reach perfection. For various reasons, the three sects of Dönmes grew close to three different Sufi orders: Yakubi Dönmes to Melamis, Karakaş Dönmes to Bektaşis, and Kapancı Dönmes, my sect, to Mevlevis. Following the Great Fire of Selanik in 1917 and the Greek-Turkish Population Exchange of 1923, two important events that caused migrations to what became the territory of the Republic of Turkey, more Dönmes followed the Sufi orders. This facilitated a smoother cultural blending in the new land. Given this background, my great-grand-uncle Mehmet Esad Dede's involvement with Mevlevis is not so surprising.

Despite all the coexistence and syncretism that took place for centuries in Selanik and later in Istanbul, much of Dönme culture and identity has been kept secret. While the observant among the Dönme community have considered concealment a principle from a religious standpoint, an important question arises: Why so much secrecy among nonpracticing Dönmes in Turkish society? The reason is not only because of religious rules barring us from speaking out, but rather due to the potential social limitations that would be inflicted on our lives. Unlike Jewish, Armenian, Greek, and Assyrian minority groups, Dönmes carried Turkish names but some were Muslim only on paper. Such practices made Dönmes seem to be part of the majority of Muslim Turks, giving them some protection in society.

What events led us to this fear of revelation? About two generations ago, life in Selanik had become difficult for my ancestors. Nationalism on the part of the Greek government and society as a whole made those who were not Greek Orthodox feel unwelcome. Dönmes obeyed the population exchange treaty that forced them to start a new life in Turkey after 1923. Adapting to a new country was challenging, and, to complicate matters, a Dönme named Karakaşzade Rüştü, who was upset with his own community, revealed the Dönmes' identities to the Turkish government prior to their departure from Selanik. Therefore, from day one, the government knew who we were. In fact, the Wealth Tax of 1942, imposed arbitrarily and exorbitantly on religious minorities (e.g., Armenians at 232 percent and Jews at 179 percent of the value of their property) (Guttstadt 2013, 75), included the Dönme, though they had Muslim identity. Some Dönme families (including mine) paid their share because they did not want to end up in the Aşkale forced labor camp in eastern Turkey for those who could not pay. It is no wonder my ancestors learned to not speak openly of their identities, and Dönme individuals were identified and taxed as minorities despite their official status as Muslims.

Despite Turkey's wide cultural diversity, the continuous influence of nationalism gave rise to cultural homogenization. This reality indicates a lack of tolerance and disregard for ethnically and religiously unique groups, which become scapegoats during times of political and economic instability. So we hide in secrecy. Society knows we exist, but exactly who is a Dönme is not known. This inability to identify Dönmes has been a greater disturbance than the existence of other minorities who are more visible, which leads to substantial efforts to try and expose us, including our religious practices and schools. As part of these witch hunts, websites listing our names have been created. Some best-selling books are filled with mostly unsubstantiated claims about our supposed conspiracies. The political right wing is especially anti-Dönme, and considers us to be the greatest internal threat to the nation. They believe that our people are an underground criminal organization, who worked closely with the secularist founder of the republic, Mustafa Kemal Atatürk,[2] who was born and raised in Selanik. They accuse us of being behind many impactful events in history, helping to establish and maintain a democratic and secular nation. Despite these efforts, the Dönmes are not easily identified. The secret nature of our beliefs and the deep integration into society serve as a social camouflage.

In my early discoveries, not only did I find out that we were different, but I also learned we had the tendency to blend in with the majority. While things have changed over the years, they have not necessarily improved for minorities in Istanbul. Regardless, I have been digesting the past through much research and exchanges with community members and analyzing our current direction on the basis of universal values. I am not willing to carry the same burden of secrecy that my forebears bore. I feel the residue of pain from years of silence, as others have filled in the blanks with their conspiracy theories about us being illegal aliens ruling the country. I have realized that my learning experience is not solely about knowing more but also about being part of the community and taking ownership. This is why I feel obligated to know everything in my history, from my earliest known Spanish ancestor, Samuel Passarell, to today's living cultural heritage.

I personally believe that practicing freedom secures freedom. We should not waste opportunities to introduce ourselves to the outside world. Although extreme nationalist ideas continue to be a threat, our existence must be recognized, and society must know who we are through our own words. This will eliminate the muddiness of "knowledge" about the Dönmes. By not speaking up about our origin, we let the majority determine whether our origin is acceptable. While I am vocal about my beliefs, I also respect the preferred secrecy of other Dönmes and choose to only reveal my own identity and not the identity of others.

To be sure, applying for Spanish citizenship added another level of constraint to our day-to-day lives from the beginning. For instance, Dönmes tiptoed in our own cemeteries to gather burial records and take photographs of gravestones in order to comply with the evidentiary requirements. Some of us were harassed by the local officials, cemetery security, or even ordinary citizens. As the first Dönme to be granted Spanish nationality, I worried and had a few sleepless nights when my name was publicly announced on the *Boletin Oficial Del Estado* in August of 2016, along with those of the hundreds of Sephardi Jews approved for the citizenship. However, I have realized that, despite the risk of being revealed, being able to connect myself back to the land where my first known ancestor, Samuel Passarell, lived is a precious achievement of my life.

The Welcome of Citizenship

Few people willingly abandon their homelands to sail away to unknown territories full of challenges. But the survival instinct forced our forebears to leave their hearts behind in the places they had known as home. This feeling has been embedded into our beings and miraculously passed down to new generations who have not migrated before. My own heart is with my family, yet a part of me feels drawn to the Iberian Peninsula and the adventure awaiting me there. My sentimental connection to the Spanish land did not emerge through the citizenship experience. Actually, the citizenship was the *outcome* of my self-discovery in the continuation of this epic and a growing sympathy to the lands where this long story originated.

April 2017, Chicago. I was in a large waiting room, where a couple of dozen people sat, each of us waiting our turn. Each held a numbered ticket and paid close attention to the announcements of the clerks who sat behind the glass partition, the numbers slowly growing. At exactly noon, the door beside the Spanish flag opened and a female officer called my name with a smile. I entered a large lobby void of furnishings. I noticed a gentleman and another lady wearing smiles as they stood with their backs against the wall. It must be the Spanish way of greeting, I thought. The gentleman, who I later learned was the consul general, showed me to his office and implied that I should enter and sit on the sofa in front of his desk.

"You are on Spanish soil now, and you soon will be Spanish. I will be conducting the process in our official language unless you want me to speak Ladino."

He then smiled and said a few words in medieval Spanish without waiting for my response. Our Ladino language borrowed many words from all the countries my ancestors had lived in. It is unlikely that there are any remaining Ladino speakers in the Dönme community, as all that remains of the bygone language in the community are crumbs of words and expressions.

"I speak some Italian and Portuguese, but I think I'd have better luck with Castilian or Galego," I told him.

The consul sifted through the paperwork in the large old-style binder, reading and signing some pages swiftly as the female clerk used the dividers to move from one document to the other. I was able to understand most of the words, and everything sounded as I would expect with reference to obtaining a passport, until I heard them say something that did not sound procedural. As I remember it, he said, "And on behalf of the Spanish King, I greatly apologize to you and your family for what has happened to your ancestors in our history, and I welcome you back to your homeland, Spain." I recalled then how I had started the application process despite the number of questions without answers: Which Spanish state authority to apply to and how? What form to fill out? What documentation to send, and to where? How to follow up? Being a Dönme added an especially difficult layer, because, given the secrecy around our origins, we do not have absolute evidence for the evaluators, such as Sephardi Jewish marriage or circumcision documents. Thankfully, I could prove that I had Passarels in my genealogy, and I also provided Vassaf's text about my Sufi great-grandfather's Jewish roots, among other paperwork. My persistence in the face of all the frustrations had brought me to this unforgettable moment.

The apology seeped into every crevice of my soul. In that moment I realized the gravity of what I had accomplished. It felt as if someone had told me I had single-handedly ended a war that had been waged against my forebears for centuries. This apology was addressed to me as an individual, but it was meant for all of the souls who had endured the sufferings caused by the Spanish Inquisition. This official apology was not a political check-box exercise or a perfunctory effort to look good in the eyes of the Western world. I felt the sincerity of it, not only in the words, but also in how I was treated by the government officials.

The female officer entered the room holding in her hand one of the forms that I had filled out, and stated, "All of your documentation seems to be complete in order for us to request a new birth certificate for you, with the exception of this particular field."

She pointed to the field with her index finger. She was right, I had forgotten to complete it. I looked the foreign word up in the Spanish-English dictionary, and translated it, "select a city."

"May I select A Coruna?"

"Why A Coruna?"

"Because I love it there, and my family and I go there every year."

"Yes, but this field is essentially asking where your ancestors are from."

Where they were from? Really? I understood this law was meant to register Jews in the very places where they were expelled from in order to remedy the recognized historic errors. While I personally appreciated the goodwill embedded in the process, it was practically impossible to identify "where we were from" in today's Spain. All I knew was that the Sephardi Jews were consequently expelled from multiple cities during the pre-Inquisition era until the Alhambra Decree of 1492. I felt fortunate to be able to identify the earliest ancestor possible, Samuel Passarell, who had lived in Zaragoza in the 1250s; therefore, I am now a *maño* (a person from Zaragoza).

It must have been a long and strenuous migration from Zaragoza to Istanbul over the centuries, with a long stopover in Selanik. Each stop had its own difficulties, which continue in some ways. Even the last one. Years ago, on my visit to the cemetery in Istanbul, I struggled to find my grandmother's grave, even with the kind help offered by the attendant. He asked, "Where was your grandmother born?" When I answered, "Selanik," he blanched. With a disgusted look, he pointed to a separate section of the Muslim cemetery where all Dönmes were buried.

Desecration

I flinched when my phone rang. It was one of my "cousins" calling. We Dönmes often call each other "cousin," as we are all related due to the centuries-long tradition of endogamy.

"Did you see the photos I sent to you?" he said.

"Let me look."

I flipped through many photos of vandalized graves in our cemetery. Unlike Muslim graves, most Dönme graves have portraits of the deceased, which were often a common target of hammer blows. Most Dönme graves are covered with a marble top, along with the head and footstones, and obelisks—all were broken with a sledgehammer. This was not the first attack, and we always expect more in the future. Community members make donations to help restore the tombstones to their original state.

Healing

In the past few centuries, we have been associated with a different social category than "Jewish." But it's important to remember we have common ancestors with the Sephardi Jews. This is helpful when trying to prove our origin to the Jewish communities, which is the first step in our citizenship applications, though not every Dönme family has the required evidence, given that family trees disguise Jewish identity after the so-called conversion.

To date, my gradually increasing curiosity has yet to reach its peak, which means I am always learning more about our roots and culture and our book, the Zohar. In this process, I have become a Dönme who is well-connected to my community. We do exist, and the sincere recognition of our existence by Spain carries tremendous positive meaning for the Dönmes and heals the souls of the deceased.

I have monumental gratitude for the elder family members, especially my grandmother and my mother who had to exert themselves to keep a secret and to equip me to protect myself. This was perhaps one of the most uncommon ways of learning about one's identity. Their journey has encouraged me to make bold moves, including embracing Spain.

Uluç Özüyener is the author of the memoir, *Hayat Kaç Kere Başlar?*" (How many times can life begin?) (Çatı 2013) and *Paslı Anahtar* (Rusty key) (Büyükada 2018), a historical novel based on family stories. As a member of a crypto-Jewish community called Sabbateans, Uluç has fewer reservations than most members of the group when it comes to sharing his family origin, traditions, and experiences. He is the first Sabbatean to become a Spanish citizen. An IT professional living in the United States, he is married and a father of three. He is also the cofounder and president of the nonprofit organization Society for Sabbatean Studies.

Notes

1. The Zohar is not considered a supplement but rather is a substitution of the Talmud upon the arrival of the messiah. It is essential to Dönmes is mainly because of its emphasis on messianic expectations. This is at the heart of the special tie between the Dönme and the Zohar.
2. In 1951, "The Law Concerning Crimes Committed against Atatürk" made insulting Atatürk a punishable crime. But Atatürk died in 1934, and the law does not allow fundamentalists to go after Atatürk, so instead they target Dönme.

Reference

Guttstadt, Corry. 2013. *Turkey, the Jews, and the Holocaust*. Cambridge: Cambridge University Press.

Part III.

Negotiating the Present

Between States and Official Communities

Chapter 8

Moriscos-Andalusíes

Historical Reparation, Reconciliation, and the Duty of Memory

Elena Arigita and Laura Galián

The institutional recognition of the Sephardi Jews and the historical decision to grant them citizenship rights inevitably bring to mind the historical memory of another expulsion, that of the Moriscos.[1] In a process that, while different, also had many similarities to that of the Sephardi Jews in the post-1492 period, the Moriscos were subjected to forced conversion to Christianity, assimilation, and ultimately expulsion from Spain in the years from 1609 to 1614. The preamble to "Law 12/2015 of 24 June, granting Spanish nationality to Sephardi Jews originating from Spain" (hereafter Law 12/2015) offers an account of historical events that focuses in particular on two periods: the first is post-1492—that is, the immediate aftermath of al-Andalus, which marks the beginning of the long period of exile; and the second is the mid-nineteenth century, a time of political instability in Spain that coincided with the development of Africanism as an ideology on which the legitimacy of the Spanish Protectorate in Morocco (1912–58) would be based. Africanism also championed a philosephardic approach in which the Jewish communities in the Protectorate were granted certain privileges compared to their Muslim neighbors (detailed by Elisabeth Bolorinos Allard, chap. 6 in this volume). As the preamble to the 2015 law notes, the measures taken to recognize the Jewish communities in Northern Africa in the nineteenth century were the first stage of a long process, one that culminated in the passing of the law, self-described as one of recognition and reconciliation, not of reparation (see Aragoneses, chap. 1 in this volume). Despite the historical parallels and the arguments put forth during the deliberations of the law in the Spanish parliament (see Aliberti, chap. 3 in this volume), there is no prospect of a law granting citizenship rights to Morisco descendants.

This chapter explores some of the underlying historical and cultural reasons for this purposeful omission. It also sheds light on another aspect of the highly complex process of reparation of past injustices, known in Spain as *memoria histórica* (historical memory) by exploring the case of the Moriscos and the parallels and differences in treatment with the Sephardi Jews. The objective is to understand the boundaries and limitations that the dominant historical narrative has imposed on the descendants of the Moriscos, as well as to investigate how Morisco demands for reparative recognition have been mobilized. To this end, it is crucial to observe how the interwoven histories of the Iberian Peninsula and North Africa are made up of various superimposed layers, in which al-Andalus is the subject of constant reinterpretation and political mobilization. The fact that there is no law for the Moriscos means that they have never been legally recognized or defined.

The terms "Morisco" and "*moriscos-andalusíes*" bears some explanation. Derived from the word "Moor," the label "Morisco" refers to Spanish Muslims who converted to Christianity between 1499 and 1526 and/or their descendants who were expelled from Spain between 1609 and 1614. An important point should be made here: in Arabic, the Moriscos and their descendants have been continuously referred to as Andalusíes, which encompasses the idea of belonging or pertaining to al-Andalus, the term for Muslim Spain as a whole.[2] Antonio Manuel Rodríguez Ramos, a scholar who also advocates for equal rights for descendants of Sephardi Jews and Moriscos, identifies the Moriscos as "Hispanics who were expelled, exiled and cast out from the Iberian Peninsula and from its official history, merely for being or for looking like Muslims or because they descended from people who were or looked like Muslims" (Rodríguez Ramos 2018a, 33).[3] Rodríguez Ramos also states that the Moriscos were falsely dubbed as foreigners and were stigmatized as such. Despite this derogatory association, he suggests that the label "Morisco" is useful, because it can be extended by analogy to the Muslims from al-Andalus and the Mudejars, who were forced into exile prior to 1609. Rodríguez Ramos proposes the term *moriscos-andalusíes,* admitting that it is far from perfect "in that it goes too far, encompassing any inhabitant of al-Andalus, Muslim or non-Muslim; while also falling short, in that it excludes the Moriscos who converted to Christianity after the conquest of al-Andalus" (Rodríguez Ramos 2018a, 42). Nevertheless, we also use this combined and more evocative term, which includes those who kept alive the memory of a people excluded first by the policies of assimilation and later by policies of "purity of blood." Morisco descendants, despite their complex Spanish, Andalusí, Muslim, and North African backgrounds, and their history of Spanish persecutions and exile, have been left out of the reparations discourses and restitutive citizenship dispensations. We examine these notions and their varying applications to Spain's Jewish and Muslim past and present, since they have been matters of political polarization in the parliament and in public debate. At stake are crucial questions: Is there a legitimate projection of the past into the present? What are the conditions of the commonplace "learning from history," if it is only specific episodes that define modern collective identity, usually those that maintain the asymmetric relations of the colonial period in the postcolonial era? In this regard, we consider that Paul Ricoeur's statement "the duty of memory is the duty to do justice" (2003, 121) serves as a guideline for exploring the relationship between the mobilization of the history of the Moriscos and the postcolonial condition of the Morisco descendants.

Reconciliation Versus Reparation: Jews and Muslims in Democracy

Although reparation can be considered a necessary condition for social reconciliation, both terms remain the subject of debate today (Méndez 2011). Used above all in the context of transitional justice after dictatorship in Latin America, these concepts have never led to broader theoretical study that goes beyond their application in a range of case studies.

In the particular case being studied here, Law 12/2015 does not claim at any time to be a reparative measure for the Sephardi Jews. It merely states, "With this Law, today's Spain seeks to take a determined step to bring about the re-encounter implicit in the definitive reconciliation with the Sephardi communities" (Law 12/2015). Although reconciliation could be understood as the culmination of a process of reparation, in this case achieved by the granting of nationality, historical reparation—a key concept in questions of justice and truth—is not mentioned in this law. For Rettberg and Ugarriza (2015), the word "reconciliation" has been viewed from many different perspectives, from that of a rhetorical resource with no specific meaning, to that of the endpoint for the construction of peace. Despite these divergent approaches, the common thread joining these definitions is the repair of broken social bonds that can lead to a collective future as a means of overcoming injustice (4).

To understand the differences between reconciliation and reparation, it is important to examine the way they are used in international law and jurisprudence. The concept of reparation is used by the United Nations to refer to processes of transitional justice and recovery of memory that took place at the end of the 1970s, with the truth commissions in Latin America, South-East Asia, and some former colonies in North Africa. According to the United Nations (UN), reparation "must cover all the damage and harm suffered by the victim and that, among other aspects, measures of restitution must be taken with the objective of ensuring that the victim is returned to the situation that they were in before" (cited in Faconi, Ortiz, and Sierra León 2020, 1939; see also Aliberti, chap. 3 in this volume; and Aragoneses, chap. 1 in this volume). In other words, the reparation must be proportional to the type of damage caused. In this sense, Law 12/2015 omits the need for reparation as a key condition for reconciliation, so complicating even more the duty to provide justice to the historic communities and completely excluding the *moriscos-andalusíes* from a still incomplete framework of reparations. The word "reconciliation," as used in Law 12/2015, has nothing to do with reparations. We can generally define reconciliation as the process by which two parties at odds over a past event reach a certain consensus as to what happened in the past and the moral conviction that it should not have happened.

The use of "reconciliation" here follows the logic of the commemorative events of 1992, a watershed year loaded with symbolism and a in Spanish and, indeed, in world history. The aim of revisiting the past served the purpose of rewriting history, from a more inclusive perspective, within the new democratic system following the death of Franco (Arigita 2009). However, both the expression "reencounter of two worlds"[4] (as an attempt to replace the phrase "the conquest of the Americas") and the word "reconciliation" (instead of reparation) bypass the recognition of the deep injustice of these historical events.

The speeches made by King Juan Carlos I of Spain at the commemorative events entitled "Sefarad 92" and "Al-Andalus 92"[5] are good examples of how the history of al-Andalus was reinterpreted by state institutions. In both cases, the king offered a conciliatory view of history, although with certain nuances that revealed slightly different approaches to the Sephardi and the Morisco legacies. In his speech to the Jewish community in the synagogue in Toledo, he said,

> We have seen moments of splendor and of decline. We have lived through periods of deep respect for freedoms and others of intolerance and persecution for political, ideological or religious reasons. The important thing is not to keep tally of the good or bad decisions we have made, but to have the will to project and to analyze the past with a view to our future, the will to work together to accomplish a noble endeavor.... The return to Sefarad, which was first timidly embarked upon in the last century, is slowly beginning to fill the

gap produced by your absence. In this way we are renewing the *convivencia* in a Spain that has consolidated its democratic system. Sefarad is no longer a nostalgic idea and is now a home in which it would be wrong to proclaim that the Hispano-Jews feel as if they were in their own homes, because this is their home, the home of all Spaniards regardless of their creed or religion. (Casa de su Majestad 1992a, ??)

In this case, the king highlighted the capacity of the Sephardi Jews to maintain cultural roots, an argument that would be central to the development of a law granting citizenship to their descendants and not to the Moriscos. He also alluded to the special treatment afforded to the Jewish community in Morocco by the supporters of colonialism in Africa during the Spanish Protectorate in North Africa.

By contrast, in his speech at the ceremony held to celebrate al-Andalus, the king also referred to *convivencia* (peaceful coexistence) and intolerance, the shared past, and the fact that the Arabic legacy has lived on in the Spanish language. He also mentioned "the Arab communities who descended from those hard-working Moriscos," who had held onto the keys of the homes they were forced to abandon. Some slight differences can be noted, however:

> Al-Andalus was, as has been made clear by experts in Arabic and Spanish historiography, the coming together of peoples that inhabited the same living space, who over the centuries grew accustomed to share and to dissent, without losing respect for diversity.... It is true that modern-day Spaniards have lived, without knowing it, in permanent contact with Arabic, through the continued use of a language molded by al-Andalusian words, and by exceptionally well-conserved popular customs and traditional arts. It is equally true that the Arabic communities who descended from those hard-working Moriscos and today live in cities with al-Andalusian tradition, such as Fez or Testur, have held on, with praiseworthy steadfastness, to the keys to their houses in Toledo or Cordoba, which they were forced to abandon when reasons of state prevailed over reason itself. But the bonds they feel with their al-Andalusian past, which bring us even closer to them, cannot allow us to forget that on occasions the nostalgia that often envelops history can conceal the real situation.
>
> This is because history, as Ibn Khaldun so rightly pointed out six centuries ago, must allow us to understand the reality of today by verifying the facts and investigating the causes that gave rise to them. And we want to approach this reality with the most positive frame of mind possible. A reality of promising joint projects, which we want to promote in the present and which we trust will be multiplied in the future. (Casa de su majestad 1992b)

There is a key difference between the two speeches. Rather than valorizing nostalgia for a displaced community being materialized in a home for the Moriscos, as with the address to the Sephardis, there is a warning that nostalgia can conceal the real situation. Referring to Ibn Khaldun as a source of authority, the king presents a future of cooperation, thus avoiding having to mention the traumatic past that culminated in the Expulsion, which he alludes to vaguely as "when reasons of state prevailed over reason itself" (1992b). In this way, history as an academic discipline is used to caution about the possible perils of nostalgia and the need to maintain analytical distance so as to build a future based on cooperation. The authoritative argument about history as a discipline has an important implication that situates the Morisco descendants in a different temporality from that of the Sephardi Jews. In the speech of the monarch, a welcome is extended to the Sephardi Jews for whom Spain "is now a home," while for Moriscos the past cannot be revived, despite al-Andalusian traditions preserved in Fez or Testur that merit praise and can only fulfill an instructive role for the present. Another important nuance in this question of temporality is the subtle reference to Africanist philosephardism in the synagogue speech: "The return to Sefarad, which was first timidly embarked upon in the last century, is slowly beginning to fill the gap produced by your absence" (1992a). This fragment has a sense of continuity that makes it possible to formulate a legal framework for the Sephardim, while the speech at the ceremony in Cordoba does not include any reference to the colonial rhetoric of Spanish-Arab brotherhood and more specifically Spanish-Moroccan brotherhood (Mateo-Dieste 2003). In other words, the two official commemoration discourses do not construct equal frameworks of recognition because the narratives are based on differentiated ways of framing temporality, positioning the relationship of the past to the present, and representing affective ties. The two speeches, then, sketch what would later gel into different recognitions of their al-Andalusian past for Sephardi Jews and Moriscos.

The Mobilization of the Past: Morisco Descendants' Search for Justice

The recognition granted to the Sephardi Jews under Law 12/2015 mobilized a campaign in support of similar treatment for the *moriscos-andalusíes*. This was articulated above all by activists in Morocco and Spain who came together in support of the duty of memory. The year 1992 was also the year in which cooperation agreements were signed between the Spanish government and the Islamic Commission of Spain (Law 26/1992, of 10 November), the Federation of Jewish Communities in Spain (Law 25/1992, of 10 November) and the Federation of Evangelical Religious Entities in Spain (Law 24/1992, of 10 November). The signing of these agreements was the culmination of a process to provide a framework for religious pluralism in Spain. It also marked the official recognition of Islam, Judaism, and Protestantism, based on the long-standing historic roots of the three religious traditions. But how did

Muslims in Spain respond to this mobilization of the past? In 1992 there were few representative voices in Spanish public life of a very diverse minority who identified themselves as Muslims. In fact, it was institutional initiatives that made more visible what became the official representation of Islam. This role fell to Mansur Abdussalam Escudero in his capacity as the representative of the Islamic Commission of Spain.[6] In his reply to a speech by Minister of Justice Tomás de la Cuadra Salcedo on the day the cooperation agreement was signed (28 April 1992), he (unlike others) referred to the agreement as a reparative instrument, which has come to correct an "injustice" (Escudero 1992, 9). He also alluded to the historical significance of this event claiming that the Capitulations of Granada were still valid and relevant today:

> The signing of this agreement has remedied a situation of injustice which has been maintained for five hundred years. In 1492, the nascent Spanish state signed another agreement with the Muslims, which was never repealed, known as the Capitulations of Granada, by which they promised to respect all their laws, their language, and their customs. . . . As we all know from history, the Capitulations were never complied with, and the Muslims, just like the Jews and the Unitarian Christians, all Spanish citizens of their time, were obliged to change their religion, to abandon their own country or in the worst cases were physically eliminated. (Escudero 1992, 9)

The year 1992 was, therefore, a key opportunity for those calling for a review of the al-Andalusian past. The speeches and events facilitated the recognition of the suffering experienced by the Sephardi Jews and, in a different way that was not so clearly expressed, experienced by the Moriscos. However, the differing discourses presented at the commemorations also laid the foundations for the arguments commonly advanced by Spanish politicians for not introducing legislation for reconciliation with the Moriscos, and for the alleged impossibility of treating them in the same way as they treated the Sephardis.

It should also be emphasized that this unequal treatment was far from new. It was based on Spanish colonial policy in Africa in the late nineteenth and early twentieth centuries, which was itself sustained by an Africanist ideology with a philosephardi current. This resulted, for example, in the extension of consular protection to Sephardi Jews and paved the way for subsequent processes of naturalization. Similar recognition has never been granted to descendants of Moriscos, although veterans from the Indigenous Regular Forces of Spain in Morocco, who were recruited to fight alongside Franco, were the main beneficiaries of the naturalization processes held after the civil war (Ojeda-Mata 2015, 43–44).

As Bolorinos Allard explains in chapter 6, in this volume, the special treatment afforded to the Sephardis in Law 12/2015, compared to the

Moriscos, is also rooted in the philosephardic movement. This process took place in parallel with the development of the Africanist movement, which sought to recover the Spanish Islamic legacy at a time when the narrative foundations of Spanish colonial aspirations were being laid.[7] However, as Bolorinos Allard notes in chapter 6, while philosephardism flourished within this historical context, "a movement to reintegrate Muslims of Iberian descent" never materialized.

The political discourses during the historical period that led to the process of naturalization of the Sephardis rejected similar treatment for the descendants of the Moriscos. Maite Ojeda-Mata exposes the weaknesses of the culturalist argument about the presumed preservation of Spanish language and culture by Sephardi Jewish descendants and observes that the ultimate objective of the politicians involved was not the reparation of a historic injustice but rather restriction of access to citizenship by imposing a series of cultural requirements on its acquisition (Ojeda-Mata 2015, 50).

In the debates that took place when Law 12/2015 was put forward, then Minister for Foreign Affairs José Manuel García-Margallo, stated that the question of granting nationality to the Moriscos "is a technical problem that must be discussed" and could not be sorted out "in a quarter of an hour" (quoted in "El Gobierno" 2015). This reply is symptomatic of the current state of the question. If, as Rodríguez Ramos argues (2020), "a identidad de razón, identidad de derecho" (for identical reasons, identical rights) as the Spanish expression goes, then the same legal solution must be applied to claims based on the same reasoning. The difficulties around the technical formulation that would allow the *moriscos-andalusíes* to be included in the law is insufficient to explain the lack of will for Sephardis and *moriscos-andalusíes* to be placed on an equal legal footing. The arguments provided by Rodríguez Ramos demonstrate that the parallels between Moriscos and Sephardim could allow for equalization. The lack of official explanations makes it clear the exclusion is not due to a legal formulation. Rather, it is traceable to the ambivalent discourses of Spanish institutions and politics (such as the speeches of the monarch in 1992) and the long-lasting, unsettled history of Spain with regard to Islam.

However, for *moriscos-andalusíes* today, the important memory issue lies not so much in receiving legal remedy for the injustice committed, but in symbolic reparation. According to Rodríguez Ramos, most of the *moriscos-andalusíes* would like some form of recognition that they belong to the Spanish nation and form an integral part thereof, together with a recognition of the injustice that was committed with their expulsion in 1609. In this sense, historical reparation would be accompanied by symbolic reparation rather than legal recognition. This would not involve returning the victims to their situation prior to the injustice, which would clearly be impossible but instead would entail legal reparation through symbols that would try to repair the irreparable, such as culture and art as concrete vehicles for implementing symbolic reparations measures (Faconi, Ortiz, and Sierra León 2020). For this reason, the duty of memory is imperative for repairing past wrongdoings.

The Duty of Memory: The Commemoration of the Four Hundredth Anniversary of the Expulsion of the Moriscos

When referring to the principle of the *devoir de mémoire* (duty of memory), a concept articulated by Paul Ricoeur, we often find that academic reflection has been accompanied by intellectual and political activism in defense of the need to repair past wrongdoings. According to Ricoeur (2003), the act of remembering keeps the object being remembered alive. For this philosopher, the duty of memory is applicable at both an ethical and a political level, and an optimal use of memory can also lead to its worst possible misuse, in that on occasion it may be confused with the work of history (118).

Morisco memory, as a paradigmatic representation of an injustice, has another important consequence for understanding and contextualizing both present-day debates and arguments justifying legal processes. Mary Elizabeth Perry (2008), a historian specializing in early modern Spain, writes of the need to distinguish between (a) the collective memory of the Moriscos (in other words, the collective memory of the generations that suffered the aftermath of the Expulsion and helped shape the narrative over the course of the sixteenth and seventeenth centuries); and (b) the mobilization of the Morisco memory today, be it of their descendants or of some other form of mobilization of historical memory. She concludes, "Morisco history challenges us to examine the politics of historical memory and to learn from the past. . . . A closer examination of context and sources raises important questions, such as why historical sources emphasize certain kinds of violence while ignoring others, why some historical experiences are so traumatic that those involved simply try to forget them in silence, why some memories of the past become respected legends used by succeeding generations to explain and justify and motivate others to support" (82).

The challenge that Perry highlights brings us back to the inescapable need to contextualize memory as a product of time and space and to recognize that the trauma and the silence of the generations who underwent the Expulsion are not transferable to later generations. Although the story of this traumatic past is deeply embodied in their identity, it takes on a new dimension for these generations as it helps explain the present and enables the construction of future projects.

Marta Domínguez takes this idea a step farther when she states that accounts of the displacement of modern-day Moriscos and Sephardis "are not 'personal' stories of loss and dispossession, but rather remote accounts of a distant past" (Domínguez Díaz 2017, 212). She collected narratives about identity from descendants of Sephardis and Moriscos from Israel and Tunisia. She noted differences between the mobilization of their accounts of history and the type of claims to which these accounts led: Moriscos and Sephardis share "the remoteness of the past" and, at the same time, "both diaspora discourses are informative of the state of Muslim-Jewish relations today." This aspect is highly significant, given that in their respective narratives, the past takes on new meaning for the present, so that antisemitism and Islamophobia "can be seen here as vehicles people use to channel and make sense of their discontent towards Europe" (226).

In this vein, Domínguez observes how, marked by the colonial experience in the Spanish Protectorate in northern Morocco, Moroccan Morisco identity can be distinguished from Tunisian Morisco identity, in that the former claim the right to be considered Andalusíes or al-Andalusians, and to have Spanish nationality as a historic community. She also points out that, within Morocco, claims of this kind are more frequent in the northern cities that were once part of the former colony (Domínguez Díaz 2017, 221).

In this way, the demands for reparation of the *morisco-andalusí* and the Sephardi past can and indeed must be observed within a more complex context of Spanish-Moroccan relations. These relations encompass not only descendants of the *moriscos-andalusíes* but also *andalucista* activists and Muslims within Spain who,[8] in their support for recognition of the Morisco past, are seeking to challenge the established discourse on historic Spanish identity linked to purity of blood. They aim to broaden this identity, to make it mixed-race, embracing what Rodríguez Ramos refers to as the "third Spain,"[9] one that was "born out of a Spain that was Morisco. Jewish. Convert. Cursed" (Rodríguez Ramos 2018b, 31). Below, we first explore the similarities and differences in the ways Morisco and Sephardi memory is mobilized in the inclusive, reparatory tone associated with the idea of reconciliation. We follow this with a look at the different ways in which their respective pasts are projected on to the present, and how these projections reverberate in complex ways through discourses about Islam in general, and the *moriscos-andalusíes* in particular, as demonstrated by Fernández and Cañete (2019) with regard to the Spanish exceptionalism toward the Maghreb and Morocco. These ambivalent discourses of the past, and, more precisely, of the colonial past, are intrinsically intertwined with the exclusion of the Morisco descendants from legal and symbolic reparations.

In 2009, within the context of the commemoration of the four hundredth anniversary of the Expulsion of the Moriscos, the Foreign Affairs Committee of the Spanish Parliament approved a *propuesta no de ley* (nonlegislative motion), calling for the injustice of the Expulsion to be recognized at an institutional level. In his speech in defense of this motion, José Antonio Pérez Tapias, a philosophy professor at the University of Granada and a member of parliament for the Izquierda Socialista (Socialist Left Party), defended this proposal as a duty of memory. It was, he argued, in line with other commemorations and in particular with the recognition awarded to the Sephardi Jews, who were granted the Prince of Asturias Award for Concord in 1990. The injustice suffered by the *moriscos-andalusíes*, he continued, also needed to be made good, as a way of furthering historical memory via institutional recognition.[10]

As part of the 2009 commemorations, the *moriscos-andalusíes* were put forward for the 2010 Prince of Asturias Award. Although ultimately unsuccessful, their candidacy was defended and actively supported by a rather widespread civil initiative. It was supported by more than three thousand personalities from the international political and cultural spheres, although the award was finally given to Manos Unidas, a Catholic Church association for the development of the world's poorest countries. The candidacy of the *moriscos-andalusíes* was truly transnational and was supported by Moroccan activists demanding a similar recognition to that afforded the descendants of the Sephardis. The public petition in support of their candidacy argued, in line with the proposal made to parliament, that the award would be "a symbolic and necessary gesture for the complete reconstruction of the Hispanic collective memory; in recognition of the exemplary way in which they [the *moriscos-andalusíes*] have consciously kept their cultural identity alive in the places where they settled; and from the perspective of brotherhood, justice and by the precedent set by the award granted 20 years ago to the Sephardi communities for the same reason" (quoted in Arigita 2019, 141).

The candidacy of the descendants of the *moriscos-andalusíes* for the Prince of Asturias Award must be seen within this framework of citizen action. Their candidacy is also a key point in the legal initiative on behalf of two communities with direct historic links to Spain, the Sephardis and the *moriscos-andalusíes*, to be granted equal legal status. The importance of recognition, at both cultural and legal levels, points to the need for a two-pronged approach in support of demands in favor *of morisco-andalusí* memory.

As a legal expert, Rodríguez Ramos played a key role in the preparation of this claim and was responsible for reviewing Article 22 of the Civil Code, from the perspective of the duty of memory. Article 22 reduces the required period of residence in Spain to two years for applicants who are members of historic communities or communities with historical or cultural links to Spain. However, it does not include the *moriscos-andalusíes* as a historical community. Rather than nationality, Rodríguez Ramos prefers to use the concept of statality. The difference lies in the fact that statality is a legal-political link between the individual and the state, which is different from but compatible with the recognition of diverse national identities; nationality is understood as "a collective memory deserving of legal protection" (Rodríguez Ramos 2018a, 39). The lack of recognition for the *moriscos-andalusíes* in Article 22 demonstrates, in his opinion, the roots of the issue being debated, which are also evidenced by Law 12/2015—namely, the tensions between Spain and Islam. As part of the campaign for the amendment of Article 22, in the second International Encounter for Education and Culture on the Alliance of Civilizations, held in Chauen in 2006, backing was given to the Chauen Declaration, which urged the authorities to recognize the preferential right of acquisition of Spanish nationality to the descendants of *moriscos-andalusíes*, placing them on an equal footing with the descendants of the Sephardis (Rodríguez Ramos 2018a, 41).

This was not the first time that the juridical and legislative pathway had been tried. In 2002, two senators from the Izquierda Unida (Unified Left) group, Manuel Cámara Fernández and José Cabrero Palomares, presented an amendment to a bill to amend the Civil Code. This proposal was rejected. Four years later, Mansur Escudero, in his capacity as the representative of the Islamic Commission of Spain, presented a nonlegislative motion to the Parliament of Andalusia on behalf of the Grupo Izquierda Unida-Los Verdes (Unified Left—Greens Group), requesting the amendment of Article 22 to include the *andalusíes* (Rodríguez Ramos 2018a, 41).

Law 12/2015 served to reinforce this awareness of the need for symbolic reparation, and this was made clear in an international congress on "the Morisco question and International Law," organized by the Fundación Memoria de los Andalusíes (Memory of the Andalusíes Foundation) and held in Rabat in April 2016. In a speech to open the Congress, the president of the foundation, Mohammed Najib Loubaris, argued that the claims in favor of the *moriscos-andalusíes* should be closely linked to international law research in Morocco, in order to quash the idea that the Moriscos' time had passed. Loubaris presented a six-point route map in which he emphasized the need to make amends for the Expulsion without this implying "any material compensation or the naturalization of the descendants, as they are not stateless," and the return to the spirit of the Capitulations, rendering the subsequent Edicts of Expulsion null and void. He also proposed to redraft the Civil Code and to hold an annual National Day for the Memory of the Moriscos (Amri, Hadri, and Loubaris Najib 2018, 19–20). The participants proposed strategies for the recognition of the Moriscos that concluded with a Declaration of the Kasaba of al-Andalus. These included, among others, a proposal to create a documentation and study center; a demand that the Moriscos be granted the same rights in the Civil Code as the Sephardis; a return to the idea of promoting the candidature of the Moriscos to the Princess of Asturias Award for Concord; and to support the idea of commemorating the memory on 9 April every year. In October 2020 Loubaris sent a letter to the president of Spain, Pedro Sánchez, in which he reminded him of their claim that the Moriscos to be given the same rights as the Sephardis, and he did so "in the name of the Morisco diaspora south of the Mediterranean and in Latin America."[11] Apart from the media interest in this initiative, it has yet to receive a reply at a political level. No steps have been taken by the government to do so.

Conclusion

This review of the claims and the mobilizations in favor of the recognition of Morisco-Andalusí memory and the construction of a solid set of legal arguments underscores the unresolved issue of the exclusion of the *moriscos-andalusíes* in the reconciliation Law 12/2015. In this chapter, we have demonstrated how the commemorative events of 1992 became foundational in the creation of a redeeming narrative of the history of 1492 and of 1609. This involved the mobilization of the past promoted by institutions of the state in order to commemorate and construct a more inclusive perspective of some of the most controversial episodes in the historical narrative of Spain as a nation-state. This new, more-inclusive narrative was therefore prepared by and for the state as part of a commemorative project, in which recognition of past mistakes formed an integral part. However, in parallel to the official discourse, the commemoration inevitably interacted with the mobilization of a political consciousness that demanded and argued in support of symbolic reparation as a duty of memory, bringing together a very diverse group of actors in both Spain and Morocco. Three decades after Mansur Escudero called for a return to the spirit of the Capitulations in the ceremony marking the official recognition of Islam as a religious minority, the associations and activists working in favor of the *morisco-andalusí* memory have constructed a set of arguments in parallel to the recognition that the state granted to the descendants of the Sephardis. Along this path, the interwoven histories between Spain and North Africa reveal the multiple layers that have been formed and help explain both the claims being made today and the silence that has often surrounded this question.

The rights of the *moriscos-andalusíes* can be made legally equivalent with those of Sephardi Jewish descendants with regard to Spanish citizenship. However, in the political, institutional, and cultural discourses, the factors that come to fore are the uniqueness and exceptionality of the Moriscos, as they figure in the monarch's 1992 speech. Yet, for various civil society actors, symbolic reparations are at the forefront of activism and the fight for justice. Beyond legal recognition, then, historical reparation needs to be accompanied by symbolic reparation.

This chapter would not be complete without a reference to the present-day context in which we are writing, in which the revival of the National-Catholic ideology by the extreme right in the Spanish Parliament and other institutions has brought historical revisionism to the center of public debate (García San Juan 2017).[12] Remembrance of the *moriscos-andalusíes* inevitably falls within this strongly polarized debate and highlights once again the restrictions imposed by the rewriting of history as a means of redeeming the state, while avoiding tackling the implications for today's diverse Spanish society of the recognition of its Muslim past.

Elena Arigita is permanent lecturer of Arab and Islamic studies in the Semitic Studies Department, University of Granada (Spain). She was a language lecturer at Cairo University and al-Azhar (Egypt), a postdoctoral researcher at the International Institute for the Study of Islam in the Modern World–ISIM in Leiden (the Netherlands), and a senior researcher at the International Institute for Arab and Muslim World Studies–IEAM Casa Arabe (Spain). She is principal investigator of RETOPEA at the University of Granada. Her research interests and publications deal with religious authority and institutionalization of Islam and the politics of inclusion and exclusion of Islam in Europe.

Laura Galián is assistant professor in the Department of Arab and Islamic Studies and Oriental Studies, Autonomous University of Madrid (Spain). She was a postdoctoral researcher at project RETOPEA: Religious Toleration and Peace (Universidad de Granada) and a Juan de la Cierva research fellow at the same university. Her research interests and publications deal with history of concepts, history of ideas, and the Middle East. In 2020 she published *Colonialism, Transnationalism and Anarchism in the South of the Mediterranean* (Palgrave Macmillan).

Notes

1. This chapter has received funding from the Spanish research project "Representations of Islam in the Glocal Mediterranean: Conceptual Cartography and History" (FEDER-MICINN: RTI2018-098892-B-100) and the European Union's Horizon 2020 research and innovation Programme under grant agreement Grant Agreement no. 770309. The contents of this publication are the sole responsibility of Elena Arigita and Laura Galián and do not necessarily reflect the opinion of the European Union.
2. By contrast, in Spanish and in the academic literature that studies the period between 1492 and 1614, these people are referred to as Moriscos. This is because the label Moriscos, which referred to many of the accused in Inquisition proceedings, was frequently found in archives of the Catholic Church. As Perceval and Forga (2010) have observed, there is a paradox in studying a group named by historians for their own purposes. Yet, Morisco descendants in post-exile North Africa carried varying labels, including, for example in Tunisia, by Spanish regional origin (e.g., Granada, Castile, etc.) or patronymics with accompanying terms identifying them as Andalusíes or Moors (De Epalza and Slama-Gafsi 2010). European travelers in North Africa noted the ethnic differences between "Andalusian Moors" and the rest of the population (40–41). In Arabic, *al-andalusī* was a name that Moriscos from the sixteenth and seventeenth centuries shared with many other immigrants of the same origin from earlier periods and was used throughout the Arab world (33).
3. Translations are our own unless otherwise noted.
4. Although there was a Spanish National Commission for the Commemoration of the 500 Years of the Discovery of America, "Encounter of the Two Worlds" was a very common expression during the commemoration. Federico Mayor Zaragoza, director general of UNESCO, in Paris on 13 March 1989 made a call for celebration with the following title: "Quinto Centenario del Encuentro de Dos Mundos." The phrase became common and was featured on stamps and coin collections in different countries. The expression "reencounter" was considered as a fresh start after the first encounter of 1492.
5. These two events commemorated and reinterpreted the very symbolic date of the fifth centenary of 1492.
6. Mansur Abdussalam Escudero (Malaga 1947-Almodovar del Río 2010) was a charismatic leader and a prominent figure in Spanish Islam at both a political and institutional level, and in terms of interreligious dialogue. In 1989 he founded the Junta Islámica, which he led until his death. He also headed the Islamic Commission (the official representation of Islam as a religious minority in dealings with the state) from its creation until he became convinced that his leadership was no longer representative of the new, diverse reality in Spain in 2006. However, he remained involved in various transnational Muslim networks. His sudden death in October 2010 interrupted his personal projects in favor of the shared use of the Mosque-Cathedral of Cordoba, and the recognition of, and reparations for, the Moriscos.

7. For a broader account of the intellectual foundations of the Africanist movement and its relationship with the construction of identity and colonial domination, see Cañete 2021.
8. The term "Andalucista" is often used to refer to the supporters of political parties in Andalusia in the late twentieth century who defined themselves as such (e.g., Partido Andalucista). In this case however, we use the term as defined by Charles Hirschkind, as an intellectual tradition that sprang from the al-Andalusian and Morisco characters in the literature of the Siglo de Oro (Golden Age). This tradition took ideological form in the nineteenth century as a movement of a small group of intellectuals who, faced with the decline and loss of the last colonies in the Spanish Empire, turned to history as a source of national renewal, through the Jewish and Muslim legacies. This movement developed alongside Africanism, and gave meaning to the idea of Hispano-Moroccan brotherhood, thereby providing an ideological basis for the Protectorate. In the twentieth century and with a key contribution from Américo Castro, *andalucismo* challenged an increasingly mainstream historiographic tradition that marginalized the al-Andalusian heritage. This was done by reinterpreting its past legacy in the present (Hirschkind 2020, 7–10).
9. This idea of a *tercera* España (third Spain) is developed in more detail by Antonio Manuel Rodríguez Ramos in his book *La huella morisca*. Charles Hirschkind places it within the broader context of contemporary debates in Spain about the historiography of al-Andalus (Hirschkind 2020, 57–58, 84–85).
10. This proposal was passed, although various political parties (Partido Popular and Convergencia y Unió) voted against it. There was also some controversy in the following weeks regarding the validity of the claim. For more about this controversy, please see Arigita (2019).
11. The letter was disseminated on social media. We obtained it from the Facebook account registered under the name "Consejo Nacional Andalusí" on 18 April 2021.
12. The historian Alejandro García San Juán (2017) warns about the recovery of this dangerous exclusive discourse in his article.

References

Amri, Kautar El, Rahma Hadri, and Mohammed Loubaris Najib, eds. 2018. *La cuestión morisca y el derecho*. Rabat: Fundación Memoria de los Andalusíes.

Arigita, Elena. 2009. "Spain—the Al-Andalus Legacy." In *The Borders of Islam: Exploring Samuel Huntingtons's Faultlines from Al-Andalus to the Virtual Ummah*, edited by Stig Jarle Hansen, Atle Mesoy, and Tuncay Kardas, 223–34. London: Hurst.

———. 2019. "Narratives on the Margins of History: Memory and the Commemoration of the Moriscos." *Journal of North African Studies* 24, no.1: 134–51. https://doi.org/10.1080/13629387.2018.1459267.

Cañete, Carlos. 2021. *Cuando África comenzaba en los Pirineos. Una historia del paradigma africanista español (siglos XV–XX)*. Madrid: Marcial Pons Historia.

Casa de su Majestad el Rey. 1992a. "Palabras de su majestad el rey a la comunidad israelita." Casa de su Majestad el Rey. https://www.casareal.es/GL/actividades/Paginas/actividades_discursos_detalle.aspx?data=4131.

———. 1992b. "Palabras de su majestad el rey en el acto institucional al-Andalus." https://www.casareal.es/EN/actividades/Paginas/actividades_discursos_detalle.aspx?data=4650.

De Epalza Ferrer, Mikel, and Abdel-Hakim Slama-Gafsi. 2010. *El español hablado en Túnez por los moriscos o andalusíes y sus descendientes (siglos XVII-XVIII)*. Valencia: Universitat de València.

Domínguez Díaz, Marta. 2017. "'Once Upon a Time Our Home Was in Spain': Comparing Diaspora Discourses among Morisco Descendants and Sephardim Today." In *Jewish-Muslim Relations in Past and Present: A Kaleidoscopic View*, edited by Josef Meri, 206–29. Leiden: Brill.

"El gobierno no concederá la nacionalidad a los descendientes de los moriscos ni a los saharauis."2015. *El Diario*. 12 January 2015. https://www.eldiario.es/politica/gobierno-concedera-nacionalidad-descendientes-saharahuis_1_4426151.html.

Escudero, Mansur. 1992. "Intervención en nombre de la Comisión Islámica de España en ocasión de la firma del Acuerdo de Cooperación con el Estado español." *Liqa' Encuentro Islamo-Cristiano* 225.

Faconi, José Liliana, Mendoza Ortiz, and Yolanda Sierra León, eds. 2020. *Reparación simbólica: cultura y arte para nueve casos de violaciones de los derechos humanos*. Bogota: Universidad Externado de Colombia.

Fernández Parrilla, Gonzalo, and Carlos Cañete. 2019. "Spanish-Maghribi (Moroccan) Relations beyond Exceptionalism: A Postcolonial Perspective." *Journal of North African Studies* 24, no. 1: 111–33.

García San Juan, Alejandro. 2017. "Al-Andalus y la resurrección de la memoria histórica nacionalcatólica." *Eldiario.es*. 28 January 2017.https://www.eldiario.es/andalucia/en-abierto/al-andalus-resurreccion-memoria-historica-nacionalcatolica_132_3613097.html.

Hirschkind, Charles. 2020. *The Feeling of History: Islam, Romanticism, and Andalusia*. Chicago: University of Chicago Press.

Law 26/1992. 1992. "Ley 26/1992 de 10 de noviembre, por la que se aprueba el Acuerdo de Cooperación del Estado con la Comisión Islámica de España" [Law 26 of 10 November approving the Agreement of Cooperation of the State with the Islamic Commission of Spain]. *Boletín Oficial del Estado*, 12 November, 1992, no. 272.

Law 25/1992. 1992. "Ley 25/1992 de 10 de noviembre, por la que se aprueba el Acuerdo de Cooperación del Estado con la Federación de Comunidades Israelitas de España" [Law 25 of 10 November approving the Agreement of Cooperation of the State with the Federation of *Israelita* (Jewish) Communities]. *Boletín Oficial del Estado*, 12 November, 1992, no. 272.

Law 24/1992. 1992. "Ley 24/1992, de 10 de noviembre, por la que se aprueba el Acuerdo Cooperación del Estado con la Federación de Entidades Religiosas Evangélicas de España" [Law 24/1992 of 10 November approving the Agreement of Cooperation of the State with the Federation of Evangelical Religious Entities of Spain]. "*Boletín Oficial del Estado*, 12 November, 1992, no. 272.f

Law 12/2015. 2015. "Ley 12/2015 de 24 de junio, en materia de concesión de la nacionalidad española a los sefardíes originarios de España" [Law 12/2015 of 24 June, granting Spanish nationality to Sephardi Jews originating from Spain]. *Boletín Oficial del Estado*, 25 June 2015, no. 151.

Mateo-Dieste, Josep Lluis. 2003. *La «hermandad» hispano-marroquí. Política y religión bajo el Protectorado español en Marruecos (1912–1956)*. Barcelona: Bellaterra.

Méndez, María Lucía. 2011. "Revisión de la literatura especializada en reconciliación." Bogota: GIZ (Deutsche Gessellschaft für Internationale Zusammenarbeit). https://library.fes.de/pdf-files/bueros/kolumbien/08551.pdf.

Ojeda-Mata, Maite. 2015. "La ciudadanía española y los sefardíes: identidades legitimadoras, ideologías étnicas y derechos políticos." *Quaderns-e* 20, no. 2: 36–52.

Perceval, J. M., and M. Forga. 2010. "Repensar la Expulsión 400 años después: del 'todos no son uno' al estudio de la complejidad morisca." *Awraq* 1: 119–136.

Perry, Mary Elizabeth. 2008. "Memory and Mutilation: The Case of the Moriscos." In *In the Light of Medieval Spain. Islam, the West and the Relevance of the Past*, edited by Simon R. Doubleday and D. David Coleman, 67–89. New York: Palgrave Macmillan.

Rettberg, Angelika y Juan E. Ugarriza. 2015. "Reconciliation: A Comprehensive Framework for Empirical Analysis." *Security Dialogue* 47, no.6: 517–40.

Ricoeur, Paul. 2003. *La memoria, la historia, el olvido*. Madrid: Editorial Trotta.

Rodríguez Ramos, and Antonio Manuel. 2018a. "Hacia la equiparación jurídica de los descendientes de moriscos-andalusíes en el derecho civil español." In *La cuestión morisca y el Derecho; Segundo Coloquio Internacional Fundación Memoria de los Andalusíes*, edited by Kaoutar el Amri, Rahma Hadri, Mohammed Najid Loubaris, 33–55. Rabat: Fundación Memoria de los Andalusíes.

———. 2018b. *La huella morisca. El al Ándalus que llevamos dentro*. Córdoba: Almuzara.

———. 2020. Interview conducted by the authors of this article. 3 November.

Chapter 9

Negotiating Historical Redress
The Spanish Law of Nationality for Sephardi Descendants and Spain's Jewish Communities

Daniela Flesler and Michal Rose Friedman

In a much publicized first visit to the Madrid Beth Yaacov Synagogue in 1992, as part of the commemoration of the five-hundredth anniversary of the 1492 Expulsion, King Juan Carlos I symbolically "welcomed home" the descendants of the expelled Jews (Juan Carlos I 1992).[1] An overwhelmingly conciliatory tone dominated the speeches of everyone present, including those of the official representatives of Spain's Jewish communities. None of the speakers asked for the official abrogation of the Edict of Expulsion, nor did any of them suggest that Spain had a debt to repay—even a moral debt—to the descendants of those expelled or to Spain's contemporary Jewish communities. The speeches, as well as the psalms and prayers selected to be read in the synagogue, were screened and approved by Spanish diplomats in advance. All speeches echoed the official message of celebrating a modern and democratic Spain that should orient itself toward the future (Lisbona 1993, 365, 367–68). The Jewish presence and setting at the official commemoration ceremony lent the act considerable symbolic legitimacy, as proof that Spain had left its intolerant past behind (Flesler and Pérez Melgosa 2020, 18–20). Twenty-three years later, in June 2015, Spanish officials and the leaders of the Federation of Jewish Communities of Spain (FCJE) celebrated the approval of Law 12/2015. As in 1992, both parties communicated a similar message, emphasizing the law's restorative nature and in the words of the FCJE, its opening of "a new period of reencounter, dialogue and coexistence" (eSefarad.com 2015).

This chapter—based in part on interviews conducted with Jewish community leaders, government officials, and other social actors who were involved in the development of the law—illustrates the essential role of Spain's Jewish communities, especially the FCJE, in the conception and implementation of Law 12/2015. Also apparent are the limits of community power and influence as partners with the state. The FCJE proposed the creation of the law, negotiated its conditions with the government, and played a central role in the review of applicants' qualifications. Despite this close cooperation, a careful examination reveals a divergence between the intentions, aspirations, and expectations held by Jewish community leaders and the Spanish government. We explore the ways in which Jewish representatives have leveraged long-standing Spanish philosephardic ideas in order to advance their advocacy efforts. This is but the latest manifestation in a long history of Jewish representatives seeking historical redress from the Spanish state. All involved in these negotiations invoked well-established philosephardic rhetoric around notions of rescue, gratitude, indebtedness, and loyalty that have served to both bolster and undermine the interests of the Jewish communities of Spain. While multiple parties may have negotiated over the law, in reality the law's final version was disproportionately shaped by conservative political interests rooted in traditional notions of Spanish national identity.

The Federation of Jewish Communities of Spain and the Origins of Law 12/2015

Spain's current Jewish community, consisting of both Sephardi and Ashkenazi Jews, numbers around 45,000 individuals, most of whom emigrated to Spain from Morocco and Argentina in the 1960s and 1970s. Moroccan Jews began arriving in Spain in substantial numbers after Morocco's independence in 1956, with their arrivals increasing especially following the 1967 Arab-Israeli War. They came from the main cities of the former Spanish Protectorate in Morocco, and from the Spanish cities of Ceuta and Melilla. The majority considered themselves to be direct descendants of Jews exiled from the Iberian Peninsula returning to their ancestral home. They took great pride in their connection to Spain's medieval Jewish past and the endurance of this legacy through their language, culture, and religious rituals. They rapidly became a numerical majority among Jews in Spain and played the largest role in establishing the official institutions that govern today's Jewish community. In the 1970s significant numbers of mainly Ashkenazi Argentine Jews emigrated to Spain as political exiles and a second wave arrived following the 2001 economic crisis.

During the 1960s, several crucial developments took place in Spain's rapprochement with world Jewry: Franco collaborated with Israel, facilitating the migration of Sephardi Jews from Egypt and Morocco to Spain; the Sephardic Museum in Toledo was created in 1964; and a Law of Religious Freedom was passed in 1967, which officially recognized Spain's Jewish associations. However, it was not until the ratification of the post-dictatorship 1978 Constitution that Spain guaranteed full religious freedom and prohibited religious discrimination. A new law of religious freedom in 1980 (Law 7/1980) allowed the establishment in July of 1982 of the FJCE, initially called Federación de Comunidades Israelitas de España (Federation of Israelite Communities of Spain), composed of the communities of Barcelona, Madrid, Ceuta, and Melilla. Samuel Toledano served as its first secretary (1982–94), followed by Carlos Schorr (1993–2003), Jacobo Israel Garzón (2004–11), Isaac Querub Caro (2011–20), and Isaac Benzaquén Pinto (2020–present).

The 1985 official recognition of religions other than Catholicism as being *de notorio arraigo* (deeply rooted) in Spain paved the way for the Cooperation Agreements signed by the Spanish government with Muslim, Jewish, and Protestant religious communities in 1992. The government's advisory commission on religious liberty came under the jurisdiction of the ministry of justice. One of the consequences of the 1992 agreements was that they forced religious groups with a high degree of internal diversity, such as Muslims and Jews, to have only one organization act as a representative and interlocutor with the state (Benasuly 2008, 116). The FCJE, which was founded by and remains governed by traditional members of the community, thus officially represents all Jewish communities in Spain from the point of view of the state. Jewish groups connected to reformist or conservative denominations are officially linked as partners, but they do not have an official vote. In our interviews with leaders of Masorti and Reform congregations, as well as with religiously unaffiliated Jews running cultural organizations, it became clear that they did not feel the FCJE represented them (Roife 2021; Sorenssen 2021). In Madrid, for example, the Masorti congregation is in the process of establishing a separate Jewish cemetery due to disparate understandings of who should be considered a legitimate Jew (Roife 2021).

In the context of Law 12/2015, the question of official representation was unclear. While the state considers the FCJE to be the official interlocutor for Spain's Jewish community, there is no (single) official legal representative of the Sephardi community in Spain, or globally. This allowed for multiple independent actors to become closely engaged in advocating for the law, including Sephardi individuals from outside Spain (Bendahan 2021). Isaac Querub, FCJE president when the law went into effect, was a major protagonist in its development. Carolina Aisen, who has served as FJCE director since 2003, and who supervises all of the organization's projects, provided continuity between Garzón and Querub's presidencies. When elected to head the FCJE in 2011, Querub, accompanied by former president Mauricio Toledano, went to speak with Alberto Ruiz-Gallardón, the newly appointed minister of justice of the conservative Popular Party (PP) (Querub 2021).[2]

Querub and Gallardón were already on familiar terms, having worked together in previous years, when Querub was president of the Jewish Community of Madrid (1996–2001) and Gallardón was president of the Regional Community of Madrid (1995–2002), and then Madrid's mayor (2003–11). In our interview with him, Gallardón credited Querub and the FCJE with the initial idea for the project: "The proposal, the idea, the request, came from the Jewish community; from Isaac Querub. . . . I have to say in his honor, that it is not an idea that would have occurred to me at that time. It was them." He described the meeting as follows:

> Isaac Querub—I say it because it is important that it be known that it was him—besides calling me to let me know he was available for anything I might need, he told me, "Alberto, we have done very important things together when you were president of the Community of Madrid, we have done very important things together when you were mayor of Madrid, but now we have to do the most important thing that should have been done since 1492." And I asked him, "What is that, Isaac?" and he said, "We have to close the historical wound that was opened with the Granada Edict of Expulsion of 1492." (Gallardón 2021)

The meaning of "closing the historical wound," however, would come to be interpreted rather disparately by the various protagonists of the law.

The Narrative of Spanish Rescue of Jews

The theme of Spanish rescue of Jews appeared in our interviews as an important structuring narrative to explain the origins and motivations for the creation of Law 12/2015. When Querub assumed the presidency in 2011, there were 4,522 pending citizenship application files awaiting approval (Aisen 2021; Mateo 2018; Querub 2021), reflecting the efforts of his predecessors in the FCJE. Between 2004 and 2011, while Garzón was president, Venezuela and Turkey had become the focal points of such efforts due to the perception that these countries' Jewish communities were under political threat. The first step the FJCE took under his presidency was to get in touch with the ministers of justice and of foreign affairs, both of which were charged with all matters pertaining to religion. These ministries had attended to what Garzón described as Spain's "essentially historic labor of supporting the Sephardim," citing the examples of the Suez Crisis of 1956, the Arab-Israeli War of 1967, and the war in the former Yugoslavia in the 1990s. In these and other instances, entrance into Spain was facilitated for a number of Sephardi Jews. Garzón explained how the Spanish government had "always wanted to maintain the position of supporting Sephardi Jews, during all times, even during Francoism" (2021). In these pre-2015 instances, the legal tool used was the *carta de naturaleza* (letter of naturalization), a discretionary granting of nationality by the government. The precedent was the 1924 Royal Decree that granted Spanish nationality to a limited number of Sephardi Jews due to the perceived benefits these Jews could offer Spain as advocates for Spanish colonial economic, political, and cultural interests (Lisbona 1993, 36–38; Ojeda Mata 2013, 145–47).

In Venezuela, in particular, there were Moroccan Jews born in the Protectorate, who had Spanish citizenship. Their children, however, could not access this status, since the Spanish law specified that their parents had to be born in Spain. Garzón argued that the designation "Spain" should be understood as including the Protectorate, and his intervention succeeded in securing citizenship for around seven hundred Venezuelan Jews (Garzón 2021). Around the same time, a parallel effort focused on Venezuela was spearheaded by Melilla-born Jewish businessman Sadia Cohen Zrihen (1935–2020). Cohen left for Venezuela in the late 1950s; he settled there and became well-integrated in the Jewish community of Caracas, as well as in social and political circles (see Perdomo 2020). Nonetheless, he maintained a bond with Spain, and helped facilitate Spanish nationality for many Venezuelan Sephardi Jews (Belilty 2021). In 2011 he founded the Madrid-based Don Juan de Borbón Foundation, connected to the Spanish crown, dedicated to fostering closer ties between Spain and Israel in the areas of culture and research. Cohen and his foundation became directly involved in advocating for Law 12/2015, alongside members of the conservative Popular Party (Prada 2014). Another figure who became prominent in advocacy for the law, initially focusing his efforts on Jewish rescue, was the Spanish businessman David Hatchwell, who served as president of the Jewish Community of Madrid (2011–17) and who currently heads the Fundación Hispanojudía, established in 2015. The foundation was created with the stated objectives of establishing a Jewish museum in Madrid; promoting relations between Israel, Spain, and Latin America; and "recover[ing] the historical memory of the role that Jews have played in the Spanish nation and in Europe over the many centuries of our history" (fundacionhispanojudia.org/). The organization counts on the support of many influential Spaniards, and Gallardón served as its vice president between 2016 and 2020.

When addressing Law 12/2015, Isaac Querub also emphasized prior rescue efforts. Both Querub and Gallardón traced a direct line between the 1924 Royal Decree and the initiatives of Spanish diplomats during World War II to issue *salvoconductos* (transit visas) for Jews fleeing Nazi persecution. Querub summarized these prior efforts to us as government actions: "On the basis of this decree, the Spanish State, through various representatives, intervened on behalf of various Jews of Sephardi origin" (Querub 2021). In other interviews, Querub also emphasized these rescue efforts as instances when Spanish diplomats "remembered and assumed responsibility for the history of Spain, of Sepharad" (Felis 2015).[3] Although these two issues—World War II rescue and Law 12/2015—are not generally thought of as interrelated, Querub sees them as such. Spanish officials' actions on behalf of Jews have been, for Querub, acts of remembrance that draw on recognizing a specific history that is not well known to most Spaniards. By connecting the law to previous Spanish rescue efforts, Jewish representatives like Querub were clearly signaling that the population they had in mind when drafting the 2015 law were Sephardi Jews and not non-Jewish descendants.

Querub seems to have said as much to *New York Times* journalist Doreen Carvajal. In 2012, Carvajal reported (and confirmed to us in a 19 February 2021 interview) that Querub told her the law was intended only for practicing Jews. Carvajal's exchange with the FCJE at this early stage in the development of the law is not surprising. After all, it was highly unusual that an organization identified with traditional Sephardi Judaism like the FCJE would consider as Sephardis people who had not been raised as Jews, or who self-identified as converso descendants, but did not necessarily plan to convert to Judaism. Garzón also confirmed that the FJCE's initiatives were directed specifically at Sephardi Jews: "We had taken up the issue of Venezuela and Turkey because they were places where Jews could find themselves in a difficult situation. . . . We had not thought of [securing Spanish nationality] for Sephardis who were not in danger, but for Sephardi Jews that were in danger" (Garzón 2021). In our interview, however, Querub insisted that the law was conceived from the beginning for anyone of Sephardi descent, no matter what their religious affiliation might be in the present, and that the law purposely did not mention the word "Jews." Aisen, who coordinated much of the application evaluation process, explained that the law did not exclude non-Jews for the simple reason that the Spanish Constitution does not allow discrimination on the basis of religion (Aisen 2021).

Like Querub and Garzón, Gallardón (2021) emphasized the Jewish rescue narrative as a precedent for Law 12/2015, and moreover highlighted his familial connection to it. In addition to what he described as his "personal convictions" motivating his involvement, he explained that his great-grandfather, José Rojas Moreno, was Spain's ambassador to Romania during World War II. He described how Rojas Moreno used the 1924 Royal Decree to provide passports to Jews in Bucharest, and Yad Vashem (Israel) later recognized him as a "righteous among the nations." The story of his great-grandfather, he explained, "was something that, in the oral history of my family, was always told and it was felt with much pride, because they did it, additionally, on their own accord, at their own risk, that is, without the official support of the Spanish government." Moreover, his paternal great-grandfather served as a medical physician in the mines of the Rif, in the Spanish Protectorate in Morocco. His true vocation, however, was writing, and he abandoned medicine and became a journalist and an author. Gallardón explained that during this period his great-grandfather "developed a very intense relationship with the Jewish community in Morocco." He emphasized that this was not "an official relationship like that of my maternal great grandfather, but a personal one.... In his memoirs he writes about all of the [Jewish] friends he had and how he attended their religious festivals."

This narrative of rescue has even deeper roots. During the Spanish-Moroccan War of 1859–60, Spanish troops encountered Sephardi Jews upon their entry into the city of Tetuán, who allegedly greeted them with shouts of, "Welcome! Long live the Spanish queen!" in their native Judeo-Spanish language (Haketia) (Alarcón 1860, 402). During the twenty-seven months that the Spanish troops occupied Tetuán, Jews and Spaniards developed a relationship of mutual benefit that would have a lasting effect for Spanish political and commercial interests in Morocco (González García 1991, 67–79). The memory of this encounter as a rescue from destitution and Muslim rule shaped later Spanish philosephardic understandings of Sephardi Jews as being indebted to Spain (Rohr 2007, 21).

Gallardón's clarification, quoted earlier—that it was the Jewish community of Spain, represented by Isaac Querub and the FJCE, who approached him regarding the need to actively confront Spain's dark past—is reminiscent of a longer tradition of Jewish advocacy in Spain. This advocacy for Jewish rights and humanitarian assistance entailed appealing to the highest authorities of the Spanish state. Jewish officials at different historical moments, including Ludwig Philippson and leaders of the consistories of Bayonne and Bordeaux in the nineteenth century, or Abraham Shalom Yahuda and Max Mazín in the twentieth century, all called on Spain to abrogate the 1492 Decree and institute religious freedom (Friedman 2019, 2020; Lisbona 1993; Manrique Escudero 2016). Reclaiming this past served as a way of bolstering Spain's self-image and international reputation, while Jews sought both pragmatic actions regarding their legal status in Spain or elsewhere and symbolic gestures of historical acknowledgment (Stein 2016).

Debts of Gratitude

In these historical exchanges between Jewish officials and their Spanish interlocutors we find a common language of indebtedness and gratitude, of Jewish indebtedness to Spain, or of Spanish indebtedness to Sephardi Jews. Such language extends to what has been formulated as the ingratitude of the Catholic monarchs toward the Jews when they expelled them, after they had benefited from the Jews' services during the conquest of Granada. Gallardón reiterated this narrative in our interview. Referencing the 1492 Expulsion, he commented, "In Spain it had an additional burden of ingratitude since Spanish Jews had financed the Catholic monarchs to aid in their expulsion of the Arabs. . . . The debt that we Spaniards have to the Jews is enormous and of course I don't think we'll ever be able to repay it" (Gallardón 2021). Among nineteenth-century reclamations by Jewish representatives addressed to Spanish authorities, the petition to abrogate the 1492 Edict, submitted by the Sephardi heads of the consistories of Bordeaux and Bayonne in the wake of the 1868 liberal revolution, stands out. These representatives also referenced a debt, stating that abrogating the edict would constitute a reparative act in memory of their ancestors, which would result in great public recognition for Spain (Manrique Escudero 2016, 56–112).

During the Franco era, Jewish leaders in Spain were pressured to lend legitimacy to government actions. Franco's government thought that having gestures of goodwill toward Spain's Jews would help his relations with the United States, which were crucial to ending the regime's international isolation after 1953 (Lisbona 1993, 143–47, 157). In 1964 Max Mazín, president of the Jewish Community of Madrid (1961–69), requested an audience with Franco to advance Spain's Jewish communities' legal recognition. Mazín emphasized that the visit was meant "to thank him for the benevolent treatment the authorities have always bestowed on us . . . to express the gratitude of the Israelite Communities of Spain for the creation of the Sephardic Center and Museum [in Toledo]" (225–26). In the meeting, Franco described his experience in the Protectorate, emphasizing the gratitude of Moroccan Jews to the Spaniards

(226–27). Once again, indebtedness and gratitude became the language of exchange between Jewish representatives and Spanish authorities.

We can still see this language at work in the characterizations of Law 12/2015. Speaking in terms similar to Mazín's more than fifty years earlier, Querub stated, "We, the Jews of Spain, are very grateful to Spanish society. . . . We feel proud of Spain" (Querub 2021). During the December 2015 ceremony in the Royal Palace celebrating the new law, King Felipe VI stated that Spain was grateful for Jews' loyalty and love: "I want to associate the word 'reencounter' with another equally relevant one: gratitude. Dear Sephardis, thank you for your loyalty and for keeping as a precious treasure your language—Judeo-Spanish or Judezmo and also Haketia—, and your customs, that are not different from our own. And thank you also for letting love prevail over rancor and for having taught your children to love this Spanish homeland" (Felipe VI 2015). Other officials, including diplomat and then director of the Centro Sefarad-Israel in Madrid, Miguel de Lucas,[4] used terms such as "privilege," and "gift," to characterize Law 12/2015. In our interview with him, he observed: "In reality, the law does not recognize the right (el derecho) to citizenship. . . . This law states that, within the juridical concept of naturalization, that it is my privilege as the government, that I grant it when I wish . . . as a gift; as a privilege it grants to whomever it wants." To de Lucas, then, the law represents a gift expressing Spain's historical gratitude, in return for a perceived Sephardi loyalty (de Lucas 2021; see also McDonald 2021, 750).

Conditions, Obstacles, Reparations

The discourse of gratitude is closely intertwined with the notion of Jewish loyalty to Spain. This notion also explains why a similar law has not been considered for descendants of Moriscos, because presumably such loyalty has been demonstrated by Jews and not Muslims. To justify the exclusivist reason for the law, and echoing a persistent philosephardic discourse, several of our interlocutors chose to emphasize certain historical moments that supposedly fit into this narrative of Sephardi loyalty to Spain and mutual indebtedness.[5] When asked about a similar law for the Moriscos, Querub responded, "I can say that we Sephardis have truly preserved, in the majority of cases, the language, many social, as well as culinary customs. . . . And moreover, we Sephardis never, never, never, have expressed hatred nor resentment towards Spain, nor Spaniards. When we have spoken about Spain and Spaniards we have always done so with respect and affection" (Querub 2021). Gallardón was equally emphatic. In relaying to us the debate in the Spanish Parliament over the amendments introduced by leftist parties to include Moriscos and Sahrawis in the law (see Aliberti, chap. 3; and Arigita and Galián, chap. 8, in this volume), he used the following argument:

> "Tell me," I said to that deputy, "where can you find a community of Arab citizens who continue to speak Spanish, who maintain Spanish culture, and who moreover maintain besides the language, the tradition . . . and when you go to their home they show you the key where their ancestors lived in Spain? Tell me, because if you can show me that, then we can also give those Arabs Spanish citizenship. . . . What the Arabs did not do is conserve their love of Spain, its language, its traditions, and its customs. But the Jews did, and therefore the Jews deserve this nationality." (Gallardón 2021)

In Gallardón's view, this tactic clinched the debate in favor of not including in the projected law "all of the descendants of Arabs who had lived in Spain."

The proposed law also introduced several strict conditions for applicants, including a costly application process, required exams in modern Spanish language and culture, demonstration of a current connection to Spain, and a three-year window (eventually extended to four) for applying. The list of requisites points toward the granting of nationality as a privilege, along the lines of de Lucas's characterization. Gallardón justified these requirements in relation to the exclusion of Morisco descendants: "The truth is, besides justifying this privilege, the reason for including the language requirement in the law was so that this same request would not be made by Arab citizens" (2021). Such an explanation demonstrates that the requirements of the law are in place to prove the veracity of the myth of Sephardi attachment and loyalty to Spain, a narrative that includes the view that Morisco descendants did not maintain a similar attachment.

Most of our interlocutors emphasized that they did not agree with the inclusion of these conditions and that they were negotiated back and forth between the FCJE and the government. Querub explained, "It was not exactly the law that we wanted. We wanted a much simpler, easier law, more automatic. But due to concerns of the Spanish state, possibly because of the issue of immigration control, etcetera, a series of requirements were put in place. The other requirement we disagreed over was that of demonstrating a current connection to Spain. I felt this was contradictory, because it was not that evident that they [Sephardis] had maintained this connection to Spain after 500 years" (2021). Aisen confirmed the FJCE's opposition to these requirements, stating, "A Sephardi person should not need to prove a current connection to Spain" (2021). They also objected, as did many others, to the fee payments and the costly requirement to travel to Spain to sign the application in the presence of a notary (lawyer). In the December 2015 Royal Palace ceremony, Querub stated his wish that the law's stricter conditions could be interpreted, as he put it, "sensibly" by those responsible for its application ("Acto solemne" 2015). Garzón (2021) also confirmed that these conditions originated with the government. Uri Benguigui, president of the Comunidad Israelita de Barcelona (2014–18), told us that he complained to the government about them. He saw these requirements as connected to an effort to limit the total number of applicants, because certain factions in the government explicitly talked of the fear of "avalanches of Jews that would arrive" (Benguigui 2021). At the time, Spanish media sources echoed such sensationalist concerns (M. González 2019; *Europa Press*, 2014). Gallardón himself confirmed this fear: "When I was trying to pass the law, there were some voices that signaled alarm, mainly about the number of Sephardi Jews who would come to Spain. They said there would be inordinate numbers, though with time it was demonstrated that this was not the case. . . . This is the reason why these time limits and precautions were put in place. . . . Today I would be in support of modifying the law to remove the time limit" (Gallardón 2021).

An ample spectrum of political parties in parliament also expressed objections. The Spanish Socialist Workers' Party (PSOE), Basque Nationalist Party (PNV), and Republican Left of Catalonia (EPC) objected, among other items, to the language and culture exams ("Proposiciones de Ley. Enmiendas"). Part of the reason why these exams were included was because the draft law, throughout its development and until 2015, also contained a revision of the procedure for naturalization through residence for immigrants living in Spain. The draft included these exams as requirements to prove immigrants' sufficient degree of integration into Spanish society, weaponizing fears of Muslim immigrants' supposed lack of integration into European societies.[6] The Popular Party (PP) decided to separate the law for Sephardi descendants from the discussion of naturalization through residency, which was debated and passed into law a few days later, on 13 July, as Law 19/2015. Notwithstanding the opposition of the FCJE, PSOE, PNV, and EPC, Law 12/2015 passed on 24 June, and included the same requirements: a Spanish language test, plus a civics and culture exam to prove Sephardi applicants' "special link with Spain," (phrased in draft Law 19/2015 as a way to prove immigrants' "sufficient degree of integration into Spanish society"). After Law 12/2015 was passed, Aisen (2021) was able to obtain an exception for these exams for applicants who were age seventy and older.

These requirements stood in contrast with Gallardón's vision of the law as a reparation of the past. He emphasized the importance of amending the past, and spoke of its purpose as "asking for forgiveness, because

Spain, like all great nations, has many chapters in its history of which it is profoundly proud, and it has many others of which it should be ashamed. . . . One of the reasons for shame is the Edict of Expulsion signed by the Catholic monarchs in 1492" (Gallardón 2021). He insisted, moreover, that "Spain can never correct the brutality of expelling sons of its *patria* [homeland]. That is absolutely irreparable, it cannot be corrected. . . . What we can do is send a clear message: first, recognize the error; second ask for forgiveness from the descendants of those affected; and thirdly . . . send a message to the new generations that there are things that should never be repeated." In speaking about how important it was that no political parties would oppose the proposed law, he stated, "It is a law that is the recuperation of the historical memory of the Spanish people."(2021). Gallardón's language choice is significant. The reference to "historical memory" is very charged in contemporary Spain, and is directly associated with ongoing discussions and debates over the Spanish Civil War and the Francoist dictatorship. That the Popular Party would be the author of a law meant to repair Spain's historical legacy as a means of fostering democratic ideals might thus appear ironic to those familiar with contemporary Spanish political struggles over the recovery of historical memory.[7]

Enacting a Common Purpose

Although official Jewish representatives expressed their dissatisfaction with the obstacles included in the law while it was being debated, they fully embraced and celebrated it once it was passed. Just as in 1992, Spanish government officials and Jewish representatives publicly presented a shared vision of Spain. These officials emphasized the need to work toward the future, as opposed to repairing the past. To convey this idea, a common metaphor was used: "You cannot remove the ugly pages of history, they are already there; the important thing is to write new positive pages with an eye toward the future" (Querub 2021). In a similar vein, de Lucas (2021) claimed that "Many dark pages of the past cannot be removed. You cannot repair that damage. It is necessary to write a new page." Indeed, the law's preamble stresses "the common determination to jointly build, in contrast to the intolerance of past times, a new space of peaceful coexistence and unity" (Law 12/2015). In this way, the preamble positioned modern democratic Spain as standing in direct opposition to its "intolerant" past, from the perspective of a pluralistic vision of national identity. During the December 2015 ceremony, King Felipe VI used the same metaphor as he proclaimed, "It is an infrequent privilege to be able to write new positive pages of history. But I am convinced that on this occasion, with this Law and ceremony that brings us together today, all of us present here today feel that we stand before one of these opportunities" (Felipe VI 2015).

In an interview with Radio Sefarad (FJCE's community radio station) on 11 June 2015, the day the law was passed, Querub joyfully declared, "We have a law that symbolically annuls the Expulsion Decree of the Catholic monarchs of 1492," and referred to the law as an instance of a society wanting to "repair an injustice" ("Un día histórico" 2015). Querub's official statements have oscillated between this vision of the law as historical reparation, the vision he originally presented to Gallardón, and a more cautious stance regarding use of the term "reparation." In our 2021 interviews, both Querub and de Lucas emphatically rejected the term "reparation": "We have never used the word 'reparation' because of its legal ramifications. Because reparation supposes political as well as economic responsibilities and we have never wanted to speak about economic issues. We never wanted to speak about reparations, not now and not in 92'. . . . I prefer the word 'rectify'" (Querub 2021). De Lucas claimed that the law "does not need to repair anything," and furthermore claimed that there was no desire (within the government) to embark on a general examination of the past. Their rejection of the term "historical reparation"—after Querub used it himself in 2015 to characterize the law—seems related to a growing awareness of the legal connotations of the term according to international law (see Aragoneses, chap. 1, and Aliberti, chap. 3, in this volume). It is not surprising that the Spanish government would try to forestall any possible future claims of material reparations by Sephardi descendants beyond the law of nationality.

A common feature of the global principle of political legitimization that Jeffrey K. Olick (2007) has described as "the politics of regret," is grounded in the idea that nations' responsibility for the wrongs of the past are performances of atonement and apology. We asked Querub and Garzón whether they would have liked Spanish officials to offer Sephardi Jews an apology, and both emphatically insisted that it was unnecessary. Explaining how he had taken part in the 1992 commemoration ceremony, Querub (2021) told us, "We were very careful not to talk about the past, but to speak fundamentally about the future, about diversity and unity. We never blamed the Spaniards for the past. In fact, the Spanish state did not yet exist in 1492." Querub's statement echoed King Juan Carlos's conciliatory tone and rhetoric on the same occasion: "What is important is not an accounting of our rights and wrongs, but the willingness to project and analyze the past in service of our future, the willingness to work together towards a noble goal" (Juan Carlos I 1992).

Expressing a similar sentiment regarding the purpose of Law 12/2015, Querub (2021) explained his lack of interest in discussing forgiveness: "I cannot change the past, not I nor anyone else. . . . The spirit of asking for forgiveness is in truth demonstrated through acts in the present and in the future, something that would make coexistence better. . . . It is very difficult to decontextualize and judge the Trastámara family, Queen Isabel, or King Ferdinand, for what they did. . . . I prefer for the current political leaders, for the current King, to say what he is saying today and that the Spanish people embrace us as they have." Garzón also thought there was no need to ask for an apology: "When somebody tells me 'I want the Edict of 1492 to be abrogated,' I say, 'For what?' It was already annulled, with a new constitution, that replaced the prior legislation" (Garzón 2021). Rejection of both historical reparation and the need for apology point to these Jewish representatives' assimilation of the position of the Spanish government and their enactment of a public facing common front.[8]

Other Jewish representatives, however, have described Law 12/2015 itself as an act of contrition. Benguigui spoke to us of its significance as completing the symbolic restitution that King Juan Carlos had begun in 1992, an idea also echoed in FJCE declarations. But he also viewed it as directly affecting Spain's Jewish community in that its symbolic significance and implied apology was directed to them: "The nationality law appeared to us as something symbolic. It was a sort of . . . symbolic restitution of something that was poorly done and that had not been done in 100 years. Jews have been in [modern] Spain for 100 years. The law, first of all, addresses or gives restitution to present day Jews who live in Spain—us, me, for example—since it is important for my government to say, 'Through this law what I am doing is asking your forgiveness'" (Benguigui 2021).

Conclusion

The enacting of a common discourse celebrating the law as symbolic of a pluralistic, multicultural, democratic Spain in which minorities are well integrated, should not obscure the fact that the FJCE had wanted a very different law, yet had to accept the government's conditions. The FJCE's perception was that otherwise there would have been no law at all (Aisen 2021). However, in their celebration of the law, FJCE representatives have uncritically endorsed and reproduced a philosephardic discourse that legitimizes essentialist and Castilian-centric nationalistic notions of Spain and Spanish culture. This endorsement was perhaps most prominent during the December 2015 ceremony at the royal palace. A young Spanish man emphasized his Sephardi family's love and loyalty to Spain, noting how in his house "the only language spoken was Castilian." Querub placed the Spanish protagonists of the law, including Gallardón and de Lucas, within the same political lineage as Senator Ángel Pulido. These men, he stated, were all *hombres de entraña* (men of substance) just like Pulido. Moreover, he connected the law to a shared Judeo-Christian tradition, vowing that Jews would defend and uphold these values in the face of "the barbaric attacks on Western civilization and the State of Israel" ("Acto solemne 2015,"). It is notable that these assertions followed the attacks on the *Charlie Hebdo* headquarters and in the Hypercacher kosher supermarket in Paris the previous January. Such statements appear to illustrate less a multicultural and multilingual Spain embracing pluralism than the idea that, to access nationality through this privileged process, Sephardis need to reaffirm conservative Castilian-centric notions of Spanishness[9] while they also distance themselves from Muslims in Europe.

Sociologist Alejandro Baer (2011) has compellingly argued that because discourses of historical memory in Spain are linked politically to the reclamations of the left regarding Francoism, the Popular Party has used a traditionally philosephardic view of Sephardi memory emphasizing a "lack of vindictiveness" to score political points against the left (106). In our interview Baer added, "The Jews are a convenient memory—they do not seek any revenge . . . they do not challenge you and enable you to bolster the idea that there are others who should be forgotten" (Baer 2021). Reinforcing this particular historical memory of Jews maintaining their love for Spain, thus, serves to delegitimize the historical memory of Francoist repression reclaimed by the left, while it also undermines historical reparation claims by Muslims. Implicitly, according to this view, in contrast to Sephardi claims [allegedly] motivated by love for Spain, these other claims would be motivated by vindictiveness.

In conclusion, our examination of the actions and discourse of official Jewish representatives and their engagement with the Spanish state over the 2015 law reveals how the assimilation of an official state discourse is a result of a prolonged historical relationship of negotiation from a disadvantaged position. Jewish representatives were heeded by Spanish officials in their request for a legal means of rescue for some Sephardi communities and were given an important role in screening and certifying applicants, even though many of these applicants would not be the ones they initially had in mind. Yet this role, despite appearances, was structured and limited by decisions beyond their control, and by the symbolic constraints imposed by philosephardic discourse.

Daniela Flesler is associate professor and chair of the department of Hispanic Languages and Literature at Stony Brook University. She is the author of *The Return of the Moor: Spanish Responses to Contemporary Moroccan Immigration* (Purdue University Press 2008). She is coeditor of *Revisiting Jewish Spain in the Modern Era* (Routledge 2013) and *Genealogies of Sepharad* (*Quest. Issues in Contemporary Jewish History* 18, 2020). She has been the recipient of ACLS and NEH Fellowships. Her most recent book is *The Memory Work of Jewish Spain*, coauthored with Adrián Pérez Melgosa (Indiana University Press 2020).

Michal Rose Friedman is the Jack Buncher Professor of Jewish Studies in the Department of History at Carnegie Mellon University. She was a postdoctoral fellow at the Herbert D. Katz Center for Advanced Judaic Studies at the University of Pennsylvania (2015), and at the Seminar in Advanced Jewish Studies at the University of Oxford (2016). She is coeditor of "Genealogies of Sepharad" a special issue of *Quest. Issues in Contemporary Jewish History* (2020) and a forum on Sephardi scholar Abraham Shalom Yahuda (*Jewish Quarterly Review* 2019). She has authored journal articles and book chapters on Jewish and Iberian history.

Notes

1. We thank Esther Bendahan and all the individuals who agreed to be interviewed for this chapter. We also thank the anonymous reviewers, and Rina Benmayor and Dalia Kandiyoti for their generous comments and careful editing. All translations are our own.
2. Rajoy was prime minister for the conservative Popular Party from 2011 to 2018.
3. Such rescue efforts were however notably undertaken by diplomats acting on their own, as they were not sanctioned by the Spanish government (see Avni 1982, Marquina, and Ospina 1987 and Rother 2005).
4. The Centro Sefarad-Israel is connected to Spain's diplomatic efforts and dependent on and funded by the ministry of foreign affairs.
5. Other historical moments present a more uncomfortable picture, in which this narrative is much more difficult to sustain. Traditional Spanish historiography has often considered Jews traitors for their supposed assistance to the Muslim conquerors in 711. Nineteenth-century Spanish scholars like Amador de los Ríos viewed this episode as proof of Jews' lack of gratitude and love toward their patria (see Friedman 2011, 97).
6. According to de Lucas (2021), the modification of these requirements happened to coincide with the passing of the law. Aisen (2021) explained that the government was modifying the law of naturalization through residency at the same time, so, from the government's perspective it made sense to include the same provisions in Law 12/2015.
7. The 2007 "Law of Historical Memory" passed by the PSOE gave rights to civil war and Francoist dictatorship victims and their descendants. The Popular Party voted

against it, claiming that it served to weaken the political consensus of the transition to democracy. On the struggle over historical memory of the Spanish Civil War and the legacy of the Franco regime in Spain, see Ruiz Torres (2007); Labanyi (2008); Faber (2018 & 2021).

8. In the April 2015 draft of Law 12/2015, the Catalan political party Convergencia i Unió suggested including the phrases "moral reparation" and "historical error reparation," which would imply, in their view, an apology to the Jewish people for the Expulsion of 1492. The amendment did not pass.

9. McDonald (2021, 750) has similarly noted in this regard that Law 12/2015 is "affirming [Sephardic Jews'] fundamental Spanishness . . . shoring up an explicitly Castilian national identity."

References

"Acto solemne con motivo de la Ley de concesión de nacionalidad española a los sefardíes de España." https://www.youtube.com/watch?v=w4KsrnR3TWo (December 2nd, 2015).
Aisen, Carolina. 2021. Zoom Interview with Daniela Flesler and Michal R. Friedman, 3 February 2021.
Avni, Haim. 1982. *España, Franco y los judíos.* Madrid: Altalena.
Baer, Alejandro. 2011. "The Voids of Sepharad: The Memory of the Holocaust in Spain." In *Revisiting Jewish Spain in the Modern Era*, edited by Daniela Flesler, Tabea Linhard, and Adrián Pérez Melgosa. Special Issue of the *Journal of Spanish Cultural Studies* 12, no. 1: 95–120.
———. 2021. Zoom interview with Daniela Flesler and Michal R. Friedman, 5 February 2021.
Belilty, Jimmy. 2021. Zoom interview with Daniela Flesler and Michal R. Friedman, 8 March 2021.
Benasuly, Alberto. 2008. "La Constitución Española de 1978 y las minorías religiosas." In *Los judíos en la España contemporánea, Apuntes históricos y jurídicos*, 105–20. Madrid: Hebraica.
Bendahan, Esther. 2021. Zoom interview with Daniela Flesler and Michal R. Friedman, 9 April 2021.
Benguigui, Uri. 2021. Zoom interview with Daniela Flesler and Michal R. Friedman, 2 April 2021.
Carvajal, Doreen. 2012. "A Tepid Welcome Back for Spanish Jews." *New York Times*, 9 December 2012. Accessed 15 March 2021. https://www.nytimes.com/2012/12/09/Sunday-review/a-tepid-welcome-back-for-spanish-jews.html.
———. 2021. Zoom interview with Daniela Flesler and Michal R. Friedman, 19 February 2021.
de Alarcón, Pedro Antonio. 1859. *Diario de un testigo de la guerra de Africa : ilustrado con vistas de batallas, de ciudades y paisajes, tipos, trajes y monumentos, con el retrato del autor y de los principales personajes, copiados de fotografías y croquis ejecutados en el mismo teatro de la guerra.* Madrid: Gaspar y Roig Editores.
de Lucas, Miguel. 2021. Zoom interview with Daniela Flesler and Michal R. Friedman, 10 February 2021.
eSefarad.com. 2015. *Aprobada la ley de nacionalidad española a sefardíes-Comunicado de la Federación de Comunidades Judías de España.* https://esefarad.com/?p=63961.

Europa Press. 2014. "Asociaciones judías esperan una avalancha de solicitudes de nacionalización de sefardíes." 9 February 2014. https://www.europapress.es/internacional/noticia-asociaciones-judias-esperan-avalancha-solicitudes-nacionalizacion-sefardies-20140209131424.html.

Faber, Sebastiaan. 2018. *Memory Battles of the Spanish Civil War: History, Fiction, Photography*. Nashville, TN: Vanderbilt University Press.

———. 2021. *Exhuming Franco: Spain's Second Transition*. Nashville, TN: Vanderbilt University Press.

Felipe VI. 2015. "Palabras de Su Majestad el Rey en el acto solemne con motivo de la Ley 12/2015." Palacio Real de Madrid, 30 November. https://www.casareal.es/ES/Actividades/Paginas/actividades_discursos_detalle.aspx?data=5550.

Felis, Clara. 2015. "Isaac Querub: 'Los hijos de Sefarad han aceptado sin rencor el silencio.'" *El Mundo* 1 June. Accessed 31 March 2021. https://www.elmundo.es/la-aventura-de-la-historia/2015/06/01/556bfd29e2704e693e8b456c.html.

Flesler, Daniela, and Adrián Pérez Melgosa. 2020. *The Memory Work of Jewish Spain*. Bloomington: Indiana University Press.

Friedman, Michal Rose. 2011. "Reconquering 'Sepharad': Hispanism and Proto-Fascism in Giménez Caballero's Sephardist Crusade." *Journal of Spanish Cultural Studies* 12, no. 1: 35–60.

———. 2019. "Orientalism between Empires: Abraham Shalom Yahuda at the Intersection of Sepharad, Zionism, and Imperialism." *Jewish Quarterly Review* 109, no. 3: 435–51.

———. 2020. "Unsettling the 'Jewish Question' from the Margins of Europe: Spanish Liberalism and Sepharad." In *Jews, Liberalism, Antisemitism: A Global History*, edited by Abigail Green and Simon Levis Sullam, 185–208. London: Palgrave Macmillan.

González García, Isidro. 1991. *El retorno de los judíos*. Madrid: Nerea.

González, Miguel. 2019. "Avalancha de solicitudes al cerrarse el plazo para que los sefardíes puedan ser españoles." *El País*, 30 September 2019. https://elpais.com/politica/2019/09/27/actualidad/1569606716_863875.html.

Israel Garzón, Jacobo. 2021. Zoom interview with Daniela Flesler and Michal R. Friedman, 24 February 2021.

Juan Carlos I. 1992. "Palabras de Su Majestad el Rey a la comunidad israelita." Sinagoga de Madrid, 31 March. Accessed 15 May 2021. https://www.casareal.es/GL/actividades/Paginas/actividades_discursos_detalle.aspx?data=4131.

Labanyi, Jo. 2008. "The Politics of Memory in Contemporary Spain." Introduction in *Journal of Spanish Cultural Studies*, Special Issue 9, no. 2: 119–25.

Law 12/2015. 2015. "Ley 12/2015 de 24 de junio, en materia de concesión de la nacionalidad española a los sefardíes originarios de España" [Law 12/2015 of 24 June, granting Spanish nationality to Sephardi Jews originating from Spain]. *Boletín Oficial del Estado*, 25 June 2015, no. 151.

Law 19/2015. 2015. "Ley de 13 de julio, de medidas de reforma administrativa en el ámbito de la Administración de Justicia y del Registro Civil." *Boletín Oficial del Estado* https://www.boe.es/boe/dias/2015/07/14/pdfs/BOE-A-2015-7851.pdf.

Law 7/1980. 1980. "Ley Orgánica 7/1980, de 5 de julio, de Libertad Religiosa." *Boletín Oficial del Estado* núm. 177, de 24/07/1980 https://www.boe.es/buscar/act.php?id=BOE-A-1980-15955.

Lisbona, José Antonio. 1993. *Retorno a Sefarad: la política de España hacia sus judíos en el siglo XX*. Barcelona: Riopiedras.

Manrique Escudero, Monica. 2016. *Los judíos ante los cambios políticos en España en 1868*. Madrid: Hebraica Ediciones.

Marquina, Antonio, and Ospina, Gloria. 1987. *España y los judíos en el siglo XX: la acción exterior*. Madrid: Espasa Calpe.

Mateo, Juan José. 2018. "El gobierno amplía hasta 2019 el plazo para que los sefardíes obtengan la nacionalidad." *El País*, 5 March 2018. https://elpais.com/poitica/2018/03/05/actualidad/1520265130_351979.html.

McDonald, Charles A. 2021. "Rancor: Sephardi Jews, Spanish Citizenship, and the Politics of Sentiment." *Comparative Studies in Society and History* 63, no. 3: 722–51.

Ojeda Mata, Maite. 2013. *Modern Spain and the Sephardim: Legitimizing Identities*. Washington DC: Lexington Books.

Olick, Jeffrey K. 2007. *The Politics of Regret: On Collective Memory and Historical Responsibility*. New York: Routledge.

Perdomo, Williams. 2020. "Continúan los homenajes a Sadia Cohen Zrihen, luchador incansable por los derechos de los sefardíes." *El Nacional*, 9 May 2020. https://www.elnacional.com/mundo/continuan-los-homenajes-a-sadia-cohen-zrihen-luchador-incansable-por-los-derechos-de-los-sefardies.

Prada, Alfredo. 2014. "La tramitación del proyecto de ley por el que se concederá la nacionalidad española a los sefardíes avanza." *España Exterior*, 11 July 2014. https://www.espanaexterior.com/noticias/alfredo-prada-la-tramitacion-del-proyecto-de-ley-por-el-que-se-concedera-la-nacionalidad-espanola-a-los-sefardies-avanza-3.

"Proposiciones de Ley. Enmiendas." *Boletín Oficial de las Cortes Generales*. Senado. X Legislatura. Núm. 509, 24 April 2015.

Querub, Isaac. 2021. Zoom interview with Daniela Flesler and Michal R. Friedman, 28 January 2021.

Rohr, Isabelle. 2007. *The Spanish Right and the Jews, 1898-1945: Antisemitism and Opportunism*. Eastbourne: Sussex Academic Press.

Roife, Gastón. 2021. Zoom interview with Daniela Flesler and Michal R. Friedman, 19 January 2021.

Rother, Bernd. 2005. *Franco y el Holocausto*. Madrid: Marcial Pons.

Ruiz-Gallardón, Alberto. 2021. Zoom interview with Daniela Flesler and Michal R. Friedman, 16 March 2021.

Ruiz Torres, Pedro. 2007. "Los discursos de la memoria histórica en España." *Hispania Nova* 7, Separata. http://hispanianova.rediris.es/7/dossier/07d001.pdf.

Sorenssen, Víctor. 2021. Zoom interview with Daniela Flesler and Michal R. Friedman, 12 February 2021.

Stein, Sarah. 2016. *Extraterritorial Dreams: European Citizenship, Sephardi Jews, and the Ottoman Twentieth Century*. Chicago: University of Chicago Press.

"Un día histórico para los sefardíes, con Isaac Querub, Presidente de la FCJE." Radio Sefarad 11 June 2015. Accessed 18 May 2021.

Chapter 10

Personal Essay
"Congratulations, You Are Portuguese!" Reflections on Identity and Nationality

Rita Ender

On 27 June 2018 I received an email from Monica, a colleague who is also my lawyer, in Portugal: "Congratulations, Rita. You are Portuguese!" Suddenly, with the stroke of an email, I had become Portuguese!

In one of his novels, José Saramago, the Portuguese novelist, wrote: "If I go to the cinema, the theater, or a concert, I know that the seat in which I am sitting does not belong to me, but I behave as if it were my rightful place in this world, a place for which I have fought and worked so hard" (Saramago 2012, 24).

At that moment, I had a similar feeling. Portugal is not a place where I feel any particular belonging, but it is a place where I can now claim rights. Of course, I did not express these sentiments in my application for citizenship, nor in those of my family members or clients. We merely tried to prove our Sephardi identity to the Portuguese state, and they decided that we belong.

I am a lawyer in Istanbul, and I have been helping Turkish clients with their application for Portuguese citizenship. My family and I were my first case. We applied in 2016, a year after the law came into effect. We wanted to apply all at the same time, and it took some convincing to get the whole the family (my sister, my father, and my mother) on board.

Why did we want to become Portuguese citizens? My sister had lived briefly in Italy and Spain, and I had lived in France. Trying to survive in Europe as Turkish citizens was as hard as being a Jew in Turkey. My sister and I knew that having European Union citizenship would make it much easier for us if one day we wanted to live in a country other than Turkey. We also both travel to Europe frequently for business and pleasure. With a Portuguese passport, we would not have to renew our Schengen visas every few years; we would be able to travel visa-free to large swaths of the world. These were the practical reasons behind our application.

There were more existential reasons, as well. I had serious concerns about Turkey's political situation and the future of the country. My concerns and worries multiplied with the June 2015 election results, in which the conservative Justice and Development Party (AK Party) won another victory, despite the publication in the press of clear evidence of corruption. I entered my thirties that summer; the party had been in power since I was eighteen. During this period, its use of power became increasingly repressive, especially after the Gezi Park resistance of 2013. The arrest of journalists, politicians acting out personal vendettas, the lack of judicial independence, the policing of speech even on social media, the rampant violations of the most fundamental human rights—I was carrying my Judaism while also trying to wrestle with all this as a citizen of Turkey. Being Jewish ought to be like having curly hair or olive skin—something natural that shouldn't require long explanations. However, being Jewish in Turkey requires a serious responsibility. For example, as a Jewish woman in Turkey, it is not a simple affair to initiate legal action against a man who is stalking you, who is sending forty to fifty emails a day, who is making collages out of various photos of you that he found on the internet, and expressing his absurd and obsessive opinions about the Jewish people. Would you be protected? Would he get the punishment he deserved? Or would he get a pat on the back from the police? Was he acting alone, or was there another power behind his actions? If there was to be a trial, would nationalists make a cause out of the hearing and come to the courthouse to shout antisemitic slogans? Would the right-wing or religious press try to turn it into a cause célèbre? Was it necessary to act alone, or would it be best to coordinate with the Jewish community?

Being safe and secure enough to take action on your own is a great luxury. I mean, it's not obvious from my clothes that I am Jewish; my Turkish is native and without accent; there's no longer a Jewish-majority neighborhood to be from. But I had chosen to put it out there from the beginning. Google knew it. It was clear that I am Jewish from my newspaper articles and books, cases I had taken on, and even just my first name, which is instantly identifiable as non-Turkish. For this reason, I kept thinking that one day I might have to escape from the land where I was born, where I grew up, where I lived—to escape from my hometown.

As these thoughts circled in my head, even before the change in the Portuguese law, I constantly checked to make sure that both my own and my family's Israeli visas in our Turkish passports were valid. Even if we would not be leaving the next day, maybe I could try my luck moving alone to France, where I had studied. But if we were to leave as a family, I thought that we could only go to Israel, even though we didn't have a close relationship with the country or with Zionism. For a long time my mother repeated, "If we have to escape from here one day, it's clear Israel is the only place that is going to welcome us. What are we going to do with Portuguese citizenship?" It took time for my sister and me to persuade her.

Fortunately, the Portuguese state did not require exams, unlike the Spanish law. In effect, Spain was telling us, "We kicked you out in the fifteenth century—now we are recalling you for a variety of reasons. But . . . first you have to take an exam on all of our culture and language that you missed during the past five hundred years." If Portugal had had such requirements, we would have never been able to persuade my mother. With the help of our father, though, we gradually broke down my mother's resistance and started to think about what evidence we had that could prove we were Portuguese.

We had a surname. After the Turkish Surname Law came into force in 1934, my paternal grandfather's family had adopted the name Ender, which means "rare." Before the change, their surname had been Albukrek,[1] which is the Turkish spelling of the Iberian Albu(r)querque, meaning "white oak" in Iberian Latin and "the land of the cork oak" in Andalusian Arabic. It is also the surname of a Spanish landowner, general, and explorer after whom Albuquerque, New Mexico, is named. Viktor Albukrek—a Jew from Ankara, like my father's family—argued that the Jewish Albukreks came to Ankara in the 1500s from the Spanish town of Alburquerque, which is located in the north of the province of Badajoz near the Portuguese border.[2] Although it is almost impossible to confirm this information, having a Portuguese surname was an important indicator for the Portuguese government. My father had kept my grandfather's primary school diploma from 1931–32, which showed our family's original surname. That diploma was an important piece of evidence for my father, my sister, and me.

There were also records of our family in the archive kept by the chief rabbinate of Turkey. Based on these records, the office of the chief rabbinate wrote a letter confirming that we were indeed Sephardic. The chief rabbi, Isak Haleva, signed.

Everyone in the family had been married according to Jewish law. We had our *ketubas* (Jewish marriage contracts) and wedding photos to be added to the application file. We kept pictures and printed invitations for all the Jewish rites of passage: *pidyons* (redemption ceremony for first-born sons), circumcisions, bar mitzvahs, *fashaduras* (baby showers). Our dead were sent off on their eternal journey according to Jewish custom and were all buried in Jewish cemeteries. The grave of my grandmother's father, Moshe Arav, whom I always called "grandfather with glasses," is in the Jewish cemetery of Bursa; on his tombstone it is written in Judeo-Spanish (Ladino): "Aki repoza el defondo de Moşe Arav. Ke su alma ke repoze en ganeden (Here rests Moshe Arav. May his soul rest in *gan Eden* [heaven]).

Already everyone in the family up to my generation could speak this ancestral language. My sister, my cousins, and I, like most in our generation, understand bits and pieces of the language, but we cannot speak it. Still, I could decode these simple Judeo-Spanish lines on my great-grandfather's gravestone because the verbs are almost the same as their French equivalents. I also knew the meaning of some of the words: for instance, I knew the word "alma" very well only because of my aunt and uncle, Janet and Jak Esim, who have been making music and singing in this language since before we were born. And in the songs that we grew up with and went to sleep to, the word comes up quite a lot. In "Alma Miya," we heard, "Alma miya vino la ora / Apartir te vas agora/ Komo i komo me ire / Sin ti Roza, komo are?" (The time has come, my dear / You are leaving now / How will I leave / Without you, Roza, how will I go on?) (Janet and Jak Esim Ensemble 2005). And in another, we listened to "Durmete mi alma, durmete mi sol / Durmete pedaso de mi korason (Sleep, my dear, sleep my sun / Sleep, piece of my heart)" (Janet and Jak Esim Ensemble 2006).

In 2014 a graduate student interviewed me about the experience of being Jewish in Turkey. When we got to discussing Judeo-Spanish, I explained that I could not give directions in the language, but I could say, "Mijor es murir mas ke sufrir / Dolores de amor, vengo a sufrir" (It is better to die than to suffer / The pangs of love, I come to suffer). This conversation inspired me to make a documentary about the Judeo-Spanish words that young Jews in Turkey still know. I called it *Las Ultimas Palavras* (The last words). By focusing on the words that Turkish-Jewish young adults knew in Spanish, I wanted to also record their feelings and views about the language. I added the documentary and the news clippings about the film to our citizenship application file. With these items, together with reams of official documents such as birth certificates and Turkish census registrations, we applied to the Jewish community of Porto and asked for a certificate of Sephardi origin. The Portuguese "law of return" stipulates that one must obtain such a certificate, issued by one of the two recognized Jewish communities in the country, either the one in Porto or in Lisbon. These groups are the arbiters of who is or is not sufficiently Sephardic. It was necessary to choose between the two congregations, and I had heard that one of our relatives had done it through Porto, so I followed their lead. Then I began correspondence with Mónica João Teixeira, an attorney who frequently works on such applications for Portuguese citizenship, and, with her assistance and the certificate from the Porto community, we submitted our application to the Portuguese state.

Neither my sister nor I nor my parents had ever been to Portugal. We were demanding our rights from a land that we had never seen. Did we really have the right? I thought a lot about that. Even though we could not speak it, we had Judeo-Spanish, our mother tongue, yes. But other than that, and some traditional dishes, did we have any other connection with the Iberian Peninsula? Were we victims of the Inquisition and what had happened in the fifteenth century? Was it not too long—more than five or six centuries—to carry on the victimization? How can a state show its regret after so many centuries?

While I was searching (but not finding) answers to these questions and our application was still being evaluated, I received an invitation from the Jewish Community of Porto to present my documentary at a cultural event it was organizing. I accepted with pleasure and in early 2017, for the first time in my life, I went to Portugal.

I went alone, but it turned out that a tour bus full of Turkish Jews had come to attend the same event. I watched Jews from the antipodes of the Sephardic world speak Judeo-Spanish amongst themselves, as these visitors from Turkey, England, the Netherlands, and elsewhere attempted to understand what Portugal meant to them as new or future Portuguese citizens.

I loved Porto. With its doors, ceramics, water, and food, the city was a poem, unlike anything I'd seen before. I never had a feeling of, "We were here once. "On the contrary, I thought there was no trace of Judaism in the city. The touristic old Jewish quarter that you find in most European city centers was absent here. Even in the synagogue and within the Jewish community, there was little sign of a deep Portuguese connection—most congregants had been born in Brazil, the UK, and a variety of countries that were not Portugal.

The screening I presented at the Kadoorie Mekor Haim Synagogue still meant a lot to me. The audience was interested and asked compelling questions. I met Mónica face to face at a dinner that evening. When I found out that she was on the committee of lawyers who prepared the law that entitled us to citizenship, I asked her a few technical legal questions and one big political question: Why was Portugal offering citizenship to us? She gave sincere answers. At the end of our conversation, my understanding was that this law passed in large part because we, global Sephardic Jewry, would increase the number of seats for Portugal in the population-apportioned EU Parliament. Win-win.

Another person I met during this trip was Ângela, a Portuguese academic, who was very interested in Jewish culture. We discussed our common intellectual interests, the Portuguese citizenship law, and our personal stories. Ângela thought her own family had Jewish roots but were among those that had converted to Christianity in the fifteenth century. When I asked why she thought so, her answers were grounded in her feelings, and frankly, at first, they struck me as absurd. But then I realized I was being unfair. We Turkish Jews always begin narrating our communal history with, "We came here from Spain (and Portugal) five hundred years ago." We have a language—medieval Spanish—that is disappearing, but none of us knows exactly from where and under which conditions our ancestors arrived in the Ottoman Empire, just as she did not know exactly why or how some of her ancestors had changed their religion.

As Marianne Hirsch, scholar of the post-Holocaust generations puts it, postmemory is always about recall, stories, and feelings:

> "Postmemory" describes the relationship that the "generation after" bears to the personal, collective, and cultural trauma of those who came before—to experiences they "remember" only by means of the stories, images, and behaviors among which they grew up. But these experiences were transmitted to them so deeply and affectively as to seem to constitute memories in their own right. As I see it, the connection to the past that I define as postmemory is mediated not by recall but by imaginative investment, projection, and creation. To grow up with overwhelming inherited memories, to be dominated by narratives that preceded one's birth or one's consciousness, is to risk having one's own life stories displaced, even evacuated, by our ancestors. It is to be shaped, however indirectly, by traumatic fragments of events that still defy narrative reconstruction and exceed comprehension. These events happened in the past, but their effects continue into the present. (Hirsch 2020)

We have an even more mediated relationship with the past. Not one, not two, but twenty or more generations have elapsed since we were expelled from Iberia. Past addresses, contemporary photos, copies of old passports . . . none of these exist. Instead of objects, we have semi-mythical stories of objects, stories of five hundred–year-old keys to Iberian houses; no one I know has ever seen such a key. We are just telling ourselves that there is continuity, not rupture, between our ancestors' lives in the fifteenth century and our lives today.

However, every personal story is a story of rupture. After applying for my family, I started to apply for other clients. Other than in divorce cases, I had never before been so privy to my clients' private lives. With some stories, proving the Sephardiness was easy, just as mine had been. For the people who lived with some sort of connection to the institutional Turkish-Jewish community, the documents that needed to be collected, and the letter of motivation addressed to the Porto community were more or less the same. But, especially after the attempted coup d'état of 15 July 2016, many more wanted to emigrate from Turkey, or at least wanted the option to do so. This significantly increased requests for citizenship applications. And now everyone was in a hurry.

In this rush, new complications emerged. Women, for instance, had a different concern from men: their names. Due to the backlog of applications, citizenship was now being granted eighteen months to two years after application. Meanwhile, people's lives and their marital status were changing. According to the laws of the Republic of Turkey, women are compelled to take their husbands' surnames whether or not they also keep or discard their own last names, in accordance with Article 187 of the Civil Code.[3] In some cases, we took this risk and applied for new citizenship with the old surname, without reporting the married surname. On paper, they appeared as two people with two different names, with their identities belonging to a man in one country but not in the other.

This reminds me of the fado "Amor Sem Casa" (Homeless love):"Hora de chegar / Hora de chegar a lugar nenhum, / Não sou de ninguém/ deixai-me ficar" [The time to arrive / time to arrive no place / I belong to no one / let me stay] (Rodrigues 1997).

Belonging to a country means adhering to legal rules. While I had developed a routine for quickly acquiring all the necessary documents in Turkey, getting these from other countries had some interesting variations. It was relatively painless to obtain these documents for a client who was born in Switzerland, but the client who was born in Dhaka, Bangladesh, was unfortunately not quite so lucky. Her father had been a submarine commander in the Pakistan Navy. One day, while his submarine was undergoing emergency repairs in Istanbul, he physically collided with my client's mother at the door of a hotel. They proceeded to fall in love, move to East Pakistan, and get married there. Almost immediately after my client was born, the India-Pakistan War/Bangladesh Liberation War broke out, and the family moved to Istanbul. In the end, we presented documents that evidenced our efforts to acquire her original paperwork. In the meantime, we thought of ways to summarize her parents' love story in order to explain how the client's Sephardic identity was transported to a country without any Jewish population at all, Sephardic or otherwise.

There were others who came knocking on my door with the hope of leaving. For example, a pair of Iranian-Jewish siblings who had traveled to Turkey for work came to see me. While praying in one of Istanbul's synagogues, they learned about the Portuguese citizenship application process, as it was on the tip of everyone's tongues at that time. As I walked them through the application process, I frankly told them that, although they were Jewish, they would not be able to provide the requisite documents, and that they were not Sephardic.[4] Looking into their eyes, but especially into the woman's, it was not easy to say this. For the thousands of Jews in Iran, Portuguese citizenship could be a salvation.

There is Sephardiness in the story of the people who lack Judaism; the number of their descendants' *ketubas* may have dwindled, but it is still possible to find sufficient documents to submit for citizenship.

I filed an application with the Jewish Community of Porto for a client who felt connected to his Sephardi identity, but, according to *halacha* (Jewish law), only his grandfather was considered Jewish.[5] While the Porto community initially sent an email approving his documents, shortly thereafter they sent a second email stating the first one had been sent in error and that they couldn't actually issue him the required Sephardic heritage certificate. Rumors circulated that the Porto community, which is very observant, had been issuing certificates based on the applicants' halachic Jewish status, despite the criteria laid out in the Portuguese laws: "The [Portuguese] Government may grant nationality by naturalisation . . . to the descendants of Portuguese Sephardic Jews, upon demonstration of the tradition of belonging to a Sephardic community of Portuguese origin, based on proven objective requirements of connection to Portugal, namely surnames, family language, direct or collateral descendancy" (Portuguese Law on Nationality 2013). I recommended that my client, who was very upset, convey his feelings to the Porto community. In one part of his heartfelt letter, written in English, he explained what he felt:[6]

> There was something very confusing; According to locals, I was considered Jewish and from time to time I had witnessed unwanted incidents. No matter what myself was not Jewish by religion, I always taught and raised as a Sephardic Jew by my grandfather and other family members. They had never excluded me or made me feel like an outsider. Consequently, I embraced and adopted a Sephardic Jewish way of life. No matter what people say, I always consider myself as a Sephardic individual. It has been more like an identity for me. As mentioned above, we had some unwanted situations such as my grandfather taking our mezuzah off our door. But I am now being told that I am not wanted or accepted by the Sephardic Jewish Community that I feel like I belong to?
> Even though I am not considered to be Jewish and approved by a Rabbi, Do I try my best to exercise Judaism; Yes. In that moment, my application for Sephardic Heritage Certification was accepted, I was thinking of when I could get my citizenship and go back to Portugal and try to get involved in the community that my ancestors belonged to and contribute in any way I can. Was I considering living there for the rest of my life? At one point, yes. But the fairy tale did not last long . . . my father on the other side of the phone [was] telling me that my application was reviewed again and is now rejected!

It was after sending this letter that my client received a final email from the Porto community, granting his certificate. The Jew who finds freedom in marrying a Jew; the Jew who marries a non-Jew; the Jew who, because of their sexual orientation, is not allowed to marry in a traditional synagogue; the Jew who is only actually half-Jewish; the Jew who has abandoned religion; the Jew who starts their day by blessing the land of Israel; the Jew who spends their day protesting the state of Israel; the Jew who does not for a moment consider any of this—all may or may not feel Jewish. In matters like these, it is not appropriate to make decisions about belonging on someone else's behalf. To do so would be to act like the Nazis, relying on pseudoscientific criteria to distinguish the Jew from the non-Jew.

At the same time, it is also necessary for institutions to act according to some clear criteria. But sometimes objective criteria can lead to unconscionable results. Thus, for example, dozens who have spent their careers insulting Jews later turned up at the door of the chief rabbinate of Turkey in order to get the documents attesting to their Jewishness. Suddenly, some people in Turkey, among them both ordinary and professional antisemites, who found a Jew in their family tree, have gone from wanting to hide this fact to wanting to demonstrate it beyond doubt. For example, one person who arranged a meeting with me started by recounting his family history. Despite some Jewish ancestry, he said, he had absolutely nothing to do with Judaism and wanted this passport to be able to easily travel to the Greek Islands. He then added, "But my son is completely Jewish." When I asked him what he meant, he answered me plainly: "He's very stingy." I advised him to write this all down word-for-word in his application letter, and he apologized.

To whom? Who deserves an apology, who has the power to forgive?

There is an earthly element to forgiveness and a divine one. According to Emmanuel Levinas (1990, 21), no one can obtain forgiveness from God for a fault committed against another person. Perhaps justice is the same way—there is both divine and earthly justice. An earthly court, such as the European Court of Human Rights (ECHR), singles out an individual's inner world when evaluating freedom of religion because, according to ECHR's criterion, the right to change one's religion or belief is recognized as an individual's right to *forum internum* (an internal forum) and is protected unconditionally. The manifestation of religion or conviction is protected by the *forum externum* (external forum), on which some conditions might be placed in the case of compelling public interest. In the *Case of İzzettin Doğan and Others v Turkey*, the ECHR comes to mind: "Internal freedom (*forum internum*): The key international instruments confirm that '[e]veryone has the right to freedom of thought, conscience and religion.' In contrast to manifestations of religion, the right to freedom of thought, conscience and religion . . . is absolute and may not be subjected to limitations of any kind. Thus, for example, legal requirements mandating involuntary disclosure of religious beliefs are impermissible."[7] With these applications, we have acquired a new citizenship by legally proving some part of our absolute and unlimited *forum internum*. We have voluntarily disclosed it to the Porto or Lisbon communities and to the Portuguese state. In this way, we also acquired a new identity, a new piece of our identity.

Suddenly, in an email, we became Portuguese.

After becoming Portuguese, I traveled to Lisbon to get my passport and identity card. There, they measured my height to record it on my ID: 1.65 cm. I was surprised. I had thought I was 1.68 cm. Maybe I'm a little different from what I thought I was. I am not sure what being Portuguese will mean to me, or my clients, in the coming years: for some, it will be proof of their heritage. For others, it will be an opportunity for their children. I hope for me and my family that it will be a chance to step outside of ourselves and discover a new part of who we are. As José Saramago has already said, "If you don't step outside yourself, you'll never discover who you are" (Saramago 2011, 27).

Rita Ender graduated from Marmara University's Law School in 2008. She has worked as a lawyer since January 2010. She has master's degrees from Galatasaray University and Panthéon-Assas University (Paris II) and has done extensive work in the field of minority rights. Ender has written for a variety of newspapers and magazines in Turkey since 2001 and is the author of five books, including *İsmiyle Yaşamak* [Living with this name, 2016], *Aile Yadigarları* [Family heirlooms, 2018], *Madam Amati* (2019), *Bir Avazda—Hamilelik Söyleşileri* [All at once—Pregnancy interviews, 2021].

Notes

Since this writing, the Jewish Community of Porto has relinquished its role in the certification process.

1. In general, before 1934 most Muslims in Turkey did not have permanent family names, though most of the non-Muslim minorities did. The Surname Law had certain stipulations about permissible surnames; one such stipulation was that it could not be "foreign," a judgment that was left to the discretion of local bureaucrats.
2. It was there that the famous explorer's family owned land, according to Viktor Albukrek in *Bir Zamanlar Büyükada* (2013, 14).

3. Although women have filed a court case claiming that this article is against the constitution and international conventions and that it promotes inequality, the practice and the law have remained unchanged.
4. Though Turkey and Iran are neighboring countries with some of the largest Jewish populations in the Middle East, the communities have different origins—one traces its story to the Spanish Inquisition, one to the Book of Esther—and now have different destinies.
5. Halachically, Judaism is transmitted by mothers. A child born to a Jewish woman is Jewish, while one born to a non-Jewish woman is not considered to be Jewish, regardless of the father's identity.
6. I am reproducing the letter as it was originally written.
7. Case of İzzettin Doğan and Others / Turkey, Application no. 62649/10, 26 April 2016, p. 29.

References

Albukrek, Viktor. 2013. *Bir Zamanlar Büyükada*. İstanbul: Adalı.
Hirsch, Marianne. 2020. "An Interview with Marianne Hirsch." https://cup.columbia.edu/author-interviews/hirsch-generation-postmemory.
Janet and Jak Esim Ensemble. 2005. "Antik Bir Hüzün." Kalan Records.
———. 2006. "Adio." Kalan Records.
Levinas, Emmanuel. 1990. *Nine Talmudic Readings*. Bloomington: Indiana University Press.
Portuguese Law on Nationality. 2013. As amended by Organic Law No. 1/2013 of 29 July.
Rodrigues, Amalia. 1997. "Segredo." EMI-Valentim De Carvalho.
Saramago, José. 2011. *The Tale of the Unknown Island*. London: Havrill Press.
———. 2012. *The Manual of Painting and Calligraphy*. Boston: Mariner Books.

Chapter 11

Personal Essay
Sefarad Postponed

Ruth Behar

1

When I learned, in the summer of 2015, about the passage of what is referred to by many as the Spanish Law of Return for Sephardic Jews, my first thought was that I should pursue it. Not much, it seemed, was asked of us. The law didn't require residency in Spain and allowed for other citizenships. Then I learned about all the paperwork that was needed. I decided it would take too much effort. Still . . . I couldn't completely let go of the possibility of becoming *espanyola*, a Sephardic Jew with a Spanish passport. Every so often, I would again think I ought to do this—for the ancestors, and because of my longstanding passion for Spain and the Spanish language.

Growing up in a Cuban Jewish family, I had always spoken Spanish. It was my first language. As a young girl, I had a vague understanding that my Turkish Sephardic grandparents had a different accent because they spoke another Spanish, a very old, very antiquated Spanish. I didn't know it was called Ladino then. I also had a vague understanding of our family's roots in Spain. That was why, when I had the opportunity to travel on a semester abroad program, I chose to go to Spain. It was the autumn of 1975, and I was nineteen. I smoked Ducados, and drank *jerez* and spent my afternoons at the Prado Museum, transfixed by Goya's black paintings. Though it was exciting to be on my own as a young woman for the first time, I never felt carefree. The *guardia civil* in their stiff green uniforms and intimidating *tricornio* hats were stationed all over Madrid. I tried never to look at them, and when I did, their gazes were so harsh they sent a chill up my spine.

I remember the silence that enveloped Madrid when Franco died in November of that year. People were afraid to cheer, to speak, to smile. Experiencing the palpable fear that oppressed an entire nation, even *after* the death of their dictator, marked me, haunted me, and I came to feel an unbreakable bond with Spain and Spaniards. I had left Cuba when I was four and a half and had not yet visited my homeland as an adult, but I'd grown up hearing the family talk about Fidel Castro and how we'd been fortunate to escape from his dictatorship. Later, I'd return to visit Cuba and embark on a series of back-and-forth trips, reclaiming my bond with my native land and finding inspiration to write poetry in Spanish and connect with the Jewish community, but that sense of fear never left me, the fear I felt for the first time in Spain, that dictators had the power to infest your soul.

Afterward, it was in Spain that I became an anthropologist, living in a small village in the northern region of León in the late 1970s and early 1980s, and returning often into the early 1990s. People were kind and welcoming and I formed close bonds with several families that I am in touch with to this day. My great-uncle Moisés, on my mother's Ashkenazi side, had questioned my desire to do fieldwork in Spain rather than in Israel. "They expelled your father's family. Why go there?," he asked. It was hard to explain. I had a strong tie to Israel; my parents and my brother and I fled to Israel in the 1960s after the Cuban revolution, and Israel was the country that gave us our freedom first, and then after a year we'd gone on to the United States. But the tie to the Spanish language and Spanish heritage had proved stronger, even though in León I struggled with being in a place so profoundly steeped in Catholicism. I didn't dare tell anyone I was Jewish. It took years for me to "come out" as a Sephardic Jew in Spain.

Always, I felt a pull toward that tragic sense of life I'd read about in Miguel de Unamuno, the darkness Goya conjured, the feeling that Spain lived with an inexpressible weight of sorrow and guilt from its conquests, its expulsions, its lost empire, its authoritarianism, its widows who dressed in black grief forever, who refused happiness. And then I was away from Spain for several years, spending time in Cuba, where I never had to hide my Jewishness, and when I went back as the new century unfolded, I discovered a different country—suddenly obsessed with its Sephardic past. It was shocking to me, this Spain where I didn't have to hide, where the cloak of intolerance had been cast aside, where statues of Lorca in Madrid and of Mercè Rodoreda in Barcelona shone in the sun and children played at the feet of literary heroes who stood for freedom.

Yet I learned soon enough that being Jewish in Spain still evoked whispers and secrets. To attend Shabbat services in Barcelona and Madrid, we needed letters from our rabbi in Ann Arbor vouching for us, and extensive security checks. The synagogues were in unmarked buildings, likely the result of antisemitic attacks on synagogues elsewhere in Europe. But once inside these well-guarded spaces, it was a relief to see living, breathing Jews celebrating Judaism in Spain.

It's vexing sometimes to observe the excessive Spanish fascination with the Jews of the past that is visible in such cultural/archaeological/touristic projects as Caminos de Sefarad: Red de Juderías. In 2004 I experienced being the exotic Sephardic Other when I participated in the summit of a group of Sephardic Jews with the last name "Behar" that took place in Béjar (Behar 2013). We converged on the town seeking our roots, and the municipal leaders were delighted to welcome us back, offering entertainment that included a dramatic reading of the Edict of the Expulsion.

You can't help feeling that they prefer "us" as specimens in a museum. Imagine the little label, as the French Sephardic author Marcel Cohen puts it in his sorrowful manifesto, *In Search of a Lost Ladino*: "Visitors wishing to listen to the snippets of fifteenth-century ballads that he still retains faithfully in his memory should exercise respect and patience, since this specimen has a horror of appearing ridiculous" (Cohen 2006, 31).

2

So, yes, I had complex, ambivalent reasons to seek out Spanish citizenship, but always the paperwork seemed daunting. Then, at the end of August of 2019, I happened to be in Miami Beach and learned that the lawyer, Luis Portero, from Málaga, would be giving an evening chat about how Sephardic Jews could obtain Spanish citizenship. The event was taking place at Temple Moses, the Cuban Sephardic synagogue that my Tía (aunt) Fanny attends and that I attend whenever I am in town. I'm not religious, but I feel at home at Temple Moses among people who remember my family from Cuba. There are many who share not only the same Turkish-Cuban Sephardic ancestry, but also the last name Behar.

I decided I'd go to the event out of anthropological curiosity. Portero had represented several people I know and was an advocate for the offer of Spanish citizenship to the Sephardim. I planned to take notes and observe how the invitation to become Spanish citizens was being presented to Sephardic Jews like me, who were on the fence about whether to go through the bureaucratic and expensive process of obtaining a Spanish passport. There were about twenty people at the event, and Portero patiently spelled out every requirement, including language and civics exams, birth and marriage documents, police and FBI records, proof of Sephardic ancestry, and connection to Spain, a requirement that could be met through support for Spain's cultural institutions. He said it was our right as Sephardic Jews to claim our Spanish citizenship, and he wanted to help as many of us as he could with our applications. Repairing a historical wrong, working for *la justicia*, he told us, inspired him as a lawyer. He spoke with conviction and stayed long past when the event was supposed to end.

It still felt like a chore to gather together all that paperwork, but I found Portero to be quite congenial and I asked if we could talk further. He was on vacation in Miami Beach with his wife and two young sons, but invited me to meet him in the lobby of his hotel the next day. As we talked, he turned on his laptop. Before I knew it, he was filling out the basic application for me, so I could get in line at the ministry of justice before the upcoming 1 October 2019 deadline. I didn't know if I'd go through with the process, but I figured it couldn't hurt to get started. He told me the biggest challenge was going to be getting a copy of my Cuban birth certificate, which would need to be notarized in Havana by the Cuban authorities as well as the Embassy of Spain. That could take a while. The rest of the paperwork would be easier, he promised.

"¿Quieres hacerlo?" he asked earnestly. Did I want to go ahead?

"Creo que sí," I responded, I thought so, and promised to let him know soon.

Before we said goodbye, he told me he'd read my book, *The Presence of the Past in a Spanish Village: Santa María del Monte* (Behar 1986), about the village in León that had been the subject of my anthropology dissertation. And he'd seen my documentary, *Adio Kerida* (Behar 2002), about the Sephardic Jews of Cuba. He smiled and asked me to let him know if I had any new books or films; he'd be interested in learning more.

I was impressed. Portero had done his research. He wasn't just seeking clients. He was on a quest to find self-conscious Sephardic intellectuals like me—"Spaniards without a homeland," as Ángel Pulido (1905), the renowned Spanish physician, anthropologist, and senator, had called us more than a hundred years ago—and restore our citizenship. Even if only a symbolic act, this mattered. It was impossible to erase the expulsion of the Jews from the history of Spain, but a different future could be imagined where we might belong again.

3

I gradually gathered my documents, and through the kindness of friends in Havana, who stood on lines and offered bribes on my behalf, I was able to obtain the birth certificate with all the required stamps and signatures in three months.

It was an extremely slow process getting the certificate of Sephardic ancestry from one of the synagogues certified to provide it in the United States, but that finally arrived. And then one day I received an email from Portero's office letting me know that the Federation of Jewish Communities of Spain (FCJE), which adjudicates the Spanish ancestry of applicants for the 2015 law, had approved my application.

By March 2020 I had almost everything in place. I needed the civics test, which I'd take at the Cervantes Institute in New York. And I needed the police and FBI criminal records check, which I'd waited on since they would expire after six months; I wanted to avoid having to request them twice (I admit that requesting these documents terrified me. I have a Kafkaesque fear of being on the radar of these officials, for my parents taught me, even after we became American citizens, never to "llamar la atención," call attention to ourselves, or do anything that could get us deported).

I was starting to fantasize about the trip to Spain, stopping at the Prado and looking at Goya's *pinturas negras* (I saw these "black paintings" as an image of the Spain of the past, devoid of Jews, not of the present that now included "us"), and then taking the train to Málaga, where Luis Portero would be waiting, the sea glistening on the horizon. Pictures would be taken, of course, as I signed the papers, as I'd seen others do on Facebook, proudly claiming—and acclaiming—their Spanish citizenship.

I hadn't told my father I was pursuing Spanish citizenship—not knowing if he'd be for or against it, and not wanting to upset him, just in case. Our relationship had always been strained, ever since I was a young girl challenging his patriarchal control, but we both took pride in the Sephardic heritage that stemmed from his lineage. I thought about how I would surprise him with the news. Maybe, I hoped, this act of embracing our shared heritage would reconcile us in ways that misspoken words and long silences couldn't.

4

We were on the precipice of the pandemic, not yet aware of how dramatically it would put a halt to life as we had known it.

Soon it became clear I wouldn't be going to Spain in May or June. Nor in July, nor in August. Nor even in September or October. The year 2020 would be cancelled. My return to Sefarad would be postponed. For is Sefarad not a dream, in the end? Even with the existence of Israel, don't we still say, "Next year in Jerusalem"?

Amid the intense focus on mortality that has been our daily lot since the pandemic, thinking about attaining Spanish citizenship has seemed trivial in the grand scheme of things. Travel has been put on hold, making plans for the future has been put on hold. We live now with an acceptance of uncertainty. We live with the threat of death looming much too close. Even with two vaccines now approved and the first recipients being vaccinated, the surges continue. We don't know how long the pandemic will last, how long it will be before the entire world goes back to "normal." We wait and we postpone, we wait again, postpone again, and so the time passes.

And yet, during these days, I've been thinking a lot about the Sephardic expulsion from Spain in 1492. I'm trying to write a novel that references that era from the point of view of a young girl, and so I've steeped myself in histories and testimonies to try to learn how the Jews of Spain experienced that trauma. I want to know what their journeys were like as they fled via Portugal or via the ports of Cádiz or Valencia to Italy or the Ottoman Empire, what they felt as they departed their homeland, what goodbyes they uttered to family who made the decision to convert to Christianity and stay. There is so much that didn't get recorded. There are so many gaps to fill with the imagination. I tell myself that the uncertainty—and huge anxiety—that I live with now, day to day, gives me a deeper understanding of that departure, that flight into exile, that stubborn faith that allowed my ancestors to sing as they left Sefarad.

5

Maybe next year this global catastrophe will be over.

Maybe by then it will be possible to continue the process of obtaining Spanish citizenship.

Maybe by then that will seem important again.

Maybe I'll travel to Málaga, after all, and sign papers. And get my picture taken. And maybe (but not likely), I'll post it on Facebook.

6

España en el corazón... I borrow that phrase, Spain in the heart, from Pablo Neruda, whose book of poems about war-torn Spain was printed and bound by soldiers of the republic who made the paper themselves in the middle of fighting; then, after their defeat, they left with thousands of others in a mass exodus, going into exile ... like the Sephardim before them.

In the words of Neruda (2005, 20–21; emphasis in original):

*Cómo, hasta el llanto, hasta el alma
amo tu duro suelo, tu pan pobre . . .*

*How, even to weeping, even to the soul,
I love your hard earth, your humble bread . . .*

Spain is in *my* heart, but always with a touch of sorrow.
But still, I want to say . . .
Let it be joyful, let that moment be joyful—
When they give me back the key . . .
Our ancestors wept so many tears.
So let it be joyful.

Ann Arbor, MI, 28 December 2020

Epilogue

It was not to be.

Or it was not meant to be, if I think in terms of Sephardic superstitiousness.

By May 2021 I began to receive a series of messages from the legal office of Luis Portero letting me know that the deadline to sign the application for Spanish citizenship was fast approaching. That deadline was 1 September 2021. Then it was 31 December 2021. No exceptions could be made. The signing before a notary had to be done in person in Spain.

An email from 29 October 2021 in Spanish and stilted English informed me, "Due to the imminent end of Law 12/2105 of June 24 regarding the granting of Spanish nationality to Sephardic originating in Spain, we urge our clients who due to various causes have not been able to attend the signing before a notary to attend as soon as possible."

I wrote back and said that with the pandemic I didn't feel it was safe to travel to Spain and asked for an extension. By 12 November 2021, I received a response letting me know that their legal office could assist me in obtaining Portuguese citizenship instead. The email noted, "Obtaining Portuguese citizenship is a less involved process than the Spanish process and their law doesn't have a deadline so you can put in the request at any time and no sociocultural knowledge is required, nor do you need to know the Portuguese language, and you do not have to travel to Portugal to sign before a notary or to take care of any paperwork."

I said I would think about it. But the truth is I didn't know what to think. I felt such a strange mix of emotions all at once. I felt fooled for having believed Spain seriously wanted to offer a home to all of us Spaniards without a country. I felt humiliated, I felt sad, I felt angry, and finally I felt it was not meant to be for a reason, that I'd been saved from some evil, I'd been lucky.

Sefarad had been postponed by the pandemic. Then it was postponed by an arbitrary deadline. *La Espanya* had wanted us to return, but only within a time slot that had a beginning and an end. It was not a forever invitation.

Come back, departed ones, while the door is open.

Now the door had closed. And there was no key. And I wept for my ancestors. Again.

Ann Arbor, MI, 10 February 2022

Ruth Behar, anthropologist and author, is the James W. Fernandez Distinguished University Professor of Anthropology at the University of Michigan, a MacArthur Fellow, and member of the American Academy of Arts and Sciences. Her acclaimed scholarly books include *The Presence of the Past in a Spanish Village*, *Translated Woman*, *The Vulnerable Observer*, *An Island Called Home,* and *Traveling Heavy*. Other works include a collection of poems, *Everything I Kept/Todo lo que guardé;* a documentary, *Adio Kerida*; the prize-winning young adult novels, *Lucky Broken Girl* and *Letters from Cuba*; and *Tía Fortuna's New Home,* a children's book on Sephardic Cuban heritage.

References

Behar, Ruth. 1986. *The Presence of the Past in a Spanish Village: Santa María del Monte*. Princeton: Princeton University Press. 2nd ed., 1991. En español: *La presencia del pasado en un pueblo español: Santa María del Monte*. Museo Etnográfico de León, 2013.

———, dir. 2002. *Adio Kerida: A Cuban Sephardic Journey*. Women Make Movies. DVD. https://vimeo.com/ondemand/adiokerida

———. 2013. "The First World Summit of Behars." In *Traveling Heavy: A Memoir in between Journeys*, 117–41. Durham, NC: Duke University Press. En español: "La primera cumbre mundial de los Behar." En *Un cierto aire sefardí: Recuerdos de mis andares por el mundo*. Madrid: Editorial Verbum, 2020: 139–65.

Cohen, Marcel. 2006. *In Search of a Lost Ladino: Letter to Antonio Saura*. Jerusalem: Ibis Editions.

Neruda, Pablo. 2005. *Spain in Our Hearts: Hymn to the Glories of the People at War/ España en el corazón: Himno a las glorias del pueblo en guerra*. Translated by Donald D. Walsh. Selection from the poem "Cómo era España" (What Spain was like), 20–21. New York: New Directions.

Pulido, Angel. 1905. *Españoles sin patria y la raza sefardí*. Madrid.

Part IV.

Sephardi Descendants

Emotions, Identities, and Bureaucracies

Chapter 12

"La Nostalgia de Sefarad Tira Mucho, Pero No Tanto"
Attachment, Sentiment, and the Ethics of Refusal

Charles A. McDonald

Introduction

In August of 2016, I received an email from "Tony," a Sephardi American expatriate living in Madrid. "Have you seen this?" Attached was an article recently published in Spain's newspaper of record, *El País*, titled "Only 2,424 Sephardim Have Applied for Spanish Citizenship" (González 2016). I had first met Tony six months earlier when I interviewed him about his experience as an applicant under Spain's 2015 citizenship law for Sephardi Jews. We had remained in regular contact because he allowed me to figuratively—and literally—look over his shoulder while he moved through the application process. His email found me not long after I'd arrived back in New York from a year spent conducting fieldwork and archival research on various projects aimed at returning Jews and Judaism to Spain. Although I had been making research trips to Spain since 2010, I had envisioned this most recent visit as the culmination of my dissertation fieldwork, which I had timed to coincide with the law's first year.[1]

Tony had long been critical of various aspects of the law, including what he considered its overly stringent qualifications; a poorly designed application platform; an unwieldy bureaucratic structure; the application fees and often-unavoidable expense of hiring genealogists and lawyers; and the fact that the law itself was temporary rather than permanent. Given that some Jewish leaders and government officials had estimated

Spain might receive as many as half a million applications in total, media outlets and Sephardi Jews alike registered surprise at early numbers that were considerably lower than anticipated (see Gladstone 2014; *La Vanguardia* 2018). The *El País* article was one of the first in a string of media reports over the next few years that suggested the law was garnering fewer applicants than expected due to many of the same issues Tony had identified (Adatto 2019; Caselli 2016; González 2018, 2019a, 2019b). In keeping with other media assessments of the law, the article concluded that the typical total cost (3,000–5,000 euros) combined with the other requirements (genealogical documentation, proof of a special connection with modern Spain, language and culture tests, and travel to Spain to sign the completed application) would likely dissuade seniors and people of limited means from applying. These bureaucratic and financial obstacles were compounded by poor preparation, inadequate staffing, and an unreliable online submission portal. For all these reasons, the article warned that the law risked ending up a fiasco. As the kicker put it, "La nostalgia de Sefarad tira mucho, pero no tanto" (Nostalgia for Sepharad pulls hard, but not that hard).

Other Gravities, Other Claims

In the 2015 law's preamble—as well as in the rhetoric of state and religious authorities—sentiments like nostalgia and love are ascribed to Sephardi descendants, while the possibility that they might feel rancor toward Spain for the Expulsion is habitually invoked only to be denied (McDonald 2021). This chapter is less concerned with how the Spanish state has envisioned the emotions and attachments of its would-be subjects than it is with the discrepancies between these visions and those expressed by Sephardi descendants themselves. Scholars writing about the Iberian citizenship laws have rightly argued that we need to attend to the ways that the act of applying for citizenship has often prompted Sephardi descendants to rethink their ancestry, identity, and attachments (Benmayor and Kandiyoti 2020). But what about those who are choosing not to apply? How ought we read their decisions? Why might some Sephardi descendants find it preferable, or even necessary, to refuse the offer of citizenship? What can those perspectives add to our understanding of the ways that people negotiate citizenship and its attendant claims, particularly in scenarios where states promote the offer of citizenship as a form of historical reparation? This chapter is about those Sephardi descendants for whom nostalgia hardly pulled at all, or for whom its pull was insufficient to counteract other forces.[2]

This is not to discount the many Sephardi descendants who welcomed these laws for a wide range of reasons (Benmayor and Kandiyoti 2020; Côrte-Real Pinto and David 2019; Goldschläger and Orjuela 2021; Shammah Gesser 2019). Nor I do I wish to overlook the significant challenges the application process presented for Sephardi descendants. Some scholars have raised concerns about the law's historical connection to the Regenerationist movement of the early twentieth century, and other philosephardic projects that cast Sephardi Jews in racial terms (McDonald 2021; Ojeda-Mata 2017; Naar, chap. 5, in this volume; see also Goode 2009). Others have pointed out the law's disregard for the heterogeneous ways that Sephardi descendants reckon belonging in favor of claiming the Spanish nation-state as the primary frame for thinking about Sephardi identity (Benmayor and Kandiyoti 2020; Goldschläger and Orjuela 2021). The law has also elicited strong critiques for its exclusion of Muslims and Morisco descendants from similar return legislation (Bastaki 2017; McDonald 2021), as discussed in the chapters in this volume by Arigita and Galian (chap. 8), and Bolorinos Allard (chap. 6).

Less frequently addressed has been the question of those Sephardi descendants who were eligible and had the means to apply, but who chose not to. I argue that any analysis of Iberian citizenship as potentially reparative must include the experiences of Sephardi descendants who refuse to participate. My aim is to consider the conditions of possibility for such decisions and some of the ways that my interlocutors made sense of them. Whether they take the form of explicit rejections, pointed critiques, or general indifference, I read these refusals as political claims. Such claims may also be cautionary, enjoining scholars against inadvertently reproducing the very rhetorics that these laws have summoned and reanimated.

A Note on Methods:
Ethnographic Fieldwork and Partial Knowledge

This discussion of the ethics of refusal among Sephardi descendants emerged from a larger book project on the return to Sepharad, of which Spain's 2015 citizenship law is but one part. My thinking is indebted to conversations that took place during fieldwork in multiple countries and across various digital platforms over a span of many years, as well as archival and textual research. As a cultural anthropologist I am perhaps more wary than colleagues in other fields may be of the epistemological claims of quantitative approaches that promise to capture and reveal the truth, if we can just determine the right sample size. Yet the question of who and what counts when moral injury, reparations, and citizenship are at stake is very much a part of the story of how the law was developed and received.³ One challenge of writing about this law is attending to the multiple, and often competing, claims about quantification without necessarily acceding to their logics. This methodological discussion is as much a reluctant response to the exhortation to distill and parcel out ethnographic data as it is an imperfect, but necessary, accounting of who and what led me here.

Tony was one of several dozen interlocutors I met in the years since plans for the Sephardi citizenship law were first announced in 2012. I also regularly communicated with people I met as far back as 2007, when I lived in Córdoba for a year and first became interested in Spain's Jewish revivals. These included the members of various Jewish communities in Madrid, Barcelona, Sevilla, and several smaller cities; officials from the Federation of Jewish Communities of Spain (FCJE) and the government; ex-patriate Jews like Tony who had been living in Spain for years; Jewish students and tourists; colleagues and collaborators; and the transnational networks that connected us. The bulk of my ethnographic research consisted mainly of participant-observation, sustained by long-term relationships of trust. As such, my classical fieldwork has spanned more than a decade and encompasses informal conversations and encounters with hundreds of people, which occurred in spaces including synagogues, bars, homes, conferences, museums, beaches, workshops, hotels, public commemorations, parties, and political demonstrations.

In order to broaden the reach of my study and include people I would otherwise not encounter during my primary fieldwork, I conducted roughly forty additional interviews between 2015 and 2019 with Sephardi descendants from Venezuela, Turkey, France, Brazil, Israel, Mexico, Argentina, the United Kingdom, and the United States. My interlocutors ranged in age from their early twenties to their late seventies, and included slightly more men than women. To meet them, I sought out referrals from existing contacts, joined online groups for Sephardi descendants and Iberian citizenship-seekers, and responded to direct queries from applicants interested in my research. Since most potential citizenship applicants were not living in Spain, the majority of our discussions took place over Skype, Zoom, or telephone, rather than in person.

Unsurprisingly, interviewing people who did not apply for citizenship under the Spanish or Portuguese schemes presented something of a challenge, since there were few obvious ways for me to locate them and little incentive for them to speak to me. Of the people I spoke to directly, I encountered only a handful who decided not to apply for either citizenship law. I did, however, learn from them about others who made similar decisions, mainly family members. Here I focus only on three exchanges, which reveal the underexplored theme of refusal among Sephardi descendants and complicate the emerging scholarly literature on the Iberian laws. I do not, nor could I hope to, speak to the full spectrum of reasons why people did not apply to the Spanish law. Sephardi descendants understood the law, its promise of return, and their relations to it in many different ways. To the extent that ethnography is imagined as authorized by its grounding in the empirical, it is the particularity rather than the generalizability of these scenes that I am interested in. This is what anthropologist Marilyn Strathern (2004) has called partial knowledge: motivated, fragmentary, and in pursuit of good connections. I draw on the words of my interlocutors not to claim them as representative cases, but to discern where unsettled histories, personal experience, and collective imaginings collide to animate a politics of refusal.

Disappointment, Frustration, Critique

In retrospect, I think that Tony's decision to forward me the *El País* article in August 2016 marked the beginning of a shift in the way that many of my interlocutors spoke about the law. Between 2012 (when proposals for the new Spanish law were first introduced) and late 2015 (when the law went into effect), most people I spoke to were excited and hopeful about the legislation. Of course, they had questions and concerns, but there was a widespread sense that the new law represented an important commitment, albeit largely symbolic, to redressing the injuries of the past and perhaps even securing a better future. Even Tony—who was as realist as they come and who had exhaustively detailed what he perceived as the law's limitations—was nevertheless eager for the law to go into effect. Indeed, he was one of the very first to apply. But as more of my interlocutors experienced the lengthy and frustrating application process themselves, and critical reports about the numbers of applicants and the obstacles they faced began to circulate, the mood noticeably darkened. Many of the people with whom I was in conversation were now being confronted by a reality that did not live up to the hopes and fantasies they had nurtured when the law existed as a mere possibility.

Phrases that I had rarely heard uttered before late 2016 began to litter the pages of my fieldnotes and transcripts: my interlocutors increasingly spoke of the law as superficial, disorganized, slapdash, and insincere. One person I interviewed in 2017 was convinced that Spain had "passed [the law] to make themselves feel good, but there was no infrastructure behind it or anything like that." Like other Sephardi descendants that I spoke to, he chose to apply to Portugal instead of Spain based on what he read in the news and heard from friends and family who were familiar with the process, which he deemed disorganized. One successful applicant, who in 2019 referred to the law as superficial, told me he felt it was deliberately limited. He speculated that this was because the government was "afraid of the anti-Jewish public in Spain." I noted this shift in language both among those I had spoken to previously and with first-time interviewees, where negative evaluations became more common over time. I am, of course, not suggesting that everyone soured on the law, or that my interlocutors uniformly felt one way or another. My point is that, if earlier narratives were largely positive, if tempered by specific critiques, the frequency and volume of negative descriptions increased as my interlocutors knew more about the practicalities of applying and how many applications were being submitted and approved. It is against this backdrop that I interpret the refusals I describe here, even as I understand them less as a direct response to low numbers than as a widening discrepancy between what my interlocutors felt had been promised and what was being delivered. Some of them believed the law could and should reunite an orphaned diasporic people with their culture and place of origin. Others hoped the law might help save vulnerable Sephardi Jews from antisemitism and political turmoil in places like Venezuela and Turkey, or in the United States and the United Kingdom, by giving them refuge in Spain. Still others insisted that the law should establish a permanent legal right to Spanish citizenship for Sephardi Jews along with a comprehensive set of legal, cultural, and educational measures that would ensure their safety in Spain.

Refusing Absolution

"Alexandra" was a middle-aged Sephardi-American woman with piercing blue-gray eyes and an intense energy that was both commanding and charming. We met in September of 2016 at a New York bakery known for its excellent babka after a mutual contact put us in touch. Wedging ourselves into two chairs on either side of a tiny white table, we made small talk as I retrieved my notebook and recorder and prepared to begin interviewing her about her plans to apply for Spanish citizenship. I was thrown off when instead *she* began grilling *me*. Why was Spain doing this? Why was it limited to a three-year window? How were they determining who was Sephardic? Would she be absolving Spain of its past by applying? If the first three questions were ones I had been grappling with for some time, the last one surprised me, because it centered not on what the abstract entity of Spain wanted, but on what Sephardi Jews in the diaspora might *not* want. Until that point, I confess, it had not occurred to me that anyone who could take advantage of the law might choose not to. I had taken for granted that it was the ethical position of the state that was most pressing; she brought a more expansive notion of ethics into view, one that was rooted in the agency of potential Spanish subjects, and that understood the act of deliberation itself as presupposing an *already present* obligation of the state to Sephardi descendants.

It wasn't until we were quite far along in the discussion that I learned that Alexandra was an attorney who had spent years working with immigrants and refugees, and so was especially attuned to the doubled-edged sword of citizenship: its capacity to simultaneously include and exclude (Mehta 1990; Stein 2016; Thomas and Clarke 2013). She told me that she was concerned about the unwarranted legitimacy that her application might confer on a law that she and other Jews considered inadequate on moral and historical grounds. Although she had agreed to meet because she was thinking about applying for the law, by the end of the conversation she seemed certain that she would be doing no such thing. I had only just returned to New York and begun puzzling through the previous year of fieldwork, so I had fewer answers to her questions than we both would have liked. Looking back on our conversation now, it strikes me that my responses hardly mattered. It's not that she was delivering a prepared monologue, as I had come to expect from some interviewees. Rather, she was reflecting in real time, as she cycled through questions, *felt* their implications, and then arrived somewhere new. She seemed disappointed, or perhaps indignant, as if she had retroactively been betrayed, and was already anticipating a betrayal that had not yet fully materialized. She was reasoning, it seemed to me, through sentiments.

As Audra Simpson astutely observes, "The primary way in which the state's power is made real and personal, affective in its capacity, is through the granting of citizenship and, in this, the structural and legal preconditions for intimacy, forms of sociability, belongings, and affections" (Simpson 2014, 18). And yet, such "affections and attachments—familial and otherwise—were often impervious to the meddling priorities of a supposedly 'rational' and reasoned state" (Stoler 2009, 2). Theoretical approaches associated with the affective turn (Clough and Halley 2007) have largely failed to address the discrepancies between those sentiments sanctioned by the state in the name of citizenship and those that subjects, or would-be-subjects, actually experience. Alexandra's investments are opaque from the perspective of theories that draw arbitrary distinctions between affect and emotion, and between either of these and reason (Ahmed 2004; Martin 2013; White 2017). As Emily

Martin writes, whatever their differences, those who subscribe to this notion of affect tend to "claim that the role of reason and rationality in politics, ethics, and aesthetics has been overvalued" (Martin 2013, S154). And they are right to make this argument.

But recognizing that reason has never been nearly as discrete, sure-footed, or effective as its proponents and critics would have us believe need not entail rejecting analyses that foreground a politics of affect that is not rooted in the unknowable depths of consciousness. Given the ways in which affect theory has reproduced mind-body dualisms that see autonomous intensities as somehow more revelatory of what we do and why, it may be more helpful to think with sentiments, which Stoler (2009, 40) defines as "judgments, assessments, and interpretations of the social and political world." To speak of sentiments is to recognize that Alexandra's emotive and ethical deliberations are already part of the same history as the Spanish state's appeals to nostalgia and love, and thus ought to be brought into the same analytic frame.

Alexandra not only maintained that applying would be tantamount to absolving Spain of its historical responsibility to Sephardi Jews. She also told me that she had been dissuaded by the fact that Spain had not made the long-term investments in education, infrastructure, and social welfare that would be necessary to combat antisemitism and make the settlement of new Jewish citizens in Spain viable. Alexandra's sense of the poverty of the law and its lack of institutional support emerged in part from her work with a nongovernmental organization (NGO) that worked on issues of historical memory and human rights. For her, post-Holocaust Germany offered a model for atonement, reconciliation, and material support (see Slyomovics 2015) that Spain could have followed if it had been serious about the return of Jews. This was a position taken by several other people I interviewed, including those who had applied for citizenship in Spain or Portugal.

Since Spain's now-expired law did not guarantee a right of return as established in other contexts, the citizenship it offers is better understood as a gift (McDonald 2021), one which attempts to foreclose, rather than address, the question of non-material reparations.[4] As Marcel Mauss (1967) has shown, gifts incur obligations; they do not just reflect relationships, but also create and sustain them. While Mauss understood the refusal of a gift as ending relations, Carole McGranahan (2016, 335) has asked us to consider refusal as a "generative act, a rearrangement of relations rather than an ending of them." In the case McGranahan describes, exiled Tibetans have preemptively refused citizenship in India and Nepal for decades on the grounds that it might void their claims on Tibet. Her account is informed by Audra Simpson, who has theorized how indigenous people participate in "calculated refusals of the 'gifts' of the state, and in vexed determinations of 'membership' and belonging in that state" (Simpson 2014, 12). This is a different sort of refusal than we are used to thinking about, one that decenters the state as the only grounds for thinking the political and inquires instead into how it is productive for those who refuse. While the relationship of Sephardi descendants to the citizenship offered by Spain and Portugal, and the political stakes of their refusal, is distinct from Tibetan refugees or Indigenous Iroquois, there are important resonances. Any state's power to grant citizenship is founded on inequality. This is perhaps especially clear when citizenship takes the form of a gift bestowed, rather than as a right demanded and enforced. Refusal recasts that relationship of inequality in favor of a political otherwise: "Refusal involves attachments, connections to a goal, relations to ambitions. It is a no committed to generating a yes" (McGranahan 2016, 335).

Alexandra evidently did not feel the love and nostalgia for Spain that state discourses suggested she would or should. The affective states I noted in our conversation had less to do with Spain's history and more to do with its failure to acknowledge that history in the present. Her indignation arose in response to what she and so many other Sephardi descendants saw as Spain's superficial treatment of historical justice and the reparative work required to enact it. Suspicious of what the acceptance of Spanish citizenship meant—and the very terms in which it was being offered—she refused to even apply. If Alexandra was being pulled at all, it was not by nostalgia for Sepharad, but rather by her attachments to other Jews and by her awareness of the ways that citizenship so often denies, rather than confers, rights. The pull of these ethical demands envisioned a more honest and lasting reparative politics for Sephardi descendants, one that might be possible someday, but not under the conditions of Spain's 2015 law.

Indifference

In early 2019, "Aarón" responded to a request for interviews I'd posted in a Facebook group for Venezuelan Jews. A few weeks later, we spoke on the phone as his son was driving him to an appointment in the Midwestern US city where they lived. Born in 1974, Aarón was—like many Venezuelan Jews his age—the child of Sephardi immigrants who had left Morocco shortly after its independence from France and Spain in 1956. When I asked him what he thought about the citizenship law, he told me there was an ethical component given the history of the Inquisition, and that the law could be a way for Spain to address what he termed its "very hard history with the Jews." Although he thought it was helpful for Spain to recognize both this history and other diasporic Sephardi Jews like him, Aarón suspected that there were ulterior motives at play. In the years since the law was first announced, he had come to believe that "it was a strategy to control the demographics . . . certain people have been growing. . . . Some areas have grown heavily in terms of the Muslim population." I gathered from his tone that such a concern on the part of the Spanish state was not unreasonable or surprising to him.

Aarón said that many Venezuelans he knew had applied for the law over the previous four years, hoping that a Spanish passport might offer them an escape from the rather grim situation at home. As for him, he already held dual US–Spanish citizenship and had been living in the United States for the past decade, so he saw no reason to apply. Aarón identified strongly with his Moroccan Sephardi ancestry and with his birthplace, Venezuela. Like Alexandra, he did not need Spanish citizenship, nor did he feel particularly attached to Spain, though he believed that Spain owed something to Sephardi descendants. Unlike her, however, he had no affective response to the law, indignant or otherwise. As he told me simply, "I don't have big emotions about it."

Aarón's emotional indifference toward Spain and the citizenship law echoed a conversation I'd had two years earlier with "Casey," an American in his mid-thirties, about his extended family. When we spoke, he had highlighted his relative privilege as an American, even at a time when antisemitism in the United States had risen dramatically since Donald Trump was elected president. As he observed, "Of all the people who deserve reparations of any kind from a state that has an opportunity to give those reparations, I guess we're low on the list for the most part. It's not like we're refugees. It's not a pressing concern. At least not here." While having a Spanish passport and the mobility that it conferred was not a pressing concern in New York, it was in Venezuela, where much of Casey's family still lived: "They're kind of screwed: all of their property and assets are in Venezuela, but they want to leave really badly." And yet, as he explained, his Venezuelan family members were unlikely to avail themselves of either the Spanish or Portuguese citizenship offers. Although his family strongly identified as Sephardi Jews, he explained that theirs was "not a deep-seated connection to Spain."

Their attachments lay elsewhere: "Especially because my Venezuelan family are Jews now—they're not crypto-Jews—if they needed to get out, I think they'd say either America or Israel. Spain would be pretty low on their list."[5] When I asked why Spain was such an improbable choice for them, he explained that Israel or America would be easier transitions, since his family had networks in both countries. But their disinterest in Spain or Portugal was not only a matter of familiarity and convenience. "From an emotional standpoint even, I think they would want to be in Israel, versus Spain or Portugal. If it were more of a refugee issue, it would be those places, versus the desire to have a passport."

"And why those places?," I asked. To begin with, Casey explained, there were more Jews in the United States and Israel. But beyond that, his family "identifies with a global Jewish culture more than they identify with a more provincial Sephardi or Spanish culture." From his family's perspective, "there is a weird sense, not that it's fake, but that becoming an actual Spaniard is a little artificial. Why are you trying to become a Spaniard? You're a Sephardic Jew. Isn't that enough?" I asked Casey whether his parents—who lived in the United States, and were eligible for Spanish or Portuguese citizenship—would consider applying. With a half-smile, he shook his head no. On this issue, there was a profound generational gap that separated him and his American cousins from their parents. His father and grandmother were still Dutch citizens; they weren't "concerned or interested" in the Iberian legislation because they felt "no need to reconcile," as the language of the law suggested they would.

For Casey's parents and grandparents, there is no inevitable correspondence between Sephardi ancestry and national attachments. Rather, emotional connections are the result of preexisting relationships and ways of wrestling with history, affinity, and solidarity. For them, Spain and Portugal are abstract and provincial places: whatever pull they may have had for earlier generations of Sephardi Jews is eclipsed by the lively social and economic ties his family now has with Israel and the United States. The older generations in his family simply don't see Spain or Portugal as important nodes in what Casey called a global Jewish culture. They harbored neither nostalgia nor rancor for Spain, nor any other sentiments. Despite his American family's anxieties about Trump and his Venezuelan family's increasingly desperate situation, they chose not to apply for either of the Iberian citizenship laws. Their refusal took the form of indifference.

Conclusion

How do Sephardi descendants respond to the gift of citizenship? What quandaries does it occasion, and what opportunities may it provide for thinking and doing politics otherwise? In different ways, each of these brief ethnographic vignettes foregrounds discrepancy as a galvanizing force for sentiments and actions. The stories unfolded by Alexandra, Aarón, and Casey echo something I have found in my other fieldwork as well: Spain's law has a way of disturbing the very histories of exile and diaspora that it claims to ameliorate or even supersede (McDonald 2019). Ironically, by casting Sephardi descendants as essentially Spanish in a fantasy of national integration and redemption, the narrative that the law seeks to enact ends up undermining itself. Like any mechanism for granting citizenship, Spain's law aims to identify and secure the right kinds of national subjects, whether through the explicit criteria for inclusion that determine who counts as a Sephardi descendant; the evidentiary, bureaucratic, and financial obstacles it requires applicants to navigate; or the tacit exclusion of Muslim and Morisco descendants.

The Sephardi histories I encountered in my fieldwork were entangled in multiple diasporas and empires, entanglements that were obscured by the neat lists of nations where descendants were (or were not) applying for Spanish citizenship. For many of my interlocutors, the law articulated a normative correspondence between sentiment and attachment that bore little resemblance to their lives. The discrepancy between their conceptions of Sephardi history, identity, and reparative justice, and those that were embedded in the law triggered a sense of misrecognition. Individual feelings of misrecognition existed alongside and sometimes in tension with other, more positive, sentiments. The experience of misrecognition did not inevitably prompt sustained critiques or refusals among people who found themselves in that position, one in which their ways of being in the world were at odds with those espoused by a state that claimed to speak to and for them. But for some of the Sephardi descendants I came to know, the law's failure to correspond with what they knew and how they felt prompted them to reassess how they might relate to Spain and to citizenship itself.

For more than a century, philosephardic thinkers promoted the return of Sephardi Jews as the solution to many of Spain's problems, even as they fretted about the possibility that Jews might continue to harbor rancor for the Expulsion (McDonald 2021). But the refusals I have described here were born not of an irrational emotional attachment to the injuries of the past, but of the inequities of the present. Rather than breaking with the past to reconcile and repair, the law appeared to some of my interlocutors (and to me) as a continuity. They refused the gift of citizenship as a rebuke not of Spain's history, but rather of its unilateral transformation of that history such that what many of them saw as an inadequate or cynical gesture of atonement could be presented as a resolution. By attending to Sephardi refusals, we are better able to take stock of a more complicated geography of belonging and ethical relations than envisioned by the law.

Charles A. McDonald is a Scholar-in-Residence at the King Juan Carlos I of Spain Center at New York University and the Managing Director of the Institute for Critical Social Inquiry at the New School for Social Research. He has previously held postdoctoral fellowships at Northwestern University and Rice University. He received his PhD in anthropology and historical studies at the New School in 2019. His work has been supported by the Social Science Research Council (SSRC), Wenner-Gren Foundation, and the Center for Jewish History. He has held visiting research positions at the Consejo Superior de Investigaciones Científicas (CSIC), Universidad Autónoma de Madrid, and the Universitat Autònoma de Barcelona. He is currently working on a book manuscript about the return of Jews and Judaism in contemporary Spain.

Notes

1. Law 12/2015 was approved in June and went into effect in October.
2. On the politics of nostalgia, see Angé and Berliner (2014); Boym (2001).
3. For a stunning analysis of the politics of counting and accountability, see Nelson (2015).
4. On Israel's Law of Return, see Kravel-Tovi (2017); Seeman (2009).
5. For recent work on the descendants of conversos and crypto-Jews, see Kandiyoti (2020) and Leite (2017).

References

Adatto, Kiku. 2019. "Spain's Attempt to Atone for a 500-Year-Old Sin." *The Atlantic*, 21 September. https://www.theatlantic.com/international/archive/2019/09/spain-offers-citizenship-sephardic-jews/598258/.
Ahmed, Sara. 2004. *The Cultural Politics of Emotion*. New York: Routledge.
Angé, Olivia, and David Berliner, eds. 2014. *Anthropology and Nostalgia*. New York: Berghahn.
Bastaki, Janan. 2017. "Reading History into Law: Who is Worthy of Reparations? Observations on Spain and Portugal's Return Laws and the Implications for Reparations." *Islamophobia Studies Journal* 4, no. 1: 115–28.
Benmayor, Rina, and Dalia Kandiyoti. 2020. "Ancestry, Genealogy, and Restorative Citizenship: Oral Histories of Sephardi Descendants Reclaiming Spanish and Portuguese Nationality." *Quest. Issues in Contemporary Jewish History* 18 (December): 1–33.
Boym, Svetlana. 2001. *The Future of Nostalgia*. New York: Basic Books.
Caselli, Irene. 2016. "Argentina's Sephardic Jews Mull Return to Spain after 524 Years." *BBC News*, 24 December 2016. https://www.bbc.com/news/world-latin-america-38328490.
Clough, Patricia Ticineto, and Jean Halley. 2007. *The Affective Turn: Theorizing the Social*. Durham, NC: Duke University Press.

Côrte-Real Pinto, Gabriela Anouck, and Isabel David. 2019. "Choosing Second Citizenship in Troubled Times: The Jewish Minority in Turkey." *British Journal of Middle Eastern Studies* 46, no. 5: 781–96.

Gladstone, Rick. 2014. "Many Seek Spanish Citizenship Offered to Sephardic Jews." *New York Times*, 19 March 2014. https://www.nytimes.com/2014/03/20/world/europe/many-seek-spanish-citizenship-offered-to-sephardic-jews.html.

Goldschläger, Arielle, and Camilla Orjuela. 2021. "Return After 500 Years? Spanish and Portuguese Repatriation Laws and the Reconstruction of Sephardic Identity." *Diaspora Studies* 14, no. 1: 97–115.

González, Miguel. 2016. "Solo 2.424 Sefardíes Han Pedido La Nacionalidad Española." *El País*, 27 August 2016. https://elpais.com/politica/2016/08/27/actualidad/1472323420_545660.html.

———. 2018. "Los sefardíes dan la espalda a su ley." *El País*, 18 November 2018. https://elpais.com/politica/2018/11/17/actualidad/1542476664_339040.html.

———. 2019a. "Los Sefardíes Ya no Son Españoles Sin Patria, Proclama El Presidente De La Comunidad Judía." *El País*, 2 October 2019. https://elpais.com/politica/2019/10/02/actualidad/1570019211_938436.html.

———. 2019b. "Sephardic Jews Rush to Apply for Spanish Citizenship before Deadline Ends." *El País*, 2 October 2019. https://english.elpais.com/elpais/2019/10/02/inenglish/1570003149_039827.html.

Goode, Joshua. 2009. *Impurity of Blood: Defining Race in Spain, 1870–1930*. Baton Rouge: Louisiana State University Press.

Kandiyoti, Dalia. 2020. *The Converso's Return: Conversion and Sephardi History in Contemporary Literature*. Stanford, CA: Stanford University Press.

Kravel-Tovi, Michal. 2017. *When the State Winks: Jewish Conversion, Performance, and Bureaucracy in Israel*. New York: Columbia University Press.

La Vanguardia. 2018. "El Gobierno amplía un año el plazo para que judíos sefardíes adquieran la nacionalidad Española." 9 March. https://www.lavanguardia.com/vida/20180309/441376394532/el-gobierno-amplia-un-ano-el-plazo-para-que-judios-sefardies-adquieran-la-nacionalidad-espanola.html.

Law 12/2015. 2015. "Ley 12/2015 de 24 de junio, en materia de concesión de la nacionalidad española a los sefardíes originarios de España" [Law 12/2015 of 24 June, granting Spanish nationality to Sephardi Jews originating from Spain]. *Boletín Oficial del Estado*, 25 June 2015, no. 151.

Leite, Naomi. 2017. *Unorthodox Kin: Portuguese Marranos and the Global Search for Belonging*. Oakland: University of California Press.

Martin, Emily. 2013. "The Potentiality of Ethnography and the Limits of Affect Theory." *Current Anthropology* 54, no. S7: S149–S158. https://doi.org/10.1086/670388.

Mauss, Marcel. 1967. *The Gift: Forms and Functions of Exchange in Archaic Societies*. Translated by Ian Cunnison. New York: W. W. Norton.

McDonald, Charles A. 2019. "Return to Sepharad: Citizenship, Conversion, and the Politics of Inclusion." PhD dissertation, New School for Social Research, New York.

———. 2021. "Rancor: Sephardi Jews, Spanish Citizenship, and the Politics of Sentiment." *Comparative Studies in Society and History* 63, no. 3: 722–751.

McGranahan, Carole. 2016. "Refusal and the Gift of Citizenship." *Cultural Anthropology* 31 no. 3: 334–41.

Mehta, Uday S. 1990. "Liberal Strategies of Exclusion." *Politics* and *Society* 18, no. 4: 427–54.

Nelson, Diane M. 2015. *Who Counts? The Mathematics of Death and Life after Genocide.* Durham, NC: Duke University Press.

Ojeda-Mata, Maite. 2017. *Modern Spain and the Sephardim: Legitimizing Identities.* Lanham, MD: Lexington Books.

Seeman, Don. 2009. *One People, One Blood: Ethiopian-Israelis and the Return to Judaism.* New Brunswick, NJ: Rutgers University Press.

Schammah Gesser, Silvina. 2019. "Virtually Sephardic? the Marketing and Reception of the New Iberian Laws of Nationality in Israel." *Lusotopie* 18: 192–217.

Simpson, Audra. 2014. *Mohawk Interruptus: Political Life Across the Borders of Settler States.* Durham, NC: Duke University Press.

Slyomovics, Susan. 2015. *How to Accept German Reparations.* Philadelphia: University of Pennsylvania Press.

Stein, Sarah Abrevaya. 2016. *Extraterritorial Dreams: European Citizenship, Sephardi Jews, and the Ottoman Twentieth Century.* Chicago: University of Chicago Press.

Stoler, Ann Laura. 2009. *Along the Archival Grain: Epistemic Anxieties and Colonial Common Sense.* Princeton: Princeton University Press.

Strathern, Marilyn. 2004. *Partial Connections.* Walnut Creek: Altamira Press.

Thomas, Deborah A., and Kamari M. Clarke. 2013. "Globalization and Race: Structures of Inequality, New Sovereignties, and Citizenship in a Neoliberal Era." *Annual Review of Anthropology* 42, no. 1: 305–25.

White, Daniel. 2017. "Affect: An Introduction." *Cultural Anthropology* 32, no. 2: 175–180.

Chapter 13

Affective Citizenship and Iberian Sephardi Descendants

Rina Benmayor

On 18 April 2018, my Spanish passport arrived in the mail, culminating an intense and challenging two-year process. For me, obtaining Spanish citizenship was charged from the very beginning with emotional significance.[1] While the passport legally signified my membership in the nation-state, it was also the material embodiment of my reclamation of an ancestral right. Its blank pages secreted the hidden holographic narratives of our Iberian Sephardi past, waiting to be revealed. The pages also enclosed stories of my lived relationship with Spain. During my first trip in the early 1960s, a *pensión* receptionist recorded my passport and immediately pulled me aside, whispering, "Eres una de mozós?" Are you one of us? Stunned, I nodded yes. I had no idea that "we" had any contemporary presence in Spain. During my doctoral studies in Spanish literature, I heard a tape of an elderly woman singing a medieval Spanish ballad in a language I instantly recognized as Ladino. That moment of recognition led to my own collection and study of Judeo-Spanish *romances* (ballads) in oral tradition (Benmayor 1979). In my fifty years as a scholar, this work still means the most to me. Recently, I discovered my surnames in medieval archived documents: Çaragoçi (Saragossi) appears as early as 1293 in Toledo, and Abenmayor in the early fifteenth century also in Toledo and other cities (León Tello 1979). These experiences were inscribed in the pages of this passport, in invisible ink.

When I first learned about the proposed citizenship law in 2012, I remember feeling overcome with anticipation. When it finally appeared in 2015, the feeling was of excitement to discover that I met every one of the qualifications. I was not prepared, however, for the stresses of the actual application process: two long years securing documents, notarizations, *apostilles* (legal certifications), translations, tests, criminal record checks, four attempts at fingerprint clearance, more signatures, and waiting, waiting for the snail mail at each step along the way. In the summer of 2018, I finally traveled to Spain on my newly minted passport, entering Europe through pre-Brexit London. I felt relief at being able to bypass the long immigration line and privileged to sail through the "E.U. Citizens Here" lane. However, arriving in Madrid, I found no immigration checkpoint and no official to greet me with my fantasized "Welcome home!" In today's digital world, hand stamping passports is a thing of the past. Such contrasting feelings of elation at the end of this long quest, finally with my prize in hand, and sudden deflation at its seeming insignificance, drove home just how emotionally laden citizenship can be.

Beginning in 2017, Dalia Kandiyoti and I initiated the Sephardic Jews and Spanish and Portuguese Citizenship Oral History project (Benmayor and Kandiyoti 2017–22).[2] The collection comprises some seventy in-depth oral histories, fourteen of which are cited in this chapter. In all the interviews we conducted, narrators[3] openly expressed feelings of pride, nostalgia, excitement, fear, frustration, and apprehension. They performed emotion through their voices and body language: their pauses in self-reflection were affective signals and vectors of meaning. More importantly, the narratives were heavily marked by stories of attachments to heritage, family, and the lived and imagined past, rather than by proud claims to a new national identity (Benmayor and Kandiyoti 2020). Transcending the legal dimensions of national membership, contemporary scholars have constructed citizenship variably as imagined (Anderson 1998), cultural (Flores and Benmayor 1997), extraterritorial (Stein 2016), and instrumental (Joppke 2019). Framed as morally reparative gestures and rooted in ancestral, historical, and cultural senses of belonging, the Spanish and Portuguese 2015 laws have facilitated another way to formulate and interpret citizenship—what I am calling "affective citizenship," kindled by feelings about the past, emotions in the present, and desires for the future.

Affective Citizenship

The turn toward the study of affect and emotion has occupied scholarship across the disciplines in recent decades. Heritage and museum studies scholars argue that studying affect and emotion "allow[s] us to deepen our understanding of how people develop attachments and commitments to the past, things, beliefs, places, traditions and institutions" (Wetherell, Smith, and Campbell 2018, 2). Scholars in the humanities, social sciences, and hard sciences have been concerned to distinguish the somatic and cognitive dimensions of affect, emotion, and feelings.[4] However, I am using the terms "affect" and "affective" in an umbrella sense, as does Anne Marie Fortier, "to designate a generic category of emotions and feelings, including embodied and sensory feelings through which we experience the world" (2017, 2). Moreover, as Sara Ahmed keenly observes: "Affect and emotion are difficult to separate, as they are entangled in the body" (quoted in Fortier 2016, 2). In this chapter, I am examining the emotions, feelings, and sentiments that come into play in the process of claiming ancestral rights. Oral histories of applicants variably express the thrill and satisfaction at the possibility of recovering this right to citizenship. They express the desire to honor family and connect with unknown forbears, curiosity and joy in discovering hidden roots, excitement at the opportunities that this passport might afford, fear of political forces in their home contexts, or anxiety and frustration over bureaucratic requirements and processes. However, these feelings embody deeper meanings and impact our understanding of ancestral citizenship.

I chose to use the term "Affective Citizenship" in my title for several reasons. Thinking about nation-state membership as *affective* suggests a dynamic relationship among the laws, the emotional responses they generate among applicants, and how these responses accept, resist, or reshape the state-intended objectives of these laws. To help explain this dynamic, Jo Labanyi's essay, "Doing Things" (2011), is quite provocative and productive for understanding the Sephardi citizenship phenomenon. Extending and expanding Sara Ahmed's formulation, that "emotions *do things*" (Ahmed 2004, 119; Ahmed 2014, 191; emphasis in original), Labanyi places a focus on "*things*," attending to the materiality of cultural practices and texts that exist in relationship to the social world and that "have the capacity to affect us" (Labanyi 2011, 231–32; emphasis in original). This conceptual extension posits a dynamic continuum that begins with affect (at the precognitive level of sensation), expresses itself corporeally through emotion and feelings, but continues beyond individual embodiment into the social sphere, through relationships with cultural forms and practices, the *things* that in turn affect thought and behavior in the real world. Oral narratives, I suggest, are emotionally laden verbal and performative texts that convey meaning at the level of bodily language and feeling in the social world of the narrator. Through affect and emotion applicant subjects share their experiences and world views, shaping and in turn *affecting* how we might understand ancestral belonging and modern citizenship.

The other reason for choosing this phrase in my title is that qualifying citizenship as affective destabilizes its static legal definition. Michalinos

Zembylas notes that citizenship may function "as a form of *felt identity* constructed by emotional bonds among those who share the same feelings of loyalty to the nation" (2014, 8; emphasis in original). In the case of citizenship for Sephardi descendants, loyalty to the nation is not a given. How are Sephardi descendants constructing belonging to Spain or Portugal when most have no intention to relocate to these ancestral homelands? As noted in the "Introduction" to this volume, the preambles to both laws make overt use of philosephardic discourses of nostalgia and return as strategies for Sephardi reintegration into the contemporary nation-states. The preamble to the Spanish law claims, "The children of Sepharad maintained an abundance of nostalgia immune to the transformation of languages and generations" (Law 12/2015). The preamble to the Portuguese law affirms, "Despite the persecutions and exile from their national territory, many Sephardi Jews of Portuguese origin and their descendants maintained . . . their Portuguese origins, along with a strong memory that led them to call themselves 'Portuguese Jews' or 'Jews of the Portuguese nation'" (Decreto Lei). Pointing to the relationship between the state and affect, Laszczkowski and Reeves argue that emotions "come to be invested in particular sites, people, material infrastructure, projects, documents, and legal enactments" (2018, 3). As legal enactments, both preambles make strategic use of emotional language inviting descendants to reimagine and reconnect to the nation-state as new citizens, illustrating the power of heritage practices to stand in for and legitimate claims to inclusion or exclusion on the basis of identity, nation, and citizenship (Wetherell, Smith, and Campbell 2018, 10).

Charles McDonald (2021) frames state claims for nostalgia and absence of rancor as a politics of sentiment, which disguises the possibility of refusal. In situating the emotional worlds of applicants at the center, as we both do, I propose a different form of refutation that is grounded in an affirmation of Sephardiness. In exploring the affective dimensions of ancestral citizenship, I propose that that, as the affective point of departure, the laws have aroused and strengthened a sense of Sephardi identity, grounded in emotions around familial history, collective memory, and cultural practices, through which descendants in turn reshape the intentions and affective meanings of the laws.

Affective Attachments and the Power of Memory

The memory of the Expulsions, from Spain in 1492 and from Portugal in 1496, and the violence of forced conversion and Inquisitorial persecutions are anchors and points of departure in today's Sephardi historical narrative, although this was not always the case (Cohen 2018). In the contemporary Sephardi imagination, the memory of exile and the feelings of trauma that it evokes (Kandiyoti 2020) speak to the existence of what historian Barbara Rosenwein calls an "emotional community," comprising "the emotions that [communities] value . . . [and] the nature of the affective bonds between people" (2010, 20). While the two Expulsions marked the physical detachment and disconnection of the Jews from Iberia, the 2015 nationality laws propose a reattachment through nation-state citizenship. As such, the Expulsions and the 2015 laws bookend these collective cultural memories, provoking a new, emotional conversation around identity, belonging, and attachment.

In her widely cited essay, Ahmed (2004, 119) emphasizes that, "Emotions . . . align individuals with communities . . . through the very intensity of their attachments." This insightful assertion prompts two questions: What are the communities to which Sephardi descendants align themselves? And how is this intensity of affective attachments manifested in conversations about the citizenship process? It is important to note that Sephardi descendants are a very heterogeneous group. Many so-called normative descendants like myself, whose familial Sephardi Jewish identity remained intact over the centuries, strongly affirm their attachments to history, genealogy, language, and other signifying cultural practices. Others, particularly younger generations who may have maintained an identity as Jews, are more distant from their specifically Sephardi roots. Among them, we might find powerful accounts of experiences of research and recovery of remote or lost familial pasts. While the citizenship laws were initially drafted with Jewish-identified Sephardis in mind (see Flesler and Friedman, chap. 9 in this volume), they also include claimants who are no longer Jewish-identified, such as the descendants of conversos, those who identify as crypto-Jews, and those whose families became Christian in more recent times through intermarriage. These applicants often expressed a new-found attachment to Sephardi identity, both documented and imaginary, in exhilarating and sometimes euphoric terms.

Understanding citizenship as affective highlights the intensity of emotional attachment expressed by descendants, conveying to us, and sometimes to themselves in the telling, the deeper meanings of this ancestral recovery. Voicing his feelings about acquiring Spanish nationality, Argentinian Marcelo Benveniste, the grandson of immigrants from the island of Rhodes and editor of the renowned online journal *E-Sefarad,* exclaimed, "I'm very moved that a decision taken by the Spanish government connects me to those ancestors of 600 years ago. And, to think that today I'm doing this because my twelfth great grandfather lived there. That history that we have lived for so long, that included an entire chain of ancestors before me. . . . I too am part of that history. I too form part of that chain" (Benveniste 2017).

With his words "me emociona" (I am moved, I am excited), Benveniste claims an affective space to explain the symbolic meaning this citizenship holds for him. He asserts that his decision to apply was a sentient response to the more than five-centuries-old collective and familial memory of the expulsion of the Sephardi Jews from Iberia, embodied by an imaginary chain of familial forebears. In this formulation, modern notions of nationality and state citizenship are intersected and reshaped by the feelings that ancestral, historical, and familial memory elicit. And while Benveniste cannot trace his bloodline beyond his grandparents, he expressed a deeply felt attachment to this long chain of imaginary great-grandfathers. His voice rose in pitch with these phrases: "That history that we have lived for so long, that included an entire chain of ancestors before me. . . . I too form part of that chain. . . . This somewhat romantic view, I like it! . . . It makes me feel very good" (Benveniste 2017). Benveniste articulates the sentiment of many normative Sephardi Jews in response to the citizenship invitation. The decision to pursue Spanish or Portuguese citizenship is grounded in emotional historical memory and to an affective claim for reparative reconnection.

If the citizenship laws call up the genealogical imaginary, uniting Benveniste with his fifteenth-century Spanish ancestors, they also invoke other aspects of heritage. For Mexican writer Myriam Moscona, the affective attachment was through and to language—Ladino. "I am a writer and [language] is what means the most to me, beyond any religious belonging," she declared. In her novel, *Tela de Sevoya* (Onion Skin), Moscona peels back the layers of her cultural past as she narrates a journey to Bulgaria. In her interview, she described the novel as a way to "dejar una memoria sobre la lengua," a way to "leave a memory of the language, leave a memory on the tongue," playing on the double meaning of the word *"lengua"* as both language and tongue (Moscona 2017). She recounted that she absorbed the ancestral family Spanish as a child, listening to her grandparents, but it was a passive language: "El ladino entró por mis oídos pero nunca salió por mi boca" (Ladino came in through my ears but never came out of my mouth), she confessed laughing. It was "the gift that my grandparents gave me, which I didn't realize at the time" (2017). If Benveniste invoked the image of an unbroken chain, Moscona used the metaphor of the Olympic torch to insert herself into her ancestral picture: "I feel like the torch has been passed on to me, like in the Olympics. . . . In my hands, I felt that the flame was dying out, and that is why I wanted to leave a memory of that language.

That language is the language of those expelled from Spain, which is me, it is in my blood, regardless of whether my ancestors came from Italy or left Toledo. I am undeniably a repository of those [cultural] traditions." Like Ladino, Spanish citizenship holds symbolic, historical, and aesthetic value for Moscona. "There is a beauty" she proclaimed, "in being able to hold that passport that was snatched from my ancestors."

Affective attachments may be celebratory and affirming, honoring the past and the present, but they often manifest themselves as feelings of nostalgia and loss. Alluding to Marianne Hirsch's concept of postmemory (2012), and citing Thomas Dodman (2018, 14) on nostalgia and the multidirectionality of memory, Dario Miccoli (2017, 62) writes, "Nostalgia can be read as a most present feeling that speaks in an indirect manner, and [is] based upon family or national *postmemories*, to and about the world in which they live: a world endowed with a 'dialectical temporality that is *both* linear and cyclical . . . at once oriented to the future and that constantly dredges up the past, thus allowing for the experience of longing both as loss *and* imaginative recall'" (62; emphasis in original).

Turkish activist "Raşel" (a pseudonym) reflected this dialectical temporality with regard to the waning of "the Jewish language." Speaking excitedly in Turkish, with French interspersed, she shared the following anecdote (italics added for emphasis):[5]

> Speaking the Jewish language [Ladino] so little has created an *incredible nostalgia* in me. . . . One day, there was a [political] meeting . . . [with] Argentinian mothers from La Plaza de Mayo . . . but the translator did not come. So, I translated the speech of that woman. I am still puzzled [about] how I was able to translate her speech! . . . I felt so happy because I felt as if the two pieces of my identity came together. Everyone around me was a leftist, Turkish, and this took place at a human rights association . . . a totally different place than my childhood. And there, I used my Spanish. . . . This was an important moment of happiness for me, a moment of rapprochement [integration]. . . . It's *euphorisant* [euphoric], something *euphorisant*. (2017; emphasis in original)

Her choice of words—"nostalgia," "happiness," "rapprochement," "*euphorisant*"—is significant. In this account, linguistic loss morphs into the happiness of recovery, and nostalgia evolves into euphoria. The very intensity of feelings that Ahmed saw as key to understanding attachment are central to Raşel's sense of cultural and political identity. Basque oral historian Miren Llona describes such stores of affective recall as "enclaves of memory," where events that are seared in memory because of the intensity of the emotions that produced them, resurface with the telling (2016, 77–78).

While Benveniste, Moscona, and Raşel anchor their pursuit of Spanish citizenship in collective cultural memory, for younger generations of descendants, attachment is often located in their lived present rather than in a distant past. Young descendants, in their twenties and thirties, often identify an affective connection to a grandparent as the motive force in claiming citizenship. For Liz Levine, a media professional in her early thirties whose immigrant grandmother was part of the historic Seattle Sephardi community, reattachment to modern Spain constituted an emotional act of honoring living generations: "I kept telling her [her grandmother], 'I'm gonna do this to honor you,' and I only wish she had lived to see the end of it. She was so alive when I started the application. I kept telling her, 'I'm gonna make this right! I'm gonna get back what your family deserved. I'm gonna take back what's ours.' And so, I'm working on it" (2018).

As suggested by these accounts, claiming ancestral citizenship involves the mobilization of individual, familial, and collective memory, resulting in a reconnection, reinforcement, and reaffirmation of Sephardiness.

The Impact of Discovery/Recovery

The development of affective attachments does not depend only on prior knowledge of a Sephardi heritage. Based on a smaller set of interviews, Goldschläger and Orjuela argue that "the passing of the laws in Spain and Portugal has contributed to activating a homeland consciousness and prompting a dialogue with the past" (2021, 109). The citizenship laws have unleashed a remarkable movement of research and dis/recovery among Jewish and non-Jewish-identified descendants (Benmayor and Kandiyoti 2020). Narratives of discovery and recovery recount search experiences and findings with an intensity of feeling that matches, if not surpasses, the power of historical identity in normative Sephardi Jews.

British-born Bernard Miller, a worldly man in his seventies with an innate facility for language learning, narrates his journey to trace his maternal ancestry to Spain and Portugal via Amsterdam. Despite his upbringing as a politically progressive liberal Jew, he notes, "I grew up in this tiny nuclear family with no knowledge of my Sephardic or, for that matter, my Ashkenazic background. . . . We simply never talked about the past" (2021). The announcement of the citizenship laws prompted his first foray into genealogy:

> I didn't even know if I would be able to trace my citizenship [ancestry]. I mean it was just . . . I wanted to be part of the Iberian history. I wanted to be connected to it for emotional reasons, intellectual reasons, not anything that I could put my finger on. . . . Just a few months ago, I put together a family tree. I traced my first full line, and it wasn't very difficult, back to 1490-ish. . . . I've gone from being part of a tiny nuclear

family which I felt was really isolated, to . . . where I feel my family is global . . . global in ways that I couldn't ever have imagined! Every day, there are new family discoveries. . . . I've got new ancestors with exciting stories and new blood relatives . . . from all over the world, which is fabulous and it's really exciting! I'd been warned this would happen, I got hooked on genealogy and I'm now a genealogy junkie. . . . So, as you can see, I get these emotional attachments. (2021)

Miller embodies Ahmed's emphasis on the emotional intensity of community bonds. He says, "I get these emotional attachments, I've got the language attachments, I've got the culture attachments when I'm in Spain." Uncovering his Sephardi past heightened his feelings of belonging, not just to Iberian roots but also to a what Goldschläger and Orjuela call a "global Sephardi identity" (2021, 109).

Genealogical discovery and research have had an equally significant emotional impact on applicants who have not been practicing Jews for generations: those of converso heritage from the sixteenth and seventeenth centuries, crypto-Jews, Dönmes, and those who converted to Christianity in more recent times. Dalia Kandiyoti's chapter (chap. 14) and Uluç Özüyener's personal story (chap. 7) in this volume offer moving examples of converso and crypto-Jewish responses to the laws, producing new identity bonds and validating hidden ones. Archival searches for genealogical evidence, the construction of elaborate family trees, and DNA testing among non-Jewish descendants serve powerful dual purposes. To descendants themselves, and primarily to the state, these forms of attachment acquire the power of concrete evidence of heritage. They also carry a distinct emotional force that sometimes leads to elevating Sephardiness to a privileged identitary position. As Ana Maria Gallegos, a multiethnic and multiracial converso descendant from New Mexico expressed it: "I've always felt, I don't know . . . I wouldn't say 'different' but I'm very happy to know who I am. Now I know our whole history and . . . I'm just very happy to identify as Sephardic" (Gallegos 2017). "Knowing who I am," declared with a tone of peaceful finality, illustrates how, through the citizenship quest, Sephardi heritage can come to predominate over the interwoven indigenous and other identity strands brought about in this geographical region through conquest, migration, and mixing (Kandiyoti 2020, 6–8).

Newly found Sephardiness among non-Jews can sometimes heighten the sense of attachment through the new country. While on a student visa in Barcelona, Justin Samuels, an African American who has traced his lineage to a nineteenth-century Sephardi slaveholder in Alabama, applied for and received both Spanish and Portuguese citizenship for himself and his mother. Initially moving to Barcelona to study film, he has taken up permanent residence in Málaga. Although his incursion into genealogical family research predated his move to Spain, he explains that, once there, the link between the country's Sephardi past and his own deepened, leading to what Goldschläger and Orjuela call a "homeland-oriented identity" (2021, 99). Amusingly, when asked how he felt about acquiring Spanish citizenship, he invoked humor and irony: "Larry David [an American Jewish comedian] said it from a different angle. He had relatives in the Holocaust and then he found out that one of his ancestors was a Confederate slave-owning Jew. . . . So he goes, 'Wow! I'm attached to two of the most racist places in the world.' And I thought, 'Wow! I'm attached to the Spanish Inquisition and slavery, so that's how I felt!'" (Samuels 2018). Genealogical research and the citizenship opportunities led Samuels to expand and affirm his intersecting multiracial, religious, and ethnic identities, born out of multiple diasporas, institutionalized racism, violence, and resistance.

References to loss and missing elements also appear in narratives of more recent Christianization. Brazilian Glayci Errúas learned through family stories that she had a Moroccan Sephardi grandfather buried in the Jewish cemetery of Manaus. In this case, the loss of Judaism was barely two generations old, the result of intermarriage. Errúas describes her intense feelings of loss through the body, the most intimate locus of affective attachment. In a quiet, contemplative tone, she recounted her discovery using striking somatic metaphors, as body parts missing, torn away, severed: "For me, personally, it's as if something were missing. When I began to discover more about my ancestors, about my roots, it was as if I were discovering myself at the same time. So, I dare say that it is the discovery of deeper knowledge . . . as if something had been torn from me, that belonged to me. At some moment, the connection was severed. Wiped out" (Errúas 2019). Acquiring citizenship brings both corporeal and emotional restoration for Errúas. Claiming reparative citizenship becomes, in her words, an act of "retaking that which was in some way yours," a way to make history whole again. In such cases, the citizenship laws produce a legitimation of identity that had been relegated in large measure to the shadows and the imagination.

In all the above cases, the emotional impact of genealogical discovery, recovery, and the search for biological legitimacy prompted by the evidence required by the laws becomes an affirmation of ancestral Sephardi identity more than an espousal of a new Spanish or Portuguese self. Consequently, feelings about ancestry emerge as key to understanding the acquisition of a new citizenship as an affective move to a kind of Sephardi citizenship. In her personal essay in chapter 4 in this volume, Colette Capriles, a Venezuelan who descends from Curaçaoan Sephardi Jews but whose family became Christian barely a generation ago, expressed it simply in this way: "When asked, I always state that I have a 'Sephardi passport,' not a Spanish one."

Longing and Return

The philosephardic nostalgia rhetoric of the Spanish and Portuguese laws cited earlier in this chapter can be read as a renewed attempt to attract and reintegrate Sephardi descendants into the modern Iberian states. However, if any cultural longing is expressed in their narratives, it is for the lands and cultures of their immediate forebears. While most state a strong desire to visit the lands of their medieval origins, very few have the intention to return to reside there. Whatever the response, it is emotionally grounded. Sephardi Jews who experienced further diasporization in the twentieth century, particularly from the Ottoman Empire to Europe or the Americas (Ben-Ur 2009; Mays 2020) often attached feelings of nostalgia not to a remote and imaginary Iberia but to the places and cultures more immediately left behind, where their centuries-long Jewish and Sephardi identities were not questioned (Naar 2015, 2016). Born and raised in Britain, one narrator who chose to be identified as "Anonymous," recalls his grandparents' feelings of longing as follows: "There was no sense in the family, at this stage in history, of a yearning for Portugal or Spain and the Iberian Peninsula. When my father and other members of family talked about the history, it was about Izmir and about Turkey that they felt . . . sentimental is not quite the right word, they felt an emotional link. There was no sense any more of having lived in Portugal or Spain. . . . For them all it was all about the Eastern Mediterranean, about Turkey" (Anonymous 2019).

In the same way, a generation removed from his Ottoman roots, Anonymous does not yearn for the Izmir of his parents or grandparents, but for what he feels may be an impending loss of his own, brought about by Brexit. In his interview, he expressed concern for the potential loss of his Europeanness within Britain. He opted for Portuguese citizenship, saying, "I think the strongest emotional thing, if and when it happens, will be actually being able to reassert Europeanness, which we've taken for granted. For all of my adult life Britain's been in the EU." Though his decision might at first glance seem instrumental—to secure a European nationality and a passport—the desire to preserve his Europeanness comes from a deeper place of fear, that of an endangered identity, and a desire to preserve its affective attachments.

Ethan Russo, a scientist in his sixties, born in the United States and whose family came from Monastir (today, Bitola), describes longing in attachment to language and cultural transmission: "This [Ladino] was a cultural longing that was passed generation by generation for 500 years and that was their mother tongue for this entire time, when they easily could have decided, 'Okay, we're gonna speak Turkish' or whatever. They just never chose to relinquish that identity. So, it was important to them and it's important to me" (2018). More tentative in ascribing an ultimate significance to acquiring Spanish citizenship, he reflected: "I look forward to getting through the process successfully and having the opportunity to find out what it really means."

Spain and Portugal justify their formulations about nostalgia for Sefarad through the possibility of an open invitation to return. "How we have missed you!" proclaimed King Felipe VI to the Sephardi community, celebrating the first group of descendants to receive citizenship (Alberola 2015). Indeed, a handful of narrators, like Gallegos and Samuels, have embraced the invitation, relocating and establishing new lives in Spain. They tell stories of highly emotional encounters and sensations that motivated such decisions. While signing her application before a Spanish lawyer, Gallegos recounted breathlessly: "As I stood in the offices in Málaga, the woman in Spanish told me that it was important that I understand that Spain was inviting me back as a direct descendant of the Sephardic Jews that were expelled during the Inquisition. . . . Oh my gosh! That was so emotional for me! I started crying and she got up from around the table and she hugged me, she gave me this really warm hug and said 'Welcome back.' It was pretty surreal!" (2018).

The welcome is a standard part of the signing ceremony, and yet it stands out in her memory as the official validation of her newly acquired Sephardi identity. She and her family have since moved to Madrid. Whether residency will eventually lead to calling herself "Spanish," or some amalgam of Spaniard and Sephardi, remains to be seen.

Jamaican artist Anna Ruth Henriques is also among the few descendants who have decided to return to their ancestral homelands. Born to a Chinese Jamaican mother and a Sephardi Jamaican father from one of the island's prominent Jewish families, Anna Ruth grew up embracing her mixed racial ancestry and her religious identity as a Jew. She went to the United States for university and then worked there for many years. Feeling oppressed by the racism she encountered, she decided to apply for Portuguese citizenship, as this would give her access to the whole of Europe. Receiving the official certificate of Sephardi heritage from the Jewish Community of Porto, she decided to visit the country and she stayed, establishing a yoga and healing retreat on a small farm in the Algarve region. Anna's return story opens with an exchange with an airport immigration officer who welcomed her home (the very encounter

I wished for and did not receive, as I lamented in my opening to this chapter):

> Okay, I'm going to just visit Portugal. Once I got on the plane, I started to feel like I was surrounded by people who were very familiar. Even though I didn't understand a word. There was something in their whole demeanor, energetically almost, and when I landed at the Lisbon airport, I really felt like I had to come home. And when the guy [immigration officer recognizing her surname as Portuguese] said to me, 'Welcome home, welcome home,' I was like, "Oh my God! This is like too many signs, you know?!" (2020)

She went on to describe her feelings upon receiving her ancestry certification: "There was something so embracing about it. The fact that that community in Portugal had considered me one of theirs, you know, in their fold . . . there was a moment of . . . like elation!" (2020; voiced emphasis in the recording).

In defining the sensation felt in the body which she comes to name as elation, Anna articulates the affective moment that sets off the process that Labanyi refers to. Multiple identities and citizenships carry with them the possibility of multiple homes and the meanings they hold. For Henriques, "Jamaica will always be home. . . . I was born there, and I feel very connected to Jamaica, but . . . I've lived all over the world. And this [Portugal] is really the only place I've felt . . . this is not temporary. I don't need to leave again. . . . It's an ancient home, you know. This is an ancient home that's now the present home." This inexplicable sensation of recognition, of feeling suddenly at home, is not an uncommon response among descendants who visit their ancestral lands. As descendants, we look for, imagine, and find familiarity in these somewhat mythologized contexts—in the way people look, dress, or socialize. We fit ourselves into the landscapes and ambiences, make them ours. We invoke our affective worlds, our senses and emotions, to explain and confirm to ourselves these responses to our Iberian pasts. Henriques's story suggests that acquiring ancestral citizenship is a profoundly affective experience that mobilizes "homeland consciousness" (Goldschläger and Orjuela 2021, 109), shaped by identity attachments to the historical (and imagined or idealized) past that produce feelings of belonging in the present.

Conclusion

When people asked me why I wanted to seek Spanish citizenship, my quick response was "Because I could." However, I came to understand that the real reason was that the laws elicited feelings within me, reminding me that I come from a history of expulsion, of repeated diasporas, and remarkable cultural persistence, and that I have an internal sense of belonging and identity attachments that have little to do with formal nationality or nationalisms. The affective attachments that motivated and gave meaning to acquiring Spanish or Portuguese citizenship, for me and others, are deeply grounded in being and, as we have seen in some cases, becoming Sephardi. This was also true for the people that Dalia Kandiyoti and I interviewed in our oral history project. The laws have inspired descendants to reflect on our place in Sephardi history, on what was taken away a half a millennium ago, and how and why that matters today.

Citizenship is not usually studied through the lens of emotion (Ho 2009), even though, as I have argued, acquiring a nationality can be a profoundly emotional experience. When examined through an affective lens, Spanish and Portuguese citizenship becomes transformed from a legal transaction of national inclusion to an affirmation of ancestral identity and reclamation of lost rights. Instead of reattachment to what are now modern nation-states, acquiring Spanish or Portuguese citizenship signifies an affective re/turn to and reinforcement of Sephardi identity—through history, genealogy, culture, and memory. Even those who seek dual or multiple citizenship for practical, instrumental reasons—ease of travel, or for educational or business opportunities—are motivated by the desire for greater mobility or sense of freedom (Ofir 2017). Those who live in politically and economically precarious circumstances might be motivated by fear and the desire for greater security that a reserve citizenship can bring (Benmayor and Kandiyoti 2020).

At the outset of this chapter, I noted that the memory of the Expulsions and the 2015 laws serve as historical and emotional bookends to each other. A close examination of applicant oral histories through the affective lens reveals how emotions "*do* things" and "do *things*" as narrators interpret and reshape the invitation to reparative citizenship to fit our individual histories and trajectories, and here I return to include myself. We convert what once was a territorial definition of belonging into one that is internally driven by affective attachments, defying physical boundaries. The affective lens brings into focus ways in which descendants construct and affirm Sephardiness. At the same time, it allows a projection of new meanings into the future. In our interview with him, US historian Victor Silverman, whose personal essay (chap. 16) also closes this volume, reflects on the emotional impact of the laws in generating a more democratic, expansive understanding of identity:

> It's like going back in time, and now I'm really Portuguese and I think that is going to have an emotional meaning. That really *is* something of who I am, and having a state recognize that is *really* important. State recognition of our identity is central, essential to all sorts

of things about modern identity. State recognition in response to who we actually *are* . . . also defines who we actually are. . . . So, I think it's really good to support those things, in this world now, in this particular time when people are making these moves to amend past wrongs, to make their societies more diverse and more multicultural and to embrace the complexities of our past and present. Those are things we need to be supporting. Those are things that would make the world a better place and make it a safer place for all of us. (2017; voiced emphases in the recording).

Both Henriques and Silverman attest to the importance of having one's identities officially and openly recognized. Recognition provides deep emotional validation. However, while Silverman lauds the state for this validation of his Portugueseness, declaring, "Now I'm really Portuguese," he does not view this identity as a validation of the state. Rather, he sees these state actions through a complex global lens, looking toward more open understanding of diversity rather than as an expression of singular and bounded nationalism. Similarly, other narrators attribute importance to the citizenship laws as examples of mutual respect and *convivencia* (peaceful coexistence) "because of the xenophobic times we are living, within and outside the European continent" (Luz 2017).

In this chapter, I have offered another reading and understanding of these historically unusual laws, from the perspective of Sephardi descendants, illustrating how they give deeper significance to attaining this European Union passport, beyond the concrete practical and transnational opportunities it may embody. The little booklets signifying national belonging, that quite probably will never be physically stamped, are an embodiment of an internal affective passport that contains the attachments that each of us carries, shaped by our different historical trajectories. Through our feelings and emotions, we construct our identities and belongings responding to who we *are*, as Silverman asserted, and who we want to be. We may travel to Spain and Portugal, and even live there, but we will most likely do so as Sephardi descendants rather than new Spaniards or Portuguese. By reacquiring the right to citizenship, descendants call on states to move beyond worn out, culturally homogeneous national interests and ideologies. Understanding the affective nature of citizenship allows Sephardi descendants to define our own ways of belonging to our countries of ancestry through different standpoints, historical experiences, and meanings, thus resisting the homogenization into a uniform, singular, and restricted understanding of Sephardi identity in a today's world.

Rina Benmayor is Professor Emerita in the School of Humanities and Communication, California State University Monterey Bay, where she taught oral history, literature, and digital storytelling. She is the author of *Romances judeo-españoles de Oriente* (Gredos 1979); and coauthor and coeditor of *Latino Cultural Citizenship* (Beacon Press 1997); *Telling to Live: Latina Feminist Testimonios* (Duke University Press 2001); and *Memory, Subjectivities, and Representation: Approaches to Oral History in Latin America, Portugal, and Spain* (Palgrave 2016; Oral History Association Book Award 2016). With Dalia Kandiyoti, she has conducted extensive oral histories with Sephardi citizenship applicants. These interviews are archived in the University of Washington Sephardic Studies Digital Collection. This chapter was developed with National Endowment for the Humanities support.

Notes

1. I extend my deepest appreciation and respect to the oral history narrators whose stories led me to the topics of emotion and affect. I also acknowledge and thank the National Endowment for the Humanities (NEH) Faculty Award for the generous funding that enabled the development and writing of this chapter. My heartfelt appreciation to my colleagues and friends, Drs. Patricia Zavella and Sherna Berger Gluck, who supported my NEH proposal; to Dr. Esther Cohen and Robin Inouye (MFCC), both professional psychologists, for their invaluable feedback on early drafts of this chapter; and to my *ermanas* Dalia Kandiyoti and Michal Rose Friedman, for their encouragement, vast insights, and constructive suggestions. *Eyvallah*!
2. "Spanish and Portuguese Citizenship for Sephardi Jewish Descendants: An Oral History Collection (2017-2022)" (Benmayor and Kandiyoti, 2017-2022) is the first and to date the most extensive collection of in-depth interviews with Sephardi descendants on the 2015 citizenship laws. The University of Washington Sephardic Studies Digital Collection is the online repository of the corpus (jewishstudies.washington.edu/sephardi-citizenship). The collection comprises some sixty interviews, running in length from sixty to ninety minutes each. The narrators come from around the globe and range in age from their twenties to their eighties. They include descendants of: Jewish-identified Sephardis; conversos (Jews who were forcibly converted to Christianity); and *Dönmes* (descended from the followers of Sabbetai Sevi). Among the narrators are also Jews who lost their Jewish and Sephardi identities through intermarriages and assimilation. Topics covered include family origins and history, connections to Ladino or Haketia, religious and cultural upbringing, motivations for seeking citizenship, experiences with the process, views on Spain and Portugal's past wrongs, and thoughts about citizenship as a form of reparation. For more detailed information on the collection and its methodology, see Benmayor and Kandiyoti (2020).
3. "Narrator" is the term preferred in oral history, rather than "informant" or "interviewee," to recognize and validate agency.
4. Jo Labanyi (2011) richly synthesizes these discussions, attending to Massumi's (2002) formulation of affect as precognitive.
5. Translated and transcribed by Defne Özözer, Boğaziçi University, Istanbul, Turkey. Italics are mine, to render the voiced emphasis in the recording.

References

Ahmed, Sara. 2004. "Affective Economies." *Social Text* 79, no. 22:2: 119. https://muse.jhu.edu/article/55780.

———. 2014. *The Cultural Politics of Emotion*. 2nd ed. Edinburgh: Edinburgh University Press. https://www.jstor.org/stable/10.3366/j.ctt1g09x4q.

Alberola, Miquel. 2015. "El Rey a los sefardíes: 'Cuánto os hemos echado de menos!'" *El País*, 20 November 2015. https://elpais.com/politica/2015/11/30/actualidad/1448887588_869275.html.

Anderson, Benedict. 1998. *Imagined Communities: Reflections on the Origin and Spread of Nationalism*. Rev. ed. London and New York: Verso.

"Anonymous." 2019. Interview conducted by Dalia Kandiyoti. 27 September, via Zoom.

Benmayor, Rina. 1979. *Romances judeo-españoles de Oriente: Nueva recolección*. Madrid: Gredos.

Benmayor, Rina, and Dalia Kandiyoti. 2017–2022. "Spanish and Portuguese Citizenship for Sephardi Jewish Descendants: An Oral History Collection (2017–2022)." University of Washington Sephardic Studies Digital Collection.

———. 2020. "Ancestry, Genealogy, and Restorative Citizenship: Oral Histories of Sephardi Descendants Reclaiming Spanish and Portuguese Nationality." *Quest: Issues in Contemporary Jewish History* 18 (December). https://www.quest-cdecjournal.it/wp-content/uploads/2021/01/9-Q18_03_Benmayor-Kandiyoti.pdf.

Ben-Ur, Aviva. 2009. *Sephardic Jews in America: A Diasporic History*. New York: New York University Press.

Benveniste, Marcelo Daniel. 2017. Interview conducted by Rina Benmayor. 2 November, via Zoom.

Cohen, Julia Philips. 2018. "El pasado como tierra ajena: Imaginando Sefarad desde el Imperio Otomano." Paper read at Seminario, Genealogías de Sefarad, Madrid, 4 July.

Decreto-Lei 30-A/2015. 2015. *Diário da República Electrónica*. 28 September 2019. https://dre.pt/pesquisa/-/search/66619927.

Errúas, Glayci. 2019. Interview conducted by Rina Benmayor, 7 February, via Zoom.

Flores, William V., and Rina Benmayor. 1997. *Latino Cultural Citizenship*. Boston: Beacon Press.

Fortier, Anne-Marie. 2016. "Afterword: Acts of Affective Citizenship? Possibilities and Limitations." Acts_of_Affective_Citizenship.pdf. Published subsequently in *Citizenship Studies* 20, no. 8: 1038–44.

Gallegos, Ana Maria. 2017. Interview conducted by Dalia Kandiyoti, 23 March, via Zoom.

Goldschläger, Arielle, and Camilla Orjuela. 2021. "Return After 500 Years? Spanish and Portuguese Repatriation Laws and the Reconstruction of Sephardic Identity." *Diaspora Studies* 14, no. 1: 97–115.

Henriques, Anna Ruth. 2020. Interview conducted by Rina Benmayor and Dalia Kandiyoti, 28 June, via Zoom.

Hirsch, Marianne. 2012. *The Generation of Postmemory: Writing and Visual Culture after the Holocaust*. New York: Columbia University Press.

Ho, Elaine Lynn-Ee. 2009. "Constituting Citizenship Through the Emotions: Singaporean Transmigrants in London." *Annals of the Association of American Geographers* 99, no. 4, 788–804.

Joppke, Christian. 2019. "The Instrumental Turn of Citizenship." *Journal of Ethnic and Migration Studies* 45, no. 6: 869.
Kandiyoti, Dalia. 2020. *The Converso's Return: Conversion and Sephardi History in Contemporary Literature and Culture*. Stanford, CA: Stanford University Press.
Labanyi, Jo. 2011. "Doing Things: Emotion, Affect, and Materiality." *Journal of Spanish Cultural Studies* 11, no. 3–4.
Laszczkowski, Mateusz, and Madeleine Reeves, 2018. "Introduction: Affect and the Anthropology of the State." In *Affective States: Entanglements, Suspensions, Suspicions*, edited by Mateusz Laszczkowski and Madeleine Reeves, 1–14. New York: Berghahn.
Law 12/2015. 2015. "Ley 12/2015 de 24 de junio, en materia de concesión de la nacionalidad española a los sefardíes originarios de España" [Law 12/2015 of 24 June, granting Spanish nationality to Sephardi Jews originating from Spain]. *Boletín Oficial del Estado*, 25 June 2015, no. 151.
León Tello, Pilar. 1979. *Judíos de Toledo*. Madrid: Consejo Superior de Investigaciones Científicas.
Levine, Elizabeth. 2018. Interview conducted by Rina Benmayor, 31 January, via Zoom.
Llona, Miren. 2016. "The Healing Effect of Discourses: Body, Emotions, and Gender Subjectivity in Basque Nationalism." In *Memory, Subjectivities, and Representation: Approaches to Oral History in Latin America, Portugal, and Spain*, edited by Rina Benmayor, María Eugenia Cardenal de la Nuez, and Pilar Domínguez, 77–92. London: Palgrave.
Luz. 2017. Interview conducted by Rina Benmayor, 12 April, via Zoom.
Massumi, Brian. 2002. *Parables of the Virtual. Movement, Affect, Sensation*. Durham, NC: Duke University Press.
Mays, Devi. 2020. *Forging Ties, Forging Passports: Migration and the Modern Sephardi Diaspora*. Stanford, CA: Stanford University Press.
McDonald, Charles A. 2021. "Rancor: Sephardi Jews, Spanish Citizenship, and the Politics of Sentiment." *Comparative Studies in Society and History* 63, no. 3:722–751.
Miccoli, Dario. 2017. "'I come from a country that is no more': Jewish Nostalgia in the Postcolonial Mediterranean." *Ethnologies* 39, no. 2: 51–68.
Miller, Bernard. 2021. Interview conducted by Dalia Kandiyoti and Rina Benmayor, 9 June, via Zoom.
Moscona, Myriam. 2017. Interview conducted by Dalia Kandiyoti, 15 March, via Skype
Naar, Devin E. 2015. "Turkinos Beyond the Empire: Ottoman Jews in America, 1893 to 1924." *Jewish Quarterly Review* 105, no. 2 (Spring): 174–205.
———. 2016. "'Sephardim Since Birth': Reconfiguring Jewish Identity in America." In *Sephardi and Mizrahi Jews in America: The Jewish Role in American Life*, vol. 13, edited by Steven J. Ross, Saba Soomekh, and Lisa Ansell: 75–104. West Lafayette, Indiana: Purdue University Press.
Ofir, Ido. 2017. Interview conducted by Dalia Kandiyoti, 29 November, via Zoom.
Raşel. 2017. Interview conducted by Dalia Kandiyoti, 18 January, via Skype.
Rosenwein, Barbara. 2010. "Problems and Methods in the History of Emotions: Passions in Context." https://www.passionsincontext.de/uploads/media/01_Rosenwein.pdf
Russo, Ethan. 2018. Interview conducted by Rina Benmayor, 10 January, via Zoom.
Samuels, Justin. 2018. Interview conducted by Rina Benmayor, 3 February, via Zoom.
Silverman, Victor. 2017. Interview conducted by Rina Benmayor, 19 December, via Zoom.
Stein, Sarah Abrevaya. 2016. *Extraterritorial Dreams: European Citizenship, Sephardi Jews, and the Ottoman Twentieth Century*. Stanford, CA: Stanford University Press.

Wetherell, Margaret, Laurajane Smith, and Gary Campbell. 2018. Introduction. "Affective Heritage Practices." In *Emotions, Affective Practices, and the Past in the Present.* Smith, Laurajane, Margaret Wetherell, and Gary Campbell, editors. New York: Routledge.

Zembylas, Michalinos. 2014. "Affective Citizenship in Multicultural Societies: Implications for Critical Citizenship Education." *Citizenship Teaching and Learning* 9, no. 1. https://www.researchgate.net/profile/Michalinos-Zembylas/publication/263762536_Affective_citizenship_in_multicultural_societies_Implications_for_critical_citizenship_education/links/553101560cf27acb0de8cf24/Affective-citizenship-in-multicultural-societies-Implications-for-critical-citizenship-education.pdf.

Chapter 14

Descendants of Conversos in the Americas

The Ancestral Past, Sephardi Identity, and Citizenship in Spain and Portugal

Dalia Kandiyoti

The long history and continuity of Sephardi Jews outside the Iberian Peninsula has been the discursive focus of official, media, and scholarly discourses about Spain and Portugal's 2015 nationality laws.[1] The preambles of both laws begin by defining "*sefardíes*" or "*sefardies*" as "Jews of ancient and traditional Jewish communities of the Iberian Peninsula" (Portugal: Decreto-Lei 2015) and as "Jews of the Iberian Peninsula" who were compelled to take the drastic path of exile and reestablished their communities in Balkan, Ottoman, and North African diasporas (Spain: Law 12/2015). As noted in the "Introduction" to this volume, loyalty, Iberian Jewish cultural retention, and nostalgia projected onto ongoing Sephardi identity has undergirded and legitimized the reparative citizenship offers. The fate of the forced converts and non-Jews with Iberian Jewish ancestry figured minimally in the construction of these official narratives. Yet, because the main criterion of eligibility is the proof of Sephardi Jewish *ancestry* by applicants of any ethnicity or faith, both Spain and Portugal have received an outpouring of petitions from non-Jewish descendants. Although it is not possible to determine their numbers currently, it is likely that they constitute a significant number of the total applications, and especially those from the Americas, probably in the tens of thousands.

These applicants include the subjects of this chapter, which is based on oral histories of seventeen individuals who have applied for citizenship and one person who planned but could not pursue the process because of timing issues. Rina Benmayor and I video-interviewed them remotely as part of a joint project on those seeking Spanish or Portuguese nationality on the basis of their Sephardi ancestry.[2] The eighteen narrators were raised in practicing or nominally Christian families in the United States and Latin America, and have sought the new nationality based on their descent from conversos who migrated to the continent from the sixteenth to eighteenth centuries. Far from constituting a homogenous group, these participants speak various languages and have differing outlooks and depth of knowledge about their Jewish ancestry and Sephardi or converso histories. For about half, the knowledge and discovery of their descent predated the citizenship opportunities. Six had converted to Judaism as adults some years ago, practice Judaism, and consider themselves Sephardi Jews; others have developed affinities through their recent investigations into converso and Sephardi genealogy and history.[3]

The chapter contributes to knowledge about contemporary converso descendants' origin narratives as well as to the conjuncture of genealogy, identity, and citizenship acquisition. The Sephardi laws, as they are often called, are unusual in the vast genealogical reach of their requirements, prompting new discoveries about ancestors, and/or bringing the lineage to a new light under the promise of citizenship. Ancestral citizenships have gained much currency in Europe (see Cook-Martín 2013; Harpaz 2013, 2019; Joppke 2005; Pogonyi 2019), and popular genealogy has received considerable scholarly attention (Kramer 2011; Nash 2002; Nelson 2016; Zerubavel 2011). But there is still a dearth of scholarship on the mutual impact of citizenship and genealogy from the point of view of new seekers of ancestral citizenship.

In this first study on converso descendants who have sought Spanish or Portuguese nationality based on their Sephardi Jewish ancestry, I seek to convey a broad sense of these particular applicants' backgrounds and views on the citizenships by focusing on three specific aspects that emerged from their stories: (1) the role of local, regional, and national narratives in the Americas in ascertaining Sephardi Jewish and converso descent; (2) attitudes toward Spain and Portugal and their relation to those local and national origins stories; and (3) ideas about Sephardi identity. I argue first that, in presenting themselves to the state as descendants of Sephardi Jews, narrators produce a new historical consciousness, which inscribes Sephardi and converso pasts into various national, regional, and communal narratives in the Americas that previously had little place for them. Second, I show that the weak or strong ties narrators may have had to Spain or Portugal, as a consequence of being Latin American or US Latina/o/x, are reconfigured through Sephardi Jewish and converso descent. Third, some narrators suggest, on the genealogical basis of the laws, the heritability of Sephardi identity and its disconnection from religion and culture.

Striving for Spanish and Portuguese citizenship can be double-edged: one accepts to be incorporated into a state on the state's terms. In most other European cases (e.g., Hungary and Bulgaria), applicants for ancestral citizenship who are outside the national territories share the ethnicity, race, and/or religion that are *dominant* in the states, thus providing the citizenship opportunity. But for converso descendants, the required genealogical and historical proof compels a backward look that tells stories about minoritization, persecution, oppressive secrecy, and cultural loss rather than those solely about connections to the preponderant identities of the nation-states. Hence, the basis of their pursuit does not involve a reincorporation based on a triumphalist or amenable Lusotropicalism (see David and Côrte-Real, chap. 2 in this volume), or Hispanism emphasizing common bonds between the colonizer and the colonized, the evangelizer and the forced convert, the enfranchised and the expelled. For some petitioners, especially those with race and class privilege in Latin America, this is a first encounter with a heritage of subjugation. For others, the crypto-Jewish experience connects to indigenous oppressions in the Americas in parallel as well as opposing ways. Hoping for a resumed status as inheritors of Iberia, the narrators relate being heirs of a past more broken than the one they had known for a good part of their lives as normative Christians in the Western Hemisphere. They often represent themselves as remnants of unsung and improbable survivals in the Americas.

The laws may impact people's narratives about themselves and their ancestors in unintended ways. As we will see in this chapter, crypto-Jewishness and Sephardi descent color not only their perceptions of Spain and Portugal but also received histories about settlements in the Americas and regional and national identities. Descent is also at the center of how some narrators view Sephardi identity in unconventional ways. Hence, the genealogical imperative of eligibility, in which descent has to be traced to specific ancestors identified in the historical record as conversos, affects the meanings of the citizenship quest in multiple ways, but in terms that are rather different from the state discourses about the loyalty and continuity of the Sephardi Jews.

Background

The narrators who are descendants of conversos are mostly of Catholic and, more rarely, of Protestant identities and/or familial backgrounds. They have applied for Spanish or Portuguese citizenship based on their ancestors who had converted to Christianity in the Iberian Peninsula, likely under duress, and migrated to the Americas in the sixteenth and seventeenth centuries despite the prohibition against converts in the conquered territories. Since they had to hide their origins in Judaism, which was banned, it is mainly the records of the Inquisitions on both sides of the Atlantic that have provided information on the persecution and murders of those accused of judaizing. But Jewish practices and stories of Jewish provenance were disseminated, both orally and in secret ways in the Americas. Conversos and their descendants moved around the Spanish and Portuguese Empires, mostly blending in with the general Christian populations. In some areas, such as today's northern Mexico or the US Southwest, familial stories of Jewish origins and some enduring practices that are presumed to be Jewish have circulated for many years.

This history of secret Judaism in the Americas, and, especially, its manifestations in contemporary communities, garnered much interest in the past few decades, in a phenomenon I have called "the converso's return" (Kandiyoti 2020). A resurgence of crypto-Jewish identity claims in the past few decades was bolstered by the work of academic historians tracing converso descendants in both Europe and the Americas (Hordes 2008; Israel 2002; Kaplan 2000; Kunin 2009; Wachtel 2001). Such studies have served the applicants' own genealogical and historical investigations and, for some, their identity shifts. The 2015 laws only increased this revival of converso consciousness, as the citizenship opportunity was advertised by lawyers and intermediary organizations and spread widely through word of mouth. Consequently, things changed: many Christians who had no previous knowledge of Jewish heritage decided to seek Spanish or Portuguese nationality and pursued genealogical research.

Many, though not all, of the eighteen narrators whose interviews are the basis of this chapter were interested in Spanish or Portuguese citizenship for reasons that included the practical, especially what Rina Benmayor and I have termed "reserve citizenship" (Benmayor and Kandiyoti 2020, 247), an alternative sought due to the lack of safety and stability in the countries of origin, or else with the goal of expanding travel, education, or residence options in the present or future. Like other US Latina/o/x featured in a 2018 front-page *New York Times* article (Romero 2018), Cristina Ramirez, an American librarian in her early forties who grew up living in different states and who converted to Judaism years before applying for Spanish nationality, spoke to me of the racism she has often experienced as a Latina, adding, "If things get really bad, I . . . like the idea of mentally having a kind of an escape route in my back pocket. If we have to leave" (2018). All the Venezuelans among these participants had already left their country relatively recently, seeing no future there, and wanted additional options. Upon hearing about this rare offer, and often with the help of their social networks who referred them to genealogy experts, lawyers, and other intermediaries, they decided to search for a Jewish background. In a related way, Eduardo Ávila, a forensics expert and father of young children who was also concerned about violence in Brazil, "decided to look for some Jews in my family," which led to the discovery of Sephardi Jews in his lineage from centuries ago (2019).

These narrators availed themselves of historiographies, church records, and paid genealogists, despite the obscurity and remoteness of the origins they needed to document to prove Sehpardi descent. Sometimes, family rumors or artifacts helped bolster the case. "Fabiana,"[4] a displaced upper-middle-class Venezuelan in her twenties, found a two-hundred-year-old family book with information and names (2020). Like many other narrators from diverse parts, she has an ancestor from Monterrey, Mexico, an area conquered by Luis de Carvajal y de la Cueva (d. 1591). This most famous converso Spaniard of the Americas, also a forebear of several of the narrators, provided services to the empire as a conquistador. But this did not help him evade the Inquisition in New Spain, which killed dozens of his family members for allegedly practicing the banned religion in secret. A genealogy expert concluded that, among the names in Fabiana's book and church records, were those belonging to converso descendants who, like Carvajal, had settled in northern Mexico. Such patronymics included Garza, Benavides, and Treviño. Names alone are not considered proof by either the Spanish or Portuguese governments, and the requirements for family trees and other genealogical evidence are elaborate: applicants must document names with vital statistics for each generation in the familial bloodline, supported by official records and historiographical studies verifying converso names and settlements. Without an obligation to demonstrate cultural ties to Sephardi Judaism, applicants need to authenticate only descent, in a continuous line back to the first historically documented Sephardi ancestor in the sixteenth or seventeenth centuries.

The six interviewees who had formally converted to Judaism as adults before the 2015 laws, often being the first or only ones in their family to do so, have a different trajectory: they identify as converso descendants and Sephardi Jews and attend religious services on a regular basis. A sense that their families were different from the surrounding community was present for several of our narrators, whether they had done the genealogical research before or after 2015. But the six converts (or reconverts) reported being compelled to learn about their ancestors or being drawn to Judaism from a young age, without having a particular reason. The sense of standing apart in some way was also spurred by some familial practices such as avoidance of pork, past practices of circumcision, and, in New Mexico, a distinct form of Spanish.

Shifting Local, Regional, and National Narratives

The nature of the narrators' relation to their Sephardi roots was one of the many questions Rina Benmayor and I asked during our interviews, but, much of the time, it generated the most detailed and lengthiest response among this group and often focused on regional histories in the Americas. Attending to these stories helps us understand how these discoveries, occasioned or furthered by the citizenship opportunity, entail much more than the relationship of a nation-state and a geographically specific culturally continuous diaspora. Furthermore, these narratives can revise the existing, dominant stories of dispersal and resettlement. The uncovering of Sephardi Jewish identity in a Christian landscape in the Americas meant turning considerable attention to the settlement story in the continent and origins in particular regions and nations, which often became the focal point of their interest and curiosity.

José Navarro, who lived in Mexico City at the time of our interview and converted to Judaism as an adult, had investigated extensively the history of Cotija, Mexico, the town of his family's origins. During our conversation, he gave me references to Mexican historians who have written about the settlement of crypto-Jews in that area of Michoacán state. He surmised from his research that his ancestors were among the Portuguese converso descendants fleeing Mexico City's Inquisition, populating the region in the late seventeenth century. He characterized the families in Cotija, established in the sixteenth century, as closed and exclusive. According to Navarro (2020), Cotijans maintained this attitude even when they were displaced as migrants in the twentieth century, for example in Chicago, where, looking and acting differently from members of other Mexican communities, they did not blend in. Acknowledging that the attitude toward the indigenous in the Cotija area and other outsiders had to do with racism, he also cited a local saying: "Vamonos para Cotija, donde son buenos cristianos, que para no perder la sangre, se casan entre primos hermanos" (Let's go to Cotija, where they are good Christians who, to preserve the blood, marry their first cousins).[5]

While not always associated with whiteness as in this case, the self-enclosure and endogamy of traditional settler or immigrant communities, very frequently in the smaller cities and towns of the Americas, was offered by the narrators more than once as a piece of evidence of the occluded Jewish past behind the dominant story of "good Christian" origins. This custom resonated with many applicants as one evidence of crypto-Jewishness that conforms to the well-documented practice of endogamy within the historical and surviving converso communities, such as those in northern Portugal and for many centuries in Mallorca, Spain (Moore 1976).

Lisiane Vilanova, a Brazilian in her forties living in Chile, reported (2019) that, growing up in the Rio Grande do Sul region of southern Brazil, she felt that her family always seemed different, apart, and self-enclosed, despite the mixed nature of ethnicities in the area, ranging from European to African and Indigenous. Emigrants from the Azores Islands and among the first to arrive in the region, her family remained more Portuguese than Brazilian. But she had always heard the same phrase: "We are from nowhere; we are nothing" (Vilanova 2019). Mystified by such lacunae in the familial narrative, Vilanova started filling in the blanks through research, discovering the trajectory of Iberian conversos. Eventually, she located through academic investigation a forebear who was known as a converso or *judeu* (Jew) in the Azores and Madeira, where he lived in the eighteenth century before settling in southern Brazil.

Filipe Azevedo, a Brazilian in his late twenties who converted to Judaism in 2017, also emphasized the regional basis of secret familial origins. Azevedo's research focused in the northeast of Brazil. He found through the internet, including in Portugal's Torre de Tombo Library site, that he had ancestors who left Spain for Portugal's Barcelos and Azores Islands, emigrating to Brazil in the eighteenth century. They changed locations from Pernambuco to Seridó, both now known as having been sites of New Christian colonies, and where since the 1970s there has been a movement to seek New Christian and Jewish roots (Feitler 2011; Liphshiz 2018). Azevedo (2020) keenly talked about the wealth of documentation of Sephardi Jews' presence in northeastern Brazil and connected this emerging body of information to some unusual practices in his own childhood Catholic home, such as the avoidance of pork and churchgoing, which he interpreted as remnant ancestral legacy practiced unknowingly by his family.[6] For him, these settler ancestors are persecuted heroes who suffered and survived and came to be severed from their Jewishness. Azevedo's conversion and quest for Spanish (rather than Portuguese) citizenship as a recovery of original belonging in Spain serves to honor these forebears. For such narrators, then, the meanings of these two genealogical citizenships, in which the family tree and not contemporary identification is the sine qua non requirement for eligibility, were located largely in the long-obscured crypto-Jewish aspects of migrations and colonial settlements in various regions that were revealed to them through research. Rather than the continuity (of Sephardi Judaism) emphasized by the official Spanish and Portuguese discourses about the laws, it was narratives of rupture and secrecy that characterized their stories of these migrations and diasporizations. And what moved many of these applicants was a different perspective on the conventional histories of the regions and nation-states to which they belong. Rather than having recourse to the normative stories about Christian Spanish or Portuguese settlement in the Americas, many remarked that their ancestors' experiences in the conquered continent were those of refuge, exile, and secrecy.

Like Navarro in Mexico and Vilanova and Azevedo in Brazil, narrators in the US Southwest also sensed that there was more to what was apparent about their families and the history of their settlements. Although they came from mostly intensively Catholic, traditional, and close-knit extended communities that identified as Spanish, Californians, New Mexicans, and Texans, they came to think that something different prevailed in their families. But they also found that this difference had permeated, secretly, the local cultures from Albuquerque, New Mexico, to Laredo, Texas, and beyond. The discovery of the nature and history of the submerged crypto-Jewish elements by those in their fifties, sixties, and seventies coincided with the resurgence of interest in the crypto-Jewish history of these areas a few decades ago (Kandiyoti 2020). Roots in northern Mexico, especially in the cities of Monterrey and Saltillo, also figured large.

While genealogical research can shape potential new social identities—or, in the case of the 2015 laws, legal identities—the unearthed knowledge about origins does not emerge from a discursively neutral context, nor does it have predictable implications. The perception of Spanish belonging as partly a crypto-Jewish one acts as a counternarrative to the dominant understanding of New Mexicans as primarily of Catholic, Spanish, and conquistador stock, with the white racialization and Christian Europeanness that this narrative entails (Nieto-Phillips 2004). The United States–born narrators were particularly explicit about how the crypto-Jewish element bears on an already racially charged situation. Paula Moya, a New Mexican professor in California, laid bare the complications of identity. Referring to the Spanish, rather than, for example, Mexican, Chicana/o/x, or indigenous identification common among Hispanic families in New Mexico, Moya explained,

> A notable aspect of my growing up was the idea that there were three groups in Santa Fe: the Spanish, the Indians, and the Anglos is what we call them, and that we had this tri-racial harmony. At the time we identified ourselves as Spanish and this was in contradistinction to Anglos and to Native Americans who I think we called the Indians at the time anyway. . . . Being Spanish in New Mexico meant not being Mexican, . . . and I rejected that on moral, intellectual, political grounds. . . . It was pretty clear to me that we all had Native heritage in addition to whatever Spanish heritage. (2020)

Although her mother had completed a genealogy many years earlier, confirming a status of *primera familia* (first family), among the first New Mexican settlers of Spanish origin, Moya had been uninterested in and skeptical about the European racialization and occlusion of violent conquest and indigeneity that such formulations implied (Nieto-Phillips 2004). Moya's acknowledgment of the foundational indigenous genealogical component and critique of the distancing of "the Mexican" in the United States is certainly not unknown to other narrators. In fact, Kathleen Alcalá, the well-known author who traced family history to Saltillo, Mexico, and whose parents were child refugees in California during the Mexican Revolution of 1910, observed,

> I had thought that one reason they might claim Jewish ancestry was to differentiate ourselves from the common person, from "los otros Mexicanos" . . . that we were special, we were from an educated background, we were different in some way. And I took that as a form of racism and thought, "Well it's probably entirely made up." Until I did the research for my first book, and this isn't made up at all. This is very clearly what our family background was. (2020)

Alcalá, who practices Judaism, also identifies as Opata. Actively involved with the Indigenous Nation, she also features its history in her novels set in the United States–Mexico borderlands region, in which the Opata characters' destinies are intertwined with the crypto-Jewish ones. Like many of the narrators, Alcalá maintains for herself a frame of mixed belongings, in which devotion to Judaism and commitment to the Opata are compatible.

Others, such as Navarro of Mexico City and Anna Guerra, a psychotherapist in Houston who was not able to apply by the Spanish deadline, were not as invested in finding out more about their Native roots, though they acknowledged them. Guerra's reason for this was that the role of indigeneity was well-known to her, but the mystery was Jewishness. And, she remarked, "I am someone who can't let a mystery go" (2020). Arnulfo Ramirez, a retired scholar who wrote a memoir about his South Texan and North Mexican family, remarked about his mixed kinship links. He was related to conquerors of northern Mexico, such as those who came on the ship with Carvajal, the persecuted converso also known as the pacifier of Indians. He explained, "When they were celebrating 1992 [quincentennial of the conquest] in different parts of the Hispanic world, in Mexico, they would say, 'I am the conqueror and I am the conquered.' You've got both in the family. You had some that were conquerors and some that were conquered" (A. Ramirez 2020). Similarly, referring to the Carvajals in her mother's bloodline and the horror of those family members burning at the stake for judaizing, Moya also observed that "they were enslaving Indians." While the new knowledge about crypto-Jewish roots does not make her change sides regarding conquerors and the conquered in the Americas, her tentative conclusion is that "there is no clean space." What emerges for Moya during the process of learning and application is "a complicated picture of people who are trying to survive." And, she reports, she is no longer dismissive about her mother's efforts at genealogy. "I have to admit that this is part of our heritage," and "I connect more to the Jewish struggle," as she explained (2020). For Moya, as for many of the other narrators, local and regional identities shifted in light of the uncovered converso history as a result of the citizenship pursuit, while approaches to other aspects of the past, such as the indigenous, did not alter in a significant way, whether participants had previously centered indigeneity or not. The narrators' rewriting of regional and imperial histories with a converso inflection demonstrate that the repair and reconnection in the citizenship process is not only vis-à-vis Spain and Portugal, but also with regard to existing narratives about settlement, conquest, and mixture in the Americas.

New genealogical discoveries can also transform some aspects of national discourses for narrators. "Cecilia," a Venezuelan Catholic in her twenties living in New York and learning for the first time about conversos in her heritage was surprised both by Spain's offer and the fact that there were Jews in her lineage, identified by a professional genealogist. She had always thought, she said, she was "more Venezuelan than an *arepa*," referring to a signature national food (2020). This comment also confirms the range of associations of Venezuelan national identity and the perception of Jewishness as non-national. The insertion of a Jewish element into the narrative of Christian origins and settlements in the Americas, then, can cause a shift in something beyond self-perception and partially reconfigure the dominant national stories of origins. The drive of some descendants to seek or publicize crypto-Jewish history in wide social and media networks during the course of pursuing new nationalities (see Pignatelli, chap. 15 in this volume) also contributes to the creation of new local and national narratives through the dissemination of new information and new identities based on the past.

Becoming Spaniards or Portuguese, or Affirming Sephardi Ancestors?

Given this investment in local histories in the Americas and the genealogical, cultural, and spiritual multiplicity many narrators identify with, how do hopeful future nationals conceive of themselves in relation to Spain and Portugal? While most explained that they did not plan to live in the Iberian Peninsula, Ana María Gallegos of northern New Mexico moved to Madrid shortly after our interview in 2018. Some expressed the desire to possibly retire, maintain a base, or return frequently, while others, applying with their young or adult children, simply wished to have the option to travel or even relocate. Most saw no permanent life change on the horizon based on the new citizenship. Whatever the practical plans of the applicants, the connection with Spain and Portugal that already figured in the heritage of the narrators in the United States and in the national stories of those in Latin America received a new life in the process of ascertaining Sephardi descent. This new connection reinforced or, in some cases, created a different and more expansive kind of historical consciousness about both Jewish and Atlantic histories. Often in the narratives, Spain and Portugal were decentered, distanced, or perceived through a Sephardi Jewish lens differentiated from the respective national identities.

Some, like Guerra, Gallegos, and Vilanova referred to above, and Elmer Sierra from Texas whose family originated from Burgos, Spain, have always identified as Spanish or Portuguese (though not to the exclusion of other belongings). Hence, becoming citizens of these Iberian countries felt natural. But for others it posed an existential problem. "Luis," a Venezuelan professional in his forties living in New York City with his wife and children, had strong doubts about becoming Spanish, though, like other Venezuelans, he was hoping the citizenship would bring relief from pressing immigration and other legal and bureaucratic hurdles and delays he faced because of his birth nationality. He explained that, while other Latin Americans do identify as Spanish via their ancestry, his family, of long-ago Basque origins, self-defined as Venezuelan patriots:

> This idea of becoming Spanish completely clashes with family tradition and with the independence of Venezuela, that is, with the configuration of especially one particular social class in Latin America [which] is constructed in opposition to Spain. So, when I went to Málaga last year to sign the citizenship application, that night I had a political conflict in my head. I was thinking of all my relatives—my grandmother would have died; both grandmothers [would have], thinking that . . . many of my cousins are applying for Spanish papers. They would not have liked it at all. And in fact, I don't feel comfortable with the idea of becoming Spanish. . . . It's what bothers me the most in all this. . . . Having discovered that I have Sephardi heritage is delightful; I think it's great. But becoming Spanish is a conflict, though . . . pragmatically speaking it seems fine. (2019)

Interestingly, he added, despite the strong Catholicism of his family, whose members are not immune to the occasional antisemitic joke, having Jewish origins was far from problematic and even a source of pride. But it was the Spanish belonging that was disjunctive with national and class identity.

Two other narrators also distanced themselves from Iberia but for different historical reasons. Notably, Maria Sanchez of Albuquerque had an elaborate narrative about Spain and Sephardism honed with years of research and participation in crypto-Jewish and normative Jewish institutions. Early on in our conversation, Sanchez (2018) cited more than once the influence of her elder, Eulogia "Loggie" "Mama" Carrasco, a charismatic well-known figure in New Mexico, who had an encompassing view of the transgenerational conscious and unconscious memory of crypto-Jewish descendants as permeated with the fear of the Inquisition (Rochlin and Rochlin 2000, 224). The Inquisition loomed large in several narrators' historical consciousness. Sanchez commented that, in her current work as a therapist for vulnerable and marginal populations in Albuquerque, she recognized the transgenerational psychological effects of living with Inquisitorial terror. Gail Gutierrez from California, who had converted to Judaism, might not go through with her application after all, because of what she perceives as enduring antisemitism in Spain. She also communicated some of this sense that, while the country is familiar ground, it is also a space of a historicized fear.

> When I'm in Spain it's like "oh I love this place. There is so much richness." . . . A part of me feels like I was there before. When I went to Cordoba I knew where everything was . . . and I had never been there before. . . . It was like a memory that came back. The same as in Granada.
> We were in Granada during [Easter] once, and . . . many times before in Spain I had seen the high holiday marching, the parades, and candles. . . . That night it terrorized me. I had to go back to the hotel. I was shaking in fear. . . . I have no idea why. . . . Some kind of genetic memory, I don't know. . . . I've been in Spain many times and lived there. I'd never had any real deep connections told to me in terms of my family and Spanish culture and Spanish history. Just experiences where I am like "this is a place I know," "this is a place where I belong," and "this is a place that scares me." (Gutierrez 2020)

Elsewhere, I referred to as paramemory the descriptions of corporeal historical memory that converso descendants have reported in testimonies and memoirs. Something beyond individual memory presents itself in the body that "experiences" the past. The body also serves as an archive in such experiences for which there may not be a precise explanation, but that has strong impact nevertheless (Kandiyoti 2020), as it does for Gutierrez who does not "trust Spain."

While the collective memory of the Inquisition is prevalent among some applicants who identify as descendants of crypto-Jews, that past does not inform reparative citizenship similarly for everyone. For many, Spain's crimes against Jews are too remote for them to hold resentment or anger. For Vilanova, who feels both Portuguese and Brazilian, Portugal's gesture shows that it is seeking to make amends and can even serve as a model for other nations (Vilanova 2019). To Navarro of Mexico City, what Spain has done is a "formal sensation of *tikkun*," in a reference to the Jewish tradition of repairing the world. Navarro believes that King Felipe's 2015 speech (Felipe VI 2015) on the occasion of the Spanish law, constituted a sincere "apology," while the Inquisition and the Expulsion are "another history; another era" (Navarro 2020).

For those who were already aware of converso ancestors, the confirmation of Sephardi Jewish ancestry in the certificates of origin issued by Jewish community organizations often were the most important and moving piece of validation in the whole process. The nonrecognition of crypto-Jewish descendants as Jews by other normative official Jewish bodies, such as specific congregations in the Americas or in Israel vis-à-vis its right of return, is sometimes perceived as a painful or problematic rejection. A sentiment of orphanhood emerges frequently in contemporary crypto-Jewish discourse. Some applicants referred to this as an ongoing issue. Elmer Sierra, a Catholic born and raised in Brownsville, Texas, told us he ascertained Levite blood via DNA ancestry testing. He expressed disappointment with Israel's nonrecognition of converso descendants as potential returnees and citizens, given its genealogical requirement to have at least one recognized Jewish grandparent. But for Sierra, whose university education was in the sciences, deep genetic ancestry is just as valid: "When you have Levite blood in you, it's perpetual. It doesn't matter if you are Muslim, Jewish, or Christian. It's written" (2020). Sierra explained that, although the new citizenship would honor his paternal ancestors, known to be church-builders in Spain, a more important motivation was to secure the right of return to Israel. He and some of his cousins hoped that the Federation of Jewish Communities of Spain, which is charged with authenticating and certifying claimants' Sephardi descent, "might be a way for us to go back" to Israel, perhaps even to settle there.

The confirmation of Sephardi Jewish descent by Spain or Portugal's official Jewish organizations, a requirement of the application, was meaningful to others as well, albeit not in relation to Israel. Azevedo also felt very satisfied to receive this document, as a recognition of his ancestors, given that he is eager to transmit this history to his prospective children. Describing his Portuguese and Brazilian forebears as heroes, because of the persecution they survived and the tenacity they showed regarding their faith, he perceived the certificate and the law as a reparation, albeit a minimal and conditional one. Like him, for Navarro, and Arnulfo Ramirez and many other narrators, the application for Spanish or Portuguese nationality entailed a closer connection with and confirmation of Jewish ancestors rather more strongly than the symbolic meanings of becoming new Spaniards or Portuguese. Navarro (2020) said it plainly: "I sought the nationality out of . . . love for an identity, for Sepharad, a very strong sentiment toward Sepharad." Using the Hebrew name for Spain, Navarro affirmed the return to Spain as a recovery of a Sephardi Jewish identity. For others, more than confirming a preexisting Iberian heritage that had already been central to national or family narratives about conquests and settlements in the Americas, the Spanish or Portuguese passport was a discovery of an entirely new way of perceiving Iberia, through a Sephardi Jewish lens. These ancestral citizenships as repair, then, may awaken or strengthen the converso descendants' Sephardi consciousness, more than restoring or cementing Spanish or Portuguese identification.

"I Am Sephardi, but I Am Not Jewish": Descent and Sephardiness

If the story of the Christian past in Iberia and the Americas shifts to incorporate a repressed Sephardi Jewish element, what kind of configuration of Sephardiness emerges from the discovery of this ancestry and its presentation to communal and national authorities? Many applicants, like much of the general public, conflate descent and identity, which also lead to unexpected interpretations of Sephardi ancestry. One narrator in his thirties who spoke to me from Barranquilla, Colombia, was very invested in obtaining Spanish citizenship and had been learning and gathering sources recently about his Jewish ancestors of Portuguese converso origin who had settled in Curaçao and who had later migrated to Colombia. Seated in front of a wall on which hung a painting of the Virgin Mary holding the baby Jesus, he told me that he is Sephardi but not Jewish (De La Rosa 2018). Similarly, Navarro (2020) reported that, since the citizenship opportunity began, some other Cotijans he knew who adopted a converso genealogy, told him "Soy sefardí pero soy católico" [I am Sephardic, but I am Catholic]. Filipe Azevedo shared the same information about his Brazilian extended family members who are applicants. Neither he nor Navarro, both of whom became observant Jews, agree with this formulation, because for them being Sephardi and being Jewish cannot be perceived as separate.

The approach to Sephardiness as something distinct from Jewishness seems to overlap with other existing distinctions in Jewish worlds between religion and ethnicity, such as cultural Jew, secular Jew, or non-Jewish Jew (Deutscher 1968). However, the formulation Sephardi but not Jewish is not an indication of lack of a particular faith or secularity per se (since it can refer to practicing Christians), nor is it cultural in the sense of ongoing Jewish practices in the absence of religious belief or worship, such as in language, cuisine, arts, or customary ritual.

Genealogical and genetic investigations commonly lead to ontological assertions ("I am 10 percent Yoruba, Irish," etc.) and are not unique to converso descendants by any means: "Genealogy—and ancestors—are used as a resource for identity work. Thus, the self, and individuality, is itself constituted through (dis)embeddedness in kinship networks" (Kramer 2011, 393). Moreover, the disaggregation and distancing of Sephardi identity from the Jewish is in tandem with the primacy of genealogical qualification for citizenship eligibility. Although the preamble of the Spanish law states that "Sephardis are Jews who lived in the Iberian Peninsula" (Law 12/2015 2015), the evidentiary requirement of ancestry allows some applicants to reach their own definition of Sephardiness primarily in terms of descent.

In a version of the well-known question of "Who is a Jew?," these reparative citizenship possibilities raise the question "Who is a Sephardi Jewish *descendant*?" The self-declaration "Sephardi but not Jewish" produces in the minds of some applicants as well as for other commentators and observers, a relatively uncommon category of the non-Jewish Sephardi who may not have religious or cultural connections to Sephardi worlds. Sephardi Jewish identity is mutable and permeable as scholars have shown (e.g., Naar 2016), and Sephardiness is often perceived as a subset of Jewishness in certain contexts of Ashkenazi-centrism, but the two are usually not separated. This formulation can suggest that Sephardiness is a blood community rather than as an ethno-religious-cultural community, as it is more frequently perceived.

In addition to occasioning discoveries of descent, then, genealogical citizenship also has the consequence of producing new definitions of collective identity. About the commonplace preference for claiming some ancestors over others, Anne-Marie Kramer argues, "Given its selectivity, the genealogical imaginary then functions as a tool through which the ties of kinship can be both acknowledged *and* disavowed" (2011, 392; emphasis in original). The formulations about Sephardiness by some converso descendants, however, point to a perception that is in between avowal and disavowal, to draw on Kramer (2011), one that changes the conventional terms of the community associated with their remote, hitherto secret, relatives. The difference between the narrators who subscribe to the notion of the non-Jewish Sephardi and those who (like Navarro and Azevedo) disapprove of it may lie in the motivations that led to the discovery. Those who gained awareness of their lineage because of the citizenship offer may not be connected to or invested in normative Judaism or practicing Jewish culture, though they may be very interested in Sephardi history. Whatever the reasons for the disavowal, we can see that the genealogical basis of the citizenship, together with the participants' own views and choices, allows the severing of Sephardism from Jewishness, so long as narrators also subscribe to an ontologically informed view of distant kin.

Sephardi forebears are not only lost and found, but also remade. And, for certain narrators, the discovery produces a new imagined community based on Sephardiness as a biological and discrete formation, with implications that need further exploration than the limited space here allows. These being still nascent ideas, we need to examine them as they unfold, depending on the success of the citizenship application and the degree of relevance of the new nationality and ancient kin to the narrators' lives. In my previous work, I had suggested that the converso's return has reinserted converso history into contemporary Sephardi and other Jewish communities and consciousness (Kandiyoti 2020). Time will tell how the unexpected thousands of converso descendants who discovered or solidified Sephardi Jewish ancestry because of the citizenship process will impact Sephardism within but also outside of the frame of Spanish or Portuguese nationality.

Conclusion

Descendants of conversos in the Americas who have applied for Spanish or Portuguese citizenship have been negotiating not only the acquisition of a new nationality but also newly found ancestors and/or the presentation of themselves to a state for the first time as descendants of Jews. Given the history of persecutions, conversions, and migrations that their lineage research has uncovered, they do not subscribe to a seamless sense of continuity and linguistic and cultural loyalty to an originary identity, which is found in formulations about the Spanish and Portuguese as well as other ancestral citizenships. The narrators present stories of secrecy and repression of or complete rupture from the lineage that is the basis of the nationality provisions. Their quest for genealogical citizenship reroutes Iberian roots: Rather than Spain and Portugal, what is at center are migrations and settlement in the Americas, and the Sephardi Jewish past and its converso detours. The obligation to present lineage in the citizenship application process yields new collective narratives and a restoration of a hidden communal past, rather than the primarily individualized self-fashioning with which consumer genealogy is identified (Nash 2002, 28). These new origin narratives lead applicants to revise the existing dominant racial, national, regional, and religious scripts to a certain extent. The genealogical consciousness produced or reinforced by the pursuit of ancestral citizenship can also lead to new definitions of identities, including the Sephardi Jewish, as primarily descent based. Reparative genealogical citizenships that bring to the fore noncontinuous histories left out of the dominant narratives of the past, like those of the conversos, may repair symbolically but often in unexpected ways, and may generate ways of being otherwise Latin American, Latina/o/x, Iberian, or Sephardi Jewish.

Dalia Kandiyoti is professor of English at the City University of New York, College of Staten Island, and the author of *The Converso's Return: Conversion and Sephardi History in Contemporary Literature and Culture* (Stanford University Press 2020), *Migrant Sites: America, Place, and Diaspora Literatures* (Dartmouth College/University Press of New England 2009), and numerous articles on contemporary Sephardi, Latinx, and migration/diaspora literatures. With Dr. Rina Benmayor, she has developed an oral history project of Sephardi descendants applying for Spanish or Portuguese citizenship. These interviews are archived at the University of Washington Libraries. Her individual chapter in this volume has been supported by a National Endowment for the Humanities fellowship.

Notes

1. I am very grateful for a faculty grant from the National Endowment for the Humanities in support of the research and writing of this article. My thanks also go to the narrators for their time and generosity in sharing their stories. In the writing of this essay, I also benefited from productive conversations with Robert Latham and Michal Friedman, and from Rina Benmayor's astute suggestions.
2. "Spanish and Portuguese Citizenship for Sephardi Jewish Descendants: An Oral History Collection (2017-2022)" (Benmayor and Kandiyoti, 2017-2022) is the first and to date the most extensive collection of in-depth interviews with Sephardi descendants on the 2015 citizenship laws. The University of Washington Sephardic Studies Digital Collection is the online repository of the corpus, which comprises some sixty interviews, running in length from sixty to ninety minutes each. The narrators come from around the globe and range in age from their twenties to their eighties. They include descendants of: Jewish-identified Sephardis; conversos (Jews who were forcibly converted to Christianity); and *Dönmes* (descended from the followers of Sabbetai Sevi). Among the narrators are also Jews who lost their Jewish and Sephardi identities through intermarriages and assimilation. Topics covered include family origins and history, connections to Ladino or Haketia, religious and cultural upbringing, motivations for seeking citizenship, experiences with the process, views on Spain and Portugal's past wrongs, and thoughts about citizenship as a form of reparation. For more detailed information on the collection and its methodology, see Benmayor and Kandiyoti (2020).
3. At the time of the interviews, the narrators were at various stages of the application process, though the majority had completed their part of the bureaucratic require-

ments and were awaiting approval from the Spanish or Portuguese governments. In the summer of 2021, after the interviews, three of the narrators received rejections from Spain, along with twenty five hundred other applicants. At this time, in the first half of 2022, there is not enough clarity or investigation about the reasons for the rejections. New interviews with these and other applicants will be necessary to better understand the impact of the rejections.

4. The names in quotation marks are pseudonyms chosen by the narrators.
5. All the translations from the Spanish or Portuguese interviews are mine.
6. Often invoked, such examples of continuity of some crypto-Jewish practices in certain regions in the Americas is supported as authentic by some scholars and contested by others (Feitler 2011; Feitler and Stuczynski 2018; Hordes 2008; Kandiyoti 2020). For an overview of dissenting perspectives on the contemporary survival of crypto-Judaism in the United States, see, e.g., Carroll (2018).

References

Alcalá, Kathleen. 2020. Interview conducted by Dalia Kandiyoti. 25 March, via Zoom.
Aragoneses, Alfons. 2016. "Convivencia and Filosefardismo in Spanish Nation-Building." *Max Planck Institute for European Legal History Research Paper Series* 5: 1–34, https://dx.doi.org/10.2139/ssrn.2798054.
Ávila, Eduardo. 2019. Interview conducted by Rina Benmayor. 1 October, via Zoom.
Azevedo, Filipe. 2020. Interview conducted by Dalia Kandiyoti. 2 July, via Zoom.
Benmayor, Rina, and Dalia Kandiyoti. 2017–22. "Spanish and Portuguese Citizenship for Sephardi Jewish Descendants: An Oral History Collection (2017–2022)." University of Washington Sephardic Studies Digital Collection.
———. 2020. "Ancestry, Genealogy, and Restorative Citizenship: Oral Histories of Sephardi Descendants Reclaiming Spanish and Portuguese Nationality." *Quest. Issues in Contemporary Jewish History* 18 (December): 219-51. https://www.quest-cdecjournal.it/wp-content/uploads/2021/01/9-Q18_03_Benmayor-Kandiyoti.pdf.
Carroll, Michael P. 2018. "The Not-So-Crypto Crypto-Jews of New Mexico: Update on a Decades-Old Debate." *Religion* 48, no. 2: 236–51.
Cecilia. 2020. Interview conducted by Dalia Kandiyoti. 24 March, via Zoom.
Cook-Martín, David A. 2013. *The Scramble for Citizens: Dual Nationality and State Competition for Immigrants.* Stanford, CA: Stanford University Press.
De La Rosa, Elías. 2018. Interview conducted by Dalia Kandiyoti. 8 November, via Zoom.
Decreto-Lei nº 30-A/2015. 2015. *Diário da República* 41, 27 February 2015: 92–93.
Deutscher, Isaac. 1968. *The Non-Jewish Jew and Other Essays.* London: Oxford University Press.
Fabiana. 2018. Interview conducted by Rina Benmayor. 9 February, via Zoom.
Feitler, Bruno. 2011. "Four Chapters in the History of Crypto-Judaism in Brazil: The Case of the Northeastern New Christians (17th–21st centuries)." *Jewish History* 25: 207–27.
Feitler, Bruno, and Stuczynski Claude B. 2018. "A Portuguese-Jewish Exception?: A Historiographical Introduction." In *Portuguese Jews, New Christians, and "New Jews:" A Tribute to Roberto Bachmann,* edited by Bruno Feitler and Claude B. Stuczynski, i–xviii. Leiden: Brill.

Felipe VI. 2015. "Palabras de Su Majestad el Rey en el acto solemne con motivo de la Ley 12/2015 en materia de concesión de nacionalidad española a los sefardíes originarios de España." Palacio Real de Madrid, 30 November 2015. https://www.casareal.es/ES/Actividades/Paginas/actividades_discursos_detalle.aspx?data=5550.

Gallegos, Ana María. 2018. Interview conducted by Dalia Kandiyoti. 23 March, via Zoom.

Goode, Joshua. 2009. *Impurity of Blood: Defining Race in Spain, 1870–1930*. Baton Rouge: Louisiana State University Press, 2009.

Guerra, Anna. 2020. Interview conducted by Dalia Kandiyoti and Rina Benmayor. 15 June, via Zoom.

Gutierrez, Gail. 2020. Interview conducted by Dalia Kandiyoti. 3 July 2020, via Zoom.

Harpaz, Yossi. 2013. "Rooted Cosmopolitans: Israelis with a European Passport—History, Property, Identity." *International Migration Review* 47, no. 1 (Spring): 166–206.

———. 2019. *Citizenship 2.0: Dual Nationality as a Global Asset*. Princeton, NJ: Princeton University Press.

Hordes, Stanley. *To the End of the Earth: A History of the Crypto-Jews of New Mexico*. New York: Columbia University Press, 2008.

Israel, Jonathan I. 2002. *Diasporas within a Diaspora: Jews, Crypto-Jews, and the World Maritime Empires (1540–1740)*. Leiden: Brill.

Joppke, Christian. 2005. *Selecting by Origin: Ethnic Migration in the Liberal State*. Cambridge: Harvard University Press.

Kandiyoti, Dalia. 2020. *The Converso's Return: Conversion and Sephardi History in Contemporary Literature and Culture*. Stanford, CA: Stanford University Press.

Kaplan, Yosef. 2000. *An Alternative Path to Modernity: the Sephardi Diaspora in Western Europe*. Leiden: Brill.

Kramer, Anne-Marie. 2011. "Kinship, Affinity and Connectedness: Exploring the Role of Genealogy in Personal Lives." *Sociology* 45, no. 3: 379–95.

Kunin, Seth. 2009. *Juggling Identities: Identity and Authenticity Among the Crypto-Jews*. New York: Columbia University Press, 2009.

Law 12/2015. 2015. "Ley 12/2015 de 24 de junio, en materia de concesión de la nacionalidad española a los sefardíes originarios de España" [Law 12/2015 of 24 June, granting Spanish nationality to Sephardi Jews originating from Spain]. *Boletín Oficial del Estado*, 25 June 2015, no. 151.

Liphshiz, Canan. 2018. "Sephardic Converts give Northern Brazil's Dwindling Jewish Communities New Life." *Times of Israel*, 29 December 2018. https://www.timesofisrael.com/sephardic-converts-give-northern-brazils-dwindling-jewish-communities-new-life.

Luis. 2020. Interview conducted by Dalia Kandiyoti. 22 January, via Zoom.

Moore, Kenneth. 1976. *Those of the Street. The Catholic Jews of Mallorca, a Study in Urban Cultural Change*. Notre Dame: University of Indiana Press.

Moya, Paula. 2020. Interview conducted by Rina Benmayor and Dalia Kandiyoti. 19 September, via Zoom.

Naar, Devin E. 2016. "'Sephardim Since Birth:' Reconfiguring Jewish Identity in America." *Sephardi and Mizrahi Jews in America: the Jewish Role in American Life*, edited by Saba Soomekh. West Lafayette, IN: Purdue University Press.

Nash, Catherine. 2002. "Genealogical Identities." *Environment and Planning D: Society and Space* 20: 27–52.

Navarro, José. 2020. Interview conducted by Dalia Kandiyoti. 1 May, via Zoom.

Nelson, Alondra. 2016. *The Social Life of DNA: Race, Reparations, and Reconciliation After the Genome*. Boston: Beacon Press.

Nieto-Phillips, John M. 2004. *The Language of Blood: The Making of Spanish-American Identity in New Mexico, 1880s–1930s.* Albuquerque: University of New Mexico Press.
Olivares, David. 2019. Interview conducted by Dalia Kandiyoti and Rina Benmayor. 29 September, via Zoom.
Pogonyi, Szabolcs. 2019. "The Passport as Means of Identity Management: Making and Unmaking Ethnic Boundaries through Citizenship." *Journal of Ethnic and Migration Studies* 45, no. 6: 975–93. Accessed 8 November 2020. https://doi.org/10.1080/1369183X.2018.1440493.
Ramirez, Arnulfo. 2020. Interview conducted by Dalia Kandiyoti and Rina Benmayor. 16 April, via Zoom.
Ramirez, Cristina. 2018. Interview conducted by Dalia Kandiyoti. 14 February, via Zoom.
Rochlin, Harriet and Fred Rochlin. 2000. *Pioneer Jews: A New Life in the Far West.* New York: Houghton Mifflin.
Romero, Simon. 2018. "Some Hispanics with Jewish Roots Pursue an Exit Strategy: Emigrate to Spain." *New York Times*, 6 November 2018. https://www.nytimes.com/2018/11/06/us/jews-sephardic-hispanic-spain-new-mexico.html.
Sanchez, Maria. 2018. Interview conducted by Dalia Kandiyoti. 13 December, via telephone.
Sierra, Elmer. 2020. Interview conducted by Rina Benmayor and Dalia Kandiyoti. 1 November, via Zoom.
Vilanova, Lisiane. 2019. Interview conducted by Dalia Kandiyoti. 1 February, via Zoom.
Wachtel, Nathan. 2001. *La foi du souvenir: labyrinthes marranes.* Paris: Seuil.
Zerubavel, Eviatar. 2011. *Ancestors and Relatives: Genealogy, Identity, and Community.* Oxford: Oxford University Press.

Chapter 15

Portuguese Citizenship for Brazilian Descendants of Sephardic Jews
A Netnography

Marina Pignatelli

Introduction

In 2015, an amendment to Portugal's Nationality Act allowed descendants of Jews who were expelled in the Inquisition to become citizens if they "belong to a Sephardic community of Portuguese origin with ties to Portugal."[1] Since that year, more than fifty thousand people who claim descent from Portuguese Jews have acquired citizenship, and a few have immigrated to Portugal.[2] It is likely that many of these applicants perceive themselves as descendants of New Christians rather than as normative Sephardic Jews.

Brazilians stand out among other foreign nationals who apply for this citizenship. They are also the most active in creating online networks of citizenship information exchange in Portuguese. What characterizes these Brazilian Sephardic-descended applicants in terms of their identity perceptions? What kind of information, ideas, concerns, and support are they seeking or sharing in these virtual communities and networks? What are their expectations regarding Portuguese citizenship and their reactions when they acquire it? I embarked on this netnographic study to address these questions, by observing and analyzing the ways in which Brazilian applicants engage with each other in virtual, online spaces.

The pursuit of Portuguese citizenship by Brazilian Sephardic descendants is fueled by several contextual factors. The renewed wave of enthusiasm for cultural and religious tourism in Portugal has contributed to a Jewish Renaissance. Since 2011, the Rede Nacional de Judiarias (Portuguese Network of Jewish Quarters) has spread to a growing number of municipalities, regions, and local Jewish communities, as has a systematic effort to compile local information on Judaism throughout the country. Many historical and political events have brought new immigrants, among them Jews, to work and live in the country. Portugal is well positioned in terms of the passport index global rankings (Global Ranking—*Passport Index, 2019*). Additionally, with the increase in terrorist and antisemitic attacks in Europe, the effects of the global economic crisis, and increased political insecurity in countries such as Venezuela and Turkey, some Jews have been seeking a safe haven in Portugal. Sephardic families who for centuries lived in European, Balkan, or Muslim countries, such as Greece, Turkey, Lebanon, Syria, France, England, but also Brazil and Israel, are getting Portuguese passports as a kind of Plan B for their lives. The quest for Portuguese citizenship is not simply instrumental: several other symbolic factors and sentimental attachments are involved. Portugal's nationality law may also be interpreted as a political strategy to advertise to Sephardic descendants that the doors of Sepharad, their ancestral homeland, are open to them. In this way, the new law projects a positive image to the international community that Portugal is reclaiming its tricultural history (Christian, Muslim, and Jewish) and asserting itself as a democratic postmodern plural nation (see Côrte-Real Pinto and David, chap. 2 in this volume).

In addition to the benefits of the explosion of heritage tourism, Jewish communities across Portugal have made other gains through Sephardic descendants abroad. With the arrival of new Jewish immigrants, the 2015 law has had the effect of expanding and reinvigorating several existing Jewish congregations. The communities of Lisbon, Porto, and, to a lesser extent, Belmonte,[3] have further benefitted from the authority granted them by the government to issue, for a fee, certificates of origin to Sephardic applicants, which is the first step in the application process.

In light of this booming interest in Portugal's Sephardic past and present, I address why and how Brazilians, the largest foreign group of citizenship applicants, perceive and construct their connections to this ancestry. I organized my project around four main questions:

1. What characterizes these applicants from Brazil in terms of their narrative identities (Ricoeur 1986), or their symbolic construction of a virtual community (Rheingold 2000)?

2. What kind of information, concerns, and support are they seeking or sharing through online networks?
3. What are their expectations regarding Portuguese citizenship?
4. What are their reactions when they acquire this new citizenship?

In exploring these questions, I found that the concept of Sephardiness, as articulated in other contexts, to be useful. For instance, Rodrigue and Stein (2012) examine Sephardiness as expressed in cultural interconnections and normative Jewishness. They argue that, by the end of the Ottoman Empire, Salonican elites had developed new collective identity narratives, based on shared citizenship and genealogy, enabling them to be simultaneously Greek and Jewish. They write, "Some tend to think of Sephardiness as a matter of inheritance: something of a hereditary cultural trait.... The Sephardic cultural world was never insular, rigidly demarcated, or the product of inbred allegiances. On the contrary, its boundaries were porous, and it bled into and was constantly infused by other Jewish and non-Jewish cultures, and vice-versa" (2012, xxxiii). Insights regarding the fluidity of Sephardic identities also have resonance for groups who have lost but seek to recuperate their connections to Sephardism and Judaism, such as descendants of New Christians. For various reasons—including nationality, genealogy, or inherited or newly found cultural affinity—many of the applicants identify with their Iberian Sephardic origins while, at the same time, maintaining other national, genealogical, or cultural backgrounds or affinities.

Netnographic Methods

Drawing on netnographic artifacts, such as social networking services (SNS) and social context theories, I conducted an exploratory online netnography. I documented and sought to analyze how Brazilian applicants engage with virtual groups in online spaces to reconstruct the narrative and symbolic meanings of Sephardiness in support of their applications. I looked at the production of insights and exchanges in the two main interactive Web 2.0 internet-based applications operating in Brazil today: Facebook and YouTube. I studied the user-generated web communications content such as posts, comments, digital photos, videos, and data produced in online interactions among Brazilians who use social media webpages as forums for investigating Portuguese Sephardic origins.

The adaptation of traditional ethnographic methods to the study of online communities includes several stages and techniques: formal entry into the group or channel, data collection of documents, apparent or passive participant online observation of selected online resources, fieldnotes, and data content analysis and interpretation (Guimarães 2003; Kozinets 2010; Skågeby 2011, 411). My first step was to identify community group message archives on Facebook and YouTube from 2015 to July 2020. I then made a list and selected an appropriate corpus to study. The above research questions served as a guide in this selection, and I took into account the level of activity in the groups, the number of active members, and the number and richness of the posts, as suggested by Kozinets (2010).

I observed four out of nine Facebook groups of Brazilian virtual communities concerned with Portuguese Jewish descent that had been created since 2015.[4] The four targeted groups included two public groups: Genealogia Portuguesa Judaica (Portuguese Jewish Genealogy), and Ancestrais Sefarditas. Certificados (Sephardic Ancestors. Certificates). I also selected two closed or private groups: Genealogia Sefardita—Brasil (Sephardic Genealogy—Brazil), and Genealogia Sefardita Documentada (Documented Sephardic Genealogy). I recorded the type of page, date of creation, founder names, number of followers, link, page photo, and description. On YouTube, I examined fourteen channels with videos related to the themes of this study. From among these, I selected and logged four videos (three amateur and one semiprofessional), based on the name, subject, author, date of creation, duration, number of views, likes, and comments.[5]

Once I had made the selection, I asked permission to become a member of the groups and channels and was asked to answer a set of filter questions. I then contacted the group administrators in order to become a virtual participant observer in each group and channel. My passive observations were both synchronous (online in real time) and diachronic, in offline resources. As this was a netnography that dealt with potentially sensitive data, I used strict formal and informal codes of ethics (netiquette).[6] Between January and October 2020, the period in which I collected the data (although for the analysis I reached back to 2015), I made a concerted effort to track the members' regular activity in the respective virtual community (Garcia et al. 2009).

To address my research questions, I looked at the kinds of information, concerns, and support the posters and commenters were seeking or sharing in the forums and their expectations and reactions regarding the Portuguese citizenship. To analyze these findings, I systematically collected and categorized the textual data items (posts, comments, and messages), considering not only recurring themes but also the relevant expressed opinions or shared experiences of the forum users. I then evaluated general user or commenter reaction to the acquisition of this new Portuguese nationality in order to capture a range of feelings related to the process of constructing Sephardic identity. Finally, I assigned each item to the appropriate category of analysis (Skågeby 2015: 121).

Virtual Communities, Identities, and Discourses

Identities and discourses are terms that help describe and understand how Brazilians form concrete web communities through the targeted use of Facebook and YouTube cyberspaces that are focused on Portuguese Sephardic origins. Identity is used to describe the social, religious, political, gendered, cultural, or ethnic realms attributed to both individuals and groups. Anthropologists have tended to focus primarily on collective identities, examining their hybrid, socially constructed, and even contested character (Mitchell 2010, 368). In this study, I consider the national and the Jewish Sephardic (ethnic-religious) identity constructions through the participants' textual discourse in order to try to understand how these may impact their developing Sephardiness.

SNS are a contemporary way to create a sense of a virtual community (Rheingold 2000). A preliminary search revealed several incipient virtual communities aimed at gathering and strengthening ties among Brazilians (though not exclusively Brazilians) who feel connected to a Portuguese Sephardic Jewish origin. For example, the public Facebook groups Genealogia Judaica Portuguesa (2015) and Ancestrais Sefarditas. Certificados (2019) reveal connections made on the basis of shared genealogy and desired citizenship, enabling the groups' members to identify simultaneously as Brazilians, descendants of Portuguese New Christians or Jews, and potentially as Portuguese citizens, hence paving their way into a sense of Sephardiness.

The discursive nexus of a Facebook group can be detected in the "About" section of each page, where the history of the group is described and page administrators post the rules of participation. Although living in different parts of Brazil or even abroad, the two or three Brazilian men and women who created each group explain the group's objectives, social and historical background, and shared intended purposes. They welcome all those interested in finding their Portuguese Sephardic genealogical origins, especially the descendants of the Jews or New Christians expelled during the Inquisition period. They expect these groups to be fruitful online spaces to exchange information and provide mutual support, especially for those who expect to apply for Portuguese citizenship, as seen, for example, in the description of one of the public groups:

"A group for those interested in Portuguese citizenship for descendants of Sephardic Jews or for [people] who want to know their origins. The aim is to gather in one place, in an organized way, the names of the Sephardic ancestors already recognized by the Israeli [Portuguese Jewish] Communities" (Ancestrais Sefarditas. Certificados 2019). The private group Genealogia Sefardita-Brasil also offers a virtual communal interconnection among those seeking to apply for Portuguese citizenship, highlighting the possibility for members to do so in a free and autonomous way, under the following terms: "This group was formed to give everyone free access to sources on the maximum number of XN [New Christians], so that anyone can write their own report, or hire someone if they did not feel safe or qualified to do so. No one will need to hire someone because the sources and documents are 'secret,' hidden, or owned by some anointed ones. NOBODY owns our history and genealogy except OURSELVES" (Genealogia Sefardita—Brasil 2019).[7]

When I explored the Brazilian groups on Facebook and on YouTube, I chose those that were heavily trafficked in terms of views and comments, and therefore rich in data. In YouTube, I examined two Brazilian Jewish genealogy videos produced by Gilberto Ventura, a Brazilian rabbi who founded the Synagogue Without Borders movement in São Paulo. The videos were *Genealogia Judaica do Brasil: Cordeiro, Barbosa, Leão, Mendes, Lopes* (Sinagoga Sem Fronteiras 2017) and *Genealogia Judaica do Brasil: Sobrenomes, História, Segredos das Escrituras e Profecias, OLIVEIRA* (Sinagoga Sem Fronteiras 2020). The purpose of the Sinagoga Sem Fronteiras (Synagogue Without Borders) movement and these videos is to rescue and host the Bnei Anusim (converso descendants) and to promote awareness of Jewish history in Brazil. Another video, *Sobrenomes Sefarditas. Você tem ascendência judaica?* (Sephardic surnames. Do you have Jewish descent?) is authored by a Brazilian group—Sinagoga Anusim Brasil (Synagogue Anusim Brazil 2019)—based in Ponta Grossa, in the state of Paraná. It was created to unite those who are engaged in finding their New Christian or crypto-Jewish origins. Additionally, I examined the ASBRAP video, *Como Identificar Ascendentes Cristãos Novos* (How to identify New Christian ancestors), produced by genealogist Marcelo Bogaciovas, founder of the Brazilian Association of History and Genealogy Researchers (ASBRAP 2016), which is active among Brazilian descendants of crypto-Jews. The video discusses Sephardic genealogical research and the granting of Portuguese citizenship.

In order to analyze the identity of the chosen Facebook group members and YouTube video viewers, I first determined who the users were and what values they held in terms of cultural orientation and social background. I checked membership lists and reviewed peoples' posts. Unfortunately, group or channel administrators were unable to provide metric data for comparative quantitative analysis. However, the data that I was able to collect revealed that members and viewers were mostly adult men and women living in very diverse parts of Brazil or abroad. Members also included foreigners, such as Portuguese, Dutch, or Argentinians. Almost all posts or video comments were written in Brazilian Portuguese, with very few exceptions in English or Spanish. I found no pattern in terms of professions, occupations, or activities among the thousands of users. Some present themselves with obvious Jewish names (e.g., Hannah Ruth, Barbara Israel, Yitzhac Cunha, Antônio Ben Avraham), while the majority have unmistakably Brazilian-Portuguese names.

For some, the genealogical search for Sephardic ancestors might simply be a pragmatic shortcut to gain a new citizenship. However, posts and comments also indicated some degree of identification with a Portuguese-Jewish background. A few constructed that identity through direct descent, like Rigoni (2020), from Santa Catarina: "Hello, happy Sunday everyone. I have Sephardic descent from Antônio Bicudo. My relationship starts with my grandmother's paternal grandparents on the side of her father." Souza (2019), a Brazilian living in Dublin, states, "My connection is with Caetano Dantas Correa, from Seridó, Rio Grande do Norte. The first of the lineage in the archives of the [Portuguese] Inquisition Tribunal was Junca Moutezinho de Barcelos." Others established their own possible connection through a crypto-Jewish family history linked to the Portuguese Northeast region, as Matheus (2020), from Rio de Janeiro posted: "On my second visit to the tiny village where my grandfather was born, in the north of Portugal, bordering with Spain, I discovered 'by chance' inscriptions in Hebrew and Jewish religious symbols in the house where he lived and where for at least seven centuries, my ancestors have lived." Finardi (2020), from São Paulo, who imagines having Portuguese-Jewish roots, writes, "I am looking for my Jewish ancestry that I am sure I have, because my maternal grandparents are from Guarda [city in Northern Portugal]." Others link the discovery of their genealogy to a preexisting sense of Sephardic identity grounded in emotions and feelings held prior to embarking on the citizenship application process. As Santos (2020) relates, "I am a mulatto, a miscegenation of the Carneiro Lopes, Cunha, Santos, Magalhães, and Gil surnames, among grandparents and great-grandparents, but something else has always burned in my heart, something that these roots had already indicated to me." Or, as Marcos (2020) put it, "I think that more important than the name is the feeling of our soul that testifies that we are Jews." Finally, some acknowledge their newfound genealogical ties to Portuguese Sephardic roots as dignifying a perception of the self, like Godoy (2020): "I am Bnei Anusim. I am always proud and grateful to my Jewish ancestors. I am returning to Jewish origins and conversion. Gratitude always to my Jewish ancestors."

Much of this SNS content shows that these Brazilians shape their identities by constructing life stories on the internet. Paul Ricoeur's concept of narrative identities (1986) is based on the notion that the self comes into being only in the processing of telling a life story, and that often humans tell and live stories (construct their autobiographies) in close interaction with the stories of a religious tradition—in this case with Sephardic Judaism. These Brazilian member/viewer identities may also be understood as voluntary identities (Thoits 1992), or chosen parts of a self, composed of the meanings that these persons attach to the multiple roles they typically play in a highly differentiated society such as contemporary Brazil. Such online narrative and voluntary identities are based on an optional search for one's connection to Portuguese-Jewish origins, which may be viewed as a process of becoming Sephardic by virtue of a reconnection to Portugal in the present as well as to its Jewish past. For these Brazilians, Portuguese-Jewish descent becomes a marker of cultural otherness, and this allows them to begin to think of themselves as belonging to a larger group than their (Brazilian) community of origin. Within the online social sphere, they gradually begin to articulate a new collective existence, one not specifically related to their country of birth and that includes, as Naar (2015) as well as Rodrigue and Stein (2012) suggest, other ancestral origins. This is also a way of privileging links to Europe through Portugal. This may indicate, as Benmayor and Kandiyoti (2020) argue, that at stake is not only a matter of the legal definition of citizenship but also the issue of belonging within the globalized context of plural cultural identification processes. Both an individual and collective sense of belonging are (re)created and reinforced in a transformative, mutually interdependent, and entangled dialectic.

Seeking and Sharing

As the various posts and comments demonstrate, these Facebook groups and YouTube videos include requests for help in developing genealogical skills for finding Sephardic ancestors. Users also ask questions about the bureaucratic intricacies of the Portuguese naturalization process. In the belief that others may assist them, these requesters reveal a willingness to undertake new identity challenges and to learn more about their origins. A few of them seem to be more resourceful and self-sufficient in their own genealogical research, particularly the group administrators themselves. This is especially evident in their answers or comments with clarifying information. For example, Leonardo Prado (2018), from São Paulo, writes: "When I started my family tree, I only had one or two dates. I've been researching and I'm already entering the seventh generation." Yacov (2018) notes, "My great-grandfather was called Salvino Iacov. I searched on websites about my Jewish descent but documents are missing. I have only one photo signed by my great-grandfather Iacov." Most of the other answers seem to be less skilled regarding genealogical research and procedural matters. Therefore, questions such as the following are common: "Hi, can you enlighten me about the surname of my paternal grandfather: Rodrigues, and my maternal grandfather: Almeida, from Minas Gerais, Mata Miraí area?" (Rodrigues 2019). Or, "Help! Could someone help me with filling in the online tree on the CIL [Comunidade Israelita de Lisboa] form?" (Smartop 2020). The commenters might be considered beginners in genealogy research and perhaps to Portuguese Sephardism, since they seem to be taking the first steps in this direction. These comments from Facebook groups and YouTube channels demonstrate that such SNS resources are productive forums for creating networks that share knowledge, perceptions, reflections, and experiences among its members. Sharing genealogical information may also be instrumental in seeding an incipient sense of Sephardism within the online community.

Thematic content analysis allowed me to find key trends and themes in the selected SNS posts and comments.[8] Among the thousands of posts I sampled were requests for help and tips given to find genealogical ancestors. They also include recommendations on how to proceed, as Queiroz (2020) suggested: "You should register your tree on genealogical sites like Geni, Family Search and MyHeritage that 'match' your relatives with many others." Others, like Fábio (2020), ask for paleographic clues: "Does anyone know how to decipher this name [on the attached photo] that is crossed out?" Others seek information regarding DNA tests: "Through the surname is it possible to be sure of being a descendant of Portuguese Jews or is a DNA test necessary?" (E. Pereira 2020).

In their posts, group participants share links and information about the 2015 law, or news from the press, books, conferences, webinars, and courses on Jewish genealogy, history, cultural heritage, and religious traditions, as well as general news concerning Israel. A few posts warn of possible fraudulent or misleading genealogists, lawyers, consultants, or alleged facilitators. For example, D'Ornellas (2020) advised, "Do not be fooled. It is not mandatory that your report be done by a genealogist unless you feel more secure.... This is not, and has never been, the Jewish community's requirement for accepting the reports."

Finally, when applicants obtain their nationality, sometimes people post special greetings or they encourage applicants in the certification process, as in this heavily "Liked" post on the group Ancestrais Sefarditas. Certificados: "Another certified cousin after years of research and four months of waiting for CIL. Don't give up, as everyone's time will come" (Mendonça 2020).

Themes and posts like the above underscore the significant role virtual communities can and do play in fostering a Portuguese-Sephardic identity among Brazilian users. For those starting out on this quest, social media may offer a new window to discover and develop a genealogical and historical consciousness. For those who already imagined descending from Portuguese Jews or New Christians, or who felt themselves to be Jews, the genealogical search strengthens and confirms a Jewish and Sephardic connection. The recourse to SNS feeds that perception, deepening shared knowledge, especially as those who have identified their Sephardic ancestors or who have obtained their certificates assist beginners in their quests.

Expectations and Reactions

In a Facebook group, Carmen Nogueira posted a provocative question: "If Sephardic citizenship did not exist, would you be interested in Portuguese Jewish genealogy?" (2020). All 121 individuals replied "Yes," followed by explanations regarding their motivations and reactions to the 2015 law. Ventura (2020), for instance, responded by stating that citizenship was a bonus for her genealogy search: "When I started my research, I knew nothing about Sephardic citizenship, and I believe that this possibility was a gift I received for researching family history." Others describe the search for their family history as a pleasant leisure pastime activity to find their true selves. Barbosa (2020) said, "Genealogy gets to be addictive, for those who appreciate history and self-knowledge. I do it as a hobby." Pinheiro, who is interested only in seeking his own roots, declared (2020): "I am looking for my Sephardic, New Christian, crypto-Jewish, Marrano origin, or whatever you want to call it, out of personal interest. I have no interest in Portuguese citizenship." Lopes replied in the same thread (2020): "Actually, my greatest interest was never citizenship, but the rescue of a story that was denied to us." Alex Pereira, (2020) added, "I've researched my genealogy since long before I even knew that Sephardic citizenship existed." Terra (2020), however, seems to be motivated to obtain a Portuguese passport and interprets his genealogic quest as a necessary but overly demanding step, remarking that: "It is the most painful citizenship of all!" Vieira further articulated Ventura's idea of citizenship being a bonus, saying, "The possibility of Citizenship is a great incentive for more people to get in touch with the history of their families. The desire to obtain a European passport does not diminish the discoveries, achievements and all the knowledge acquired along the way. I would like the right to citizenship to remain, so that more people have the possibility of contact with their origins. . . . The granting of Citizenship by the Portuguese government is a symbolic reparation" (Vieira 2020).

Still in the same thread of responses to Nogueira's post, Branco (2020) introduces a new related question: "If your Portuguese passport does not give you direct access to the Schengen area and/or to 180 countries where you can enter without a visa, would you still want to BE Portuguese?" (emphasis in original). All the answers were again affirmative, suggesting that, for these members, the Portuguese passport and/or Portuguese-ness is more important than strategic access to Europe. Addressing Branco's question, Nogueira (2020) opens the possibility for subjectivity, concluding, "This is a very personal matter. Many people think only of the European passport, while others are sensitive to their family history."

Although relevant to the issue of citizenship, these questions and responses focus on why people decide to look for their ancestors and do not focus on the reasons for applying for the Portuguese naturalization. In fact, in the analyzed SNS samples, narratives about citizenship are rarely produced. Vieira's reference to "symbolic reparation" is an exception. One possible explanation for this absence may be that these SNS were created specifically to help members with genealogy and proof of Jewish descent. The attainment of citizenship is for some secondary and for others even dispensable. At most, members post on Facebook digital versions of their certificates of origin issued by the Lisbon or Porto communities but obscuring their personal data. Rather, they write about their feelings of joy and gratitude for their accomplishment. In a highly "Liked" Facebook post, some refer to the time it took them to gain the certificate and name those who helped them during the process: "Today I was happy to receive my long-awaited CIL Certificate by Antônio Rodrigues Alvarenga! It was 3 years doing the research on my genealogy! I would like to thank the help and support of several friends who directly or indirectly took part in this achievement!" (Silva 2020). Images of new Portuguese passports and/or identity cards are an even greater rarity in these SNS. Some group participants, however, are more sophisticated in their expectations and add further thoughts on the subject, such as Lessa (2020), who states, "Now, Israel must accept Brazilian Jews as Jews." Another post laments, "What good is it, we have [the Jewish] DNA in our blood, but the Jews do not accept us. . . . Pure nonsense!" (Wal 2019).

Whether a genealogical quest results from a mere personal search for one's roots or from a strategy to obtain a new instrumental citizenship, self-perception is affected when Sephardic Jewish or New Christian descent is found. Sometimes, a sense of Jewishness through a Sephardic lineage may arise. That newly found identity may also impact the way these Brazilians expect to be seen by others, as Lessa's and Wal's comments reveal. Regarding genealogy searches as a first step toward self-discovery, Mizael asserted, "I want everything from my Jewish heritage. It is interesting that after knowing that I have it, this gives me a feeling of belonging that I cannot describe. It is strange, I spent my whole life without knowing it and when I knew, I feel very connected to Judaism. The whole [of] Brazil needs to know its hidden roots. This will bring a renaissance to the Brazilian people" (Mizael 2020).

Even after getting his Portuguese nationality, Aboab (2019) justifies why he dislikes Portugal: "I am a Sephardic Jewish descendant of Rabbi Isaac Aboab da Fonseca's family and I have no intention of living in Portugal because the Portuguese government burned alive many of my relatives, and those who survived lost all their assets during the diabolical Catholic Inquisition." The ways these Brazilians share their feelings about Sephardic Judaism, as in the case of Mizrael, or about the Portuguese state interventions in Jewish identity and belonging in the past, as in the case of Aboab, may illustrate how they are in a process of discovering, constructing, and (re)defining their own voluntary Jewish identity. For some Brazilians, this process started prior to efforts to gain the Portuguese-Sephardic passport, or even regardless of such efforts. The Sephardic genealogical quest, in which participation in these virtual communities plays a considerable role, seems to reflect a widening of identity through research. The discovery of *the* Sephardic ancestor seems to confirm and reinforce the person's preexisting essential self-perception. For others, it was the desire to gain a new citizenship that turned them into beginners in the family-tree process. When *the* Sephardic ancestor is finally found—and, even more importantly, when the certificate from one of the Portuguese Jewish communities is obtained—a sense of belonging to the Portuguese-Sephardic realm often awakens. In these SNS communities, Brazilians act according to their imagined, felt, or documented inherited Jewish, or particularly Portuguese Sephardic, shared identity. The online spaces are not only inexpensive and practical but also may contribute to structure and sustain Sephardiness.

We cannot assume, however, that choosing to produce such identity narratives in specific SNS online platforms such as the ones that shaped this research means that members produce these same reflections on self-perception in other contexts of their everyday life. Since identities are relational, socially constructed, and potentially hybrid and situational, these virtual community members may be affiliated with other parallel collective identity forums, including their own family realms or professional networks where Sephardiness is not an associative tie. Therefore, we may surmise that a rather more performative social media identity is being produced instead.

Conclusion

As a sister-nation, Brazil has a shared past with Portugal and is one of the countries where Jews and New Christians fleeing from the Inquisition found a home. Their descendants have been looking for those ties, particularly since 2015, and have created several online structures, namely on the SNS, for mutual help purposes. This chapter has observed the kinds of information, the motives, and the effects linked to the genealogical search shared on those services and suggests how these may impact the construction of Sephardiness.

The Brazilians in this study are of diverse ages, genders, occupational, and locational backgrounds. In SNS, they are in a process of creating their Sephardiness as a chosen, voluntary identity, planted in symbolic, cultural, historical, and religious grounds linked to the Portuguese Jewish realm. They may be considered active co-players in the broader network of agents committed to recovering and uplifting Sephardic perspectives in the internally diverse Jewish world. Among these agents in Portugal or Brazil are those facilitators that are directly involved in the naturalization process, such as law firms, civil government officials, professional genealogists, or the Lisbon and Porto Jewish communities. In the appendix to this chapter, Santos and Bento illustrate some of the challenges that Jewish community evaluators face in assessing wideranging types of evidence for certification—genealogical, historical, and cultural. Also included in this study are other Jewish and non-Jewish groups, such as other Portuguese or Brazilian Jewish communities and associations, the Portuguese Network of Jewish Quarters, or the Portuguese state itself, with its 2015 law and establishment in 2019 of the National Day in

Memory of the Inquisition Victims. The Facebook groups and YouTube channels studied comprise a small but exemplary part of the online and in-person social networks engaged—each with its own diverse scale, motivations, and purposes—in the reimagination and regeneration of Sephardism today.

Marina Pignatelli is a cultural anthropologist and associate professor at the Social and Political Sciences Institute, University of Lisbon. She has authored *Cadernos de Orações Cripto-Judaicas e Notas Etnográficas de Judeus e Cristãos-Novos de Bragança* (Etnográfica Press 2019), *Os Judeus e Cristãos-Novos no Mundo Lusófono* (Edições Colibri 2017), "The Origins and Religious Practices and Identities of the Honen Dalim Jewish Community in Mozambique" (*Journal of Modern Jewish Studies* 2, no. 15, 2015), and *A comunidade israelita de Lisboa* (Universidade Técnica de Lisboa 2000). Currently, she studies Marranos in Portugal. She is a board member of the Portuguese Anthropological Association and researcher at the Centre for Research in Anthropology (CRIA).

Notes

1. I would like to thank the volume coeditors, Dalia Kandiyoti and Rina Benmayor, for their insightful comments and their painstaking and clarifying revisions to this article.
2. According to the Portuguese Ministry of Justice and the Registry and Notary Institute, the number of requests for nationality by descendants of Sephardic Jews numbered 137,087 applications; of those, 300 requests have been refused, 80,102 are still pending, and 50,685 passports have been granted, from 2015 to the beginning of 2022 (Lusa/Diário de Notícias 2022). In 2020, 20,892 (65 percent) of applicants were Israeli (Carmo 2022).
3. The Jewish Community of Belmonte (JCB) was consulted during the drafting of Law 30-A/2015. In 2019, under the same act, the JCB was granted permission to issue certificates to citizenship applicants, along with Lisbon and Porto. However, the JCB certificates are not recognized by the government civil services.
4. Several other private groups can also be found on Facebook, dedicated specifically to New-Christians. They also assist possible descendants with genealogic research. These were not included in the study, due to their small size.
5. A few professional or semiprofessional Facebook pages or YouTube channels were also listed but were not considered in the selected sample, since they are extensions of consulting enterprises' blogs or websites with clear commercial purposes. On YouTube, unregistered users can watch and comment but not upload videos to the site, while registered users can upload an unlimited number of videos and add comments.
6. The netiquette procedures I followed included attaining the virtual groups' administrators informed consent to conduct the observation. Because users are dispersed over various discussion groups and forums and not always reachable for questioning (Skågeby 2009), individual informed consent was not possible. Also, because these

posts are public and users may control their own privacy settings, such consent was not viewed as required.
7. All translations from the Portuguese are mine.
8. The units of meaning coded for analysis were themes and concepts in the posts, called "items." I transcribed the exact texts of the posts to be used as indicators and/or items.

References

Aboab, Nooriel. 2019. *I Am a Sephardic Jewish Descendant Of Rabbi Issaac Aboab Da Fonseca's Family*. YouTube. Video. ASBRAP. Como Identificar Ascendentes Cristãos Novos, April 2019. https://www.youtube.com/watch?app=desktop&v=mASS fKZXWtE&t=19s.
ASBRAP. 2016. "Como Identificar Ascendentes Cristãos Novos." YouTube. Video. 41:59, January 29, 2016. https://www.youtube.com/watch?app=desktop&v=mASSfKZX WtE&t=19s.
Barbosa, Kaique. 2020. "Genealogy Gets to Be Addictive." Facebook. Genealogia Judaica Portuguesa, 21 July 2020. https://www.facebook.com/groups/1404360236538563.
Benmayor, Rina, and Dalia Kandiyoti. 2020. "Ancestry, Genealogy, and Restorative Citizenship: Oral Histories of Sephardi Descendants Reclaiming Spanish and Portuguese Nationality." In *Genealogies of Sepharad ('Jewish Spain')*, edited by Daniela Flesler, Michal R. Friedman, and Asher Salah. *Quest. Issues in Contemporary Jewish History.* 18: 219–51. https//: doi.org/10.48248/issn.2037-e41X/10981.
Branco, Vanda. 2020. "If Your Portuguese Passport Does Not Give You Direct Access to the Schengen Area." Facebook. Genealogia Judaica-Portuguesa, 21 July 2020. https://www.facebook.com/groups/1404360236538563.
Carmo, Daniela. 2022. "Mais de 30 mil descendentes de sefarditas já se naturalizaram desde 2015." *Público,* 2 January 2022. https://www.publico.pt/2022/01/02/sociedade/ noticia/30-mil-descendentes-sefarditas-ja-naturalizaram-desde-2015-1990464.
D´Ornellas, Rodrigo. 2020. "Do Not Be Fooled." Facebook. Genealogia Sefardita—Brasil, 26 March 2020. https://www.facebook.com/groups/sefarditagenealogia.
Fábio, Dinêila. 2020. "Does Anyone Know How to Decipher This Name." Facebook. Genealogia Sefardita—Brasil, 27 November 2020. https://www.facebook.com/ groups/sefarditagenealogia.
Finardi, Eva. 2020. "I am Looking for My Jewish Ancestry." Facebook. Genealogia Sefardita Documentada, 30 October 2020. https://www.facebook.com/groups/6034 18636804903.
Garcia, Angela Cora; Standlee, Alecea I.; Bechkoff, Jennifer; Cui, Yan. 2009. "Ethnographic Approaches to the Internet and Computer-Mediated Communication." *Journal of Contemporary Ethnography* 38, no.1: 52-84. https://journals.sagepub .com/doi/10.1177/0891241607310839.
Genealogia Judaica-Portuguesa. 2015. Facebook Public Group. https://www.facebook .com/groups/1404360236538563.
Genealogia Sefardita Documentada. 2019. Facebook Private Group. https://www.face book.com/groups/603418636804903/.
Genealogia Sefardita—Brasil. 2020. Facebook Private Group. 27 November 2020. https:// www.facebook.com/groups/sefarditagenealogia.

Global Ranking—Passport Index, 2019, Henley and Partners. Archived from the original and retrieved 14 August 2019. https://www.henleypassportindex.com/assets/2019/Q3/HPI%20Report%20190701.pdf.

Godoy, Cassia. 2020. *I Am Bnei Anusim. I Am Always Proud*. YouTube. Video, ASBRAP Como Identificar Ascendentes Cristãos Novos, April 2020. https://www.youtube.com/watch?app=desktop&v=mASSfKZXWtE&t=19s.

Guimarães, Mário. 2003. "Doing an Online Ethnography." Unpublished Seminar Report. Department of Sociology, University of Surrey.

Kozinets, Robert V. 2010. *Netnography—Doing Ethnographic Research Online*. London: Sage. https://www.researchgate.net/publication/267922181_Netnography_Doing_Ethnographic_Research_Online/link/5c575bb3a6fdccd6b5e0f5fd/download.

Law 30-A/2015. Decreto-Lei n.º 30-A/2015 de 27 de Fevereiro. Diário da República n.º 41/2015, 2º Suplemento, Série I de 2015-02-27. Ministério da Justiça: 92 – 93. https://dre.pt/dre/detalhe/decreto-lei/30-a-2015-66619927.

Lessa, Paulo. 2020. *Now, Israel Must Accept Brazilian Jews as Jews*. YouTube. Video. Genealogia Judaica do Brasil: Sobrenomes, História, Segredos das Escrituras e Profecias. OLIVEIRA. March 2020. https://www.youtube.com/watch?app=desktop&v=EPOSbzK_-sA.

Lopes, Sostenes. 2020. "Actually, My Greatest Interest Was Never Citizenship." Facebook. Genealogia Judaica-Portuguesa, 21 July 2020. https://www.facebook.com/groups/1404360236538563.

Lusa/Diário de Notícias. 2022. "Portugal rejeitou 300 em quase 57 mil processos de naturalização de judeus sefarditas." 6 February 2022. https://www.dn.pt/sociedade/portugal-rejeitou-300-em-quase-57-mil-processos-de-naturalizacao-de-judeus-sefarditas-14564419.html.

Marcos, Cristiano. 2020. *I Think That More Important Than the Name*. YouTube. Video. Sobrenomes Sefarditas. Você tem ascendência judaica? March. https://www.youtube.com/watch?app=desktop&v=LlrluL47Kt8.

Matheus, Wagner. 2020. "On My Second Visit to the Tiny Village." Facebook. Genealogia Sefardita—Brasil, 12 January. https://www.facebook.com/groups/sefarditagenealogia.

Mendonça, Renise. 2020. "Another Certified Cousin After Years of Research." Facebook. Ancestrais Sefarditas. Certificados, 23 September. https://www.facebook.com/groups/559148357967483.

Mitchell, J. Clyde. 2010. "Identity." In *The Routledge Encyclopedia of Social and Cultural Anthropology*, edited by Alan Barnard and Jonathan Spencer, 368–69. Abingdon, UK: Routledge.

Mizael, MXWL. 2020. *I Want Everything from My Jewish Heritage*. YouTube. Video. Jewish Genealogia Judaica do Brasil: Sobrenomes, História, Segredos das Escrituras e Profecias. OLIVEIRA, July. https://www.youtube.com/watch?app=desktop&v=EPOSbzK_-sA.

Naar, Devin E. 2015. "'Sephardim since Birth': Reconfiguring Jewish Identity in America." In *Sephardi and Mizrahi Jews in America. An Annual Review of the Casden Institute for the Study of the Jewish Role in American Life*, vol. 13, edited by Steven J. Ross, 75–104. West Lafayette, IN: Purdue University Press.

Nogueira, Carmen. 2020. "If Sephardic Citizenship Did Not Exist." Facebook. Genealogia Judaica-Portuguesa, 21 July 2020. https://www.facebook.com/groups/1404360236538563.

Pereira, Alex. 2020. "I've Researched My Genealogy Since Long Before." Facebook. Genealogia Judaica-Portuguesa, 21 July 2020. https://www.facebook.com/groups/1404360236538563.
Pereira, Elpinio. 2020. *Through the Surname Is It Possible To Be Sure Of Being A Descendant.* YouTube. Video. Genealogia Judaica do Brasil: Sobrenomes, História, Segredos das Escrituras e Profecias, OLIVEIRA, February 2020. https://www.youtube.com/watch?app=desktop&v=EPOSbzK_-sA.
Pinheiro, Claudio Jr. 2020. "I Am Looking for My Sephardic." Facebook. Genealogia Judaica Portuguesa, 9 July 2020. https://www.facebook.com/groups/140436023638563.
Prado, Leonardo. 2018. "When I Started My Family Tree." Facebook. Genealogia Judaica Portuguesa, 22 August 2018. https://www.facebook.com/groups/1404360236538563.
Queiroz, Arthur de. 2020. *You Should Register Your Tree on Genealogical Sites.* YouTube. Video. Genealogia Judaica do Brasil: Cordeiro, Barbosa, Leão, Mendes, Lopes, April. https://www.youtube.com/watch?app=desktop&v=_wPVXuUA8pw.
Rheingold, Howard. 2000. *The Virtual Community: Homesteading on the Electronic Frontier.* London: MIT Press.
Ricoeur, Paul. 1986. "Life: A Story in Search of a Narrator." In *Facts and Values: Philosophical Reflections from Western and Non-Western Perspectives,* edited by M.C. Doeser and J. Kray, 34–68. Dordrecht: Martinus Nijhoff.
Rigoni, Gustavo. 2020. "Hello, Happy Sunday." Facebook. Genealogia Sefardita—Brasil, 22 November 2020. https://www.facebook.com/groups/sefarditagenealogia.
Rodrigue, Aron, and Sarah Abrevaya Stein, eds. 2012. *A Jewish Voice from Ottoman Salonica: The Ladino Memoir of Sa'adi Besalel a-Levi.* Stanford, CA: Stanford University Press.
Rodrigues, Judith. 2019. *Hi, Can You Enlighten Me About The Surname.* YouTube. Video. Genealogia Judaica do Brasil: Sobrenomes, História, Segredos das Escrituras e Profecias, OLIVEIRA, June. https://www.youtube.com/watch?app=desktop&v=EPOSbzK_-sA.
Santos, Daniel. 2020. *I Am a Mulatto, A Miscegenation of the Surnames.* YouTube. Video. Genealogia Judaica do Brasil: Sobrenomes, História, Segredos das Escrituras e Profecias, OLIVEIRA, November 2020. https://www.youtube.com/watch?app=desktop&v=EPOSbzK_-sA.
Silva, Fábio. 2020. "Today I Was Happy to Receive My Long-Awaited CIL Certificate." Facebook. Genealogia Sefardita—Brasil, 25 June 2020. https://www.facebook.com/groups/sefarditagenealogia.
Sinagoga Anusim Brasil. 2019. "*Sobrenomes Sefarditas. Você tem ascendência judaica?*" YouTube. Vídeo, 43:27, July 2019. https://www.youtube.com/watch?app=desktop&v=LlrluL47Kt8.
Sinagoga Sem Fronteiras. 2017. "*Genealogia Judaica do Brasil*: Cordeiro, Barbosa, Leão, Mendes, Lopes". YouTube. Video, 29:37, July 3 2017. https://www.youtube.com/watch?app=desktop&v=_wPVXuUA8pw.
———. 2020. "*Genealogia Judaica do Brasil: Surnames, History, Secrets of the Scriptures and Prophecies. OLIVEIRA*". YouTube. Video. 1:49:43, June 21 2020. https://www.youtube.com/watch?app=desktop&v=EPOSbzK_-sA.
Skågeby, Jorgen. 2009. "Exploring Qualitative Sharing Practices of Social Metadata: Expanding the Attention Economy." *Information Society* 25, no.1 (January): 60–72.

———. 2011. "Online Ethnographic Methods." In *Handbook of Research on Methods and Techniques for Studying Virtual Communities,* edited by Ben Kei Daniel, 410–28. Hershey PA: Information Science Reference (an imprint of IGI Global).

———. 2015. "Interpreting Online Discussions: Connecting Artefacts and Experiences in User Studies." *Qualitative Report,* 20, no. 1: 115–29. https://nsuworks.nova.edu/tqr/vol20/iss1/9/.

Smartop, Florêncio. 2020. "Help! Could Someone Help Me with Filling in." Facebook. Genealogia Judaica Portuguesa, 27 July 2020. https://www.facebook.com/groups/1404360236538563.

Souza, Thiago. 2019. "My Connection Is with Caetano." Facebook. Genealogia Sefardita Documentada, 10 July 2019. https://www.facebook.com/groups/603418636804903.

Terra, Marcelo. 2020. "It Is the Most Painful Citizenship of All!" Facebook. Genealogia Judaica Portuguesa, 21 July 2020. https://www.facebook.com/groups/1404360236538563.

Thoits, Peggy A. 1992. "Identity Structures and Psychological Well-Being: Gender and Marital Status Comparisons." *Social Psychology Quarterly* 55, no. 3 (September): 236–56.

Ventura, Lilith. 2020 "When I Started My Research, I Knew Nothing." Facebook. Genealogia Judaica Portuguesa, 21 July 2020. https://www.facebook.com/groups/1404360236538563.

Vieira, Maria. 2020. "The Possibility of Citizenship Is a Great Incentive." Facebook. Genealogia Judaica Portuguesa, 21 July 2020. https://www.facebook.com/groups/1404360236538563.

Wal. 2019. *What Good Is It, We Have [the Jewish] DNA in Our Blood.* YouTube. Video. Genealogia Judaica do Brasil: Sobrenomes, História, Segredos das Escrituras e Profecias, OLIVEIRA, December 2019. https://www.youtube.com/watch?app=desktop&v=EPOSbzK_-sA.

Yacov, Marcelo. 2018. *My Great-Grandfather Was Called Salvino Iacov.* YouTube. Video. Genealogia Judaica do Brasil: Cordeiro, Barbosa, Leão, Mendes, Lopes, August 2018. https://www.youtube.com/watch?app=desktop&v=_wPVXuUA8pw.

Chapter 15 Appendix

Certifying Origins for Sephardic Descendants in Portugal
A Snapshot of the Evaluation Process

Teresa Santos and Heraldo Bento

Designing a Certification Process

Complementing Marina Pignatelli's account of the Brazilian applicants (chap. 15, in this volume), this appendix details the role and some of the challenges faced by the Jewish Community of Lisbon (CIL; Comunidade Israelita de Lisboa) in evaluating and certifying descendant ancestries. The CIL and the Jewish Community of Porto (CIP; Comunidade Israelita de Porto) are the two Jewish community institutions authorized by the Portuguese government to evaluate proof of ancestry.[1] The CIP serves Jewish applicants, whereas the CIL serves a broad and diverse swath of descendants, regardless of present-day religious affiliation. The universe of Sephardic descendants also responds to different diasporic and historical patterns, creating an applicant pool of considerable heterogeneity. Each applicant has different goals and expectations about becoming Portuguese and requires a tailored deployment of certification criteria.

The 2015 law created an interesting relationship between religious communities and the government. Initially, the two main questions with regard to assessing applications were, How should genealogical proof of ancestry be presented? And who should analyze it? Prior to the law's promulgation, meetings were held to discuss the intricacies of such a large-scale and unusual task as certifying ancestry and to set up the certification departments in Lisbon and Porto. These Jewish communities faced becoming extensions of governmental institutions, working with the ministries of justice and foreign affairs. They also embraced the responsibility as part of their own congregational development strategies. Once the law was published, it took time to understand its requirements and possibilities, range, and limits. Those who would be involved in this new initiative to obtain Portuguese nationality—official government agencies, lawyers, other intermediaries between applicants and evaluators, and evaluators themselves—needed to understand the scope and details of the law as well as the historical particularities of the applicant populations. The main questions were, To whom is the law addressed? And who falls outside its purview? Is the law only for Jews? Does it extend to all descendants of Sephardic Jews? Who will be considered eligible to become a Portuguese citizen under this law? These questions required a significant amount of historical reading and research to grasp the full scope and complexity of Sephardic descent today.

Following the provisions of the law and the principles of the Portuguese Constitution that prohibit religious discrimination, the CIL opened its certification to all descendants. Certification requires that applicants present a genealogical tree going back as many generations in the direct bloodline as possible, to the oldest known Sephardic descendant with a historical connection to Portugal. Family trees must be presented in generational order, based on birth, marriage, or death records, or other kind of civil documents such as wills. However, the ability to document one's genealogy across so many centuries posed a challenge to both applicants and evaluators. Normative Sephardic Jews from the Ottoman Empire, for example, ran into the lack of extant records earlier than the late nineteenth century. Those who descend from conversos who fled Portugal in the sixteenth and seventeenth centuries, settling in Amsterdam, London, or in the Americas (e.g. Curaçao or Brazil), had access to community, Inquisition, and Catholic Church records. Sephardic community archives and historical scholarship also came into play as well as evidence of collective rituals in well-known diasporic communities. Still, for those whose ancestors left Judaism and became Catholic or Muslim, the challenge to reconstruct a coherent line of Portuguese Sephardic descent was much greater, as they had to reach back much farther into the genealogical past.

The first point to be verified in the certification process was the historical accuracy of the documents presented. This challenged applicants to present sufficient and objectively accurate information, as opposed to merely having a Portuguese or Sephardic surname, or evidence derived from common myths such as lighting candles on Friday night, or stories heard from grandparents that seemingly correlated with the idea of a Jewish lineage. The communities had to invest a significant amount of effort into understanding the range of possibilities of what could be presented as proof of ancestry. Sometimes an application could be subjected to three rounds of review. The collection of documents could be substantially different from one applicant to the next, as travel and migration patterns produced a greatly diversified population of Sephardic descendants. Various kinds of documents might be presented: cultural, religious, social, historical, or genealogical. Often, for example, applicants might present diasporic migration routes to support their applications when more precise documentation was not available. However, lack of sufficient genealogical evidence also increased the chances that the application would be denied.

To address the interpretation of the evidence submitted by applicants, the CIL engaged professional historians and other experts to ensure that evidence was reliable and found in trustworthy sources. Sometimes stricter evidentiary criteria might be used for one group over another. Evaluators tried to find patterns through cross-referencing historical and genealogical data provided by different applicants. But ultimately it became the responsibility of the applicant to provide as much information as possible. Along with taking diasporic history and processes of adaptation and acculturation into account, political events and crises in other countries might affect the certification process. Examples are the political crisis in Brazil between 2014 and 2016 that resulted in the impeachment of its president; the increased fear among Turkish Jews after the failed coup in 2016; the Brexit referendum results; increased antisemitic activity in France and the United Kingdom; the spread of poverty in Latin American countries; and the expiration of Spain's citizenship law for Sephardic descendants on 1 October 2019.

A Data Snapshot

Below are several charts that give a breakdown of the applications to Portugal, between 2015 and the end of November 2020. The Instituto de Registos Centrais e do Notariado (IRCN; Institute of Registries and Notary) reported receipt of 82,923 applications, broken out by year:

Based on the IRCN data from 2015 through 2020, applications were received from eighty-six different countries, meaning that evaluators had to consider the present-day provenance of the applications as well as historical patterns of migration pertinent to each country. The CIL's tally showed that the majority of applications were from Brazil, Israel, and Turkey, totaling 12,792 applicants, followed by a surge in 2020 from

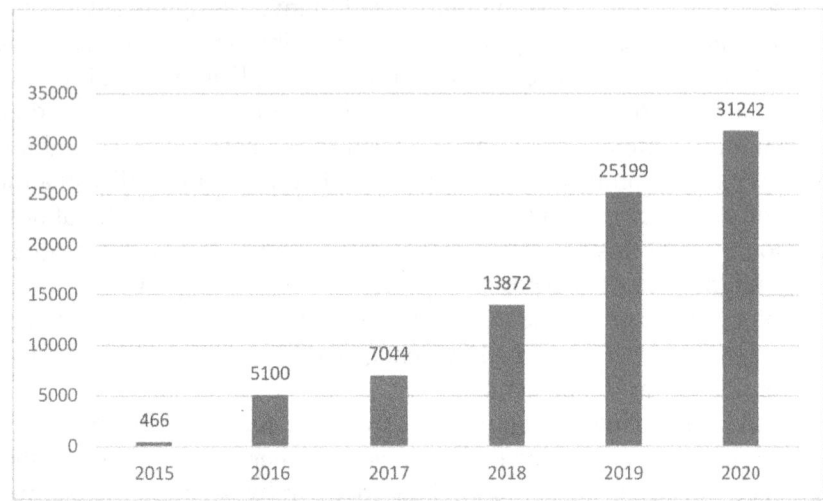

Figure 15.1. Number of Sephardic applications for Portuguese citizenship by year. Graph produced by Santos and Bento, based on raw data provided to the authors by IRCN.

Latin America (Colombia, Mexico, and Venezuela). These tallies do not include applications sent to the Porto Jewish community.

The numbers from Brazil, Israel, and Turkey respond to historical and cultural ties with those countries. Brazil is the country with the largest Portuguese immigration beginning in the sixteenth century. Israel, and Palestine before 1948, were places of Sephardic migration for many centuries. Turkey contained the largest Sephardic population during the Ottoman Empire and was spared annihilation during World War II. The surge of applications in 2020 from Colombia, Mexico, and Venezuela are accounted for by the fact that they have large populations of converso descent. These countries also find themselves in varying degrees of social, economic, and political precarity, including their citizens who seek forms of out migration. In addition, given that during medieval and early modern times there was considerable back-and-forth movement of Sephardic Jews between Spain and Portugal, the CIL decided to entertain applications from Jews of Iberian origin who could claim some connection to Portugal.

Evidentiary Profiles

To illustrate the range of evidence confronting CIL evaluators and the challenges faced by applicants in documenting their ancestry, we profile and contrast dossiers from Israel and Brazil, countries with very different

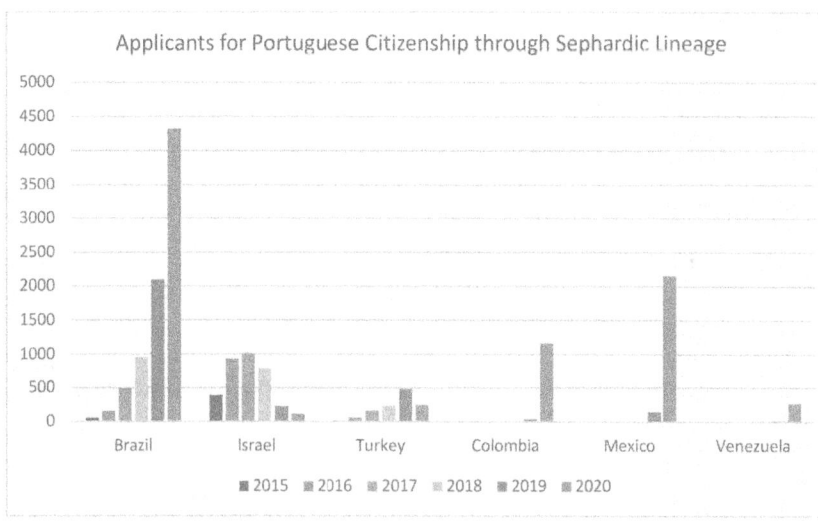

Figure 15.2. Countries with largest number of applications, by year. Graph produced by Santos and Bento, using raw data provided by the CIL, November 2020.

applicant pools. Applicants from Israel are normative Jews of Sephardic ancestry, while a large number of Brazilian applicants, though not all, are descended from converts. Additionally, we give a sense of the range of complex backgrounds and processes of the candidates through the example of the Sabbateans, or Dönmes, from Turkey. While all applicants are asked to submit their personal data and a genealogical tree, such documents become more meaningful if they are supported by other relevant information regarding family history and Sephardic ancestry. Some submit personal statements where they write emotively about their histories, the joy of coming closer to their familial pasts, their feelings toward Portugal, or cultural aspects of belonging, such as customs and habits, orally transmitted memories, and other information not implicit in the required vital statistics or genealogical charts.

The largest number of applicants, 63,236, come from Israel. A great majority have parents or grandparents who were born in Sephardic diasporic communities and speak or spoke Ladino. Given twentieth-century political transformations and migrations, Israeli applicants or their families might actually originate from North Africa (Morocco, Algeria, Libya, Tunisia), from Northern Europe, from Eastern Europe (Macedonia, Romania, or other countries involved in World War II), and from countries of the former Ottoman Empire (Turkey, Greece, or other Balkan countries). Most Israeli Sephardis present genealogical evidence that goes back from one to three generations. Given the political histories and upheavals in Sephardic communities over the centuries, especially in the Ottoman Empire from whence many Israeli Sephardic Jews descend, archival genealogical documentation is difficult to find even if it has survived. Rare are the cases of applicants who can show more than five generations in their family tree. Unlike the descendants of conversos, they are incapable of documenting fifteen generations dating back to the first known Sephardic ancestor.

Israeli Sephardis present supporting documents of a more cultural, social, and religious nature, attesting to continuity in the present day of their Sephardic Jewish identities. Religious cultural evidence might include certificates of *brit milah* (circumcision) rituals, bar and bat mitzvahs, Sephardic *ketubot* (marriage contracts), or letters reporting activities in a Sephardic synagogue, letters from intimate family friends who were rabbis or from the head rabbi in a Sephardic synagogue, old religious books belonging to the family that contain traces of Sephardic traditions, photographs of tombstones, and other visual proof of lineage.

Evidence of a more political nature might include reporting diasporic family histories, travel documents with stamps of laisser-passer from Morocco or Turkey, old passports that include all members of a family (passport holder, spouse, children, parents), and lists of names/surnames connected with Sephardic families; these are all also commonly presented. Evaluators may also encounter cultural documentation, such as certificates of participation in a Sephardic cultural association or institution, declarations of donations to Jewish institutions, activities by the applicant or an ancestor, handwritten letters in *solitreo* (Ladino cursive), audiovisual recordings of applicants speaking Ladino, dictionary entries of family profiles, personal letters recounting histories transmitted orally within the family, surnames and historical descriptions of places of settlement, academic or journalistic articles about the life of a prominent family member in Sephardic community of a certain city or country, and applicant memoirs recounting family history and/or journeys in search of roots. These are the more common supporting documents presented by Israelis.

Brazilian applicants, the second largest in number, include two very different groups: Jews and non-Jews. Among non-Jews, the CIL has received applications from entire families that may include anywhere from ten to thirty members. Family members get in touch with each other through online networking (see Pignatelli, chap. 15 in this volume), and personally know their extended families, including second- and third- (and sometimes more) degree relatives. Marcelo Guimarães, president and founder of the Associação Brasileira dos Descendentes dos Judeus da Inquisição (ABRADJIN; Brazilian Association of Jewish Descendants from the Inquisition) (anussim.org.br), explained in an informal conversation that, since its founding in 2000, there have been approximately 1,500 members and thousands of followers, all of whom have a strong ethnic sense of collectivity and identity. For descendants of sixteenth- and seventeenth-century converts, getting Portuguese nationality often has more to do with a symbolic, emotional identity process than with instrumental motives such as securing a job opportunity in Europe. Although their forebears converted to Christianity many centuries or generations ago, these descendants feel that they are paying their respects to their Jewish ancestors, and they are sensitive to and conscious of the terror those ancestors experienced during the Inquisitions in Portugal and later in Brazil. As illustrated by two personal statements that follow, the transmission of memory is so important that descendants carry the suffering of their ancestors across the generations. As one Brazilian of converso descent summed up the decision to apply, "It is because I believe the reparation that Portugal seeks is fair in recognizing the right of descendants of those who were expelled that I took the initiative to ask for my Portuguese nationality. I believe this is a way to minimize the damage caused by the brutality of the Inquisition" (ABRADJIN, anussim.org.br). Another applicant affirmed, "Today this reintegration is finally being proposed by the Portuguese state. And as a member of an expelled family, I have come to apply for it [citizenship], with the certainty that ... I would be very proud to see the whole family become—again—Portuguese" (ABRADJIN, anussim.org.br).

Because non-Jewish Brazilian applicants cannot present cultural or religious evidence, they must rely mainly on civil and Inquisition records to constitute a proper genealogical report. However, in contrast to normative Jewish applicants, converso descendants must document each generation in the direct bloodline with vital records. Genealogical reports from non-Jewish applicants may also include paleographical transcriptions, inventories or testaments, inquisitorial testimonies, and accusations of judaizing. Reports must be signed by expert professional genealogists or historians and include their résumés. These genealogy reports are very costly and those who lack the resources must invest their own time to research and produce the equivalent of a professional report. In the personal statements accompanying their applications, some also commonly refer to ritualistic remnants within their families as evidence of their Jewish ancestry, such as Shabbat candle-lighting on Friday evenings, or covering mirrors after the death of a family member. Since 2015, Brazilian converso descendants have intensified claims to their Sephardic identity and seek public recognition of it, discussing on online platforms the problems they face in doing the research required by the process. These applicants usually have Portuguese surnames and mostly come from the Brazilian federal states of Bahia, Ceará, Mato Grosso, Minas Gerais, Paraíba, Pernambuco, Rio de Janeiro, Rio Grande do Norte, or São Paulo.

Brazilian Jews, on the other hand, come mainly from the Amazon region, Rio de Janeiro, and São Paulo, having entered the country during the nineteenth and twentieth centuries. Some migrated from the Ottoman Empire (Turkey, Greece), from North Africa (Morocco, Algeria, Libya), from the Middle East (Syria, Lebanon), and from Eastern Europe (Poland, Ukraine). These applicants include fewer generations in their genealogical history for reasons stated previously about large gaps in records. They present similar kinds of documentation as Israeli applicants, perhaps adding ship manifests attesting to their moment of arrival.

An entirely different group of applicants from the Israelis and Brazilians, smaller in number but facing even greater evidentiary difficulties, are descendants of seventeenth-century Ottoman converts to Islam. Followers of Sabbatai Sevi, the Sephardic rabbi who claimed to be the messiah, they are known as Sabbetaians, or Dönmes (as Uluç Özüyener's personal essay, chap. 7 in this volume, describes). Turkish citizens today, they trace their ancestry to the city of Salonica, and to Spain and Portugal before that. This group faces great difficulty in the certification process, as CIL historians and evaluators had to study their history in depth to understand their special relationship to Sephardism and their status as descendants. Recognizing this, Dönme applicants normally submit more than one report issued by a recognized world expert; they also trace each generation in their families back to the time of the conversion to Islam. Often included in their evidence are orally transmitted family heritage stories, burial records, images from specific Dönme cemeteries, or accounts of ancient connections to Sephardic synagogues.

These profiles give a glimpse in to the wide range of historical and cultural documentation that the CIL receives and of the expertise required of ancestry certifiers. They also underscore the importance of working in expert teams to ensure that each application is given full consideration.

Teresa Santos has a master's degree in anthropology from the University of Lisbon. Her thesis is on transnationalism and affective geographies. From 2015 until March 2021 she collaborated with the Jewish Community of Lisbon on the certification of Sephardic origins for descendants seeking Portuguese citizenship. Currently, she is employed by Martins Castro International Consultancy, providing historical and juridical services to applicants for Portuguese citizenship and legalizing all matters concerning living and working in Portugal.

Heraldo Bento completed an undergraduate degree in anthropology at the University of Lisbon, with a focus on the pursuit of Portuguese citizenship by descendants of Sephardic Jews and the opportunities presented by the Portuguese nationality law. He is currently a master's student in anthropology, interested in crypto-Judaism, faith, and religiosity as constituents of symbolic identity.

Note

1. Since this writing, the CIP has relinquished its role in the certification process.

Chapter 16

Personal Essay

The Fez in the Water—Exile and Return

Victor Silverman

It was a hot summer day in 1909 when my teen-aged grandfather, Isaac Benjoya, boarded a ferry in the harbor of Izmir, Turkey, to take him across the Aegean Sea to Greece and to the ocean liner that would carry him to the United States.[1] A handsome, stylish, but poor young man from a minority religious group, he wore the required fez of a subject of the Ottoman Empire. He looked over the rail at the city thinking, I imagine, of his parents left behind. As the ferry sailed into Izmir Bay, his thoughts turned to the adventure ahead of him. Always one for the dramatic gesture, he grabbed the fez from his own head and threw it into the churning water behind the ship. He watched it bob and sink, knowing he was done with a city and a country that had been his family's home for hundreds of years.

Three years later, my grandmother, Dolsa Nahum, arrived in the United States, along with her older sister, Reyna, and niece, Rebecca, on the SS *Laura*, a ship full of Jews, Armenians, and Greeks. When she and my grandfather married in 1917, they moved to Cuba to try a new country where, as Spanish-speaking Sephardic Jews, they could understand the language and enjoy a pleasanter climate than that in New York. Life in Cuba proved hard, and after a year away from their families they bought return tickets. But the United States had joined World War I while they were away, suddenly transforming them from adventuring young marrieds into enemy aliens. Instead of returning to Brooklyn, they spent the rest of the war in Key West under house arrest ordered by the US government. While living in a room of the local rabbi, my grandfather did odd jobs and scoured the palm-lined streets for kosher food for my observant grandmother. No longer Ottoman, they were not yet American.

My grandfather's moment of leave-taking from Turkey proved exciting yet bittersweet for him—he never saw his father again. My grandparents' detention when they returned to the United States in 1918 underscored the fragility of their immigrant status. To find security in their new country, they chose to become US citizens—he in 1929, she in 1942. Despite his internment, my grandfather came to believe deeply in the American Dream, telling me how much he loved the country that had welcomed him in the end. Their experiences provide me origin stories rooted in rootlessness but with a happy ending, a willingness to let go of one country for another.

Migration, exile, and diaspora, and their complicated relationships with identity and place, with memory and present experience, run through my family's history. As Sephardic Jews, we descend from people forcibly expelled in a moment of fanatical Catholic empire building by Spain and Portugal more than five hundred years ago. My ancestors, unlike my grandparents, could not choose their homes and nationality. Still, the Ottoman Empire's relatively tolerant, confessionally-ordered society welcomed them as subjects of a new sovereign, the sultan. Becoming Americans transformed them again. Now that I, along with my extended family of sons, cousins, and aunt, have decided to "exercise the right of return" to obtain Portuguese citizenship, I find myself confronting profound questions of exile and arrival, of belonging and longing (Decreto-Lei 2015).

When I receive my Portuguese citizenship, I will also get a new birth certificate, the Portuguese state rewriting my history as it seeks to rewrite its own. My newly issued birth certificate will somehow reach back into the past to find the infant Victor, born in New York City in the middle of the last century, a US citizen, as American as apple pie. Documentary time travel will then make me Portuguese at birth. States made claims on the bodies of my forebearers; Portugal will now claim me. The birth certificate signals, on the face of it, simply that I have entered its system of record-keeping. And it gives me benefits—a European Union passport! Portuguese health care! Refuge! But it also disrupts who I am in ways I had not expected. Losing and gaining citizenship and nationality have marked important transitions in our family history, both in living memory and in ancient legend. Citizenship in Portugal offers "integration into the national community," as the 2015 law puts it (Decreto-Lei 2015). By "integrating" us into the nation where our ancestors lived half a millennium ago, the law promises my family and me that we can be part of something that we (both the Portuguese and the Sephardim) have told ourselves we had lost.

My mother, Rachel, and her three sisters, as young women growing up in depression and war, felt different than those around them in the bustling, polyglot New York City of mid-century. Part of a small community of Sephardim in Brighton Beach, Brooklyn, they literally and figuratively lived at the margins of the city. Few outside the community could figure out what or who they were: "You're not Jewish. You Puerto Rican or something?" (My uncle Larry figured it out, dubbing them the "Boreka Babies.") They looked for an opening to change their lives and the society around them. The way that radicals fought for justice for all, for the unemployed, for workers, for the oppressed, as well the thrill of the fight, drew them to the Communist Party. But equally important, I believe, was the Party's paradoxical attempt to blend the US radical tradition with internationalism. Although criticized as purveyors of an "alien ideology," the Party proclaimed in 1936, "Communism is Twentieth Century Americanism" (Bennett 1988, 329; Draper 2003, xv). The party's internationalist Americanism promised a world in which the Boreka Babies' identities—as women, as Jews, as Sephardim, as children of immigrants who had learned English in school—no longer made them outsiders. The critical alienation from the mythos of US freedom and opportunity that led them to communism, grew from an older Sephardic identity as part of an exile minority in Turkey and Brooklyn, an identity that the right of return to Portugal may upset.

My grandmother, her sisters, and their friends often sat in folding chairs or on the brick stoops of their modest homes in Brighton Beach, critiquing, in Ladino, the style and appearance of passing people—"So and so is an elephant," "Who would wear something like that?"—most likely while nodding and smiling at the uncomprehending strangers. Their snobbishness, my mother explained to me, came out of their cultured superiority. I believe it really arose from the insecurity and alienation of impoverished immigrant women with limited English skills in a society that had little idea who they were and valued them even less. Still, the names of my *Tia Reyna*, the eldest sister of my grandmother, and my *Tia Sultana*, her sister-in-law, seemed appropriate to their regal bearing: two queens in one family in Brighton! The ladies shelling beans or sewing shirts while perched on their chairs in the Brooklyn afternoon formed my aunt queens' fractious, but also intimate, court. Their outsider camaraderie sustained them, as it had in Izmir.

In going through my mother's books after she passed away a few years ago, I was surprised that she had loaded her shelves with volumes on the Spanish and Portuguese "Golden Age" and on the Expulsion, but had little on the five hundred years after. Her romantic nostalgia for Sefarad, for al-Andalus of *la convivencia,* the era of remembered Muslim-Catholic-Jewish harmony, allowed her to tap into a vein of cultural nationalism that contradicted her political radicalism. It suited her emotional politics and family history to think of herself as Iberian, not Turkish. Like my grandfather, she rejected that history. Perhaps they abandoned Turkishness because Jews, with the second-class status of *dhimmis* in a Muslim-ruled land, while much better off than their coreligionists in Christian Europe, remained subject to periodic violence. Also, as acculturating Americans, being Turkish, the orientalized Other of Christian European fever dreams, a land of enemy aliens, remained problematic. Spain, in contrast, carried a romantic but fully occidental meaning. Nonetheless, despite the fez in the water, the centuries had made us Turkish, too.

I once had a conversation with my host at a B&B in the tourist town of Foça on the entrance to Izmir Bay, a city with a bloody past of ethnic cleansing and turmoil during the 1910s and 1920s. Once the largely Greek Orthodox town of Phocaea, today there is almost no trace of that community, no people, no churches, not even names. They do call many of the pretty old houses lining the waterfront, like my B&B, "Greek" houses. I asked my host about the tragic intertwined past. "We are all the same people," he replied thoughtfully. "We listen to the same music, we eat the same food, we look the same." Both Greeks and Turks mobilized ethnoreligious hatred to create national power, a process that tore apart the Ottoman system of rule through *millet*s (religion-based communities) and left Izmir in ashes. If empires formed the "prison house of nations," as romantic nationalists claimed in the nineteenth century, then the dawn of the nation-state and its form of ethnicity-based citizenship occurred on death row of that prison (Tefft 1852, 15). Nationalists everywhere created their states amidst displacement and death, the creation of modern Turkey and Greece being no different. My immediate family luckily left before the fires arrived for that lovely city on the Aegean. Maybe that is what allows me to see through the tears and blood brought on by nationalism to glimpse another truth, one that my host also knew: "We are all the same people."

Nonetheless, it must have been difficult to recognize this cultural unity in a troubled past that left no community untouched. Inflamed by the "blood libel" that Jews killed Christian babies for their rituals, Greek Orthodox fanatics periodically attacked Sephardic neighborhoods in Izmir. My great-uncle Moshon, a barrel-chested bear of a man, joined a street gang to defend his Jewish neighborhood after one of those attacks. Sephardic official culture stressed loyalty to the sultan, and some Sephardim had been willing accomplices to Ottoman atrocities against

Orthodox Greeks, particularly in repressing Greek independence one hundred years before (Fleming 2008). Genocidal violence against Jews, Greeks, Roma, Albanians, Armenians, Kurds, Turks, and Syrians bathed their intertwined histories in blood. We are all the same people, yes, but we are also all divided by a common past.

As children, my mother and her three sisters had to share a single bed. Crowded and intimate, they loved each other deeply but also could be bitterly cruel to each other at times. Even in their later years, as divorcées and widows, they refused to talk to each other for months after some slight. Yet they would still lie side by side at night, the Boreka Babies' antagonism sustained by profound intimacy. The defensive form of community—my uncle's gang, my aunts' snobbishness, the Boreka Babies' shared bed—helped them survive an indifferent and all-too-often hostile world. This defensive culture formed my personality as well. I knew we weren't like the Ashkenazi Jews who predominated in my or my mother's neighborhoods, certainly not like the Catholics or Protestants. Not like Italians or like African Americans or Puerto Ricans. Did this sense of alienation flow from my family's peculiar dysfunctions, or was it because we were Sephardim?

Finding the particualrly Sephardic sources of our alienation has not been easy. In my family, we have no key to a home in Sefarad carried for generations and treasured in the hope of eventual return. Other than my sense of exile and alienation, I have no knowledge of our family before the late nineteenth century. There are no documents, no memories. There are no family stories of towns or ancient homes in Portugal or Spain. We have the food, the language, the names, the culture of the Sephardim. But beyond my great-grandparents, the story dims into a general tale of ancient Sephardic glory and exile, partly imagined and mostly forgotten.

Instead, I have only bits and pieces of stories of the recent past that stuck in my youthful mind. My great-grandmother knew the incantations to rid someone of the evil eye. A great-great-uncle was backgammon champion of Izmir. My grandmother's family was rich enough to own a winery, my grandfather's poor enough that they lived in the same hut with their animals and worked for my grandmother's relatives. Even though these stories flow from the recent past, I don't know if they are true or false, or if I misremember them. When my mother and her sisters would reminisce in their later years, the discussions all too often deteriorated into arguments over details and characters, ending finally with an exasperated, "That's not how I remember it!"

We know the first names of my Sephardic great-great-grandparents—Calomira, Mordecai, Moshe, Sasbona, Abram, Oro, Jacob, Rashel—but only half of their *alkunyas* (surnames), Benjoya, Daniel, Nahum, Israel.

Beyond that, the onomastic and genealogical story fades out—no one in my family has had the resources or the skills to visit Izmir to search through records that survived wars and fires. So, all that remains are historical traces—language, food, culture, our sad eyes, strong shoulders, a tendency to melodramatic gesture, a troubling strain of bipolar disorder, and vaguely remembered feelings of loss and nostalgia. These are our complicated inheritance from our myriad ancestors. They make up stories that are harder than documents to read and even more recondite for an understanding of our nationality. After five hundred years, that's not how anyone remembers it.

My mother was convinced that our family came from Sevilla. "Why do you think so?" I asked after she returned from a trip to Spain some years ago. I don't know what sort of answer I expected: maybe that she had seen evidence of Benjoya or Daniel or Nahum families there. Maybe she found a reference at an archeological site? She looked at me, slightly surprised at my obvious ignorance. "I just feel it," she answered with finality. There was no arguing with her. Ironically, when it came time to apply for citizenship, we applied to Portugal not Spain because the process was easier for the non-Spanish speaking members of the family. But then I found a documentary hint of a connection to Portugal that my mother's feeling had missed—a variant of Benjoya found in a community of Porto. My mother, famous for having a *kabeza de piedra* (a head of stone), would probably have snorted at this alternative origin story. But after visiting there a couple times, seeing the evening light on the old city and smelling the Atlantic air flowing up the Douro, I just feel it.

Despite a lack of documents, I certainly descend from refugees who became exiles in foreign lands, an inheritance that tempers my ability to feel a part of any group. Will Portuguese citizenship change that sense? The answer is likely as ambiguous as my family history is unknown. My ancestors fled five hundred years ago, but the exact dates they fled or where they went directly, I do not know. Portugal at first had seemed a refuge for exiles from Castilian fanaticism after the conquest of Granada in 1491. King Manuel's shifting treatment of Jews and Muslims soon soured that welcome. "We have fled from the lion only to fall into the jaws of the bear," wrote a refugee from Spain upon hearing Manuel's Expulsion Edict of 1496 (Soyer 2007, 192). Manuel needed popular religious fanaticism and a Castilian alliance to fuel Portuguese imperial ambitions, so he forced Jews and Muslims to convert, flee, or die. They became exiles in a foreign land because of a devil's brew of empire-building and hate that the twice-exiled Solomon Ibn Verga lamented "was evil and bitter in the extreme" (Yerushalmi 1976, 1).

Edward Said poignantly described exile as "an unhealable rift between the self and the true home: its essential sadness can never be surmounted" (Said 2000, 176). The exile's alienation, nonetheless, provides an emotional source for the incisive intellectual lineage that most informs my thought. The quintessentially modern condition, critical separation from roots, from dogma, and from the given order, focused the keen intellects of exiles and émigrés Karl Marx, Theodor Adorno, Max Horkheimer, W.E.B. Du Bois, Hannah Arendt, Edward Said, to name but a few whose thought informs my own. But the "unhealable rift" from the "true home" is a high price to pay for intellectual acuity. Certainly, for the generations locked in what the UN calls "Protracted Refugee Situations," growing up in camps in Gaza or Kenya or India, the wounds still hurt (Finch 2015). I doubt those stuck in squalor at the US border have discovered that their journey brought them closer to critical theory in the abstract, but I remain convinced they see the world more clearly than most of us (Schaffer and Smith 2004).

Though descended from exiles, I am not an exile. I can only imagine the raw pain of fleeing a home, the wrenching tears of dislocation, the fear of death, the looming shadow of disaster. To experience exile is to know directly the loss of connection to ancient land, to the national community, to neighborhood, to home. But it also calls up the effort to preserve memories, to recall the smell of the air of home, to hold on to the tone of the light, and to still hear the music of the language. My grandparents and their parents in Izmir before them saved some of their language and culture and community. However much they mixed with the peoples and cultures of the Aegean world, they remained in some ways Iberian exiles. This preservation lasted because of the culture of the Sephardim but, as importantly, because Ottoman rule depended on keeping their multitude of subject peoples divided. My identity is both my own and yet also fits the needs of the state, then and now.

José Rebeiro e Castro, leader of Portugal's centrist People's Party and a backer of the law of return, explained of the forced conversion and exile of the Sephardim: "We would like that this never happened" (AP Television 2015). It is not easy to face up to a nation's historical wrongs. As a citizen of the United States, a country with far too many unacknowledged crimes, I can sympathize with Rebeiro e Castro's wish. The Sephardim, he explains, "are Portugal. . . . They are part of us that we ourselves tore off." He hopes the recognition of the past separation and current effort to reconstruct the Portuguese nation as one that includes Jews, will "open a happier stage" (Ribeiro e Castro 2020).

For the Portuguese and the Spanish, who not so long ago emerged from decades warped by fascism and empire, their sense of self-identity as modern tolerant states in a democratic Europe means they must recognize and reject the brutal wrongs of the past. Portugal has played a positive role in Europe's all too often distressing response to migration and the ongoing global refugee crisis (Organisation for Economic Co-Operation and Development [OECD] 2019). Still it has been hard for many Portuguese to acknowledge their country's brutal past as slave traders and as a colonial power (Ames 2018). I hope the invitation to Sephardic Jews is a first step in this difficult process. Indeed, it fits a reasonable political and national goal of healing. Paula Teixeira da Cruz, the Portuguese minister of justice when the legislation for Sephardic citizenship passed, admitted that the law did not offer "historical reparation" because "there is no way to repair what has been done" (*Público* 2015). Recent changes to the law, prompted in part by the corrupt offer of citizenship to Russian oligarchs without Sephardic heritage, further underline the tenuousness of such repairs (Marques 2022). It is true for the dead. It is true for the lost centuries of disconnection from home in Porto or Lisbon or Sevilla or Granada. The exile cannot be undone even when it is over for some.

At times, national regret can be an exercise in signaling virtue rather than real confrontation with the past. In *Eichmann in Jerusalem*, Hannah Arendt criticized postwar Germans for their spurious feelings of guilt: "It is quite gratifying to feel guilty if you haven't done anything wrong: how noble! Whereas it is rather hard and certainly depressing to admit guilt and repent." Yet, as she explained later in the same volume, "Every generation by virtue of being born into a historical continuum is burdened by the sins of the fathers as it is blessed with the deeds of the ancestors" (Arendt 2006, 261, 298). Rebeiro e Castro and his colleagues would like to ease the weight of their county's past. Like all empires, there are many Portuguese burdens that weigh on the present "like a nightmare on the brains of the living," to adapt Karl Marx's phrase from *The 18th Brumaire of Louis Bonaparte*. Marx mocked French bourgeois revolutionaries as those who "anxiously conjure up the spirits of the past to their service" (Marx 2006, 215). In contrast, the liberals of Portugal, Spain, the United States, and elsewhere conjure up present-day descendants of the victims of their ancestors' crimes as a way to command national demons to fly back into the ether.

The historic traumas of the Sephardim hardened over centuries into an amber of old nightmares, ancient language, and faded memory. Just as survivors of fascism, of totalitarian camps, fear the knock on the door, I feel the outlines of that inherited amber when I learn of intolerance anywhere around me. The urge to flee to safety remains strong, reenforced by all too recent disasters—the resurgence of racist and antisemitic violence in the Trump era underscores that it can happen anywhere. The rabbi who provided certification of my current connection to the Sephardic community here in the San Francisco Bay Area asked me why we wanted Portuguese citizenship. Did we want to migrate? I answered that it was a good thing Portugal had done and it should be acknowledged. Then I added: "A Jew can never have too many passports." He laughed. "Yes, I have three!"

As a scholar, I study internationalism as a social and political movement as well as those who move more individually across the boundaries of nation, race, religion, and gender. On reflection, I now realize that I do so because I identify with those I have studied, particularly the practical internationalists who cooperated across borders to survive the most destructive moments of human history. And I try to find in history and politics the people who looked at another person and didn't see a passport, baptismal certificate, or racial and gender category, but rather found another human being—a neighbor, a brother, a sister.

The lesson to be drawn from the personal and the larger history of exile, migration, and identity can a be a nationalist one: "It always happens to the Jews." Or the lesson can be universal: "It can happen to anyone." I have chosen the universal lesson and reject a nationalist vision that relies on ethnic or religious identity. Nationalist solutions, as Arendt understood of Israelis and Palestinians, create new exiles in place of the old. "Refugees and the stateless have attached themselves like a curse" to the nation state, she wrote (Arendt 1973, 290). In a way, I have made a choice similar to the choices my grandfather and mother made. He tossed the political culture of the Ottomans into the water along with his fez in order to join a society that promised, at least, to accept him fully. I choose not to wear an identity that posits my own risk as the central political fact of life. Although I live with the constant awareness that disaster may come in the form of the mob or the state, I recognize it may come not only for me, but also for people very different from me. The best way forward, as my mother and her sisters similarly concluded, was to declare that we are all in this together. They became Communists to fight for the universal, not the particular solution. They were tragically wrong to seek it in a communism that perverted their dreams of a better world to serve the brutal interests of a totalitarian regime. Yet they were absolutely right that it was the best dream. Five hundred years is too long to remember the past with much precision, let alone to claim that such a terrible moment of history is what defines my nationality now. But it, nonetheless, defines my humanity.

I wrote this chapter in my office looking out at a typically foggy spring morning in the Bay Area of California, far from my ancestral homelands—Turkey, Portugal, Brooklyn—remembering that I, too, rejected places that claimed me. If New Jersey, where I grew up, had required a fez I would have tossed mine onto Interstate 80 heading west when I got the hell out. But now it is unlikely I will abandon California despite fires, droughts, and overcrowding—If this beautiful, troubled place is home, why in the end did I apply to return to Portugal?

My hope for humanity and my distrust of nationalism don't blind me to the emotional significance of national citizenship. For the Portuguese to exorcise their ancient and not so venerable ghosts, we Sephardim must be welcomed back to the national community. In turn, as my cousin says, "They owe us." The Portuguese and Spanish have held out a hand, offering an apology for a five-hundred-year-old wrong. It is a way to embrace nation without creating new exiles. Whatever my caveats and criticisms (Why not include the Muslims expelled by the Catholics? Why the Expulsion and not the slave trade or colonialism?), it is right to take the proffered hand in the spirit of regret and reunification that they give it. Someone in the future may not remember it that way, but that's inevitable.

Victor Silverman is an Emmy-award winning filmmaker and historian. He is professor emeritus of history at Pomona College. A scholar of US and international studies, he was the Fulbright/García Robles US Studies Chair at ITAM in Mexico City in 2022.

Note

1. I am grateful to the coeditors, Rina Benmayor and Dalia Kandiyoti, for the opportunity to reflect on family, citizenship, exile, and homeland. Thanks to Miguel Tinker Salas for his comments and to my family, particularly Ellen Benjoya Skotheim and Rachel Wolf Kerbrat, for their eager correction of my occasionally faulty memory.

References

Ames, Paul. 2018. "Portugal Confronts Its Slave Trade Past." *Politico*, 6 February 2018. https://www.politico.eu/article/portugal-slave-trade-confronts-its-past/.
AP Television. 2015. *Citizenship Plan Approved for Sephardic Jews*. YouTube video. https://www.youtube.com/watch?v=MtKbf_J4IzA.
Arendt, Hannah. 1973. *The Origins of Totalitarianism*. New York: Houghton Mifflin Harcourt.
Arendt, Hannah. 2006. *Eichmann in Jerusalem : A Report on the Banality of Evil*. New York: Penguin Classics.
Bennett, David Harry. 1988. *The Party of Fear: From Nativist Movements to the New Right in American History*. Chapel Hill: University of North Carolina Press.

Decreto-Lei. 2015. "Decreto-Lei 30-A/2015, 2015-02-27." *Diário da República Eletrónico*. 2015. https://dre.pt/pesquisa/-/search/66619927/details/maximized.
Draper, Theodore. 2003. *The Roots of American Communism*. New Brunswick, NJ: Transaction.
Finch, Tim. 2015. "In Limbo in World's Oldest Refugee Camps: Where 10 Million People Can Spend Years, or Even Decades." *Index on Censorship* 44, no. 1: 53–56. https://doi.org/10.1177/0306422015569438.
Fleming, Katherine E. 2008. *Greece—a Jewish History*. Princeton, NJ: Princeton University Press.
Marx, Karl. 2006. *18th Brumaire of Louis Bonaparte*. https://www.marxists.org/archive/marx/works/1852/18th-brumaire/index.htm.
Marques, Ana Christina. 2022, March 16. "Judeus Sefarditas: Decreto-Lei aumenta controlo e exige ligação a Portugal. *Observador*. https://observador.pt/2022/03/16/judeus-sefarditas-decreto-lei-aumenta-controlo-e-exige-real-ligacao-a-portugal.
Organisation for Economic Co-Operation and Development (OECD). 2019. "Finding Their Way: The Integration of Refugees in Portugal." https://www.oecd.org/migration/mig/finding-their-way-the-integration-of-refugees-in-portugal.pdf.
Público. 2015. "Descendentes de judeus sefarditas já vão poder pedir a nacionalidade." 29 January. https://www.publico.pt/2015/01/29/politica/noticia/descendentes-de-judeus-sefarditas-ja-vao-poder-pedir-a-nacionalidade-1684394.
Ribeiro e Castro, José. 2020. "A lei contra os judeus." *Observador*, 26 May 2020. https://observador.pt/opiniao/a-lei-contra-os-judeus.
Said, Edward W. 2000. *Reflections on Exile and Other Essays*. Cambridge: Harvard University Press.
Schaffer, K., and S. Smith. 2004. *Human Rights and Narrated Lives: The Ethics of Recognition*. New York: Palgrave Macmillan.
Soyer, François. 2007. *The Persecution of the Jews and Muslims of Portugal: King Manuel I and the End of Religious Tolerance (1496–97)*. Leiden: Brill.
Tefft, B. F. 1852. *Hungary and Kossuth: Or, An American Exposition of the Late Hungarian Revolution*. J. Ball. https://books.google.com/books?id=W5ZhAAAAcAAJ.
Yerushalmi, Yosef Hayim. 1976. *The Lisbon Massacre of 1506 and the Royal Image in the Shebet Yehudah*. Cincinnati, OH: Hebrew Union College Press.

Coda

Directions in Citizenship and Historical Repair

Dalia Kandiyoti and Rina Benmayor

Our vision for *Reparative Citizenship*, the first academic volume about the Spanish and Portuguese nationality laws for Sephardi descendants, has involved exploring a set of questions about the past and the present, as we outlined in the "Introduction" to this volume. Through the incisive reflection and scholarship of our contributors, we gain cross-disciplinary insights into the evolution of nationality and citizenship as well as the possibilities of and limits to new practices of historical redress. Coalescing in this volume are several areas of inquiry: the study of citizenship, Iberian Jewish and Muslim history, memory, and diasporization, along with contemporary politics in Spain and Portugal, topics that are often treated separately. Together, the chapters provide a multidimensional examination of the laws at the various levels of states, communities, and individual seekers of these new nationalities. They move forward our understanding of inclusion and exclusion within historical and new citizenship regimes, collective memory, and the politics of reconciliation.

The twenty-one collaborating authors also give voice to the potential "new Spaniards" and "new Portuguese" seeking, accepting, or refusing returns, whether actual or symbolic, on their own terms. As the chapters show, the meanings of citizenship are not only contained in state discourses and practices; the laws are given new significations by the applicants themselves. Their views are also important in terms of advancing knowledge about nonterritorial nationals, an inclusion that the beneficiaries negotiate from a distance. The book as a whole is an argument for maintaining in conjunction top-down and bottom-up perspectives in the study of citizenship and historical repair. This diversity of views reveals, among other things, the gaps and overlaps between the presumed petitioners that figure in state discourses and the practices and responses of actual beneficiaries. In sections devoted to legal and political processes, historical contextualizations, community and institutional analysis, and the beneficiaries' own experiences, it becomes apparent that the ideological and practical apparatuses of the laws continue to rest on narratives about expulsion, diaspora, empire, and state (re)formation that are repeated and revised at various critical historical periods. State-produced narratives about the belonging and citizenship of Sephardi Jews have adapted to political and historical circumstances, retaining a redemptive core invented more than a hundred years ago. The authors in this volume trace these relevant events and discourses over time, which helps us understand the role of historical crimes in the modern reinventions of Spain and Portugal's national identities.

These evolving narratives about the events and victims have also fed into the citizenship initiatives in complex ways. However, as many of the chapters show, at all times such dominant narratives have been subjected to negotiation and contestation by communities and individuals. Moreover, the contributions take into account both normative and non-normative Sephardi Jewish identities such as those of descendants of conversos and Dönmes, as well as of individuals who refuse to apply and those who are excluded from laws that aim to repair, namely communities of Morisco ancestry. As a result, *Reparative Citizenship* demonstrates the importance of understanding the nonhomogeneous nature of the identities that are rendered static or invisible in official discourses and the kinds of responses such representations elicit.

In addition to contributing to the study of nationality and citizenship through analytical and experiential perspectives on these unique laws, *Reparative Citizenship* also makes an intervention in Sephardi studies and Jewish studies more broadly, in several ways. The essays demonstrate the contemporary relevance of Iberian Jewish history, which is often relegated to a phenomenon of the distant past. The book also advances the conceptualization of modern Sephardi identity. It traces crucial aspects of the development of Sephardiness, also pointing to the emergence of new, contemporary narratives of Sephardi belonging by converso and Dönme descendants, non-Jewish subjects, and those individuals who have lost the connection to their heritage, including younger generations who may still be Jewish-identified. Furthermore, the chapters provide insight about the role of contemporary states, including the Iberian ones, in the construction of Sephardi history and belonging. *Reparative Citizenship* also expands existing work that analyzes the role of Sephardism in shaping Spanish and Portuguese national identities.

As such, this volume adds to the growing critical scholarship in Luso-Hispanic Studies regarding the Jewish presence in Iberia and, in two chapters, the Muslim presence as well.

Nationality for Sephardi descendants is an incomplete project that has a long history in Spain and Portugal as well as an uncertain future. With the closure of the application period in Spain and potential restrictions on the open-ended provision in Portugal, a range of explorations still lies ahead. Given some time, we will discover the consequences of the laws for their beneficiaries as well as new implications for the practices of nationality, identity, memory, and reparations. Most basically, we will need to investigate what recipients of Spanish or Portuguese nationality will "do" with this citizenship, and what they will feel and think about it. How many will relocate to the Peninsula? Will they consider being Spanish or Portuguese part of their identities? Will they learn the languages? Will they undertake diasporic practices such as voting or connecting to wider networks outside of the Peninsula or to other countries in the European Union? Many applicants networked in person or online to share the burdens of the complicated process, creating new ties or strengthening existing ones. This was especially visible among the converso and Dönme descendants whose search for the proof of ancestry was facilitated through such connections. Will these associations, some based on new ideas about kinship, continue in the future? And how will the applicants who were rejected feel and act? Will some of the eligible individuals who did not apply be able to do so? It remains to be seen whether Spain will renew its offer and what the impact of Portugal's late 2022 alterations in its requirements will be. Will Morisco descendants and Western Saharans and their advocates be successful in new attempts at creating a possibility for nationality acquisition? More widely, will there be an expansion beyond the Iberian Peninsula of nonresidential citizenship as a mode of symbolic reparation, reincorporation, and reconciliation? And what will be the practices and meanings generated by these new citizenship regimes?

To explore these and other questions, it will be necessary to extend the work *Reparative Citizenship* has begun in the study of nationality, historical reparations, and Sephardi Jews. The investigation of collective memory, a key notion common to both the state and nonstate discourses, also bears expansion beyond the work accomplished in this volume. Further theorizations of Sephardi and Morisco memory today in relation to the Spanish and Portuguese past and present; the critical study of relationship between official memory and citizenship legislation; the changing relevance of deep ancestry to both state and grassroots discourses of reparations; the importance of multivocality in the study of new citizenship and identity formations; the role of community, commercial, and other intermediaries between the individuals and the states; and the development of new networks that these laws have brought into being: these are just a few of the areas that these unique laws signal for future scholarship and writing. We hope this volume acts as a springboard for such inquiries into the significance of offering citizenship as a form of repair.

Index

Abascal, Santiago, 148
Abd el-Krim, Muhamed, 144
Aboab, Nooriel, 288
Abravanel, Jacques (1932–2012), 127, 128
Abravanel family, 112, 116, 117, 127, 128
Adio Kerida (documentary film), 216
affect, 8. *See also* affective citizenship; emotions; nostalgia; sentiment
affections, 229
affective attachment, return, 26–27, 229
emotion and, 229, 239–40
notion, theory of, 230
affective citizenship, Iberian Sephardi descendants. *See also* affect; belonging; citizenship; emotions; homeland consciousness; identities; oral history
attachments and power of memory, 241–45
belonging, 239, 240–41
citizenship and identity, 251–52
collective memory, 241–45
emotions and, 238–43, 248–52
genealogy and citizenship, 245–47
and Ladino, 243–44
nostalgia and return, 242, 244, 248–50
Africa, 3, 16, 18
African Americans, 48, 246–47
Africanism, philosephardism and, 24, 138–43, 147, 165, 170, 172
Agamben, Giorgio, 39, 40–41, 47, 78
Ahmed, Sara, 144, 240, 242, 244, 246
Aisen, Carolina, 186, 188, 192
Albukrek, Viktor, 204, 211n2
Alcalá, Kathleen, 265
Alcheh y Saporta, Isaac, 108–10, 112, 116–19, 122–23, 127, 130
Alegría and Armonía (Joy and Harmony) cultural association, 101
Alfonso X (King of Castile), 156

Alfonso XIII (King of Spain), 118, 119, 142
Almeida, José Carlos Pina, 56
Almosnino, Moses, 117, 123
Amazigh communities, 144, 145, 148
American Joint Distribution Committee, 121, 129
"Amor Sem Casa" (Homeless love), 208
ancestry. *See* descent
andalucistas, 174, 180n8
Anderson, Benedict, 40, 42
Anderson, Warwick, 55
Andrejevic, Mark, 55
Anholt, Simon, 54–55, 58, 60, 64
Anti-Defamation League, 146
antisemitism, 10, 16–17, 40–41, 58, 101
absence of, 59, 61
Brexit and, 297
discrimination and, 59, 65, 82, 146, 174, 278
philosephardism and, 9, 109–10
Arab-Israeli War (1967), 184, 187
Arendt, Hannah, 310, 311, 312
Argentina, 62, 184, 226
Aronczyk, Melissa, 55
ASBRAP (Brazilian Association of History and Genealogy Researchers), 282
Ashkenazi Jews, 15, 58, 95, 98, 99, 184, 308
assimilation, 40, 95, 101, 126, 158, 193, 196–97, 253n2, 273n2
Assmann, Aleida, 46, 49
Atatürk, Mustafa Kemal, 154, 158, 162n2
Austria, 2, 21, 47–48, 63, 78
Austria-Hungary, 115
Ávila, Eduardo, 261
Avni, Haim, 10
Azevedo, Filipe, 263, 264, 269, 270

Balkan Wars, 3, 9, 16, 113, 115

Barbosa, Kaique, 286
Barros Basto, Artur, 16, 58–59, 60, 62
Basic Law, Germany, 47, 78
Basques, 83–84, 88, 139, 193
Bauböck, Rainer, 78
Behar, Ruth, 216
Bejarano, Enrique, 141
belonging
    ancestral sense of, 239-40
    collective memory and, 3, 21
    community and, 95, 98
    ideal of, 140
    identity and, 25, 27, 242, 246
    mixed belongings, 265
    national, 316
    new meanings of, 6, 252
    Portuguese law, 209
    refusal and, 234
    recovery of, 2, 27, 263
    sense of, 98, 251, 284, 288
    Sephardi belonging, 27, 316
    state-transcending conception, 20
Benguigui, Uri, 193, 196
Ben-Jacob, Baruch, 123, 130
Benjoya family, 304–9, 312
Benoliel Ruah, Joshua, 62
Benveniste, Marcelo, 242–43, 244
Benzaquén Pinto, Isaac, 185
Bevernage, Berber, 44
bin Laden, Osama, 148
blood brotherhood, 140, 142
Bogaciovas, Marcelo, 282
Boletín Oficial del Estado, 30n3
Bolívar, Simón, 23, 100, 102
Borges, Jorge Luis, 120
Branco, Vanda, 287
brand loyalty, 54, 65
Brazil, 62, 206, 226, 261, 263–64, 278–89, 297–301
Brazilian Association of History and Genealogy Researchers (ASBRAP), 282
Brazilian descendants of Sephardic Jews, Portuguese citizenship for
    ancestry and genealogy, 281–88
    netnographic methods, 27–28, 277–81, 290n6
    Portuguese Network of Jewish Quarters, 278

Sephardiness, 279, 289
SNS, 279–80, 281, 284–90
virtual communities, identities, and discourses, 280, 281–84
Brexit, 239, 248, 297
Broudo, Isaac, 130
Bruguera Batalla, Rafael, 89
Bulgaria, 20, 243
Burgos, Carmen de, 116, 146

Cabrero Palomares, José, 176
cadastral document, 123
Calderwood, Eric, 142, 146
Caligiuri, Andrea, 44
Cámara Fernández, Manuel, 176
Cañete, Carlos, 175
Cansinos Assens, Rafael, 120
Capriles family, 23, 95–102
Capriles Teixeira, Joseph, 23, 99–100
Carasso, Isaac, 120
Carrasco, Eulogia "Loggie," 268
Carvajal, Doreen, 188
Carvajal y de la Cueva, Luis de, 261, 265
Case of İzzettin Doğan and Others v Turkey, 210–11
Castells, Manuel, 79
Castro, Américo, 8
Catalá, Rafael, 74
Catalan Parliamentary Group, 83–84, 85, 88
Catholic Church, 1, 7, 8, 96, 175, 296
    conversions, 53, 99
    expulsions, 49, 195
cemeteries, 158–59, 161–62, 205
Cervantes Institute, 107–9, 217
CGNE (General Council of Spanish Notaries), 30n3
Champalimaud Foundation, 65
Charlie Hebdo, 197
Chávez, Hugo, 102
children, citizenship, descent and, 80, 91n5, 100, 187, 267
    in Germany, 47, 97
    Spanish Law 12/2015 and, 12, 241
CIL (Jewish Community of Lisbon), 28, 285–87, 295–98, 300, 302
CIP (Jewish Community of Porto), 205, 206, 209, 249, 295
citizenship, 30n2, 39, 48, 217, 241, 243, 269. *See also* affective citizenship,

Iberian Sephardi descendants;
    Portuguese citizenship for Sephardi
    Jewish descendants; reparative
    citizenship; Spanish citizenship for
    Sephardi Jewish descendants
  Dönmes with Spanish, 159–61
  dual, 2, 6, 11, 13, 42–43, 47
  genealogy and, 245–47
  identity and, 251–52, 317–18
  instrumental, 288
  reparation and, 21, 37–38, 75–79
  reparations, 5–6, 50, 172–73, 175–78,
    287, 317
  symbolic, 243
Cohen, Marcel, 215
Cohen Zrihen, Sadia, 187
Colombia, 30n3, 101, 270, 298
Community of Portuguese Speaking
    Countries (CPLP), 56
*Como Identificar Ascendentes Cristãos
    Novos* (How to Identify New
    Christian Ancestors) (video), 282
Comunidad Israelita de Barcelona, 121, 192
concentration camps, 10, 44, 47, 96,
    126–30
Congress of Deputies, Spanish parliament,
    86, 89, 91n6
conversions, 18
  to Christianity, 1, 3, 53, 99, 207, 301
  to Judaism, 263, 268
converso descendants, in the Americas
  background, 257–62
  genealogy, 27, 258–61, 263–66,
    269–73, 286
  local, regional and national narratives,
    262–66
  Sephardiness, 270–72
  Spain, Portugal and Sephardi ancestors,
    266–70
conversos, 14–15, 20, 27, 188, 246
  indigeneity, 265–66
  the Inquisition, 168
  Portugal, 16, 18
  Spain, 145–46
convivencia (peaceful coexistence), 8, 11,
    23–24, 35–36, 138, 144, 169, 252,
    307
Cooperation Agreements, Spain, 170, 171,
    185

cord of tradition, 140, 149n1
Corkill, David, 56
Costa, António, 61
Costa, Joaquin, 140
Covid-19 pandemic, 14, 26, 63, 66, 217–18
CPLP (Community of Portuguese
    Speaking Countries), 56
crypto-Jews, 232, 246, 263, 274n6, 283.
    See also conversos
  converso descendants in the Americas,
    259–60
  nonrecognition of, 269
Cuadra Lasarte, Sabino, 79, 81
Cuadra Salcedo, Tomás de la, 171
Curaçao, 21–23, 94–95, 98–100, 270

De Belém Roseira, Maria, 57, 58, 60, 63
decolonization, 56, 90n5
Decree-Law 30-1/2015, Portugal, 1–2,
    4–5, 30n2, 37, 48–49. *See also*
    Portuguese citizenship for Sephardi
    Jewish descendants
Degeneration (Nordau), 111–12
Del Pulgar, Fernando, 116
De Lucas, Miguel, 191, 192, 194, 195,
    197, 198n6
democracy, Jews and Muslims in, 167–70
denationalization, 21
denaturalization, 47
descent, Brazilian descendants of
    Sephardic Jews and, 27–28,
    277–81, 290n6. *See also* Portuguese
    citizenship, certifying origins;
    Portuguese citizenship for Sephardi
    Jewish descendants
  Sephardiness and, 270–72
Development, Relief, and Education for
    Alien Minors Act (DREAM Act), 6
devoir de mémoire (duty of memory), 25,
    167, 170, 173–78
Díez González, Rosa María, 81–82, 85
Dirección General de Seguridad Jurídica y
    Fe Pública (DGSJFP), 30n3
D. João III (King of Portugal), 16
Dodman, Thomas, 244
"Doing Things" (Labanyi), 240
Domínguez, Marta, 174
Dönmes (Sabbateans), 14, 19, 20, 155–58,
    162n2, 246, 302

Cemetery desecration, 161
Ladino and, 154–55, 156, 159–60
nationalism and, 158
Sabbatai Sevi and, 155, 156, 302
Salonica (Selanik) and, 24, 154, 156–58, 161
secrecy and, 157–58
with Spanish citizenship, 159–61
Sufism and, 156–57
Wealth Tax and, 157
Zohar and, 156, 162, 162n1
D'Ornellas, Rodrigo, 285–86
Drahi, Patrick, 65
DREAM Act (Development, Relief, and Education for Alien Minors Act), 6
Dreyfus affair, France, 41
Dreyfus case, Portugal, 58–59
dual citizenship, 2, 6, 11, 13, 42–43, 47
Dueñas Martínez, María del Carmen, 85
duty of memory (*devoir de mémoire*), 25, 167, 170, 173–78

Egypt, 10, 185
Eichmann in Jerusalem (Arendt), 311
Elias, Norbert, 90n2
elites, 19, 40, 57, 113–14, 279, 311
Elorriaga Pisarik, Gabriel, 83, 84
emotions, 27, 238–43, 246, 248–52. *See also* affect; affective citizenship; nostalgia; sentiment
"Encounter of the Two Worlds," 179n4
Errúas, Glayci, 247
Esadnâme (Vassaf), 156
Escudero, Mansur Abdussalam, 171, 176, 178, 179n6
Esim, Janet and Jak, 205
Los españoles sin patria de Salónica pamphlet, 108
Españoles sin patria y la raza sefardí (Pulido), 139
Espinar Vicente, José María, 39, 42
ethnographic fieldwork and partial knowledge, 225–27
ethno-nationalism, 138
European Union (EU), 59, 60, 66, 287, 305
expulsions, 37–38, 45–46, 48–49, 195, 305
Morisco, 137–38, 145
moriscos-andalusíes and commemoration of, 173–77
from Portugal, 2–3, 4, 15, 16, 18, 53, 58–59, 64, 241–42, 309
from Spain, 73, 74, 76–77, 83, 109, 110–11, 126, 137, 175, 183, 186, 190, 194, 196, 215, 224, 241–42
extraterritoriality, 113–16, 119, 239
Ezratty, Salomon, 115, 116, 129

Fábio, Dinêila, 285
Facebook, 28, 279–87, 290, 290nn4–5
familial memory, 84, 88, 243
Fantasmas precursores (Yurman), 102
Federation of Jewish Communities of Spain (FCJE), 13, 25, 74, 170, 226
citizenship and, 217, 269
Law 12/2015 and, 183, 184–86, 188, 192
Felipe VI (King of Spain), 1, 13, 77, 191, 194–95, 249, 269
Ferdinand (King of Spain), 196
Fernández Parrilla, Gonzalo, 175
The final words (*Las Ultimas Palavras*) (documentary film), 25, 205, 206
Finardi, Eva, 283
Flesler, Daniela, 144
Fögen, Marie Theres, 48
Forga, M., 179n2
Fortier, Anne Marie, 240
4 Gerações em Lisboa (*Four generations in Lisbon*) (Lisbon Municipality and Benoliel Ruah), 62
France, 41, 45, 231, 278, 297
Franco, Francisco, 5, 121, 145, 147, 171, 185, 190
death of, 8, 10, 168, 214
historical memory and, 194
Freyre, Gilberto, 22, 55–56
Friedman, Michal, 139

Gallegos, Ana Maria, 246, 249, 266–67
Ganivet, Ángel, 140
García Figueras, Tomás, 142
García-Margallo, José Manuel, 87–88, 172
García San Juán, Alejandro, 180n12
Garzón, Jacobo Israel, 185, 186–89, 193, 195, 196
Gattegno, Leon, 130
Genealogia Judaica do Brasil (video), 282
genealogy, 98–100, 280–85, 287–89. *See also* descent

Index 323

Brazilian descendants of Sephardic Jews and, 27–28, 277–81, 290n6
citizenship and, 245–47, 264
converso descendants in the Americas and, 27, 258–61, 263–66, 269–73, 286
General Council of Spanish Notaries (CGNE), 30n3
Germany, 2, 17, 37, 63, 97
concentration camps, 10, 44, 47, 96, 126–30
laws, 46–47, 78
post-Holocaust, 230
Gezi Park resistance (2013), 203
Ghana, 2, 21, 37, 38, 46, 48
Gil, Rodolfo, 139
Giménez Caballero, Ernesto, 141–42, 146
Glick Schiller, Nina, 42
Godinho, Ana Mendes, 61, 62
Godoy, Cassia, 284
Goldschläger, Arielle, 245, 246, 247
González Laya, Arancha, 107
Goytisolo, Juan, 144
gratitude, 162. *See also* loyalty
certificates of origin and, 287
discourse of, 191
historical redress and debts of, 190–91
to Jewish ancestors, 284
with Jewish loyalty to Spain, 191
loyalty and, 25, 184, 191
Spanish nationality as sign of, 129
Great Depression, 110, 125
Great Fire of Salonica (Selanik), 123, 157
Greece, 2, 9–10, 63, 78, 115, 117, 307
nationalism and, 157
Spanish connection to interwar, 121–26
World War II, 110, 126–30
Greek-Turkish Population Exchange, 157
Guerra, Anna, 265, 267
guilt
collective, national, 49, 311
four types, 75
Gutierrez, Gail, 268

Hague Convention (1930), 41
Haketia, 2, 8, 191, 253n2, 273n2
Haleva, Isak, 204
Hatchwell, David, 187
Henriques, Anna Ruth, 249–50, 252

heritage, recovery of, 242, 270
Herzog, Chaim, 74
Hirsch, Marianne, 207, 244
Hirschkind, Charles, 180nn8–9
Hispanicity (*hispanidad*), 9, 23, 140, 141, 142
hispanidad (Hispanicity), 9, 23, 140, 141, 142
Hispanism, 8, 138, 140–42, 259
Historical Memory law, Spain (2007), 5, 12, 78, 80, 91n5, 198n7
historical redress
conditions, obstacles, reparations, 191–94
debts of gratitude, 190–91
FCJE and origins of Spanish Law 12/2015, 183, 184–86, 192
Spanish rescue of Jews and, 186–90
Holocaust, 13, 45, 49, 61–62, 230, 247
concentration camps, 10, 44, 47, 96, 126–30
memory, 12, 207
survivors, 2, 78, 97
homeland, 90n1, 109–11, 140, 146, 160, 194, 216
homeland consciousness, 245, 250
Homeless love ("Amor Sem Casa"), 208
How to Identify New Christian Ancestors (*Como Identificar Ascendentes Cristãos Novos*) (video), 282
La huella morisca (Rodríguez Ramos), 180n9
human rights, 46, 75, 203, 210–11

Iberian Peninsula, 13, 15, 30n1, 38, 45–46, 138, 139, 140, 144, 166, 206, 269. *See also* affective citizenship, Iberian Sephardi descendants; Muslims of Iberian descent
Ibn Khaldun, 169
Ibn Verga, Solomon, 309
Ibn Ziyad, Tariq, 144
ICTJ (International Center for Transitional Justice), 5
identities, 28, 58, 74, 78–79, 210–11, 241, 242, 244, 246, 247, 249, 278
citizenship and, 251–52, 317–18
descent and Sephardiness, 270–72
passports and, 94, 95–96

virtual communities, discourses and, 280, 281–84
Ignatieff, Michael, 44
Iñarritu García, Jon, 85, 88
India, 3, 42–43, 208, 230, 310
Indigenous people, 231, 259, 264–65
Inquisition
    Portuguese, 4, 7, 15, 16, 18, 53, 58, 62
    Spanish, 7, 99, 156, 160, 231, 247, 268
In Search of a Lost Ladino (Cohen, M.), 215
Instituto de Registos Centrais e do Notariado (IRCN), 30n3, 67n10, 297
instrumental citizenship, 239, 248, 278, 288
International Center for Transitional Justice (ICTJ), 5
IRCN (Instituto de Registos Centrais e do Notariado), 30n3, 67n10, 297
Isabel (Queen of Spain), 115, 196
Islam, 8, 156, 170, 175, 176, 178
Islamophobia, 174
Israel, 45, 61–62, 64–65, 75, 174, 278, 288
    Arab-Israeli War, 184, 187
    Franco and, 185
    Sephardic population, 297–300
Italo-Ottoman war (1911–12), 114–15

Jagoda, Flory, 107–8
Jané i Guasch, Jordi, 82, 84, 85, 87
Jaspers, Karl, 75
Jewish Community of Belmonte (JCB), 290n3
Jewish Community of Lisbon (CIL), 28, 285–87, 295–98, 300, 302
Jewish Community of Porto (CIP), 205, 206, 209, 249, 295
Jewish laws, 204, 209, 210
Jews, 3. *See also* Ashkenazi Jews; crypto-Jews; Sephardi Jews
"Jews of Portugal and the Spanish-Portuguese Jewish Diaspora" conference (2018), 62
Joppke, Christian, 11
Joy and Harmony (Alegría and Armonía) cultural association, 101
Juan Carlos I (King of Spain), 12, 73–74, 77, 168–70, 183, 195–96
Judaism, 3, 8, 59, 113, 170, 263, 268
Judeophobia, 10, 16
Judeo-Spanish. *See* Ladino
justice, 58, 231
    moriscos-andalusíes and search for, 170–73
    transitional, 5, 22, 75, 76, 80, 167–68

Kabbalah, the, 156
Kaneva, Nadia, 54
Katalan Hadash (New Catalan) synagogue, 117, 122–26
Kozinets, Robert V., 280
Kramer, Anne-Marie, 271
Kristallnacht, 97

Labanyi, Jo, 240, 253n4
Ladino (Judeo-Spanish), 2, 8, 207, 213, 238, 253n2, 299–300, 306
    Dönmes and, 154–55, 156, 159–60
    memory and, 243–44
    In Search of a Lost Ladino, 215
    songs, 107–8
    Las Ultimas Palavras and, 25, 205, 206
Laszczkowski, Mateusz, 241
Law 12/2015, Spain, 1–2, 12, 30n2, 167, 191, 196, 235n1, 241. *See also* refusal, ethics of; Spanish citizenship for Sephardi Jewish descendants; Spanish parliamentary debates, 2015 nationality law
    end of, 90, 219–20
    FCJE and, 183, 184–86, 188, 192
    preamble, 257
    reception of, 13–15
    reconciliation versus reparation, 167–70
    reparative citizenship and, 4–5, 46, 48–49, 50n1
    World War II and, 188
Law 19/2015, Spain, 193
Law of Religious Freedom, Spain (1967), 185
laws of return. *See* nation branding; Portuguese citizenship for Sephardi Jewish descendants; refusal, ethics of
Lehmann, Ana, 61
Lessa, Paulo, 288

Levinas, Emmanuel, 210
Levine, Liz, 245
Lévy, Sam, 129
Libya, 114
Lisbon, 28, 62, 285–87, 295–98, 300, 302
Lisbon massacre (April 1506), 16–17
Llamazares Trigo, Gaspar, 81–85, 88–89, 90n4
Llona, Miren, 244
long-distance nationalism, 42–43, 48, 49–50
Lopes, Sostenes, 286
Loubaris, Mohammed Najib, 176–77
loyalty, 14, 20, 25, 27, 109, 113, 146, 156, 192, 197, 257, 259, 307. *See also* gratitude
   brand, 54, 65
   citizenship and, 6, 21, 40–41, 43, 184, 191, 241
   converso descendants and, 259, 272
   gratitude and, 25, 184, 191
   identity and cultural, 272
   longing and, 8
   multiple, 41, 42
   nostalgia and, 12
   questionable, 41, 110, 115, 117–18, 122, 146
Luso-Hispanics, 20, 317
Lusophony, 56
Lusotropicalism, 22, 55–56, 259

Madariaga, María Rosa de, 144
Mahzor Katalan, title page of, 124
Manifiesto de Cartagena (Bolívar), 100
Manos Unidas, 175
Manuel I (King of Portugal), 16, 58, 59, 309
Marcos, Cristiano, 283–84
Marín, Manuela, 139
Marranos, Portugal, 16, 59, 286
   defined, 67n5
Martin, Emily, 229–30
Martín Corrales, Eloy, 144, 148
Marx, Karl, 310, 311
Massumi, Brian, 253n4
Mauss, Marcel, 230
Mayor Zaragoza, Federico, 179n4
Mazín, Max, 189, 190–91
McDonald, Charles, 199n9, 241

McGranahan, Carole, 230
Mehmed Esad Dede, 156–57
memory, 46, 62, 81, 94, 207
   affective attachments and power of, 241–45
   collective, 3, 4, 11–13, 20, 55–56, 59, 148, 173, 175–76, 241, 244, 245, 268, 315, 317
   duty of, 25, 167, 170, 173–78
   historical, 102, 165, 166, 173, 175, 187, 194, 197, 230, 243, 268
   Holocaust, 12
   paramemory, 268
   politics, 38
   Portuguese law of return and collective, 55–56
   recovery of, 168, 194
   recovery of familial, 83–84, 88, 242
   Spain and Historical Memory law, 5, 12, 78, 80, 91n5, 198n7
Menéndez Pidal, Ramón, 139
Mesquita Nunes, Adolfo, 57, 58, 61, 63
Mexico, 30n3, 262, 264, 298
Miccoli, Dario, 244
Milgram, Avraham, 17
Miller, Bernard, 245–46
millet system, Ottoman Empire, 15, 307
Mizael, MXWL, 288
Montreux Treaty (1937), 10
Moors, 24, 143–45, 166, 179n2
Moriscos, 3, 11, 14–15, 82, 149n4. *See also* Muslims of Iberian descent
   defined, 166, 179n2
   expulsions, 137–38, 145
moriscos-andalusíes
   commemoration of expulsion of, 173–77
   defined, 166–67, 179n2
   descendants and search for justice, 170–73, 175–77
   historical revisionism and, 178
   Jews and Muslims in democracy, 167–70
   Sephardi Jews and, 167–70
   Spanish citizenship and, 166–67
Morocco, 24, 41, 138–48, 169–71, 174–78, 184–85, 189
Moscona, Myriam, 243–44
Moya, Paula, 264–66
Muchnik, Natalia, 138

Mucznik, Esther, 57, 58, 59
Muslims, 7–8, 14–15, 63, 66, 155–56, 167–70, 185, 193
Muslims of Iberian descent. *See also* Moriscos; *moriscos-andalusies*
  expulsions, 137–38
  philosephardism and Africanism, 24, 138–43, 147
  Sephardi Jews and, 23–24, 138, 142–49

Naar, Devin E., 284
Nahum family, 304–6, 308–9
names, 261
  surnames, 98, 204, 208, 211n1, 238, 282–83, 285, 296
nationalism, 42–43, 48–50, 138, 157
nationality laws. *See also* Law 12/2015, Spain; nation branding
  Portuguese Decree-Law 30-1/2015, 1–2, 4–5, 30n2, 37, 48–49
nation branding, Portuguese citizenship for Sephardi Jewish descendants and, 43, 50n2, 58, 66
  collective memory, 55–56
  concept of, 53, 54, 66
  Lusotropicalism, 22, 55–56, 259
naturalization, 16, 39
  Basic Law in Germany and, 78
  denaturalization, 47
  Portugal, 30n3, 67n9, 284, 287, 289
  process and proof, 6
  as reparation, 79
  Spain, 9, 17, 41, 119, 171, 193
Navarrete, T. A., 101
Navarro, José, 262, 264, 265, 268–70
Nehama, Joseph, 115, 123–24, 126, 129
Nehamas, Alexander, 129
neo-philosephardism, 11, 12, 14
Neruda, Pablo, 218–19
Netherlands, 98, 99, 101, 109, 115
netnographic methods, 27–28, 277–81, 290n6
New Catalan (Katalan Hadash) synagogue, 117, 122–26
New Christians, 2, 18, 277, 288–89. *See also* conversos
  colonies, 263
  Facebook groups, 28, 279, 281–82, 286, 290n4

New Mexico, 204, 246, 262, 264–65, 268
Nkrumah, Kwame, 48
Nogueira, Carmen, 286, 287
Nordau, Max, 111–13, 117, 120, 121, 130
North Africa, 7–8, 139, 142, 144, 148, 299
nostalgia, 8, 26, 29, 146, 169, 223–24, 230
  rancor and, 233, 239, 241, 244, 248
  recovery and, 244
  for Sepharad, 249, 307, 309

Ojeda-Mata, Maite, 9, 13, 172
Olabarría Muñoz, Emilio, 82, 84
Olick, Jeffrey K., 75, 90n2, 195
Onion Skin (*Tela de Sevoya*) (Moscona), 243–44
oral history, 21, 189, 253n2
oral history project, 3, 13, 19, 30n4, 239, 251, 253n2, 273n2
orientalism, 23, 110
Orjuela, Camilla, 245, 246, 247
Ottoman Empire, 2, 7, 9, 119, 279, 304–5
  Italo-Ottoman war, 114–15
  millet system, 15, 307

Palestine, 10, 113, 129, 298, 312
Passarell, Samuel, 155–56, 158, 159, 161
passport, 60, 238–39, 278, 287, 305
  Capriles Teixeira, 23, 99–100
  genealogy as history, 98–99
  identity and, 94, 95–96
  Sephardi passport, 7, 98, 248
peaceful coexistence (*convivencia*), 8, 11, 23–24, 138, 144, 169, 252, 307
Perceval, J. M., 179n2
Pereira, Alex, 286
Perry, Mary Elizabeth, 173
Le Peuple judéo-espagnol (Pulido), 112
Pew Research Center, 146
Philip III (King of Spain), 137
Philippson, Ludwig, 189
philosephardism, 9–11, 13, 23–24, 30n5, 125–26, 127, 184, 189, 197, 225, 234, 248
  Africanism and, 24, 138–43, 147, 165, 170, 172
  antisemitism and, 9, 109–10
  language and discourse, 121–22, 191, 196, 241
  nationalism and, 196, 197

neo-, 11, 12, 14
  racial regeneration and, 111–13,
    129–30
  reflected back to Spain, 116–19
  Sephardi community in Salonica and,
    109, 110, 111–13, 116–19, 129–30
Pinheiro, Claudio, Jr., 286
Portero, Luis, 215–17, 219
Portugal, 16-19, 56, 65, 67n1, 115,
    203, 278. *See also* Portuguese
    citizenship, certifying origins;
    Portuguese citizenship for Sephardi
    Jewish descendants
  Decree-Law 30-1/2015, 1–2, 4–5,
    30n2, 37, 48–49
  expulsion from, 2–3, 4, 15, 16, 18, 53,
    58–59, 64, 241–42, 309
  Inquisition, 4, 7, 15, 16, 18, 53, 58, 62
  naturalization, 30n3, 67n9, 284, 287, 289
  slavery and, 55, 311
Portuguese citizenship, certifying origins,
    28
  certification process, 295–97
  data snapshot, 297–98
  evidentiary profiles, 298–302
  number of applicants by year, 298
Portuguese citizenship for Sephardi Jewish
    descendants, 17-18, 46, 67n9,
    207, 290n2. *See also* Brazilian
    descendants of Sephardic Jews;
    converso descendants, in the
    Americas; Decree-Law 30-1/2015;
    nation branding; Portuguese
    citizenship, certifying origins
  benefits of, 305–6
  documentary proof, 25, 205–6, 208,
    209
  emotion and, 248–51
  identity and, 210–11
  reasons to apply, 202–4, 209, 251, 278,
    287
  reparation in historical context, 15–19
  requirements, 19, 60, 63, 66, 204, 219,
    277
Portuguese Foundation for Science and
    Technology, 62
Portuguese Network of Jewish Quarters
    (Rede Nacional de Judiarias), 278
Portuguese Republic (1911–26), 16

Prado, Leonardo, 285
Prat, Pedro de, 118–19
preambles, citizenship laws. *See also*
    Portuguese citizenship for Sephardi
    Jewish descendants; Spanish
    citizenship for Sephardi Jewish
    descendants
  Portugal, 8, 18, 48–49, 241, 257
  Spain, 8, 12–13, 18, 48–49, 77, 84,
    165, 194, 224, 241, 257, 271
*The Presence of the Past in a Spanish
    Village* (Behar), 216
Primo de Rivera, Miguel, 9, 119, 143
Prince of Asturias Award for Concord, 12,
    175
Princess of Asturias Award for Concord,
    177
Pulido, Ángel, 8–9, 41, 109, 117, 121, 139,
    197, 216
  Hispanism and, 141–42
  philosephardism and, 111–13, 130, 143

Queiroz, Arthur de, 285
Querub, Isaac, 74, 185–89, 191–97

"race science," 109–10, 111, 121
racial regeneration, 111–13, 129–30
Ramirez, Arnulfo, 265, 269
Ramirez, Cristina, 260
Rebeiro e Castro, José, 310, 311
Rebelo de Sousa, Marcelo, 61
reconciliation, 5, 37, 38, 48, 75–77, 89,
    147, 316
  politics of, 315
  post-Holocaust Germany with, 230
  reencounter and, 1, 48, 82–83, 191
  reparation versus, 167–70
recovery
  of familial memory, 83–84, 88, 242
  of heritage, 242, 270
  Iberian Sephardi descendants, 245–48
  of memory, 168, 194
  nostalgia and, 244
  of original belonging, 263
  of Sephardi ballads, 140
Rede Nacional de Judiarias (Portuguese
    Network of Jewish Quarters), 278
reencounter *(reencuentro)*, 1, 48, 73–74,
    82–83, 90n1, 168, 179n4, 191

Reeves, Madeleine, 241
Refusal, ethics of, and Spanish citizenship for Sephardi Jewish descendants
  absolution refused, 228–31
  disappointment, frustration, critique, 227–28
  indifference, 231–33
Regenerationist movement, 149n2, 225
Reich Citizenship Law, Germany (1935), 46–47
reparation, in historical context, 1–3, 20, 165–68, 193, 195, 269. *See also* reparations; reparative citizenship
  citizenship and, 4–7
  Portugal, 15–19
  reception of Spanish Law 12/2015, 13–15
  Spanish nationality and Sephardi Jewish past, 7–13
  symbolic, 5–6, 50, 172–73, 175–78, 287, 317
reparations, 4–5, 21, 37, 38. *See also* reparation
  citizenship and, 75–79
  historical redress with conditions, obstacles and, 191–94
  naturalization as, 79
  politics, 22, 46, 75–77, 79, 89, 195, 207
  reconciliation versus, 167–70
  reparations in, 79–88
  in Spanish parliamentary debates, 79–88
  symbolic, 5–6, 50, 172–73, 175–78, 287, 317
Reparations Agreement between Israel and West Germany, 75
reparative citizenship, 4–7, 21, 37, 47, 50n1. *See also* reparation, in historical context; reparations
  historical injustices of distant past, 43–46, 48, 49–50
  transformations in twentieth century, 38–43
reserve citizenship, 251, 260
Rettberg, Angelika, 167
return, 1, 3, 48, 242, 244. *See also* nation branding; refusal, ethics of
  affective attachment, 26–27, 229
  to Africa, 141

collective memory and Portuguese law of, 55–56
conversos, 260, 272
Iberian Sephardi descendants with longing and, 248–50
to Judaism, 18, 23
restitution and, 76
right of, 3, 12, 48, 230, 269, 305–6
Sephardi community in Salonica and, 119–21
Revah, Isaac, 129
Ribeiro e Castro, José, 57, 59, 60, 67n2
Ricoeur, Paul, 167, 173, 284
Rif War, 143–44, 145, 148
Righteous Among the Nations, 59, 129, 189
right of abode, 2, 10, 37, 43, 46, 48
Rigoni, Gustavo, 283
Rodrigue, Aron, 279, 284
Rodrigues Alvarenga, Antônio, 287
Rodríguez Ramos, Antonio Manuel, 166, 172, 174, 176, 180n9
Rohr, Isabelle, 9
Rojas Moreno, José, 189
Romero de Radigales, Sebastian, 129
Ronde Klip plantation, 100
Ronny, Shabrina Amelia, 42
Roque, Ricardo, 55
Rosenwein, Barbara, 242
Rothwell, Michael, 57, 58, 67n11
Ruiz-Gallardón, Alberto, 6, 11, 73–74, 186–95, 197
Russo, Ethan, 248–49
Rüştü, Karakaşzade, 157

Saavedra, Eduardo de, 142
Sabbateans. *See* Dönmes
Sahrawis, 81–82, 84, 88, 90n5, 192
Salazar, António de Oliveira, 15–18
Salonica. *See* Sephardi community, in Salonica
Saltiel, David, 107
Saltiel, David Saadi, 130
Saltiel, Shemtov, 122–23
Sampaio, Jorge, 59
Samuels, Justin, 246–47, 249
Sanchez, Maria, 267–68
Sánchez, Pedro, 177
Santa María la Blanca synagogue, 77

Santos, Daniel, 283
Saramago, José, 26, 202, 211
Schorr, Carlos, 185
Die Schuldfrage (Jaspers), 75
Schwarz, Samuel, 16
Sciaky, Leon, 114, 120
Sefarad (film), 62
Selanik, 24, 154, 156–58, 161
Senate, Spanish parliament, 84, 87, 89, 91n6
sentiment, 26, 140, 234, 241. *See also* affect; nostalgia
Sepharad, 8, 12, 30n1, 188, 225, 231, 241, 269. *See also* Spain
Sephardi community, in Salonica
   cadastral document, 123
   Cervantes Institute and, 107–9
   documents for Abravanel, Jacques, 127, 128
   Dönmes and, 161–62
   extraterritoriality, 113–16, 119
   Holocaust, 126–30
   Katalan Hadash synagogue, 117, 122–26
   philosephardism and, 109, 110, 111–13, 116–19, 129–30
   photograph of Alcheh y Saporta, 108
   return to Spain, 119–21
   Spain and routes of nationality, 7–13
   Spanish connection in interwar Greece, 121–26
   title page of *Mahzor Katalan*, 124
Sephardic Surnames (*Sobrenomes Sefarditas*) (video), 282
Sephardi Jews, 2-3, 7–13, 45, 61, 65, 98, 101, 167–70, 185, 186-191, 234, 245, 271. *See also specific topics and* Spanish Citizenship for Sephardi Descendants and Portuguese Citizenship for Sephardi Descendants
"Sephardi" vs. "Sephardic," 30n1
Sephardi Jews, with Muslims of Iberian descent and, 23–24, 138, 142–49
Sephardi laws, 258
Sephardim. *See* Sephardi Jews
Sephardiness, 23, 28, 208, 209, 241, 245, 246, 251, 270–72, 279, 281, 289, 316

'Sephardi passport,' 7, 98, 248. *See also* passport
"Sephardi," vs. "Sephardic," 30n1
   Dönmes and, 161–62
   Spain and routes of nationality, 7–13
Serbia, 20
Sevi, Sabetay, 155, 156, 302
Shaheed, Farida, 46
Sierra, Elmer, 267, 269
Silva Rego, María del Carmen, 81, 87, 89
Silverman, Victor, 251–52
Simon, Herbert, 55
Simpson, Audra, 229, 230–31
Sinagoga Anusim Brasil, 282
slavery, 5, 18, 44, 56, 246, 247
   Ghana and, 37, 48
   Portugal and, 55, 311
SNS (social networking services), 279–80, 281, 284–90
Soares, Mário, 18, 59
Sobrenomes Sefarditas (Sephardic surnames) (video), 282
social networking services (SNS), 279–80, 281, 284–90
Sousa Mendes, Aristides de, 17, 59–60
Southwest, US, 204, 246, 262, 264–65, 267–69
Souza, Thiago, 283
Spain, 7-15, 81, 84, 89, 145–46. *See also* Law 12/2015 Spain; Spanish citizenship for Sephardi descendants
   antisemitism in, 82
   Cooperation Agreements, 170, 171, 183
   expulsions from, 73, 74, 76–77, 83, 109, 110–11, 126, 137, 175, 183, 186, 190, 194, 196, 215, 224, 241–42
   FCJE, 13, 25, 74, 170, 183–86, 217, 226, 269
   historical memory and, 194
   Historical Memory law, 5, 12, 78, 80, 91n5, 198n7
   Inquisition, 7, 99, 156, 160, 231, 268
   interwar Greece and, 121–26
   Israel and, 187
   Law 19/2015, 193
   Law of Religious Freedom, 185
   naturalization, 9, 17, 41, 119, 171, 193
   passports, 238–39

philosephardism reflected back to, 116–19
return to, 119–21
Sepharad, 8, 12, 188, 225, 231, 241, 269
Spanish citizenship for Sephardi Jewish descendants, 10, 30n4. *See also* converso descendants, in the Americas; Law 12/2015; refusal, ethics of; Spanish parliamentary debates
  Covid-19 pandemic and, 26, 217–18
  document collection, 216, 217
  Dönmes with, 159–61
  as gift, 26, 231, 233–34
  reasons to apply, 213–15, 232, 250–51
  requirements, 19, 41, 63, 66, 204, 213, 215–16, 219, 223–24, 239
  Sephardi Jews and routes of, 7–13
  symbolism of, 46
Spanish Civil War, 5, 78, 81–82, 84, 88, 121, 147
Spanish parliamentary debates, 2015 nationality law
  Congress of Deputies, 81, 86, 91n6
  legislative activity summary, 86–87
  reencuentro, 73–74, 83, 90n1
  reparations and citizenship, 75–79
  reparations in, 79–88
  reparations politics, 22, 75–77, 79, 89
  Senate, 84, 87, 89, 91n6
  timeline, 80, 91n6
  transitional justice and, 22, 75, 76
Stein, Sarah Abrevaya, 30n6, 190, 279, 284
Strathern, Marilyn, 227
Sufism, 156–57, 160
surnames, 98, 204, 208, 211n1, 238, 282–83, 285, 296
Synagogue Without Borders movement, 282

Tansey, Oisín, 57
Tardà i Coma, Joan, 84
Teixeira, Mónica João, 206–7
Teixeira da Cruz, Paula, 1, 311
Tela de Sevoya (Onion Skin) (Moscona), 243–44
Terra, Marcelo, 286–87

terrorism, 148, 197, 268, 278, 301
Texas, 264, 267, 269
Toledano, Mauricio, 186
Toledano, Samuel, 185
Torre do Tombo, 65
tourism, 11, 18, 61–62, 64–65, 278
transitional justice, 5, 22, 75, 76, 80, 167–68
Trump, Donald, 149n6, 232, 312
Turkey, 2, 4, 21, 24-25, 66, 125, 153-162, 188-211, 228, 248, 278, 297–99, 302, 304–7
  Case of İzzettin Doğan and Others v Turkey, 210–11
  Surname Law, 204, 208, 211n1
  Wealth Tax (1947), 157

Ugarriza, Juan E., 167
Las Ultimas Palavras (The final words) (documentary film), 25, 205, 206
UN. *See* United Nations
Unamuno, Miguel de, 139–40, 214
United Nations (UN), 46, 75, 168, 310
United States (US), 6, 17, 45, 115, 121, 129, 233, 245–47
  Sephardi migration to, 3
  Southwest, 204, 246, 262, 264–65, 267–69
University of Washington Sephardic Studies Digital Collection, 30n4, 253n2
Urbano de Sousa, Constança, 57, 60
US. *See* United States
useable past, 109, 122

Van Dunen, Francisca, 67n7
Van Ham, Peter, 54
Varum, Celeste, 57, 62
Vassaf, Hüseyin, 156, 160
Venezuela, 30n3, 94, 96–99, 101–2, 186–87, 228
  converso descendants and, 260–61
  Sephardic population, 298
Ventura, Gilberto, 282
Ventura, Lilith, 286, 287
Ventura Santos, Ricardo, 55
Vieira, Maria, 287
Vilanova, Lisiane, 263, 264, 267, 268
virtual communities, genealogy and, 280–89
Volcic, Zala, 55

Waldron, Jeremy, 45
Wolfe, Stephanie, 76, 80
World Sephardi Federation, 61
World War I, 3, 23, 109–10, 120–21, 127, 143, 304
World War II, 3, 10, 110, 126–30, 188–89, 298

Yacov, Marcelo, 285
Yad Vashem, 129, 189

Yahuda, Abraham S., 117, 118, 121, 189
Yahudi Dönmesi, 153–55
YouTube, 28, 279–83, 284, 290, 290n5
Yurman, Fernando, 102

Zarattini, Ioly, 99
Zembylas, Michalinos, 240–41
Zohar, 156, 162, 162n1
Zorrinho, Carlos, 57, 59

www.ingramcontent.com/pod-product-compliance
Lightning Source LLC
Chambersburg PA
CBHW070802040426
42333CB00061B/1788